CROCKFORD'S

Clerical Directory

APPENDIX,

1861:

GIVING THE

NAMES, ADDRESSES, AND OTHER PARTICULARS OF CLERGYMEN

OMITTED IN

THE CLERICAL DIRECTORY FOR 1860,

AND OF

CLERGYMEN WHO HAVE BEEN SINCE ORDAINED.

PUBLISHED ANNUALLY.

London:

CROCKFORD'S CLERICAL JOURNAL AND DIRECTORY OFFICES,
10, WELLINGTON-STREET, STRAND, W.C:

1861.

PREFACE.

THE CLERICAL DIRECTORY APPENDIX FOR 1861 has been prepared in deference to the wishes of many of the Subscribers of the work, who have urged its publication on the ground of economy, and as being likely to increase the sphere of usefulness of the DIRECTORY. It was originally the intention of the Conductors of the work to bring out a full and complete edition every year. This announcement was made in the preface of last year's issue; and, in fulfilment of it, the necessary preparations were entered into to publish the work at the appointed time. However, before proceeding far in the task, numerous letters were received from Subscribers and well-wishers of the CLERICAL DIRECTORY, advocating a biennial instead of annual issue of the complete work. It was contended that a supplement of new names and list of deceased clergymen would be quite sufficient to keep up the general correctness of the book in the interval of the two years, and that the reduced price of the publication in this form would enable many members of the Church, otherwise not inclined to purchase the work, to become regular Subscribers.

It is in order to give this very reasonable proposition a fair trial that the Conductors of the CLERICAL DIRECTORY have ventured on the publication of the present APPENDIX. It is an attempt to meet the wishes of the majority of the Subscribers of the work, and nothing more. The Conductors of the CLERICAL DIRECTORY are as desirous as ever to publish the work annually, but will let the result decide whether this form of publication, or the biennial mode of issue, with alternate Supplements, will be generally preferred.

APPENDIX

TO

Crockford's Clerical Directory,

1861.

It is requested that this Work be cited as "CROCKFORD'S CLERICAL DIRECTORY."

ACLAND, Charles Lawford, *Southgate, Edmonton, Middlesex.*—Jesus Coll. Camb. B.A. 1856, M.A. 1859, Deac. 1859, Pr. 1860, both by Bp of Lond; C. of Trin. Ch. Gray's-inn-road, Lond. 1859.

ACOCK, Edgar Morton, *Carmarthen.*—Magd. Coll. Oxon. B.A. 1859; Deac. 1860, by Bp of Salis; Vice-Prin. of the South Wales Training Coll. Carmarthen, 1860; formerly Asst. Mast. in King's Sch. Sherborne, Dorset.

ADAIR, Hugh Jenison, *Westbury, Wells, Somerset.*—Ch. Ch. Oxon. B.A. 1859; Deac. 1859, Pr. 1860, both by Bp of B. and W; C. of Westbury-cum-Priddy, 1859.

ADAM, Stephen Condon, *Hampstead-terrace, Soho-park, Birmingham.*—St John's Coll. Camb. B.A. 1858; Deac. 1858, Pr. 1859, both by Archbp of York; Assoc. Sec. for the Irish Church Missions to the Roman Catholics, West Midland Dist. 1860; formerly C. of Holy Trinity, Wicker, Sheffield, 1858-60.

ADAMS, Augustus Crichton, *Rochester.*—St Bees Theol. Coll; Deac. 1856, Pr. 1857, both by Bp of Lich; C. of St. Nicholas, Rochester, 1859; formerly C. of Winster, Derbyshire, 1856-59.

ADAMS, Charles Vernon, *Shere, Guildford, Surrey.*—St Peter's Coll. Adelaide; Deac. 1860, by Bp of Winch; C. of Shere, 1860.

ADAMS, William Joshua, *Dolphinholme, near Lancaster.*—Gon. and Cai. Coll. Camb. B.A. 1859; Deac. 1859, Pr. 1860, both by Bp of Manch; C. of Dolphinholme, 1859.

ADDISON, John Aspinall, *Brixton, Devon.*—St John's Coll. Camb. B.A. 1838, M.A. 1842; Deac. and Pr. 1839; late P. C. of Churchdown, Gloucestershire, 1852-56; formerly Warden of St Mary's Coll. Windermere.

ADDISON, John Cramer, *Wootton-under-Wood parsonage, Aylesbury, Bucks.*—P. C. of Wootton-under-Wood, Dio. Oxon. 1860 (Patron, Duke of Buckingham; P.C.'s Gross Inc. 80*l* and Ho; Pop. 253).

ADDISON, Richard, *Bishop's Hull School, Taunton.*—Literate; Deac. 1856, by Bp of Capetown, Pr. 1858, by Bp of Lich; Mast. of Bishop's Hull Sch. 1860; formerly C. of St Peter's Collegiate Church, Wolverhampton, 1858-59; C. of Sopley, Hants, 1859-60.

ADDISON, William Fountaine, *Reading, Berks.*—Wadham Coll. Oxon. B.A. 1840; C. of St Giles's, Reading, 1856; formerly P.C. of Dorchester, Oxfordshire, 1850-56.

AIREY, John Postlethwaite, *Stretford, near Manchester.*—Qu. Coll. Oxon. B.A. 1858; Deac. 1859, Pr. 1860, both by Bp of Manch; C. of Stretford, 1859.

AITKEN, James, *Woodmansterne, Epsom, Surrey.*—Exon. Coll. Oxon. B.A. 1850, M.A. 1853; Deac. 1852, Pr. 1853, both by Bp of Winch; C. of Woodmansterne, 1859; late C. of Beddington, Surrey; formerly C. of Wallington, Surrey.

AITKENS, Albert, *Christchurch, Hants.*—St John's Coll. Camb. B.A. 1850; Deac. 1851, Pr. 1852; C. of Christchurch, Hants.

AKERS, George, *Northfleet, Gravesend, Kent.*—Oriel Coll. Oxon. B.A. 1859; Deac. 1860, by Bp of Roch; C. of Northfleet, 1860.

ALDER, George, 17 *Duke-street, Portland-place, London.*—Qu. Coll. Camb. Chancellor's Medallist, 1859, B.A. 1860; Deac. 1860, by Bp of Lond; C. of St John the Evangelist, Fitzroy-square, St Pancras, Lond. 1860.

ALDOM, John Wesley, *Penistone, Yorkshire.*—Trin. Coll. Dub. B.A. 1849, M.A. 1852; Deac. 1855, Pr. 1859, both by Bp of Rip; C. of Penistone, and Head Mast. of Penistone Gram. Sch. 1855.

ALDRIDGE, Robert, *Knowl Hill parsonage, Twyford, Berks.*—Chich. Dio. Coll; Deac. 1849, Pr. 1850, both by Bp of Chich, P.C. of Knowl Hill, Dio. Oxon. 1859 (Patrons, Trustees; P.C.'s Gross Inc. 100*l* and Ho; Pop. 750); late C. of North and South Tidworth, Wilts.

ALLAN, Hugh, *St Paul's parsonage, Portland-square, Bristol.*—Wadh. Coll. Oxon. B.A. 1856, M.A. 1859; Deac. 1859, Pr. 1860, both by Bp of G. and B.; C. of St Paul's, Bristol, 1859.

ALLAN, William, 17 *Upper Stamford-street, Lambeth, London.*—Worc. Coll. Oxon. B.A. 1859; Deac. 1860, by Bp of Winch; C. of St Andrew's, Lambeth, 1860.

ALLCROFT, William Rowley, *Belton rectory, Bawtry, Lincolnshire.*—Literate; Deac. 1831, Pr. 1832, both by Archbp of York; P.C. of West Butterwick, Lincolnshire, Dio. Linc. 1852 (Patron, V. of Owston; P.C.'s Gross Inc. 95*l*; Pop. 860); C. of Belton, Isle of Axholme; Editor of *Read's History of the Isle of Axholme*, 8vo. Caldicott, Gainsborough, 1860, 16*s*.

ALLEN, Richard, *Kirkburn vicarage, Driffield, Yorkshire.*—St Cath. Coll. Camb. B.A. 1842, M.A. 1845; Deac. 1842. Pr. 1843, both by Archbp of York; C. of Kirkburn, 1855; formerly C. of Driffield, 1842-55.

ALLEN, Robert, *Nottingham.*—Literate; Deac. 1859, Pr. 1860, both by Bp of Linc; C. of St Mary's, Nottingham, 1859.

ALLEN, Thomas Kingdon, 81 *Preston-street, Bradford, Yorkshire.*—Literate; Deac. 1857, Pr. 1858, both by Bp of Rip; Incumb. of St Philip's, Girlington, Bradford, Dio. Rip. 1860 (Patrons, Trustees of the Rev. Chas. Simeon; Incumb.'s Gross Inc. 150*l*; Pop. 3000); formerly C. of St Andrew's Bradford, 1857-60.

B

ALLNUTT, Thomas, *Bucklesham rectory, Ipswich.*—St Cath. Coll. Camb. B.D. 1856 ; Deac. 1844, Pr. 1845, both by Bp of Peterb ; C. of Bucklesham, 1856.

ALLSOP, Richard Winstanley, *Coleshill, Highworth, Wilts.*—Emman. Coll. Camb. S.C.L 1855; Deac. 1856, Pr. 1857, both by Bp of Oxon ; C. of Coleshill, 1857 ; formerly C. of Shrivenham, Berks, 1856-57.

ANDREWS, John Marshall, 38 *Argyle-square, Euston-road, London N.W.*—King's Coll. Lond ; Deac. 1853, Pr. 1854, both by Bp of Lond ; P.C. of St Jude's, St Pancras, Dio. Lond. 1858 (Patron, V. of St Pancras ; Pop. 8429); late C. of St Jude's, St Pancras, Lond.

ANDREWS, Septimus, 18 *Great College-street, Westminster, London.*—Ch. Ch. Oxon. B.A. 1855, M.A. 1858 ; Deac. 1857, by Bp of Oxon ; Asst. Mast. of Westminster Sch. Lond. 1860 ; formerly Fell. of St Peter's Coll. Radley, near Abingdon, 1857-60.

ANDREWS, William, *Houghton-on-the-Hill, Leicester.*—Linc. Coll. Oxon. B.A. 1859 ; Deac. 1859, Pr. 1860, both by Bp of Peterb ; C. of Houghton-on-the-Hill, 1859.

ANDREWS, William, *Postwick rectory, near Norwich.*—Univ. of Edinb. M.D. 1835 ; Deac. 1848, Pr. 1850 ; C. of Postwick, 1859 ; formerly R. of The Knysna, Cape Town, 1848-59.

ANSTEY, Charles Christopher, *Fyzabad, Oude, East Indies*—Caius Coll. Camb. B.A. 1849, M.A. 1852 ; Deac. 1850, Pr. 1851, both by Bp of Worc ; Chap of the East India Govern. of Fyzabad, 1860 ; late C. of Hillmorton, near Rugby, 1854-59 ; formerly C. of Calthorpe, Leicestershire, 1853-54 ; previously C. of Evesham, Worcestershire, 1850-53.

ANTIGUA, The Right Rev. William Walrond JACKSON, Lord Bp of Antigua, *Clare Hall, Antigua.*—Codrington Coll. Barbadoes, Licen. Theol ; Consecrated Bp of Antigua, 1860 (Episcopal Jurisdiction, the Islands of Antigua, Nevis, St Christopher, Montserrat, the Virgins, and Dominica ; extent, 751 square miles ; Pop. 106,372 ; Number of Clergy, 35 ; Gross Inc. of See, 2000l from the Consolidated Fund) ; his Lordship was formerly Chap. to the Forces in Barbadoes.

ARCHER, Edward, *West Barkwith rectory, Wragby, Lincolnshire.*—R. of West Barkwith, Dio. Linc. 1860 (Patron, the present R ; Tithe—R. 84l ; Glebe, 113¼ acres ; R.'s Gross Inc. 280l and Ho ; Pop. 143) ; late Chap. to the Wandsworth and Clapham Union, Surrey ; formerly C. of Rochford, Essex.

ARDEN, George, *North Bovey rectory, Exeter.*—Wadh. Coll. Oxon. B.A. 1840, M.A. 1842 ; Deac. 1842, Pr. 1843, both by Bp of Exon ; R. of North Bovey, Dio. Exon. 1859 (Patron, Earl of Devon ; Tithe—R. 328l ; Glebe, 25 acres ; R.'s Gross Inc. 355l and Ho ; Pop. 600); Dom. Chap. to the Earl of Devon ; formerly R. of Winterbourne-Came w Whitcombe, Dorset, 1847-58; Author, *A Manual of Catechetical Instruction,* Masters, 1851, 2s ; *Breviates from Holy Scripture,* John W. Parker, Lond. 1856, 2s; *Lectures on Confirmation and Holy Communion,* ib. 1857, 1s: *The Cure of Souls,* ib. 1858, 2s 6d.

ARMFIELD, Henry Thomas, *Armley parsonage, near Leeds.*—Pemb. Coll. Camb. B.A. 1858; Deac. 1859, Pr. 1860, both by Bp of Worc ; C. of Armley, 1860 ; formerly 2nd Mast in Qu. Eliz. Gram. Sch. Atherstone, Warwickshire, 1859-60.

ARMITSTEAD, Henry Sidney, *Ashford-Carbonel, Ludlow, Shropshire.*—Ch. Ch. Oxon. B.A. 1859 ; Deac. 1860, by Bp of Heref ; C. of Little Hereford and Ashford-Carbonel, 1860.

ARMSTRONG, Edmund Frederick.—King's Coll, Lond. Theol. Assoc ; Deac. 1859, Pr. 1860, both by Bp of Lich.

ARMSTRONG, Rowley, *Ripley, Yorkshire.*—St Bees Theol. Coll. 1854-55; Deac. 1856, Pr. 1857, both by Bp of Chest ; C. of Ripley, 1857 ; formerly C. of Bollington, Cheshire, |1856-57 ; Author, *Sermon on the Mount,* in verse (six parts), Wertheim and Co. 1850.

ARNOLD, Frederick, 99 *Cambridge-street, Pimlico, London.*—Ch. Ch. Oxon. B.A. 1860 ; Deac. 1860, by Bp of Lond ; C. of St Gabriel's, Pimlico, Lond. 1860.

ARTHUR, Pellew, *Guildford, Surrey.*—Trin. Coll. Camb. B.A. 1859 ; Deac. 1860, by Bp of Winch ; Asst. Mast. at the Gram. Sch. Guildford, 1860.

ARUNDELL, Thomas, *Hayton vicarage, near York.*—St John's Coll. Camb. B.A. 1851 ; Deac. 1852, Pr. 1853, both by Bp of Winch ; V. of Hayton w Bealby, Dio. York, 1860 (Patron, Archbp of York ; V.'s Gross Inc. 325l and Ho ; Pop. Hayton, 220 ; Bealby, 305) ; formerly C. of Christ Ch. Blackfriars, Lond. 1852-54 ; C. of All Saints, Gordon-square, Lond. 1854-55 ; P.C. of St Peter's, Hammersmith, Middlesex, 1856-60.

ASHE, Thomas, *Silverstone, Towcester, Northants.*—St John's Coll. Camb. B.A. 1859 ; Deac. 1859, Pr. 1860, both by Bp of Peterb ; C. of Whittlebury-cum-Silverstone, 1860 ; Author, *Poems,* 8vo. Bell and Daldy, 1859, 5s.

ASHLEY, George Edward, *The Close, Lichfield.*—Oriel Coll. Oxon. B.A. 1854 ; Deac. and Pr. 1856, both by Bp of Lich ; late C. of St Mary's, Lichfield, 1856-60.

ASHLEY, John Marks, *Cobham terrace, Greenhithe, Kent.*—Caius Coll. Camb. LL.B. 1859 ; C. of Swanscombe, Kent, and Even. Lect. at St. Mary's, Greenhithe ; formerly C. of St Ethelburga, Lond ; Author, *The Relations of Science,* 1855 ; *Chapters on the Fathers of the Church,* 1859.

ASPLEN, George William, *Perse Grammar School, Cambridge.*—Corpus Coll. Camb. B.A. 1849, M.A. 1852 ; Deac. 1859, Pr. 1860, both by Bp of Ely ; 3rd Mast. Perse Gram. Sch. Camb ; C. of Stapleford, near Cambridge, 1859 ; Author, *Sketch of a Trip to Killarney and the South of Ireland,* 16mo. Bennett, Bishopsgate-street. Lond. 1858. 1s.

ATCHESON, Robert Steven Eden, *Houghton-le-Spring, Durham.*—Trin. Coll. Camb. B.A. 1853, M.A. 1857 ; Deac. 1858, Pr 1859, both by Bp of Carl ; C. of Houghton-ie-Spring, 1860 ; formerly C. of Dalston, Cumberland, 1858-60.

ATKINSON, George Barnes, *Trinity Hall, Cambridge.*—Trin. Ha. Camb. B.A. 1856, M.A. 1859 ; Deac. 1857 ; Pr. 1858, both by Bp of Ely ; Fell. and Asst. Tut. Trin. Ha. Camb.

AUDEN, Thomas, *Dedham, Colchester, Essex.*—St John's Coll. Camb. B.A. 1858 ; Deac. 1859, Pr. 1860, both by Bp of Roch ; C. of Langham, near Colchester ; Mast. of the Dedham Gram. Sch.

AVENT, John, *Capenhurst, Chester.*—Caius Coll. Camb. B.A. 1859 ; Deac. 1860, by Bp of Chest ; C. of Capenhurst, 1860.

BABINGTON, John, *Peterborough.*—Magd. Coll. Camb. B.A. 1814, M.A. 1817 ; Deac. 1814, Pr. 1815 ; Hon. Can. of Peterb. Cath!. 1849 ; formerly R. of Cossington, Leicestershire, 1820-59.

BACON, Francis, *Hundleby, Spilsby, Lincolnshire.*—St John's Coll. Camb. B.A. 1846, M.A. 1849 ; Deac. 1850, Pr. 1851 ; V. of Hundleby, Dio. Linc. 1860 (Patron, Lord Willoughby d'Eresby ; Tithe—V. 4l ; Glebe, 62 acres ; V.'s Gross Inc. 100l ; Pop. 562.)

BAGGE, James, *Crux-Easton rectory (Hants), near Newbury, Berks.*—St John's Coll. Camb. Jun. Opt. and B.A. 1814, M.A. 1818 ; Deac. 1814, Pr. 1815, both by Archbp of York ; R. of Crux-Easton, Dio. Winch. 1843 (Patron, the present R ; Tithe—R. 200l ; Glebe, 26 acres ; R.'s Gross Inc. 206l and Ho ; Pop. 105) ; Author, *Two Sermons* (preached at St Peter's, Hereford), 1817 ; *Letter to Sir Geo. Crewe, Bart. on the subject of the Derby Assize Ball,* 1821 ; *Remarks upon the Controversy between the Rev. Geo. Wilkins, Vicar of St Mary's, Nottingham, and the Rev. J. B. Stuart,* 8vo. Hatchards, 1823 ; *Sufficiency of the Scriptures, and Salvation by Grace* (An Answer to the Rev. Mr. Barter's *Few Words to Lord Shaftesbury*) ; *A Sermon* (preached at Old Shoreham, on the death of Mr. Payne), 1829 ; *Twelve Sermons* (preached at Melton Mowbray), ib. 1835 ; *Church-rates binding on Dissenters as well as Churchmen* (A Sermon), ib. 1837 ; *Popery in Alliance with Treason* (A Sermon), ib. 1838 ; *The Gawthorne Correspondence and the Rev. W. B. Barter,* 8vo. Painter, 1852.

BAGOT, Frederick, *Harpsden rectory, near Henley-on-Thames.*—Ch. Ch. Oxon, B.A. 1844, All Souls Coll. B.C.L. and D.C.L; R. of Harpsden, Dio. Oxon. 1859 (Patron, All Souls Coll. Oxon; R.'s Gross Inc. 700*l* and Ho; Pop. 215); late R. of Rodney-Stoke, Somerset, 1846–59; formerly Fell. of All Souls Coll. Oxon.

BAGSHAW, William Salmon, *Thrapstone rectory, Northants.*—St John's Coll. Camb, B.A. 1860; Deac. 1860, by Bp of Peterb; C. of Thrapstone, 1860.

BAILEY, Anthony Winter, *Panton rectory, Wragby, Lincolnshire.*—St Cath. Coll. Camb. B.A. 1852, M.A. 1855; Deac. 1852, Pr. 1853, both by Bp of Peterb; C. of Panton, 1860; formerly C. of Nailstone, Leicestershire, 1852–54; C. of Cadeby, Leicestershire, 1854–56; C. of St George's, Everton, Lancashire, 1856–60.

BAILEY, John Allanson, 13 *Catherine-street, Liverpool.*—Caius Coll. Camb. B.A. 1857; Deac. 1857, by Bp of Ely; Pr. 1858, by Archbp of Cant; C. of St Bride's, Liverpool, 1860; formerly C. of St Stephen's, Tonbridge, Kent, 1858–60.

BAILEY, Richard Philip Spry.—Univ. Coll. Dur. Licen. Theol; Deac. 1859, Pr. 1860, both by Bp of Oxon.

BAILEY, Thomas John.—Corpus Coll. Camb. B.A. 1860; Deac. 1860, by Bp of Chich.

BAILLIE, John, 68 *Westbourne-terrace, Bayswater, London.*—Univ. Edinb. and Caius Coll. Camb. B.D; Deac. 1857, Pr. 1858, both by Bp of Lond; Min. of Percy Episcopal Chapel, Rathbone-place, Oxford-street, Lond; formerly Min. of the Free Ch. of Scotland; Author, *Memoir of Hewitson* (10th edit); *Missionary of Kilmurry* (15th edit); *Adelaide L. Newton* (12th edit), *The Revival* (14th edit); *Life of Capt. W. Thornton Bates, R.N.* (new edit); *Life-Studies* (new edit); *Rivers in the Desert, a Narrative of the Awakening in Burmah* (new edit); *Grace Abounding, a Narrative of Facts, illustrating the Revival in Ireland and England*; *Scenes of Life, Historical and Biographical, chiefly from Old Testament times*; and other works.

BAINES, Joseph, *Coventry-road, Birmingham.*—Trin. Coll. Dub. 1858; Deac. 1860, by Bp of Worc; C. of Andrew's, Borderley, Birmingham, 1860.

BAIRD, William, 339 *City-road, London.*—Linc. Coll. Oxon. Sch. 1856, B.A. 1859; Deac. 1859, Pr. 1860, both by Bp of Lond; C. of St Matthew's, City-road, Lond. 1859; Author, various *Articles* in Periodicals.

BAKER, George Augustus, *Ibstone rectory, Tetsworth, Oxfordshire*—St John's Coll. Camb. B. 1811, M.A. 1815; Deac. 1811, Pr. 1812, both by Bp of B. and W; R. of the United R.'s of Fingest *w* Ibstone, Dio. Oxon. 1841 (Patrons, Bp of Oxon. and Merton Coll. Oxon. altern; Tithe—R. 230*l*; Glebe, 120 acres; R.'s Gross Inc. 350*l* and Ho; Pop. Fingest, 15; Ibstone, 310); Author, *The Unitarian Refuted*, 8vo. Cruttwell, Bath, 1818, 5*s*.

BAKER, George Bayldon, 4 *Park-terrace, Cambridge.*—St Cath. Coll. Camb. B.A. 1858; Deac. 1860, by Bp of Ely; C. of Ch. Ch. and the Abbey Ch. Camb. 1860.

BAKER, Samuel Ogilvy, *Muchelney, Langport, Somerset.*—St John's Coll. Camb. B.A. 1858; Deac. 1859, Pr. 1860, both by Bp of B. and W; C. of Muchelney *w* Drayton, 1859.

BAKER, Stephen Cattley, *Usk, Monmouthshire.*—St John's Coll. Camb. Coll. Prizeman, 1834, Jun. Opt. and B.A. 1837; Deac. 1837, Pr. 1838, both by Archbp of York, V. of Usk, Dio. Lland. 1860 (Patron, W. A. Williams, Esq. Llangibby Castle; Tithe—Imp. 252*l* 10*s*; V. 285*l*; Glebe, 1 acre; V.'s Gross Inc. 300*l*; Pop. 2180); formerly Chap. to the Usk County House of Correction, 1852–60; formerly V. of Skenfrith, Monmouthshire, 1846–52; Author, *Cambridge Crepuscular Conversations*, Hall, Cambridge, 1837; *The Soul's Foundation,* Edinburgh, 1846; *The Building of God,* ib. 1846; *Early Grace* (a Memoir), Kennedy, Edinburgh, 1846; 1*s* 6*d*; *A few Words from the late Curate* (a Tract), Taylor, Colchester, 1846; *The Blessed, or the First Psalm practically considered in Six Meditations,* Seeleys, 1855, 6*d*; *Reasons for a Reformatory for Monmouthshire,* 1856; various *Reports* and *Contributions* to Periodicals.

BAKER, William John, *Whaddon, Stony-Stratford, Bucks.*—St John's Coll. Camb. B.A. 1853, M.A. 1856; Deac. 1856, Pr. 1857, by Bp of Lich; C. of Whaddon.

BALDWIN, Octavius de Leyland, *Flamborough, Bridlington, Yorkshire.*—Brasen. Coll. Oxon. B.A. 1860; Deac. 1860, by Archbp of York; C. of Flamborough, 1860.

BALL, Thomas Preston, *Sefton, near Liverpool.* Trin. Coll. Dub. B.A. 1849, M.A. 1857; Deac. 1850, Pr. 1852; C. of Sefton, 1855.

BALLS, Orlando Charriere, *Bedford-street North, Liverpool.*—St Cath. Coll. Camb. Sch. 1853, B.A. 1856, M.A. 1859; Deac. 1858, Pr. 1859, both by Bp of Chest; C. of St Mary's Edge-hill, Liverpool; Mast. of the Liverpool Collegiate Institution.

BALSHAW, Edward, *Norton, Stockton-on-Tees, Durham.*—St John's Coll. Camb. Jun. Opt. B.A. 1858; Deac. 1858, by Bp of Dur; Mast. of the Gram. Sch. Norton, 1859; formerly Asst. C. of St Thomas, Stockton-on-Tees, 1858–59.

BANKES, Frederic, *Bishop's Hull, Taunton.*—Magd. Ha. Oxon. Lusby Sch. 1843, B.A. 1847, M.A. 1852, B.D. 1860; Deac. 1849, Pr. 1851, both by Bp of Worc; Head Mast. of Bishop's Hull Sch. 1860; formerly Head Mast. of the Dio. Gram. Sch. Grahamstown, Cape of Good Hope, 1853–55; Principal of St Andrew's Coll Grahamstown, 1855–60; Author, *The Worship of the Body; being a few plain words about a plain duty,* Masters; *Cultus Animæ, or an Arraying of the Soul; being Prayers and Meditations which may be used in Church before and after Service; adapted to the days of the week,* J. H. Parker; *The Work of the Ministry (an Ordination Sermon at St George's Cathedral, Grahamstown),* 1855; *Our Warning and our Work; two sermons preached in St George's Cathedral, Grahamstown, on occasion of the decease of Bp Armstrong,* 1856; *The Observance of Holy Days, a duty in the English Church; a sermon preached in St Andrew's College Chapel, Grahamstown.*

BANKS, William Thomas, 76 *Station-street, Burton-on-Trent, Staffordshire.*—Trin. Coll. Dub. B.A. 1860; Deac. 1860, by Bp. of Lich; Asst. C. of Holy Trinity, Burton-on-Trent, 1860.

BARCLAY, Henry Alexander, *Ipswich, Suffolk.*—Ch. Ch. Oxon. B.A. 1854, M.A. 1857; Deac. 1857, Pr. 1858, both by Bp. of Oxon; Sub. Mast. of Qu. Eliz Gram. Sch, Ipswich; formerly Asst. Mast. in Trin. Coll. Glenalmond.

BARDSLEY, John Waring, 57 *Elizabeth-street, Liverpool.*—Trin. Coll. Dub. B.A. 1859; Deac 1859, Pr. 1860, both by Bp. of Chest; C. of St. Luke's Liverpool, 1860; formerly C. of Sale, Cheshire, 1859–60.

BARFF, Henry Tootal, *Church-Fenton, Tadcaster, Yorkshire.*—Trin. Ha. Camb. B.A. 1858; Deac. 1859; C. of Church-Fenton.

BARLOW, Thomas Disney, *Oby, near Norwich.*—Trin. Coll. Dub. B.A. 1849; Deac. and Pr. 1854; C. of Oby, 1860; formerly C. of Creggan, Dio. Armagh, Ireland.

BARNACLE, Henry, *Altrincham, Cheshire.*—St. John's Coll. Camb. B.A. 1858; Deac. 1858, Pr. 1860, by Bp of Manch; C. of St. George's, Altrincham, 1860; formerly C. of St. Oswald's, Manch. 1858–60.

BARNARD, Thomas, *Throop House, Christchurch, Hants.*—Exon. Coll. Oxon. B.A. 1852; Deac. 1854, Pr. 1855, both by Bp of G. and B; C. of Holdenhurst, near Christchurch, 1856.

BARNES, Ismay, *Great Berkhamsted, Herts.*—Magd. Coll. Camb. B.A. 1857, M.A. 1860; Deac. 1858, Pr. 1859, both by Bp of Roch; C. of Great Berkhamsted, 1858.

BARNES, William, ... —Literate; Deac. 1860, by Bp of Lich.

BARNES, William, *Rotherham, Yorkshire.*—St Bees Theol. Coll; Deac. 1858, Pr. 1859, both by Archbp of York; C. of Rotherham, 1858.

BARNETT, James Lewis, *John-street, Hull.*—Magd. Ha. Oxon. B.A. 1859; Deac 1859, Pr. 1860; C of Christ Ch. Hull.

BARNETT, Robert Leighton, *Woburn, Bucks.*—St Peter's Coll. Camb. B.A. 1859; Deac. 1859, Pr. 1860, both by Bp of Oxon; C. of Woburn, 1859.

BARRET, Tufnell Samuel, *St George's parsonage, Barrow-in-Furness, Lancashire.*—Ch. Ch. Oxon. B.A. 1856, M.A. 1859; Deac. 1857, Pr. 1858; Incumb. of St George's, Barrow-in-Furness. Dio. Carl. 1860. (Patron, Duke of Devonshire; Incumb.'s Gross Inc. 140*l* and Ho; Pop. 4000); formerly C. of St Michael's, Hereford, 1857-58; Incumb. of Rusland, Lancashire, 1858-60.

BARRY, William Thomas, *Banchory-Ternan, near Aberdeen.*—Trin. Coll. Camb. B.A. 1850; Deac. 1851, Pr. 1852, both by Bp of Rip; P.C. of Banchory-Ternan, 1859; late C. of Coaley, Gloucestershire, 1855-59.

BARTER, Henry, *Bradford-on-Avon, Wilts.*—Merton Coll. Oxon. B.A. 1858; Deac. 1859, Pr. 1860, both by Bp of Salis; C. of Bradford-on-Avon, 1859.

BARTLETT, Alfred John, *Hammersmith, Middlesex.*—King's Coll. Lond. Theol. Assoc; Deac. 1860, by Bp of Lond; C. of St Stephen's, Hammersmith, 1860.

BARTLETT, Philip, *Icklesham, Rye, Sussex.*—Trin. Coll. B.A. 1856, M.A. 1859; Deac.1857, Pr. 1858, both by Bp of Chich; C. of Rye Harbour, Icklesham, 1857.

BARTLETT, Robert Edward, *St. Mark's parsonage, Whitechapel, London.*—Trin. Coll. Oxon. B.A. 1853, M.A. 1855, Denyer Theol. Prize 1856: Deac. 1856, Pr. 1859; Incumb. of St. Mark's, Whitechapel, city and dio. Lond. 1860 (Patron Bp of Lond; Gross Inc. 80*l* and Ho; Pop. 16,000); formerly of Trin. Coll. Oxon, 1854-60.

BARTLETT, Robert Leach, *Thurloxton, Bridgwater, Somerset.*—Wadham Coll. Oxon. B.A. 1848; Deac. 1849, Pr. 1850, both by Bp of Salis; R. of Thurloxton, Dio. B. and W. 1860; Patron, Lord Portman; Tithe, — R. 93*l* 14*s*. (R.'s Gross Inc. 170*l*; Pop. 192); formerly C. of Durweston, Dorset.

BARTON, John, *Sherfield, Romsey, Hants.*—Wadham Coll. Oxon. B.A. 1853; Deac. 1854, Pr. 1855; both by Bp of Winch; C. of Sherfield.

BARWIS, William Cuthbert, *Chipping Norton, Oxfordshire.*—Pemb. Coll. Camb. B.A. 1847, M.A. 1850; Deac. 1849, Pr. 1849, both by Bp of Rip; C. of Chipping Norton, 1858; formerly C. of St. James's, Leeds, 1848-51; P.C. of Christ Ch. 1851-55.

BASKERVILLE, Charles Gardiner, 10, *Johnson-street, Bath.*—Gon. and Cai. Coll. Camb. B.A. 1856; Deac. 1856, Pr. 1857; both by Bp of B. and W; Chap. to the Penitentiary, Bath, 1858 (Patrons, the Committee; Stipend, 200*l*) formerly Asst. C. of St James, and Min. of Corn-street Chapel, Bath.

BATEMAN, Gregory, *Ulrome House, Ulrome, Yorkshire.*—Trin. Coll. Camb. B.A. 1833, M.A. 1837; Deac. 1836, Pr. 1837, both by Bp of Lich; Patron of Ulrome V. Dio.York; formerly Crown Chap. in Van Diemen's Land, 1839-47; Author of various Sacred *Poems* and many *Sermons*.

BATTY, Robert Eaton, *Linton House, near Shipton, Yorkshire.*—Brasen. Col. Oxon. B.A. 1846; M.A. 1848; Deac. 1846, Pr. 1847, both by Bp of Oxon; C. of Linton, 1860; late Incumb. of the Donative of Wragby, Yorkshire, 1851-59; Author, *History of Baptismal Fonts, with Four Lithographs of Norman Fonts in Bucks,* 8vo. J. H. Parker, 1842, 2*s*; *Sermon on Fasting,* 1849; *Historic Sketch of Pontefract Castle,* 1852; *Sermon on the Life and Character of Wellington,* 1852.

BAUGH, William Joseph, *Farnham, Hants.*—Magd. Ha. Oxon. B.A. 1855; Deac. 1856, by Bp of B. and W; Pr. 1857, by Bp. of G. and B; C. of Farnham.

BAYLEY, William Rutter, *Summertown, Oxford.*—Oriel Coll. Oxon. B.A. 1858, M.A. 1860, Deac. 1859, Pr. 1860; Asst. C. of Summertown, 1859.

BAYLISS, William Wyke, *Brecon, S. Wales.*—St. John's Coll. Camb. Sch. 1856, B.A. 1858; Deac. 1858, by Bp of Norw. Pr. 1860, by Bp of St David's; C. of St Mary's, Brecon, 1860; formerly C. of St. Mark's, Lakenham, Norwich, 1858-59; C. of Ashwellthorpe, Norfolk, 1859-60.

BAYNE, Thomas Vere, *Christ Church, Oxford.*—Ch. Ch. Oxon. B.A. 1852, M.A. 1855; Deac. 1855, Pr. 1856, both by Bp of Oxon; Student and Tutor of Ch. Ch.

BAYNES, Charles Alexander, *Copford, Colchester, Essex.*—Trin. Coll. Camb. B.A. 1855; Deac. 1858, Pr. 1859; C. of Copford, 1859.

BAZELY, John, *Bury, Petworth, Sussex.* —Brasen. Coll. Oxon. B.A. 1857, M.A. 1860; Deac. 1858, Pr. 1859; C. of Coldwaltham w Hardham, near Petworth.

BEASLEY, Thomas Calvert, *Wellingborough, Northants.*—Trin. Coll. Camb. B.A. 1859; Deac. 1859, Pr. 1860, both by Bp of Peterb; C. of Wellingborough, 1859.

BEAUMONT, George Richardson, *Clithero, Lancashire.*—Literate; Deac. 1856, Pr. 1858, both by Bp of Rip; Asst. Mast. of Clitheroe Gram. Sch. 1850; C. of Hurst-green. Whalley, 1856.

BEAUMONT, William Beresford, *Church Stretton, Shropshire.*—Ch. Ch. Oxon. B.A. 1853; M.A. 1855; Deac. 1858, Pr. 1859, both by Bp of Heref; formerly student of Ch. Ch. Oxon. 1852-60; Asst. C. of Church Stretton, 1858-60.

BECK, Andrew, *Lavenham, Suffolk.*—Gon. and Cai. Coll. Camb. B.A. 1855, M.A. 1858; Deac. 1855, by Archbp of York, Pr. 1857, by Bp of Ely; C. of Lavenham, 1856; formerly C. of Kirk Fenton, Yorkshire, 1855-56.

BECK, James, *Parham, Steyning, Sussex.*—Corpus Coll. Camb. B.A. 1839, M.A. 1842; Deac. 1842, Pr. 1843, both by Bp of Salis; R. of Parham, Dio. Chich. 1859 (Patroness, Baroness de la Zouche; Tithe—R. 133*l*; Glebe, 15 acres; R.'s Gross Inc. 180*l*; Pop. 60); formerly C. of Pulborough, Sussex, 1852-57.

BECKWITH, George, *Brown Knot, Drigg, Whitehaven, Cumberland.*—New Coll. Oxon. B.A. 1858; Deac. 1858, Pr. 1859, both by Bp of Carl; C. of Drigg, 1858.

BEDFORD, Henry, *Frome Selwood, Somerset.*—Emman. Coll. Camb. S.C.L. 1854, LL.B. 1857, ad eund. Oxon. 1857; Deac. 1854, Pr. 1855, both by Bp of Exon; C. of Frome Selwood, 1860; formerly C. of St. James, Exeter, 1854-56; C. of Frome Selwood, 1856-58; C. of Wilmslow, Cheshire, 1858-59; C. of All Saints, Boyne Hill, Maidenhead, 1859-60.

BEEBY, William, *Birkby, Maryport, Cumberland.*—St John's Coll. Camb. B.A. 1856; Deac. 1856, Pr. 1857, both by Bp of Carl.

BEEDHAM, Maurice John, *Claverley, Bridgnorth, Shropshire.*—Gon. and Cai. Coll. Camb. B.A. 1857; Deac. 1858, Pr. 1859; C. of Claverley, 1859.

BELL, John Harrison, *Kirkley, Lowestoft, Suffolk.*—St John's Coll. Camb. B.A. 1822, M.A. 1827; Deac. 1823, Pr. 1824; R. of Kirkley, Dio. Norw. 1860 (Patron, the Hon. M. Irby; Tithe—R. 137*l* 10*s*; Glebe, 19 acres; R.'s Gross Inc. 170*l*; Pop. 799); late P. C. of Noak-hill, Essex, 1855-60; formerly Head Master of the Brentwood Gram. Sch.

BELLAMY, Franklin, *Devonport, Devon.*—St Aidan's Theol. Coll; Deac. 1854, Pr. 1855, both by Bp of Linc; C. of St. Paul's, Devonport, 1859; formerly C. of Trinity Ch. Nottingham, 1854-55; C. of Baumber w Sturton, Lincolnshire, 1855-57.

BELLAMY, Joseph, *St Michael's vicarage, Isle of Man.*—Literate; Deac. 1860, by Bp of S. and M; C. of St Michael's, Isle of Man, 1860.

BENHAM, William, *St Mark's College, Chelsea, London.*—King's Coll. Lond. Theol. Assoc. 1857; Deac. 1857, Pr. 1858, both by Bp of Lond; Tutor in St Mark's Coll. and Government Lect. on English Literature.

BENNETT, Edward Kedington, *Cheveley, Newmarket, Cambs.*—Univ. Coll. Oxon. B.A. 1858; Deac. 1858, Pr. 1859, both by Bp of Ely; C. of Cheveley, 1859; formerly C. of Swynshead, Hunts, 1858-59.

BENNETT, Hugh, *Elmley Castle vicarage, Pershore, Worcestershire.*—Worc. Coll. Oxon. B.A. 1840, M.A. 1843; Deac. 1840, Pr. 1841; V. of Elmley Castle, Dio. Worc. 1860 (Patron, Bp of Worces; Tithe—App. 412*l*, V. 130*l*; Glebe, 30 acres; V.'s Gross Inc. 195*l* and

Ho; Pop. 400); formerly C. of Lyme Regia, Dorset, 1841-51; C. of Whitwick, Leicestershire, 1852-56; Fell. of Worc. Coll. Oxon. 1840-59; Travelling Secretary for S.P.G. in Dio. York, 1856-60; Author, *Plain Statement of the Grounds on which it is contended that Marriage within the prohibited degrees is forbidden in Scripture*, Rivingtons, 1849, 1s 6d.

BENNETT, James Hatchard, *Solihull, Warwickshire.*—Exon Coll. Oxon. B.A. 1850, M.A. 1857; Deac. 1856, Pr. 1857, both by Bp of Roch; Mast. of Solihull Gram. Sch.

BENNETT, Stephen, *Uphill, Axbridge, Somerset.*—Oriel Coll. Oxon. B.A. 1845, M.A. 1848; Deac. 1850, Pr. 1851, both by Bp of Heref; C. of Uphill, 1860; formerly C. of Wyre-Piddle and Throckmorton, Worcestershire.

BENNITT, William, *Aylesbury, Bucks.*—Trin. Coll. Oxon. B.A. 1859; Deac. 1859, Pr. 1860, both by Bp of Oxon.; C. of Aylesbury, 1859.

BEN-OLIEL, Maxwell Mochluff, *Barbon, Kirkby Lonsdale. Westmoreland.*—St. Aidan's Theol. Coll; Deac. 1860, by Bp of Carl; C. of Barbon, 1860.

BERRY, Edward Fleetwood, *Tullamore rectory, King's Co. Leinster, Ireland.* — Trin. Coll. Dub. B.A. 1839; Deac. 1840, Pr. 1841; R. of Kilbride, Tullamore, Dio. Meath, 1843 (Patron, Bp of Meath; Tithe—R. 104l; Glebe, 5 acres; R.'s Gross Inc. 110l; Pop. 800); formerly C. of Tullamore, 1840-43; Author, *Lectures on Irish History*, Curry & Co. 1859.

BEST, William Edward, ... Corpus Coll. Camb. B.A. 1859; Deac. 1859, by Bp of Oxon. Pr. 1860, by Bp of Lich; formerly C. of Aylesbury, Bucks, 1859-60.

BETTS, John, *Upton St. Leonard's parsonage, near Gloucester.*—Qu. Coll. Camb. B.A. 1829; Deac. 1829, Pr. 1831, both by Bp of B. and W; P.C. of Upton St Leonard's, Dio. G. and B. 1860 (Patron, Bp of G. and B; Tithe—App. 678l 8s, Imp. 7l; Glebe, 29 acres; P.C.'s Gross Inc. 110l and Ho; Pop. 1094); formerly C. of Wollastone, Gloucestershire; formerly Asst. C. of Avening, Gloucestershire.

BEWSHER, Thomas, *Mungrisdale parsonage, near Penrith.*—St Cath. Coll. Camb. LL.B. 1856; Deac. 1856, Pr. 1857, both by Bp of Carl; C. of Mungrisdale, 1856 (Stipend, 100l.)

BIGGINS, Matthew Bennett, ... —St Bees Theol. Coll; Deac. 1860, by Bp of Lich.

BILLING, Robert Claudius, *Langford, Bristol.* —Worc. Coll. Oxon. B.A. 1857; Deac. 1857, Pr. 1858, both by Bp of Roch; Asst. Assoc. Sec. to the Ch. Miss. Soc. 1860; formerly C. of St Peter's, Colchester, 1857-60.

BILLINGTON, George Henry, *Wimborne St Giles's, Dorset.*—Emman. Coll. Camb. B.A. 1849, M.A. 1852; Deac. 1850, Pr. 1851; C. of Wimborne St Giles 1859; formerly C. of Westbury *in dextrâ parte*, Shropshire.

BINNEY, John Erskine, *Chiselhurst, Kent.*—Brasen. Coll. Oxon. B.A. 1858; Deac. 1859, Pr. 1860, both by Archbp of Cant; C. of St Nicolaus, Chiselhurst, 1859.

BIRCH, Frederick, *Milton-Abbas vicarage, Blandford, Dorset.*—New Inn Ha. Oxon. B.A. 1849; Deac. 1851, Pr. 1852, both by Bp of Worces; C. of Milton-Abbas; late C. of St Thomas, Haverfordwest, Pembrokeshire.

BIRD, John, *Albion-street, Hull.*—Trin. Coll. Dub. B.A. 1855; Deac. 1857, Pr. 1858, both by Bp of Lich; C. of St Mary's, Hull.

BIRD, Robert James, *Sandwich, Kent.*—St Aidan's Theol. Coll; Deac. 1859, Pr. 1860, both by Archbp of Cant; C. of Sandwich, 1859; formerly C. of Bexley, Kent.

BIRLEY, Alfred, *Astey Bridge, Bolton-le-Moors, Lancashire.*—Balliol Coll. Oxon. B.A. 1855, M.A. 1857; Deac. 1856, Pr. 1857, both by Bp of Manch; P.C. of Astley-bridge, Dio. Manch. 1859 (Patrons, Crown and Bp of Manch. alternately; P.C.'s Gross Inc. 150l; Pop. 2996); formerly C. of Chorley, Lancashire.

BIRLEY, Robert, 10, *Boundary-street, Hulme, Manchester.*—Balliol Coll. Oxon. B.A. 1847, M.A. 1852; Deac. 1850, Pr. 1852, both by Bp of Linc; Incumb. of St Phillip's, Hulme, Dio. Manch. 1860 (Patrons, Trustees; Pop. 8000); formerly C. of Holy Trinity, Hulme.

BISHOP, Henry Halsal, ... Chr. Coll. Camb. B.A. 1859; Deac. 1859, Pr. 1860, both by Bp of Lond; C. of All Souls, Marylebone, Lond. 1859.

BLACKER, Maxwell Julius, 27, *Gloucester-terrace, St. George's-road, Pimlico, London.*—Mert. Coll. Oxon. M.A. 1857; Deac. 1848, Pr. 1849; C. of Mary-the-less, Princes-road, Lambeth, Lond. 1858.

BLAGDEN, Henry, *St Neot's, Hunts.*—Trin. Coll. Camb. B.A. 1855, M.A. 1858; Deac. 1855, Pr. 1856, both by Bp of Ely; Sen. C. of St Neot's; formerly Asst. of St Mark's, Torwood, Devon.

BLAGG, Michael Ward, *Codrington College, Barbadoes.*—King's Coll. Lond. 1st Cl. Theol. Certif. 1856; Deac. 1856, Pr. 1857, both by Bp of Salis; Chap. of the Trust Estates of the S.P.G. Barbadoes, 1860; formerly C. of Powerstock, Dorset, 1856-60; Author, *Christ the Second Adam*, Three Sermons preached during Advent, 1858, 8vo. Masters, 1859.

BLAIR, James Samuel, *Long Benton, Northumberland.*—St Bees Theol. Coll; Deac. 1855, Pr. 1856, both by Bp of Manch; C. of Long Benton, 1858; formerly C. of Heathery-Cleugh, Durham, 1855-58.

BLAKE, William, *Dalston vicarage, Carlisle.*—Trin. Coll. Camb. B.A. 1845, M.A. 1848; Deac. 1846, by Bp of Winch. Pr. 1847, by Bp of Exon; C. of Dalston; formerly Chap. of High Legh, Cheshire.

BLATCH, William, *Perth, Scotland.*—Univ. of Edinburgh, Pantonian Theol. Stud; Deac. 1849, Pr. 1850, both by Bp of Edinburgh; Incumb. of St John's, Perth, 1855; Author, *Two Lectures on Historical Confirmation of the Scriptures*, Mason, 1843, 1s; *Lessons for the Living from the Experience of the Dying*, Johnstone, Edinburgh, 1850, 1s; *Memoir of Bishop Low, with Sketches of recent Scottish Ecclesiastical History*, Rivingtons, 1856, 7s; *Holding the Truth in Love, a Sermon on the Eucharistical Controversy*, Grant, Edinburgh, 1858; *The Bondage of Popery, a Sermon on the Tricentenary of the Reformation*, Grant, Edinburgh, 1859.

BLICK, Joseph Johnson, *Buxton, Norwich.*—St John's Coll. Camb; Deac. 1857, Pr. 1858, both by Bp of B. and W; C. of Buxton, 1860; formerly C. of Bath-easton, Bath, 1857-60.

BLISS, Thomas, *Clevedon, Somerset.*—Trin. Coll. Dub. B.A. 1839; Deac. 1840, Pr. 1841, both by Bp of B. and W; C. of Christ Church, Clevedon, 1859; late C. of Nailsea, 1857-59; formerly C. of Wraxall, near Bristol.

BLISSARD, John Charles, *Tunbridge Wells, Kent.*—St John's Coll. Camb. B.A. 1859; Deac. 1860, by Archbp of Cant; C. of St John's, Tunbridge Wells, 1860.

BLUNT, Abel Gerald Wilson, *Rectory-house, Church-street, Chelsea, London, S.W.* — R. of St Luke's, Chelsea, Dio. Lond. 1860 (Patron, Earl Cadogan; Tithe—R. 218l; R.'s Gross Inc. 1200l and Ho; Pop. 31,997); formerly P.C. of Crewe Green, Cheshire, 1856-60.

BLUNT, Arthur Henry, *Leckhampton, near Cheltenham.*—Pemb. Coll. Camb. B.A. 1858; Deac. 1859, Pr. 1860, both by Bp of G. and B; C. of St Philip's, Leckhampton, 1859.

BLUNT, Richard, Frederick Lefevre, *St Luke's rectory, Chelsea, London.*—King's Coll. Lond. Theol. Assoc. 1827; Deac. 1857, Pr. 1858; Sen. C. of St Luke's, Chelsea, 1860; formerly C. of St Paul's, Cheltenham, 1857-60.

BLYTH, Edward Kerslake, ... St John's Coll. Camb. B.A. 1860; Deac. 1860, by Bp of Norw.

BLYTH, Edward Hamilton, *Stoke, Grantham, Lincolnshire.*—Univ. Coll. Oxon. B.A. 1857; Deac. 1858, Pr. 1859, both of Bp of Chest; C. of Stoke-cum-Easton, 1859; formerly C. of Dunham Massey, Cheshire, 1858-59.

BLYTH, Frederick Cavan, *Kirkby rectory, Sleaford, Lincolnshire.*—Oriel Coll. Oxon. B.A. 1859; Deac. 1859, Pr. 1860, both by Bp of Linc; C. of Kirkby w Asgarby, 1859.

BOGLE, Michael James, *Scarborough, Yorkshire.*—Clare Coll. Camb. B.A. 1859; Deac. 1859, Pr. 1860, both by Archbp of York; C. of St Thomas's, Scarborough, 1859.

BOLLING, Edward James, *Little Cressingham, Watton, Norfolk.*—Univ. Coll. Oxon. B.A. 1850, M.A. 1853; Deac. 1853, by Bp of Manch; R. of Little Cressingham, Dio. Norw. 1859 (Patroness, Mrs. Ann Baker; Tithe—App. 5*l* 14*s*; R. 365*l* 9*s* 4*d*; R.'s Gross Inc. 400*l*; Pop. 252); late C. of Little Lever, Bolton-le-Moors.

BOMPAS, William Carpenter, *Sutton, Alford, Lincolnshire.*—Literate; Deac. 1859, by Bp of Linc; C. of Sutton, 1859.

BONE, William, *Holme Low, near Carlisle.*—Literate; Deac. 1860, by Bp of Carl; C. of St Paul's, Holme Low, 1860.

BONNEY, Thomas George, *St John's College, Cambridge.*—St John's Coll. Camb. B.A. 1856, M.A. 1859; Deac. 1857, Pr. 1860, both by Bp of Lond; Fell. of St John's Coll. Camb; Math. Mast. of St Peter's Coll. Westminster, Lond; Fell. of the Geological Society.

BONUS, Edward, *Tring, Herts.*—Corpus Coll. Camb. LL.B. 1857, B.A. 1858; Deac. 1859, Pr. 1860, both by Bp of Oxon; C. of Buckland, near Tring, 1859.

BORRADAILE, Robert Hudson, *Farnham, Surrey.*—St John's Coll. Camb. B.A. 1858; Deac. 1860, by Bp. of Winch; C. of Farnham, 1860.

BORTON, Charles, *Hartest rectory, Bury St Edmund's, Suffolk.*—R. of Hartest w Boxted R. Dio. Ely, 1853 (Patron, the Crown; R.'s Gross Inc. 670*l*. and Ho.; Pop. Hartest, 832, Boxted, 201).

BOURKE, Thomas, *Hyde, near Manchester.*—Trin. Coll. Dub. B.A. 1854; Deac. 1858, Pr. 1859, both by Bp of Exon; C. of St Paul's, Gee Cross, Werneth, near Manchester, 1860; formerly C. of Sampford Courtenay, Devon, 1858–60

BOURNE, Charles Johnston, *Crawley, near Winchester.*—Ch. Ch. Oxon. B.A. 1859; Deac. 1860, by Bp of Winch; C. of Crawley, 1860.

BOUSFIELD, George Benjamin Richings, *12 Round Hill crescent, Brighton.*—St Edm. Ha. Oxon. B.A. 1847; Deac. 1847, Pr. 1848, both by Bp of Norw.

BOUSFIELD, Henry Newham, *Stockwell, Surrey.*—Qu. Coll. Camb. B.A. 1832; Deac. 1832, Pr. 1833; C. of St Michael's, Stockwell. Author, *Sermon of One Syllable,* 12 pp.

BOWEN, Craufurd Townsend, *Skelton, Redcar, Yorks.*—St. Bees Theol. Coll; Deac. 1859, Pr. 1860, both by Archbp of York; C. of Skelton w Brotton, 1859.

BOWLES, William, *Erpingham, Aylsham, Norfolk.*—Corpus Coll. Camb. B.A. 1849; Deac. 1849, Pr. 1850, both by Bp of Norw; C. of Erpingham, 1859; formerly C. of Tunstead, and Chap. to the Smallburgh Union, Norfolk, 1854–59.

BOYS, Charles, *Wing rectory, Uppingham, Rutland.*—Merton Coll. Oxon. B.A. 1833, M.A. 1836; Deac. and Pr. 1835; R. of Wing, Dio. Peterb. 1839 (Patron, Ld. Chan; Glebe, 140 acres; R.'s Gross Inc. 330*l*. and Ho; Pop. 320); formerly V. of Shalford, Essex, 1835–39.

BOYCOTT, William, *Wheatacre-Burgh rectory, Norfolk, near Beccles, Suffolk.*—Magd. Coll. Camb. B.A. 1820, M.A. 1820; Deac. 1821, Pr. 1822; R. of Wheatacre-Burgh, Dio. Norw. 1829 (Patron, the present R; Tithe—R. 374*l*; Glebe 16 acres; R.'s Gross Inc. 400*l*. and Ho; Pop. 350).

BOYD, Archibald, *13, Sussex-gardens, Paddington, London, W.*—Trin. Coll. Camb. B.A. 1823, M.A. 1834; P.C. of Paddington, Dio. Lond, 1859 (Patron, Bp of Lond; P.C.'s Gross Inc. 1200*l*; Pop. 4293); late P.C. of Christ Church, Cheltenham, 1842–59; Hon. Can. of Gloucester Cathedral, 1857.

BOYS, Charles, *Stert, Devizes, Wilts.*—Corpus Coll. Camb. B.A. 1849, M.A. 1857; Deac. 1851, Pr. 1852; C. of Stert, 1858.

BRADDELL, Alexander, *46, Molesworth-street, Dublin.*—Trin. Coll. Dub. B.A; formerly Incumb. of St. Martin's-at-Palace, Norwich, 1853–60.

BRADLEY, Edward, *Denton rectory, Stilton, Hunts.*—Univ. Coll. Dur. B.A. and Licen. Theol. 1849; Deac. 1850, Pr. 1852, both by Bp of Ely; R. of Denton w Caldecote, Dio. Ely, 1859 (Patrons, Exors of the late Capt. Wells; R.'s Gross Inc. 150*l*. and Ho; Pop. 82); late P.C. of Bobbington, Staffordshire, 1857–59; formerly C. of Leigh and Bransford, near Worcester, 1854–57; Author of several works under the pseudonym of "Cuthbert Bede."

BRADSHAW, John Mills, *Mahon Cottage, Monmouth.*—Linc. Coll. Oxon. B.A. 1858, M.A. 1860; Deac. 1859, by Bp of Lland; C. of Llanvanor, Llangattock, Monmouth, 1859.

BRAITHWAITE, Robert, *Cheltenham.*—Literate; Deac. 1859, Pr. 1860, both by Bp of G. and B; C. of St. Mary's, Cheltenham, 1860.

BRAMSTON, William Mondeford, *Lamborne, Berkshire.*—Balliol Coll. Oxon. B.A. 1856, M.A. 1859; Deac. 1859, Pr. 1860, both by Bp of Oxon; C. of Lamborne w Eastbury, 1860.

BRANFOOT, Thomas Redhead, *Great Ilford, Essex.*—Trin. Coll. Oxon. B.A. 1834, M.A. 1842; Deac. 1836, Pr. 1837, both by Bp of Jamaica; C. of St. Mary's, Great Ilford, 1854; formerly Dom. Chap. to the Bp of Jamaica and Ecclesiastical Commissary for Port Royal; Author, *Sermon on Colonial Bishoprics,* Rivingtons, 1842.

BRASS, Henry, *10, Hampton-place, Brighton.*—Corpus Coll. Camb. B.A. 1854; Deac. 1855, Pr. 1856, both by Bp of Roch; C. of St Stephen's, Brighton, 1859; formerly C. of Holy Trinity, Brompton, Kent, 1855–57; C. of Tooting, Surrey, 1857–59.

BRATHWAITE, Francis Gretton Coleridge, *Banbury, Oxfordshire.*—Balliol Coll. Oxon. B.A. 1858; Deac. 1859, Pr. 1860, both by Bp of Oxon; C. of Banbury, 1859.

BREN, Robert, *Papworth St Agnes, St Ives, Hunts.*—Ch. Miss. Coll. Islington; Deac. 1848, by Bp of Lond, Pr. 1850, by Bp of Colombo; C. of Papworth St Agnes, 1859; formerly Missionary at Ceylon, 1849–59; Author, *Hinduism and Christianity Contrasted* (in Tamul), Ceylon.

BRENDON, William Edward, *Stretford rectory, near Manchester.*—Deac. 1851, Pr. 1853, both by Bp of Exon; R. of Stretford, Dio. Manch. 1860 (Patrons, D. and C. of Manch; Tithe—Imp. 430*l*; glebe, 20 acres; R.'s Gross Inc. 200*l*. and Ho; Pop. 4998); late C. and Asst. Chap. of St Andrew's Manchester; formerly C. of St Mary's Church, Torquay, Devon.

BREWSTER, Herbert Charles, *Bulwell rectory, Notts.*—Qu. Coll. Oxon. B.A. 1853; Deac. 1855, Pr. 1856, both by Bp of Heref; C. of Bulwell, 1860; formerly C. of Lucton, Herefordshire, 1855–56; C. of More, Shropshire, 1856–57; Asst. C. of Bulwell, 1857–60.

BRICE, Edward, *Brinkworth, Chippenham, Wilts.*—Linc. Coll. Oxon. B.A. 1856; Deac. 1856, Pr. 1857, both by Bp of G. and B; C. of Brinkworth, 1859; formerly C. of Heytesbury and Tytherington w Knook, Wilts.

BRIDGES, William, *The Union, Bridge-street, Manchester.*—Deac. 1845, Pr. 1846; Chap. of the Manchester Workhouse, 1860; late C. of St. Peter's, Preston, Lancashire, 1858–60; formerly P.C. of Lysse, Hants, 1847–58.

BRIERLEY, Edwin, *Great Broughton, Workington, Cumberland.*—St. Bees Theol. Coll; Deac. 1858, Pr. 1859; C. of Bridekirk, near Workington, 1858.

BRIGSTOCKE, Martin Whish, *Tretire, Ross, Herefordshire.*—Trin. Coll. Dub. B.A. 1849, M.A. 1853; Deac. 1852, by Bp of Lich. Pr. 1855, by Bp of Heref; C. of Tretire w Michaelchurch, 1859; formerly C. of Huntington, Herefordshire.

BRISTOW, William James, *Christ Church, Oxford.*—Balliol Coll. Oxon. B.A. 1857, M.A. 1860; Deac. 1859, Pr. 1860, both by Bp of Oxon; Chap. of Chr. Ch. Cath. Oxford, 1859.

BRODIE, Robert, *Downend, near Bristol.*—St Edm. Ha. Oxon, B.A. 1817, M.A. 1821; Deac. and Pr. 1817, both by Bp of Bristol; formerly C. of Clifton, Bristol, 1817-22; P.C. of Mangotsfield *w* Ch. Ch. Downend, Bristol, 1822-59.

BRODRIBB, William Jackson, *Wootton-Rivers vicarage, Pewsey, Wilts.*—St John's Coll. Camb; R. of Wootton-Rivers, Dio. Salis. 1860 (Patrons, St John's Coll. Camb. and Brasen. Coll. Oxon. altern; Tithe—R. 405*l*; Glebe, 50 acres; R.'s Gross Inc. 480*l* and Ho; Pop. 427); late Fell. of St John's Coll. Camb.

BROOK, James, *Helme parsonage, near Huddersfield.*—Worces. Coll. Oxon. B.A. 1854; Deac. 1854, by Archbp of York; Pr. 1857, by Bp of Rip; P.C. of Helme, Dio. Rip. 1858 (Patrons, Wm. Brook, Esq. and V. of Almondbury; P.C.'s Gross Inc. 120*l* and Ho; Pop. 800*l*); formerly C. of Cottingham, Yorkshire, 1854-56; C. of Meltham-Mills, Yorkshire, 1857-58.

BROOKE, Joshua Ingham, *East Retford, Notts.*—Univ. Coll. Oxon. B.A. 1859; Deac. 1860, by Bp of Linc; C. of East Retford, 1860.

BROOKE, William, *Moulton, Spalding, Lincolnshire.*—King's Coll. Camb. B.A. 1833, M.A. 1836; C. of Moulton.

BROOKES, John Henry, *Preston-Deanery, near Northampton.*—Brasen. Coll. Oxon. B.A. 1845, M.A. 1848; Deac. 1846, Pr. 1847; V. of Preston-Deanery, Dio. Peterb. 1859 (Patron, Langham Christie, Esq; V.'s Gross Inc. 200*l*; Pop. 65); formerly C. of Stoke-Bruerne, Northants; formerly Fell. of Brasen. Coll. Oxon.

BROWN, James Smith, *Wisbech, Cambs.*—St. Cath. Coll. Camb. B.A. 1848, M.A. 1851; Deac. 1850, Pr. 1851, both by Bp of Linc; C. of St Peter's, Wisbech.

BROWNE, Edward Harold, *The Close, Exeter, and Newnham, Cambridge.*—Emman. Coll. Camb. Wrang. and B.A. 1832, M.A. 1835, B.D. 1855; Deac. 1836, Pr. 1837, both by Bp of Ely; Norrisian Professor of Divinity in the Univ. of Camb. 1854; Can. Res. of Exon. Cathl. 1858; formerly Vice-Prin., and Prof. of Hebrew, at St Dav. Coll. Lampeter, 1837-49; V. of St Kenwyn *w* St Kea, Cornwall, 1849-57; Preb. of Exon. Cathl. 1849-58; V. of Heavitree, Devon, 1857-58; Author, *An Exposition of the XXXIX. Articles*, 2 vols. 8vo. 22*s*. 6*d*; 2nd edit. (in 1 vol.) 1854, 16*s*; 3rd edit. 1856, 16*s*; various *Pamphlets* and *Sermons.*

BROWNE, John George Colton, *Dudley, Worcestershire.*—Corpus Coll. Camb. B.A. 1858; Deac. 1858, Pr. 1859, both by Bp of Worc; C. of Dudley, 1858.

BROWNE, Sidney Spanswick, *Westport house, Grimsby.*—St Bees Theol. Coll; Deac. 1856, Pr. 1858; C. of Hornsea, Hull, 1860; formerly C. of St John's, Wolverhampton, 1857-58; C. of St Paul's, Paddington, near Pendleton, Manchester, 1858-60.

BRUCE, William Samuel, *10 Tollington-park, Upper Holloway, London.*—Gon. and Cai. Coll. Camb. B.A. 1859; Deac. 1860, by Bp of Lond; C. of St. Mark's, Holloway, 1860.

BRYAN, Hugh, *5 Canning-place, St. Margaret's, Leicester.*—Clare Coll. Camb. LL.B. 1859; Deac. 1859, Pr. 1860, both by Bp of Peterb; C. of St. Margaret's-cum-Knighton, Leicester, 1860.

BRYAN, William Bryan, *Haigh Hall, Wigan, Lancashire.*—C. of Haigh.

BRYANS, Francis Richard, *Duddon, Tarvin, Cheshire.*—Brasen. Coll. Oxon. B.A. 1858; Deac. 1859, Pr. 1860, both by Bp of Chest; C. of Duddon, 1859.

BUCKE, Benjamin Walter, *5 Delamere-crescent, Upper Westbourne-terrace, London, W.*—King's Coll. Lond. and St. John's Coll. Camb; Deac. 1850, Pr. 1852, both by Bp of Norw; Sen. C. of Trinity Ch., Marylebone, Lond; Dom. Chap. to the Marquis of Westmeath; late C. of Rendlesham, Suffolk; Author, *Pastoral Addresses.*

BUCKLAND, William, *Camborne, Cornwall.*—Worc. Coll. Oxon. B.A. 1860; Deac. 1860, by Bp of Exon; C. of Camborne, 1860.

BUCKLE, John, *Ashperton vicarage, Ledbury, Herefordshire.*—St Mary Ha. Oxon. 3rd Cl. Lit. Hum. 1843, B.A. 1844, M.A. 1847; Deac. 1844, Pr. 1845, both by Bp of Heref; V. of Stretton-Grandison *w* Ashperton, Dio. Heref. 1859 (Patron, Rev. J. Hopton; V.'s Gross Inc. 550*l* and Ho; Pop. Stretton-Grandison, 147, Ashperton, 517; formerly C. of Ashperton.

BUCKLE, Edward Valentine, *Banstead, Epsom, Surrey.*—Linc. Coll. Oxon. B.A. 1853, M.A. 1855; Theol. Coll. Wells, 1853; Deac. 1854, Pr. 1855, both by Bp of Oxon; C. of Banstead, 1859; formerly C. of Dallington, near Northampton, and C. of Tadmarton, Oxfordshire.

BUCKLEY, Charles Frederick, *Old Trafford, Manchester.*—Corpus Coll. Camb. B.A. 1849; Deac. 1849, Pr. 1850; C. of Holy Trinity, Hulme, Manchester.

BUCKLEY, Felix, *Buckland Monachorum, Plymouth.*—Merton Coll. Oxon. B.A. 1858; Deac. 1858, Pr. 1859, both by Bp of Exon; C. of Buckland Monachorum, 1858.

BUCKSTON, Henry, *Rugeley, Staffordshire.*—St John's Coll. Camb. B.A. 1856, M.A. 1859; Deac. 1857, Pr. 1858, both by Bp of Lich; C. of Rugeley, 1857.

BULL, Robert Cooke, *Park Cottage, Cambridge.*—Emman. Coll. Camb. B.A. 1859; Deac. 1859, Pr. 1860, both by Bp of Ely; C. of St Andrew the Great, Cambridge, 1859.

BULLOCK, George Frederick, *Buckfastleigh vicarage, Ashburton, Devon.*—Qu. Coll. Oxon. B.A. 1849, M.A. 1852; Deac. 1858, Pr. 1859, both by Bp of Exon; V. of Buckfastleigh, Dio. Exon 1859 (Patrons, Trustees of the late Rev. M. Lowndes; Tithe—V. 200*l*, Glebe, 33 acres; V's Gross Inc. 300*l* and Ho; Pop 2910); formerly C. of Widdecombe-in-the-Moor, Devon, 1858-59.

BULMER, Edward, *The Close, Norwich.*—St Pet. Coll. Camb. Sch. 1852, B.A. 1855, M.A. 1858; Deac. 1855, Pr. 1856, both by Bp of Heref; Asst. Min. Can. of Norw. Cathl; formerly C. of Moreton-on-Lugg, Herefordshire.

BUNBURY, Thomas Edwin George ... ...—St John's Coll. Oxon, B.A. 1860; Deac. 1860, by Bp of B. and W.

BUNCOMBE, Charles Joseph, *40 Holgate-road, York.*—Literate; Deac. 1855, Pr. 1856, both by Archbp of York; V. of St Mary's, Bishophill Junior, City and Dio. York, 1857 (Patrons, D. and C. of York; Tithe—70*l*; Glebe, 35 acres; V.'s Gross Inc. 140*l*; Pop. 3500); formerly C. of St Lawrence, York, 1855-57.

BURD, Charles, *Lapworth, Hockley Heath, Warwickshire.*—St John's Coll. Camb. B.A. 1856; Deac. 1857, Pr. 1858, both by Bp of L. and C; C. of Lapworth, 1860; formerly C. of Lee-Brockhurst, Shropshire, 1858-59.

BURGES, Richard Bennett, *Waddesdon, near Aylesbury, Bucks.*—Trin. Coll. Dub. B.A. 1851; Deac. 1851, Pr. 1852; R. of Waddesdon, third portion; Dio. Oxon. 1860 (Patron, Duke of Marlborough; R.'s Gross Inc. 175*l*; Pop. 1743); late C. of Steeple-Claydon, Bucks; formerly C. of Norton, Durham; Author, *Sermons* in the "Church of England Magazine."

BURGESS, William Roscoe, *West Derby, Liverpool.*—Gon. and Cai. Coll. Camb. B.A. 1859; Deac. 1860, by Bp of Chest; Asst. C. of St. James's, West Derby, 1860.

BURKITT, James, *8 Mer-Vue, Queenstown, Co. Cork.*—Trin. Coll. Dub. B.A. 1856, M.A. 1859; Deac. 1858, by Bp of Meath; Pr. 1859, by Bp. of Cork; Chap. of Mission to Seamen, Cork.

BURKITT, William Esdale, *Charlton, near Salisbury.*—Exon. Coll. Oxon. B.A. 1855; Deac. 1856, Pr. 1857, both by Bp of Lland; C. of Charlton, 1859; formerly C. of Caldicot, Monmouthshire.

BURLAND, Charles Wherwood, *Arreton vicarage, Isle of Wight.*—Linc. Coll. Oxon. B.A. 1853, M.A. 1856; Deac. 1854, by Bp of Rip. Pr. 1855, by Archbp. of York; C. of Arreton, 1857.

BURN, Robert ... ... —Trin. Coll. Camb. B.A. 1852, M.A. 1855 ; Deac. 1860, by Bp. of Lich.

BURNABY, Henry Fowke, *King's College, Cambridge.*—King's Coll. Camb. B.A. 1858 ; Deac. 1859, Pr. 1860, both by Bp of Linc. ; Fell. of King's Coll. Camb.

BURRELL, John, *West Stockwith parsonage, near Gainsborough.*—Univ. Coll. Dur. Licen. Theol. 1841 ; Deac. 1842, Pr. 1848, both by Bp of Dur ; Incumb. of West Stockwith, Dio. Linc. 1860 (Patrons, Trustees of W. Huntingdon ; Glebe, 90 acres ; Incumb.'s Gross Inc. 240*l* and Ho ; Pop. 1200) ; formerly P. C. of Byrness, Northumberland, 1842-59.

BURRELL, John Fletcher, *St. Giles's-road, Norwich.*—King's Coll. Lond. Theol. Assoc ; Deac. 1857, Pr. 1858, both by Bp of Norw ; C. of St. Peter Mancroft, Norwich, 1859 ; formerly C. of St. Stephen's, Norwich, 1857-1859.

BURROUGHES, Robert, *Ketton (Rutland), near Stamford, Northants.* — Oriel Coll. Oxon, B.A. 1859 ; Deac. 1859, Pr. 1860, both by Bp of Peterb ; C. of Ketton *w* Tixover, Rutland, 1859.

BURROWES, Henry, 19, *Regent square, Gray's Inn-road, Lond.*—Trin. Coll. Dub. B.A. 1858 ; Deac. 1858, Pr. 1859 ; Sen. C. of Regent-square Ch. Lond. 1860 ; formerly C. of Raddanstown and Sullamore, Dio. Meath. Ireland.

BURTON, Charles James, *Shadwell Lodge, Carlisle.*—Qu. Coll. Oxon. B.A. 1813, M.A. 1816 ; Deac. 1815, by Bp of L. and C. Pr. 1816, by Bp of Salis ; V. of Lydd. Dio. Cant. 1821 (Patron, Archbp of Cant ; Tithe—V. 1609*l*; Glebe, 28 acres ; V.'s Gross Inc. 1800*l* and Ho ; Pop. 1605) ; Chan. of the Dio. of Carl. 1855 ; Hon. Can. of Carl. Cathl. 1857 ; formerly P.C. of Ash-next-Sandwich and Norrington *w* Wymeswould, Kent, 1817-1821 ; Author, *View of the Creation of the World,* 1836.

BURTON, Edward, *Brigstock, Thrapstone, Northants.*—Bp Hat. Ha. Dur ; Deac. 1860, by Bp of Peterb : C. of Brigstock, 1860.

BUSS, Septimus, 46, *Camden-street, Kentish-town, London.*—King's Coll. Lond. B.A. 1858 ; Theol. Assoc. 1860 ; Deac. 1860, by Bp of Lond ; C. of Regent square Ch. St Pancras, Lond. 1860.

BUSSELL, John Garrett, *Newark-upon-Trent vicarage, Notts.*—Trin. Coll. Oxon. B.A. 1829 ; V. of Newark-upon-Trent, Dio. Linc. 1835 (Patron, the Crown ; Tithe — App. 147*l* 2*s* 10*d*, Imp. 367*l* 17*s* 2*d*, V. 209*l* 19*s* 6*d* ; V.'s Gross Inc. 440*l* and Ho ; Pop. 7553) ; Preb. of Carlton-cum-Thirlby in Linc. Cathl. 1859 ; Rur. D. of the Deanery of Newark ; Surrog. for Dio. Linc.

BUTCHER, John Henry, *Exeter.*—Emman. Coll. Camb. B.A. 1850 ; Deac. 1851, Pr. 1852 ; Asst. Mast. of the Free Gr. Sch. of St John's Hospital, Exeter ; formerly C. of Clavering, Essex.

BUTLER, Arthur Gray, *Rugby, Warwickshire.*—Oriel Coll. Oxon. B.A. 1859 ; Deac. 1860 ; Asst. Mast. at Rugby Sch ; Fell. of Oriel Coll. Oxon.

BUTLER, Henry Montagu, *Harrow, Middlesex.*—Trin. Coll. Camb. B.A. 1855, M.A. 1858 ; Deac. and Pr. 1859, both by Bp of Lich ; Head Mast. of Harrow Sch. 1859 ; formerly Fell. of Trin. Coll. Camb. 1856-59.

BUTT, James Acton, *Three Counties Asylum, Arlesey, Beds.* — Worc. Coll. Oxon. B.A. 1853, M.A. 1859 ; Deac. 1855, by Bp of Winch. Pr. 1856, by Bp of G. and B ; Chap. to the Three Counties Asylum, near Arlesey, 1860 ; formerly C. of Skeyton, Norfolk.

BYNG, The Hon. Francis, *Little Casterton rectory, near Stamford.*—Ch. Ch. Oxon. B.A. 1856, M.A. 1858 ; Deac. 1858, Pr. 1859 ; R. of Little Casterton, Dio. Peterb. 1859 (Patron, Lord Chesham ; R.'s Gross Inc. 254*l* and Ho ; Pop. 120) ; formerly C. of Prestwich, Lancashire, 1858-59.

BYRTH, Henry Stewart, *Earlstown, Warrington, Lancashire.*—Brasen. Coll. Oxon. B.A. 1854, M.A. 1856 ; Deac. 1856, Pr. 1857, both by Bp of Lond ; C. of Newton-in-Makerfield, near Warrington, 1859 ; formerly C. of Bow, Middlesex, 1857-59.

CADMAN, William, 5, *Upper Harley-street, London, W.*—St Cath. Ha. Camb. B.A. 1839, M.A. 1842 ; Deac. 1839, Pr. 1840, both by Bp of Ely ; R. of Holy Trin. St Marylebone, Dio. Lond. 1859 (Patron, the Crown ; R.'s Gross Inc. 1030*l* ; Pop. 11,640) ; late R. of St George the Martyr, Southwark, Lond. 1852-59.

CAMERON, Francis Marten, *Crowhurst rectory, Battle, Sussex.*—Ch. Ch. Oxon. B.A. 1846, M.A. 1849 ; Deac. 1847, Pr. 1848, both by Bp of Linc ; R. of Crowhurst, Dio. Chich. 1859 (Patron, T. Papillon, Esq ; R.'s Gross Inc. 320*l* and Ho ; Pop. 400) ; formerly P.C. of Brockham Green, Surrey, 1849-59 ; Author, *Shall there be a National Church?* Darling, 1856.

CAMERON, William, 37 *Georgiana-street, Camden-town, London.*—Qu. Coll. Camb. B.A. 1856, M.A. 1860 ; Deac. 1858, Pr. 1859, both by Bp of Lond ; C. of St Stephen's, Camden-town, 1858.

CAMIDGE, Charles Edward, *Sheffield, Yorks* —Wadham Coll. Oxon. B.A. 1859 ; Deac. 1860, by Archbp of York ; C. of Sheffield, 1860.

CAMPBELL, Alexander Burrowes, *Exmouth, Devon.*—Trin. Coll. Dub. B.A. 1830 ; Chap. to Earl Cowley, 1858 ; late P.C. of Great Redisham, Suffolk ; Author, *Sermons on the Death of William III ; On the Scottish Episcopacy ; A Humiliation Sermon ;* occasional *Sermons.*

CAMPBELL, William Adderley, *Clapham, Surrey.*—Worc. Coll. Oxon. B.A. 1860 ; Deac. 1860, by Bp of Winch ; C. of All Saints, Clapham, 1860.

CANCELLOR, John Henry, *Send, Ripley, Surrey.*—Trin. Coll. Camb. B.A. 1856, M.A. 1859 , Deac. 1857, Pr. 1858, both by Bp of L. and C ; C. of Send, 1859 ; formerly C. of Breaston, Derbyshire.

CANDY, Henry Houston, *Althorne vicarage, Maldon, Essex.*—Trin. Coll. Camb. B.A. 1852 ; Deac. 1853, Pr. 1854, both by Bp of Worc ; R. of Crixeth, alias Cricksea *w* Althorne V. Dio. Roch. 1860 (Patron, J. H. Candy, Esq. Little Hampton, Sussex ; Tithe—R. 247*l*, Glebe, 241 acres ; V. 156*l* 12*s*, Glebe 6¼ acres ; R.'s and V.'s Gross Inc. 450*l* and Ho ; Pop. Crixeth, 167, Althorne, 430) ; formerly C. of Althorne.

CANDY, Herbert, 3 *Victoria terrace, Bradford-on-Avon, Wilts.*—Linc. Coll. Oxon. B.A. 1857, M.A. 1859 ; Deac. 1857, by Bp of Lich. Pr. 1859 by Bp of Norw ; C. of Bradford-on-Avon, 1860 ; formerly C. of Moreton, Norfolk, 1858-59 ; C. of Buckland-Newton, Dorset, 1859-60

CAREW, John Warrington, *Strawley, Stourport, Worcestershire.*—Trin. Coll. Camb. LL.B. 1860 ; Deac. 1860, by Bp of Lond ; C. of Shrawley, 1860.

CAREY, Adolphus Frederick, 77 *Gloucester-street, Belgrave-road, London.*—Wadham Coll. Oxon. B.A. 1845, M.A. 1848 ; Deac. 1847, Pr. 1848, both by Bp of Peterb ; Asst. Min. of St. Matthew's Chapel, Spring Gardens, Lond, 1859 ; formerly British Chap. at Lugano, Switzerland, 1858-59 ; Author, various *Tracts.*

CARLISLE, The Hon. and Right Rev. Samuel WALDEGRAVE, Lord Bp of Carlisle, *Rose Castle, Cumberland.*—All Souls' Coll. Oxon. B.A. 1839, M.A. 1842 ; Deac. 1841, Pr. 1842, both by Bp of Oxon ; Consecrated Bp of Carlisle, 1860 (Episcopal Jurisdiction, Cumberland, Westmoreland, and parts of Lancashire ; Gross Inc. of See, 4500*l* and Residence ; Pop. 277,911 ; Acres, 1,459,840 ; Deaneries, 7 ; Benefices, 262 ; Curates, 47 ; Church Sittings, 48,472) ; his Lordship was formerly Fell. of All Souls Coll. Oxon. 1839 ; Public Exam. 1846 ; Select Preacher, 1846 ; Bampton Lect. 1854 ; Can. Res. Treas. and Preb. of Calne in Salis. Cathl. 1857-60 ; R. of Barford St Martin, near Salisbury, 1844-60 ; Author, *Way of Peace, or Teaching of Scripture concerning Justification, Sanctification, and Assurance* (set forth in four Sermons preached before the Univ. of Oxon. in 1847-48), 2nd edit. 12mo. 3*s*. ; *The Bible in Italy in 1851* (a Speech delivered before the Bedford Auxiliary Bible Soc.), 2 edit. 1852, 3*d* ; *Grieve not the*

Holy Spirit of God, and *Christ Crucified the Christ for this and every Age* (two Sermons before the Univ. of Oxon); *New Testament Millennarianism, or the Kingdom and Coming of Christ, as taught by Himself and His Apostles* (set forth in eight Sermons preached before the Univ. of Oxon. being the Bampton Lectures for 1854), 8vo. Hamilton and Adams.

CARRINGTON, Robert, *Camberwell, Surrey.* —Corpus Coll. Camb. B.A. 1859; Deac. 1859, Pr. 1860, both by Bp of Winch; C. of Camden Ch. Camberwell, 1859.

CARTER, Arthur Richard, *Spennymoor, Ferry hill, Durham.*—Qu. Coll. Oxon. B.A. 1860; Deac. and Pr. 1860, both by Bp of Dur; C. of Whitworth and St Paul's, Spennymoor, 1860.

CARTWRIGHT, Anson William Henry, *Brimley house, Teignmouth, Devon.*—Qu. Coll. Camb. B.A. 1856; Deac. 1859, by Bp of Worc. Pr. 1860, by Bp of Salis; Sen. C. of St Michael's, Teignmouth, 1859.

CARY, Lucius Ormsby, ... —Trin. Coll. Camb. B.A. 1860; Deac. 1860, by Bp of Chich.

CASS, William Anthony, *Horbury, Wakefield.* Literate; Deac. 1854, Pr. 1855, both by Bp of Rip; C. of Horbury, 1854.

CASTLEMAN, William Henry, *Crawley, near Winchester.*—Trin. Coll. Camb. B.A. 1859; Deac. 1860, by Bp of Winch; C. of Crawley, 1860.

CASTLEY, Elias, *Darlington, Durham.*—St Bees Theol. Coll; Deac. 1858, Pr. 1859, both by Archbp of York; C. of St John's, Darlington, 1860; formerly C. of Hinderwell, Yorkshire, 1858-60.

CAUTLEY, George Spencer, *Nettleden (Bucks), near Tring, Herts.*—Pemb. Coll. Camb. B.A. 1829; Deac. 1831, Pr. 1832; P.C. of Nettleden, Dio. Oxon. 1857 (Patrons, Guardians of the Earl of Brownlow; P.C.'s Gross Inc. 60*l*; Pop. 107.)

CAVE-BROWNE-CAVE, Edward Farsyde, *Hugglescote, near Ashby-de-la-Zouch.*—Jesus Coll. Camb. B.A. 1856, M.A. 1859; Deac. 1857, Pr. 1858, both by Bp of Manch; C. of Hugglescote-cum-Donington-the-Heath, 1858; formerly C. of Penwortham, near Preston, 1857-58.

CAWLEY, Thomas, *Naseby, near Welford, Northants.*—Wadham Coll. Oxon. B.A. 1860; Deac. 1860, by Bp of Peterb; C. of Naseby, 1860.

CAY, Christopher, ... —Emman. Coll. Camb. B.A. 1860; Deac. 1860, by Bp of Winch.

CHALMERS, John, *2 Belvedere terrace, Brighton.* —Kg. Coll. Lond. Theol. Assoc; Deac. 1851, Pr. 1851, both by Bp of Heref; P.C. of St Stephen's, Brighton, Dio. Chich. 1857 (Patron, V. of Brighton; P.C.'s Gross Inc. 450*l*; Pop. 1000); late P.C. of St Leonards-on-Sea, 1856-57.

CHAMBERLAIN, Frederick Townshend, *Allport cottage, Whitchurch, Shropshire.*—St Aidan's Coll. 1851, Trin. Coll. Dub. B.A. 1856; Deac. 1853, Pr. 1854, both by Bp of Chest; C. of Whitchurch, 1859; formerly C. of Holy Trin. Chester.

CHAMBERLAIN, Samuel, *Shrewton vicarage, Devizes, Wilts.*—Wadh. Coll. Oxon. B.A. 1859; Deac. 1860, by Bp of Salis; Asst. C. of Maddington, near Devizes, 1860.

CHAMBERS, William Hampson, *Dalston, Middlesex.*—Bp Cosin's Ha. Dur. Theol. Licen. 1859; Deac. 1859, Pr. 1860, both by Bp of Lond; C. of St Matthias, Bethnal-green, Lond. 1859.

CHAMPNEYS, William Weldon, *St Pancras vicarage, Gordon-square, London.*—Brasen. Coll. Oxon. B.A. 1828, M.A. 1831; Can. Res. of St Paul's Cathl. 1851 (value 1000*l*.); V. of St Pancras, Dio. Lond. 1860 (Patron, D. and C. of St Paul's Cathl; V.'s Gross Inc. 1700*l* and Ho; Pop. 13,314); formerly R. of Whitechapel, Lond. 1837-60.

CHANDLER, Henry Christian David, *Haverfordwest, Pembrokeshire.* — Gon. and Cai. Coll. Camb. B.A. 1859; Deac. 1860, by Bp of St David's; C. of St Mary's, Haverfordwest, 1860; Author, *Various Tracts* for the "Weekly Tract Society."

CHAPMAN, Dawson Francis, *4 Regent-street, Preston.*—Trin. Coll. Dub. B.A. 1856, M.A. 1859; Deac. 1856, Pr. 1857, both by Bp of Manch; C. of Par. Ch. Preston, 1859; formerly C. of Trin. Ch. Blackburn, 1856-59; Author, *A New Year's-Eve Sermon,* Blackburn, 1856; *Morning and Evening Prayer for persons much employed,* Preston, 1858.

CHARLESWORTH, Edward Gomersall, *2 Mount-pleasant, Darlington, Durham.*—St Bees Theol. Coll. 1852; Deac. 1853, by Archbp of York, Pr. 1854, by Bp of Rip; C. of Holy Trin. Darlington, 1860; late C. of St Mark's, Old-street, Lond. 1859-60; formerly C. of Kirby-on-the-Moor, Yorkshire; previously C. of Scammonden, Yorks.

CHARLTON, Charles, *St Paul's parsonage, Alnwick, Northumberland.*—St John's Coll. Camb. B.A. 1841, M.A. 1844; Deac. 1842, Pr. 1843, both by Bp of Peterb; L.C. of St Paul's, Alnwick, Dio. Dur. 1846 (Patron, Duke of Northumberland; P.C.'s Gross Inc. 200*l* and Ho; Pop. 3065); formerly C. of Slipton, Northants, 1842-43; C. of Cranford, Northants, 1843-44.

CHARSLEY, Robert Harvey, *Oxford.*—St Mary Ha. Oxon. B.A. 1853, M.A. 1856; Deac. 1853, Pr. 1855; Chap. of the Radcliffe Infirmary, and of the Industrial Training Sch. Oxford.

CHEPMELL, William Henry, *Jesus College, Oxford.*—Magd. Ha. Oxon. B.A. 1841, Jesus Coll. Oxon. M.A. 1843; Deac. 1842, Pr. 1843; Fell. of Jesus Coll. Oxon; formerly C. of St Peter-le-Bayley, Oxford.

CHOLMELEY, Waldo, *Hambleton, Garstang, Lancashire.*—St Bees Theol. Coll; Deac. 1856, Pr. 1857, both by Bp of Manch; C. of Hambleton, 1858; formerly C. of Churchkirk, Lancashire, 1856-58.

CHOLMONDELEY, George James, *Canterbury, New Zealand.*—St Aidan's Theol. Coll. 1858; Deac. 1858, by Bp of Norw. Pr. 1859, by Bp of G. and B; formerly C. of Lydney w Aylburton, Gloucestershire, 1858-60.

CHRISTIAN, Frederick White, *Tinwell (Rutland), near Stamford, Northants.*—Trin. Ha. Camb. B.A. 1859; Deac. 1859, Pr. 1860, both by Bp of Peterb; C. of Tinwell, 1859.

CHRISTIE, James John, *Carolgate, Retford, Nots.*—St John's Coll. Camb. B.A. 1855, M.A. 1858; Deac. 1856, Pr. 1857, both by Bp of Lond; 2nd Mast. of the Gram. Sch. East Retford, 1860; formerly Math. Lect. at the Training Coll. Highbury, Lond, 1855-57.

CHRITCHLEY, John Martyn, *The Temple, Brighton.*—Trin. Coll. Dub. B.A. 1858; Deac. 1859, by Bp of Chich; C. of Clayton w Keymer, near Brighton, 1859.

CLARK, Francis Storer, *26 High-street, Ipswich, Suffolk.*—St John's Coll. Camb. B.A. 1858; Deac. 1859, Pr. 1860, both by Bp of Norw; C. of St Margaret's, Ipswich, 1859.

CLARK, John Meek, *Magdalen College, Cambridge, and Oxford and Cambridge University Club, Pall-mall, Lond.*—Magd. Coll. Camb. B.A. 1856; Deac. 1857, Pr. 1859; Fell. and Lect. of Magd. Coll. Camb.

CLARK, William Robinson, *St Mary Magdalene vicarage, Taunton, Somerset.*—V. of St Mary Magdalene, Taunton, Dio. B. and W. 1860 (Patron, the present V; V.'s Gross Inc. 300*l* and Ho; Pop. 5837); formerly C. of St Matthias, Birmingham.

CLARKE, David George, *Brecon.* — Jesus Coll. Oxon. Sch. 1858, B.A. 1860; Deac. 1860, by Bp of St Dav: C. of St Mary's, Brecon, 1860.

CLARKE, John, *Winlaton, near Newcastle-on-Tyne.*—Qu. Coll. Cork, B.A. 1858, ad eund. Univ. Coll. Dur. Licen. Theol 1860; Deac. 1860, by Bp of Dur; C. of Winlaton, 1860.

CLARKE, William Graset, *Charlton-Abbots, Winchcombe, Gloucestershire.*—Oriel Coll. Oxon. B.A. 1844, M.A. 1846; Deac. 1845, Pr. 1846; P.C. of Charlton-Abbots, Dio. G. and B. 1859 (Patron, J. C. Chamberlayne, Esq; P.C.'s Gross Inc. 42*l*; Pop. 112); formerly C. of Iccomb, Gloucestershire.

CLAY, George Hollis, *Aspatria, near Carlisle.* —Clare Coll. Cam. B.A. 1860; Deac. 1860, by Bp of Dur; C. of Aspatria, 1860.

CLAYFORTH, Henry, *Darfield, Barnsley, Yorkshire.*—Trin. Coll. Dub. B A. 1857; Deac. 1857, Pr. 1858, both by Archbp of York; C. of the first Mediety of Darfield, 1857.

CLEGG, John ... ...
—Magd. Ha. Oxon. B.A. 1860; Deac. 1860, by Bp of B. and W.

CLEMENTS, Jacob, *Gainsborough vicarage, Lincolnshire.*—Oriel Coll. Oxon. B.A. 1842, M.A. 1845; Deac. 1843, Pr. 1844; V. of Gainsborough, Dio. Linc. 1859 (Patron, Bp of Linc) V.'s Gross Inc. 650*l* and Ho; Pop. 4419); Preb. of Corringham in Linc. Cathl. 1859; formerly P.C. of Upton St Leonard's, near Gloucester, 1846–59; Author, *The Farmer's Case, with regard to Education, plainly stated* (Pamphlet), Rivington, 8vo. 1851, 6d.

CLEMENTS, William Frederick, *Colchester, Essex.*—King's Coll. Lond. A.K.C. 1860; Deac. 1860, by Bp of Roch; C. of St Peter's, Colchester, 1860.

CLIFFORD, Henry Marcus, *Scawby Brigg, Lincolnshire.*—Wadh. Coll. Oxon. B.A. 1856; Deac. 1858, Pr. 1859, both by Archbp of York; C. of Scawby, 1859.

CLOUGH, John, *Harpham Field House, Low-thorpe, Yorks.*—Brasen. Coll. Oxon. B.A. 1857; Deac. 1859, Pr. 1860, both by Archbp of York; C. of Burton Agnes and Harpham, 1859.

CLULEE, Charles, *South Benfleet, Rayleigh, Essex.*—Qu. Coll. Birmingham, Theol. Stud; Deac. 1860, by Bp of Roch; C. of South Benfleet, 1860.

CLUTTERBUCK, John Balfour, *Leighterton. rectory, Wotton-under-Edge, Gloucestershire.*—St Peter's Coll. Camb. B.A. 1855; Deac. 1856, Pr. 1857; R. of Boxwell w Leighterton, Dio. G. and B. 1857 (Patron, R. F. Huntley, Esq; R.'s Gross Inc. 325*l* and Ho; Pop. 250); formerly C. of Tresham, Gloucestershire, 1856–57.

CLUTTERBUCK, Lorenzo, *Bidford (War-wickshire), near Bromsgrove.*—Trin. Coll. Dub. B.A. 1855, M.A. 1858; Deac. 1857, Pr. 1858, both by Bp of Worc; C. of Bidford and Salford, 1857; C. of Exhall-cum-Wixford, 1858.

COBBOLD, The Ven. Robert Henry, *Broseley rectory, Shropshire.*—St Peter's Coll. Camb. Sen. Opt. B.A. 1843, M.A. 1846; Deac. 1844, Pr. 1845, both by Bp. of Norw; R. of Broseley w Linley R. Dio. Heref. 1859 (Patron, Lord Forester; Glebe, 12 acres; R.'s Gross Inc. 480*l*; Pop. 5000); late V. of Field Dalling, Norfolk, 1858–59; formerly Archd. of Ningpo, Victoria, 1836–58; Author, *Questions on the Collects*, Hamilton and Adams, 8vo. 1847; *The Chinese at Home; or, Pictures of the Chinese*, small 8vo. John Murray, 1859.

COCHRANE, David Crawford, *Burton-on-Trent, Staffs.*—Trin. Coll. Dub. B.A. 1857, M.A. 1860; Deac. 1859, Pr. 1860, both by Bp of Lich; C. of Holy Trin. Burton-on-Trent, 1859.

COCKE, Frederick Heysett, *Norwell, Newark, Notts.*—Magd. Coll. Camb. B.A. 1846; Deac. 1847, by Bp of Exon. Pr. 1857, by Bp of Linc; C. of Norwell w Carlton.

COCKETT, Francis John, *Yardley-Hastings, near Northampton.*—St Aidan's Theol. Coll; Deac. 1860, by Bp of Peterb; C. of Yardley-Hastings, 1860.

CODD, Samuel ... ...
—St Bees' Theol. Coll; Deac. 1859, Pr. 1860, both by Bp of Lich.

CODRINGTON, Henry, *Goathurst, Bridgwater, Somerset.*—St John's Coll. Camb. B.A. 1832; Deac. 1832, Pr. 1833, both by Bp of B. and W; C. of Goathurst; Author, *Family Prayers*, 1 vol. Hamilton and Adams, 1845; Various *Pamphlets* and *Tracts*.

COLLETT, Anthony, *Dover, Kent.*—Trin. Coll. Camb. B.A. 1859; Deac. 1859, Pr. 1860, both by Archbp of Cant; C. of St Mary's, Dover, 1860.

COLLIER, Herbert Augustus, *Carrington, Boston, Lincolnshire.*—Gon. and Cai. Coll. Camb. B.A. 1859; Deac. 1860, by Bp of Linc; C. of Carrington, 1860.

COETLOGON, Charles Prescott de, *Ches-terton, Warwick.*—Exon. Coll. Oxon. B.A. 1860; Deac. 1860, by Bp of Lond; C. of Chesterton, 1860.

COLLINS, Richard, *St Saviour's vicarage, Leeds.*—Univ. Coll. Oxon. S.C.L. 1848, B.A. 1857, M.A. 1858; Deac. 1851, Pr. 1858; V. of St Saviour's, Leeds, Dio. Rip. 1859 (Patrons, Trustees; Tithe—V. 27*l*; Pop. 6000).

COLLINS, Thomas, *Newcastle-under-Lyme, Staffs.*—Sid.-Suss. Coll. Camb. B.A. 1856; Deac. 1859, Pr. 1860, both by Bp of Lich; C. of St George, New-castle-under-Lyme, 1859; 2nd Mast. of Newcastle Gram. Sch.

COLLYNS, Charles Henry, 23 *Upper Camden-place, Bath.*—Ch. Ch. Oxon. B.A. 1841, M.A. 1844; Deac. 1843, Pr. 1844; Class. Asst. Mast. and Prof. of French at Kg. Edw. VI. Sch. Bath; Author, *Translation of the Works of St Pacian, Bishop of Bar-celona, in the " Library of the Fathers,"* 8vo. Rivingtons, 1844.

COLTON, William Charles, 4 *King street, Leeds.*—Qu. Coll. Oxon. B.A. 1836; Deac. 1836; V. of Baston, Lin-colnshire, Dio. Linc. 1836 (Patron, Ld. Chan) V.'s Gross Inc. 250*l*; Pop. 863).

COLWILL, James, *Lyncombe, near Bath.*—Magd. Coll. Camb. Sch. 1856, B.A. 1859; Deac. 1859, Pr. 1860, both by Bp of B. and W; C. of Lyncombe, 1859.

COOK, Christopher, *St Neot, near Liskeard, Cornwall.*—St Dav. Coll. Lamp; Deac. 1850, Pr. 1851, both by Bp of Lland; C. of St Neot's, 1860; formerly P.C. of Llanvihangel, Pontymoil, Monmouthshire, 1851–55; P.C. of Mamhilad, Abergavenny, Monmouthshire, 1855–58.

COOKE, George Frederic, *Taunton, Somerset,* —New Coll. Oxon. B.A. 1859; Deac. 1859, Pr. 1860, both by Bp of B. and W; Asst. C. of St Mary Magdalen, Taunton, 1859.

COOKE, George Robert Davies, *Kelfield, Escrick, Yorks.*—Ch. Ch. Oxon. B.A. 1859; Deac. 1860, by Archbp of York; C. of Stillingfleet, near Escrick, 1860.

COOLEY, William Lake Johnson, *Renning-ton parsonage, Alnwick, Northumberland.*—Bp Hat. Ha. Dur. B.A. 1857, M.A. 1860; Deac. 1856, Pr. 1857, both by Archbp of Cant; P.C. of Rennington w Rock P.C. 1860 (Patron, V. of Embleton; Glebe, 4 acres; P.C.'s Gross Inc. 130*l* and Ho; Pop. Rennington, 260, Rock, 250); formerly C. of St Mary, Romney Marsh, Kent, 1856–57; C. of Dymchurch, Kent, 1857–58; C. of New-burn, Newcastle-on-Tyne, 1858–60.

COOMBE, Alexander Barn, ... Univ. Coll. Oxon. B.A. 1860; Deac. 1860, by Bp of Winch; C. of Christ Ch. Bermondsey, Lond. 1860.

COOMBES, Jeremiah, *Grammar School Cottage, Stockport, Cheshire.*—Literate; Deac. 1859, Pr. 1860; both by Bp of Chest; C. of Stockport Great Moor, 1859; Asst. Mast. of Stockport Gram. Sch.

COOPER, Edward Henry, *Coddenham, Need-ham Market, Suffolk.*—Univ. Coll. Dur. Theol. Licen. 1857; Deac. 1858, Pr. 1859, by Bp of Norw; C. of Cod-denham, 1859.

COOPER, Edward James, *Hawes, Bedale, Yorks.*—Qu. Coll. Oxon. B.A. 1853, M.A. 1857; Deac. 1854, Pr. 1855, both by Bp of Rip; P.C. of Hawes, Dio. Rip. 1860 (Patron, V. of Aysgarth; P.C.'s Gross Inc. 150*l*; Pop. 1708); formerly C. of Gasforth, near Leeds, 1857–60.

COOPER, Mark, *The Deanery, Southampton.*—St John's Coll. Camb. Coll. Prizeman, B.A. 1828, M.A. 1831; Deac. 1828, Pr. 1829, both by Archbp of York; R. of St Mary's, Southampton, Dio. Winch. 1860 (Patron, Bp of Winch; R.'s Gross Inc. 1000*l* and Ho; Pop. 8190); for-merly V. of Bramshaw, Hants, 1840–60; Author, *Three Tracts on Confirmation*; various *Tracts* and *Sermons*.

COOPER, Thomas, 67 *Branch-road, Blackburn, Lancashire.*—Chr. Coll. Camb. B.A. 1860; Deac. 1860, by Bp of Manch; C. of St. Peter's, Blackburn, 1860.

COOPER, Thomas John, ... Univ. Coll. Oxon; B.A. 1860; Deac. 1860, by Bp of Lich.

COPELAND, George Dale, *Wigan, Lancashire.* —Literate; Deac. 1859, Pr. 1860, both by Bp of Chest; of St. Thomas, Wigan, 1859.

CORDEAUX, Henry Taylor, *Chevening, Sevenoaks, Kent.*—St. John's Coll. Camb. B.A. 1857; Deac. 1857, by Bp of Roch. Pr. 1858, by Bp of Ely; C. of Chevening, 1859.

CORFE, Nelson Benjamin, *Awre, Newnham, Gloucestershire.*—Worc. Coll. Oxon. B.A. 1860; Deac. 1860, by Bp of G. and B; C. of Awre, 1860.

CORNALL, Richard, 34, *Clarence-grove, Everton, Liverpool.*—St. Bees Theol. Coll; Deac. 1859, Pr. 1860, both by Bp of Chest; C. of Christ Ch. Everton, 1859.

CORNFORD, Edward, *Stroud, Gloucestershire.*—St. John's Coll. Camb. B.A. 1855; Deac. 1856, by Bp of Exon, Pr. 1857, by Bp of Grahamstown; C. of Stroud, 1859; formerly Chap. to Bp of Grahamstown, 1857–58; Author, various *Papers in South African and other periodicals.*

CORNISH, Charles John, *Debenham vicarage, Suffolk.*—Corpus Coll. Oxon. B.A. 1856; Deac. 1858, by Bp of Exon; Pr. 1859, by Bp of Norw; V. of Debenham, Dio. Norw. 1859 (Patron, Lord Henniker; Tithe—V. 282*l*; V.'s Gross Inc. 300*l.* and Ho; Pop. 1653); formerly C. of Sidbury, Devon, 1858–59.

CORNWALL, Arthur Walton, *Barnham, near Chichester.*—Bp Hat. Ha. Univ. Dur. Licen. Theol. 1851; Deac. 1851, Pr. 1853, both by Bp of Chich; V. of Barnham, Dio. Chich. 1860 (Patron, Bp of Chich; V.'s Gross Inc. 80*l*; Pop. 149); late C. of Lower Beeding, Sussex; formerly C. of Horsham, Sussex; previously C. of Flimwell, Sussex.

CORSER, Richard Kidston, *Pewsey, Wilts.*—Corpus Coll. Camb. B.A. 1858; Deac. 1858, Pr. 1860; C. of Wilcot, Wilts, 1858.

COTES, Peter, *Litchfield rectory, Andover-road, Hants.*—Wadh. Coll. Oxon. 2nd Cl. Lit. Hum. and B.A. 1824, M.A. 1827; Deac. 1826, Pr. 1827, both by Bp of Lond; R. of Litchfield, Dio. Winch. 1832 (Patron, W. Kingsmill, Esq; Tithe—R. 400*l*; R.'s Gross Inc. 430*l* and Ho; Pop. 85); formerly C. of Wherwell, Hants, 1826–31; C. of Shaw-cum-Donnington, Berks, 1831–32; Author, various *Sermons* and *Pamphlets,* Hatchards.

COVEY, Richard, *High Wycombe, Bucks.*—Sid.-Suss. and Gon. and Caius Coll. Camb. B.A. 1859; Deac. 1860, by Bp of Oxon; C. of High Wycombe, 1860 (Stipend, 80*l.*)

COWAN, Charles Ernest Randle, ...—Caius Coll. Camb. B.A. 1859; Deac. 1859, Pr. 1860, both by Bp of Winch.

COX, Thomas, *Stockwell, Surrey.*—King's Coll. Lond. Theol. Assoc; Deac. 1860, by Bp of Winch; C. of Stockwell Chapel, 1860.

COX, George William, *Tivoli, Cheltenham.*—Trin. Coll. Oxon. S.C.L. 1849, B.A. and M.A. 1859; Deac. 1850, by Bp of Oxon. Pr. 1851, by Bp of Exon; Asst. Mast. in Cheltenham Coll. 1859; formerly C. of Salcombe Regis, Devon, 1850–54; C. of St Paul's, Exeter, 1854–59; Author, *Poems, Legendary and Historical,* 8vo. Lond. Longman, 1850, 10*s* 6*d*; *Tales from Greek Mythology,* 12mo. ib. 1861, 3*s* 6*d*; various *Papers* and *Essays* in *Magazines* and *Periodical Publications.*

COXHEAD, John James, 1 *Surrey-street, Strand, London.*—Corpus Coll. Oxon. B.A. 1860; Deac. 1860, by Bp of Lond; C. of St Clement Danes, Strand, Lond. 1860.

CRAIG, Allen Tudor, *Wanstead, Essex.*—Wadh. Coll. Oxon. B.A. 1858; Deac. 1859, Pr. 1860, both by Bp of Lond; C. of Wanstead, 1859.

CRALLAN, Thomas Edward, *Warminster, Wilts.*—Emman. Coll. Camb. B.A. 1849, M.A. 1857; Deac. 1849, Pr. 1850, both by Bp of Chich; Head Mast. of Lord Weymouth's School, Warminster, 1857; formerly 2nd Mast. of Lewis Gram. Sch. 1849–51; C. of Newick, Sussex, 1851–57.

CRASTER, Thomas Henry, *Mansfield, Notts.*—Univ. Coll. Oxon. B.A. 1857, M.A. 1860; Deac. 1860, by Bp of Linc; C. of St John's, Mansfield, 1860.

CRAVEN, Samuel, 71 *Vicarage-place, Walsall, Staffs.*—Sid.-Suss. Coll. Camb. B.A. 1855; Deac. 1855, Pr. 1856; C. of St Matthew's, Walsall, 1857; formerly C. of Lower Mitton, Worcestershire, 1855 57.

CRAWFURD, Charles Walter Payne, *Bourton-on-Water, Moreton-in-Marsh, Gloucestershire.*—Brasen. Coll. Oxon. B.A. 1847, M.A. 1850; Deac. 1849, Pr. 1850; C. of Bourton-on-Water, 1858; formerly C. of Snettisham, Norfolk.

CRAWLEY, Charles David, *Warminster, Wilts.*—Ch. Ch. Oxon. B.A. 1858; Deac. 1860; C. of Warminster, 1860.

CRESWELL, Samuel Francis, *Tonbridge, Kent.*—St John's Coll. Camb. B.A. 1859; Deac. 1860, by Archbp of Cant; C. of Hildenborough Chapelry, Tonbridge, 1860; Asst. Mast. at Tonbridge Sch; Contributor to "*Annals of Nottinghamshire,*" Simpkin and Marshall.

CRICHLOW, Henry M'Intosh, *Puddletown, Dorset.*—Trin. Coll. Camb. B.A. 1827, M.A. 1834; Deac. 1833, by Bp of Exon, Pr. 1834, by Bp of B. and W; C. of Puddletown, 1859.

CRIPPS, William Richard, *Diocesan Training College, Chester.*—Chr. Coll. Camb. B.A. 1860; Deac. 1860, by Bp of Chest; C. of Little St John's, Chester, 1860.

CROFTON, Edward, 2 *Clarence-terrace, Southsea.*—St. Mary Ha. Oxon. B.A. 1858, M.A. 1859; Deac. 1858, Pr. 1859; Asst. C. of St Paul's, Southsea, 1860; formerly C. of Patcham, Sussex, 1858–60.

CROKER, William Foord, *Sidmouth, Devon.*—Trin. Ha. Camb. B.A. 1856, M.A. 1859; Deac. 1858, Pr. 1859, both by Bp of Exon; C. of Sidmouth, 1858.

CROOK, James, *Smethwick, near Birmingham.*—Bp Hat. Ha. Dur. B.A. 1855; Deac. 1855, Pr. 1856; C. of St Matthew's, Smethwick.

CROSLAND, Jonathan, *Berkley, Frome, Somerset.*—Bp Cos. Ha. Dur. Licen. Theol. 1859; Deac. 1859, Pr. 1860, both by Bp of B. and W; C. of Berkley, 1859.

CROSSMAN, Charles Danvers, ...—Worc. Coll. Oxon. B.A. 1859; Deac. 1860, by Bp of Oxon.

CROWDEN, Charles, *Merchant Taylor's School, Suffolk-lane, Cannon-street, London.*—Linc. Coll. Oxon. B.A. 1859; Deac. 1860, by Bp of Lond; Assist. Mast. at Merchant Taylor's Sch. Lond. 1860; C. of St Margaret's, Lothbury, Lond. 1861.

CRUSE, Francis, 4 *Gladstone-place, Southwark, London.*—St Edm. Ha. Oxon. B.A. 1851; Deac. 1851, Pr. 1852; P.C. of St Jude's, Southwark, Dio. Winch. 1856 (Patrons, Trustees; Pop. 6547); formerly C. of Great Warley, Essex; Author, *Village Sermons,* Nisbet, 1855, 5*s.*

CUDLIP, Pender Hodge, *Buckfastleigh, Ashburton, Devon.*—Magd. Ha. Oxon. B.A. 1859; Deac. 1860, by Bp of Exon; C. of Buckfastleigh, 1860.

CUPPAGE, Robert Jackson, 6 *Crescent-place, Glasgow.*—Trin. Coll. Dub. B.A. 1853, 1st Cl. Sen. Divinity, 1854; Deac. 1854, Pr. 1855, both by Bp of Carl; P.C. of St John's, Glasgow, 1860; late C. of Monk's Kirby, near Lutterworth; formerly C. of Haigh, Lancashire; Author. single *Sermons.*

CURRIE, Frederick Hill, *Elm, Frome, Somerset.*—Wadh. Coll. Oxon. B.A. 1858; Deac. 1858, Pr. 1859, both by Bp of B. and W; C. of Elm, 1859; formerly C. of Kingsbury, Somerset, 1858–59.

CURRIE, Maynard Wodehouse, *Mentmore vicarage, Leighton Buzzard, Bucks.*—Trin. Coll. Camb. B.A. 1852, M.A. 1856; Deac. 1852, Pr. 1854; V. of Mentmore, Dio. Oxon. 1860 (Patron, Baron Mayer de Rothschild; Tithe—R. 190*l.*; V.'s Gross Inc. 200*l.* and Ho; Pop. 356); formerly C. of Banbury, 1852–54; C. of Saltwood, Kent, 1854–58; C. of Longworth, Berks, 1858–60.

CURRY, Henry Thomas, *Tunstall rectory, Woodbridge, Suffolk.*—Trin. Coll. Camb. B.A. 1835, M.A. 1838; Deac. 1835, Pr. 1836; R. of Tunstall, Dio. Norw. 1859 (Patron, the present R; R.'s Gross Inc. 400*l.* and Ho; Pop. 676); late Min. of Leaven Heath, Suffolk, 1841–59.

CUSTANCE, Charles William Neville, *Uxbridge, Middlesex.*—Corpus Coll. Camb. B.A. 1858; Deac. 1859, Pr. 1860; C. of Uxbridge, 1860.

CUTLER, Charles Septimus, *Darley, Matlock, Derbyshire.*—St John's Coll. Camb. Sch. 1854, B.A. 1856; Deac. 1858, Pr. 1860, both by Bp of Lich; C. of Darley, 1858.

CUTLER, Henry George Gervase, 14, *Norfolk-square Brighton.*—St John's Coll. Oxon. B.A. 1852; Deac. 1853, Pr 1854, both by Bp of Roch; C. of Christ Ch. Brighton, 1860; late C. of Mortlake, Surrey, formerly C. of East Donyland, Essex.

———◆———

DALTON, James, *Church-Broughton, near Derby.*—Worc. Coll. Oxon. B.A. 1853, M.A. 1856; Deac. 1855, Pr. 1856; C. of Church-Broughton w. Scropton, 1857; formerly C. of Ingleby, Greenhow, near Northallerton, 1855-57.

DALTRY, Thomas William, *Hambledon, Horndean, Hants.*—Trin. Coll. Camb. B.A. 1855, M.A. 1859; Deac. 1858, by Bp of Chich; C. of Hambledon, 1859; late C. of Petworth, Sussex, 1858-59.

DAMPIER, Augustus, *Egham, Surrey.*—St John's Coll. Oxon. B.A. 1857; Deac. 1859, Pr. 1860; C. of Egham, 1859.

DANBY, Samuel, *Christ Church parsonage, Belper, Derbyshire.*—St David's Coll. Lamp. B.D. 1853; Deac. 1841, by Bp of Linc. Pr. 1842, by Archbp of York; P. C. of Christ's Ch. Bridge-hill, Belper, Dio. Lich. 1859 (Patrons, Crown and Bp of Lich. alternately; P.C.'s Gross Inc. 200*l.* and Ho; Pop. 2794); Chap. of the Belper Union, 1859; late P.C. of St Paul's, King's-cross, Halifax; 1847-59; formerly C. of Malton, Yorks. 1841-43; C. of Huddersfield, 1843-47.

DANIELL, Egerton Frederic, *Kinson, Wimborne, Dorset.*—Ch. Ch. Oxon. B.A. 1856; Deac. 1857, Pr. 1859, both by Bp of Oxon; C. of Canford Magna w Kinson, Dorset, 1858.

DANSDAY, John Henry, 1A *St James's-terrace, Victoria-park, London.*—King's Coll. Lond. Theol. Assoc. 1858; Deac. 1858, Pr. 1859, both by Bp of Lond; C. of St James's the Less, Victoria-park, Lond. 1860; formerly C. of All Saints, Gordon-square, St Pancras, Lond. 1858-60.

DARBY, Edward George, *Kinoulton, near Nottingham.*—St John's Coll. Camb. B.A. 1859; Deac. 1860, by Bp of Linc; C. of Kinoulton, 1860.

DARBY, John Lionel, *Newburgh, Ormskirk, Lancashire.*—Trin. Coll. Dub. B.A. 1854; Deac. 1856, Pr. 1857, both by Bp of Chest; P.C. of Newburgh, Dio. Chest. 1859 (Patron, the Earl of Derby; P.C.'s Gross Inc. 90*l;* Pop. 900).

DARBY, Thomas, *Audley, Newcastle-on-Lyme, Staffs.*—St John's Coll. Camb. B.A. 1855; Deac. 1857, Pr. 1857, both by Bp of Lich; Head Mast. of Audley Gram. Sch. 1858 (Patrons, 19 Trustees); formerly C. of Chesterton, Staffs. 1856-58.

DAVENPORT, George, *Claremont House, Belgrave-road, Edgbaston, Birmingham.*—Qu. Theol. Coll. Birmingham; Deac. 1857, Pr. 1858; C. of St Luke's, Birmingham, 1858; formerly C. of Tamworth, Staffs. 1857-58.

DAVIES, Charles Robert Ferguson, *Withiell-Florey, Dulverton, Somerset.*—Trin. Ha. Camb. B.A. 1860; Deac. 1860, by Bp of B. and W; C. of Withiell-Florey, 1860.

DAVIES, David, *Ystradffm, near Llandovery.*—St Dav. Theol. Coll. Lamp; Deac. 1860, by Bp of St David's; C. of Ystradffyn.

DAVIES, Evan Hughes, ...—St Aidan's Theol. Coll; Deac. 1859, Pr. 1860, both by Bp of Lich.

DAVIES, Huson Silvester, *Rostherne, Knutsford, Cheshire.*—Pemb. Coll. Oxon. B.A. 1857, M.A. 1859; Deac. 1859, Pr. 1860, both by Bp of Chest; C. of St Mary's, Rostherne, 1859.

DAVIES, John Lane, *Appledore, Tenterden, Kent.*—St Aidan's Theol. Coll; Deac. 1850, Pr. 1860; C. of Appledore w Kenardington.

DAVIES, Thomas Lewis Owen, ... —Exon. Coll. Oxon. B.A. 1857, M.A. 1860; Deac. 1859, Pr. 1860; both by Bp of Winch.

DAVIS, Edwin John, *Lingfield-road, Wimbledon, Surrey.*—Magd. Ha. Oxon. B.A. 1851; Deac. 1859, by Bp of Lond; Asst. C. of St Barnabas, Kensington, Lond. 1860.

DAVIS, William Smith, *Tonge parsonage, Middleton, Lancashire.*—Corpus Coll. Camb. B.A. 1858; Deac. 1859, Pr. 1860; P. C. of Tonge w Alkrington, Dio. Manch. 1860 (Patron, R. of Prestwich; P.C.'s Gross Inc. 170*l* and Ho.; Pop. 6500); formerly C. of Prestwich, Lancashire, 1859-60.

DAVY, Archibald, *Great Barr, near Birmingham.*—Trin. Coll. Camb. B.A. 1856, M.A. 1859; Deac. 1856, Pr. 1857; C. of Great Barr.

DAVYS, Owen William, *Wheathampstead rectory, near St Alban's.*—St John's Coll. Camb. B.A. 1851, M.A. 1852; Deac. 1852, Pr. 1853, both by Bp of Peterb; R. of Wheathampstead, Dio. Roch. 1859 (Patrons, Bp of Peterb; Tithe—R. 782*l;* Glebe, 40 acres; R.'s Gross Inc. 850*l.* and Ho; Pop. 1908); formerly R. of Stilton, Hunts; 1853-59; Author, *An Architectural and Historical Guide to Peterborough Cathedral,* Whittaker and Co. 1s.

DAWES, George, *Breaston, near Derby.*—Trin. Coll. Dub. and Bp Coll. Ha. Dur. B.A. 1856; Deac. 1856, Pr. 1857, both by Bp of S. and M; C. of Breaston, 1859; formerly C. of Fenny Drayton, Warwickshire.

DAWSON, Arthur Altham, 23 *Cumberland-street, Pimlico, London.*—Trin. Coll. Dub. B.A. 1855; Deac. 1855, Pr. 1857, both by Bp of Salis; C. of St Gabriel's, Pimlico, Lond. 1860; formerly C. of Bremhill w Highway, Wilts, 1855-60.

DAWSON, Benjamin Smith, *St Teath, Camelford, Cornwall.*—Exon. Coll. Oxon. B.A. 1858, M.A. 1860; Deac. 1859, Pr. 1860; both by Bp of Exon; C. of St Teath, 1859.

DAWSON-DAMER, Lionel Digby William, *Came rectory, near Dorchester.*—Trin. Coll. Oxon. B.A. 1856, M.A. 1858; Deac. 1857, Pr. 1858, both by Bp of Linc; R. of Winterbourne-Came w Faringdon, Dio. Salis. 1859 (Patron, Hon. G. L. D. Damer; R.'s Gross Inc. 260*l* and Ho; Pop. 190).

DAY, George, *Barton-on-Humber, Lincolnshire.*—Magd. Coll. Oxon. B.A. 1858; Deac. 1859, Pr. 1860; C. of Barton-on-Humber, 1859.

DAY, Henry George, 7 *Bristol-terrace, Brighton.*—St John's Coll. Camb. B.A. 1854, M.A. 1857; Deac. 1859, Pr. 1860, both by Bp of Ely; Asst.-Mast. of Brighton Coll; Fell. of St John's Coll. Camb.

DAY, Hermitage Charles, *Frindsbury, near Rochester.*—Brasen. Coll. Oxon. B.A. 1855, M.A. 1858; Deac. 1856, Pr. 1857, both by Bp of Lich; late C. of Battlefield, Shrewsbury, 1856-58.

DAY, Maurice Fitzgerald, 22 *Hatch-street, Dublin.*—Trin. Coll. Dub. M.A; Incumb. of St Matthias Ch. Dub; Chap. to the Lord-Lieutenant of Ireland.

DAY, Russell, *Eton, near Windsor.*—King's Coll. Camb. Craven Univ. Sch. B.A. 1850, M.A. 1853; Deac. 1857; Asst.-Mast. at Eton Coll; formerly Fell. of King's Coll. Camb.

DEACLE, Thomas Hicks, *Bawburgh, near Norwich.*—St John's Coll. Camb. B.A. 1840, M.A. 1844; Deac. 1841, Pr. 1842, both by Bp of Norw; V. of Bawburgh, Dio. Norw. 1860 (Patrons, D. and C. of Norw; Tithe—App. 227*l.* and 93 acres of Glebe; V.'s Gross Inc. 130*l;* Pop. 460); late C. of Holy Trinity, Bungay, Suffolk.

DEACON, George Edward, *Sidmouth, Devon.*—Corpus Coll. Oxon. B.A. 1831, M.A. 1834; Deac. 1834, Pr. 1835, both by Bp of Oxon; formerly C. of St. Giles, Oxford, 1836-39; C. of St Lawrence, Exeter, 1839-40; C. of Rawmarsh, Yorkshire, 1840-42; C. of Ottery St Mary, Devon, 1842-53; C. of Sidmouth, 1853-57; Author, *Sermons, The Church Catholic,* the 48th series in *Sermons for Sundays,* &c., edited by Rev. A. Watson, Masters, 1846; *Baptismal Regeneration not left an Open Question by the Church of England,* Wallis, Exeter, 1850; *Beautiful Churches, a Partial Realisation of the Earnest Expectation of the Creature,* Perry, Sidmouth, 1859.

DEANE, Charles Henry, *Magdalen College, Oxford.*—Magd. Coll. Oxon. B.A. 1855, M.A. 1857; Deac. 1856, Pr.1857, both by Bp of Oxon; Fell. of Magd. Coll. Oxon.

DEANS, James, *Crediton, Devon.*—St. John's Coll. Camb. B.A. 1833, M.A. 1836; Deac. 1833, by Bp of Roch; Pr. 1833, by Bp of Linc; Chap. of the Collegiate Ch. of Crediton, Dio. Exon. 1837 (Patrons, Twelve Governors chosen from the parishioners; Chap.'s Gross Inc. 250*l* and Ho); Surrog. for Dio. Exon; formerly C. of Attercliffe, Sheffield, 1833-34; C. of Wadworth, Doncaster, 1834-37; Lect. of Rotherham, Yorkshire, 1836-37.

D'EVELYN, John William, *Armoy rectory, Ballymoney, Ireland.*—Trin. Coll. Dub. and Camb. B.A. 1842, M.A. 1845; Deac. 1843, Pr. 1844, both by Bp of Norw; R. of Armoy, Dio. Connor, 1851 (Patron, Bp of Down and Connor; Tithe—R. 200*l*; Glebe, 38 acres; R.'s Gross Inc. 245*l*. and Ho; Pop. 1400); formerly V. of Stanford, Norfolk, 1845-51.

DENHAM, Augustus Frederick, *Mablethorpe, Alford, Lincolnshire.*—Trin. Coll. Dub. B.A. 1857; Deac. 1857, Pr. 1858, both by Archbp of York; C. of Mablethorpe, 1860; late C. of Barmston, Yorks.

DENNE, Richard Henry, *Elbridge house, near Canterbury.*—Univ. Coll. Oxon. B.A. 1856, M.A. 1859; Deac. 1857, Pr. 1858, both by Bp of Chich.

DENNING, Stephen Poyntz, *St Andrew's College, Bradfield, Reading.*—Univ. Coll. Dur. B.A. 1848; M.A. 1851; Deac. 1851, by Bp of Dur. Pr. 1852 by Bp of Worc; Head Mast. of St Andrew's Coll. Bradfield, 1859; late Head Mast. of the Worc. Cathl. Sch; formerly Censor of Bp Hat. Ha. Durham.

DENNY, John, *Wellington, Shropshire.*—St. Bees Theol. Coll; Deac. 1858, Pr. 1859, both by Bp of Lich; C. of All Saints, Wellington, 1860; formerly C. of Riddings, Derbyshire, 1858-60.

DE QUETTEVILLE, Philip, *East Dean, Romsey, Hants.*—St. Peter's Coll. Camb. B.A. 1853, M.A. 1856; Deac. 1855, Pr. 1858; C. of East Dean.

DEVON, Edward Beachcroft, *Barrington, Ilminster, Somerset.*—St John's Coll. Oxon. B.A; Deac. 1860, by Bp of B and W; C. of Barrington and Shepton-Beauchamp, 1860.

DICKINSON, George Charles, *Hull, Yorks.*—St. Aidan's Theol. Coll; Deac. 1860, by Archbp of York; C. of the Mariners' Ch, Hull, 1860.

DIMOND-CHURCHWARD, Marcus Dimond, ...—Chr. Coll. Camb. B.A. 1860; Deac. 1860, by Bp of B. and W.

DIMONT, Charles Harding, *Stone, Staffs.*—Literate; Deac. 1859, Pr. 1860, both by Bp of Lich; C. of Chr. Ch. Stone, 1859.

DINGLEY, Samuel Richard, *Nunton, near Salisbury.*—Literate; Deac. 1859, Pr. 1860, both by Bp of Salis; C. of Nunton, 1859.

DIX, Edward, *Uphill House, Weston-upon-Mare.*—C. of Newlyn, near Probus, Cornwall.

DIX, Thomas Woodrow, *South Lopham, Thetford, Norfolk.*—Ch. Ch. Oxon. B.A. 1857; Deac. 1858, Pr. 1859, both by Bp of Norw; C. of South Lopham.

DIXON, Robert, *Cathedral School, Hereford.*—St John's Coll. Camb. B.A. 1857, M.A. 1860; Deac. 1859, Pr. 1860, both by Bp of Heref; C. of St Nicholas, Heref. 1860; formerly C. of St John's, Heref. 1859-60.

DIXON, Thomas Morrison, ...—St Bees Theol. Coll; Deac. 1860, by Bp of Carl.

DOBREE, James Bonamy, *Battle, Sussex.*—Corpus Coll. Camb. B.A. 1857; Deac. 1858, by Bp of Exon. Pr. 1860, by Bp of Chich; C. of Battle, 1860; formerly C. of Washfield, Devon.

DODD, Henry Philip, *Ramsgate.*—Pemb. Coll. Oxon. B.A. 1851, M.A. 1854; Deac. 1852, Pr. 1853, both by Archbp of Cant; C. of St George's, Ramsgate, 1859; formerly C. of Rusthall, Kent.

DODD, James, *Whitstable, Kent.*—King's Coll. Lond. Theol. Assoc; Deac. 1858, by Bp of Lich. Pr. 1859, by Archbp of Cant; C. of Whitstable *w* Seasalter, 1859.

DODWELL, Henry John, *St John-street, Bedford.*—Exon. Coll. Oxon. B.A. 1848, M.A. 1858; Deac. 1859, by Bp of Ely, Pr. 1860, by Bp of Winch; C. of Ravensden, near Bedford, 1860; formerly Jun. Class. Mast. of Bedford Gram. Sch. 1859-60.

DOLLING, James Ratcliffe, *Sharrington, Thetford, Norfolk.*—Worc. Coll. Oxon. B.A. 1859; Deac. 1859, Pr. 1860, both by Bp of Norw; C. of Sharrington, 1859.

DOLPHIN, John Maximilian, *Scampton, near Lincoln.*—Oriel Coll. Oxon. B.A. 1860; Deac. 1860, by Bp of Linc; C. of North Carlton, near Lincoln, 1860.

DONAGAN, Henry Robert, 17 *Victoria-street, Bradford, Yorkshire.*—Literate; Deac. 1858, Pr. 1860, both by Bp of Rip; C. of Christ Ch. Bradford, 1858.

DONNISON, James Watson Stote, *Mendham, Harleston, Norfolk.*—Univ. Coll. Oxon. B.A. 1830, M.A. 1835; Deac. 1831, Pr. 1832, both by Bp of Linc.

DORAN, John Wilberforce, ...—St John's Coll. Camb. Sch. 1855, B.A. 1857, by Bp of Ely; Deac. 1858, by Bp of Roch; Min. of St Thomas, Bethnal-green, 1859; formerly C. of Histed, Essex.

DORIA, Andrew, *Blackley Rectory, near Manchester.*—Pemb. Coll. Camb. B.A. 1856; Deac. 1856, Pr. 1857, both by Bp of Manch; C. of Blackley, 1858; formerly C. of Harpurhey, near Manchester, 1856-58.

D'ORSEY, Alexander James Donald, *Corpus Christi College, Cambridge.*—Corpus Coll. Camb. B.D. Deac. 1846, Pr. 1847, both by Bp of Glasgow; English Lect. at Corpus Coll. Camb. 1860; formerly Missionary Chap. to the English in Spain, and to English Sailors in Spanish Ports; Author, *English Grammar*, 2 vols; *Introduction to Composition*; *Colloquial Portuguese Grammar*; *Letter to the Archbishop, of Canterbury*; *Letter to Lord Brougham*; various *Sermons*.

DOUGHTY, Ernest George, *Appleby, Westmoreland.*—Trin. Coll. Camb. B.A. 1859; Deac. 1859, Pr. 1860, both by Bp of Carl; C. of St Michael, Appleby, 1859.

DOUGHTY, Thomas, ...—St Bees Theol. Coll; Deac. 1860, by Bp of Lich.

DOUGLAS, Charles, *Roper-street, Whitehaven.*—St. Bees Theol. Coll; Deac. 1856, Pr. 1857, both by Bp of Lich; C. of Holy Trin. Whitehaven, 1860; formerly C. of Bloxwich, near Walsall, 1856-58; C. of St Michael, Isle of Man, 1858-60.

DOUGLASS, Thomas Wingfield, *Northampton.*—Clare Coll. Camb. B.A. 1859; Deac. 1859, Pr. 1860, both by Bp of Peterb; C. of St Peter's, Northampton, 1859.

DOWDING, Charles, *Priston rectory, near Bath.*—Qu. Coll. Oxon. B.A. 1829; Deac. 1830, Pr. 1831, both by Bp of B. and W; R. of Priston, Dio. B. and W. 1859 (Patron, W. V. Jenkins, Esq; R.'s Gross Inc. 400*l* and Ho; Pop. 308); formerly C. of Maperton, Somerset.

DOWDING, William, *Verwood, Cranborne, Dorset.*—Merton Coll. Oxon. B.A. 1838, M.A. 1842; Deac. and Pr. 1841; C. of Verwood *w* West Moors, 1856.

DOWLAND, Edmund, ...—St John's Coll. Camb. B.A. 1857, M.A. 1859; Deac. 1859, Pr. 1860, both by Bp of Chich.

DOWSON, Charles, *Lound rectory, Lowestoft, Suffolk.*—Exon. Coll. Oxon. S.C.L. 1848; Deac. 1850, Pr. 1851; R. of Lound, Dio. Norw. 1859 (Patron, Benjamin Dowson, Esq; Tithe—R. 415*l*; Glebe, ?? acres; R.'s Gross Inc. 460*l* and Ho; Pop. 439); formerly R. of Morborne, Hunts. 1858-59; formerly V. of Lesi..., Northumberland, 1854-58.

D'OYLY, Charles John, 15 *Gloucester-place, Portman-square, London.*—Trin. Coll. Camb. Jun. Opt. and B.A. 1843, M.A. 1845; Deac. 1844, Pr. 1845, both by Bp of L. and C; Min. of St Mark's, Long-acre, Lond. and Chap. to Lincoln's Inn, 1860; formerly Min. of St John's, Broad-court, St Martin's-in-the-Fields, Lond. 1855-60; Author, *The True Faith of a Christian*, J. W. Parker, 1856, 2*s* 6*d*; *A Few Words upon Election*, Bell and Daldy, 1858.

DRAKE, Edward Tyrwhitt, *Chalfont St. Giles, Bucks.*—Magd. Coll. Camb. B.A. 1857, M.A. 1860; Deac. 1860, by Bp of Oxon; C. of Chalfont St. Giles, 1860.

DRAKE, John, *Frome, Somerset.*—Trin. Coll. Camb. B.A. 1859; Deac. 1859, Pr. 1860, both by Bp of B. and W; C. of Christ Ch. Frome, 1859.

DRAKE, William Thomas Tyrwhitt, ... —Trin. Coll. Camb. B.A. 1858; Deac. 1858, by Bp of Oxon. Pr. 1860, by Bp of Linc; formerly C. of Bray, near Maidenhead.

DRAWBRIDGE, William Barker, *Rochester.* —Caius Coll. Camb. LL.B. 1857; Deac. 1855, Pr. 1856, both by Archbp. of York; C. of St Margaret's, Rochester, 1859; late C. of Burghfield, Berks; formerly C. of Stensall and Haxby, Yorks; previously C. of St Lawrence, Reading.

DREW, Andrew Augustus Wild, *Benenden, Staplehurst, Kent.*—Trin. Coll. Camb. B.A. 1859; Deac. 1860, by Archbp. of Cant; C. of Benenden, 1860.

DREW, James, ... —St. John's Coll. Camb. B.A. 1854, M.A. 1857; Deac. 1860, by Bp of B. and W.

DROUGHT, Henry, *Walker, near Newcastle.*— Literate; Deac. 1859, Pr. 1860, both by Bp of Dur; C. of Walker, 1859.

DUCKWORTH, Robinson, *Trinity College, Oxford.*—Univ. Coll. Oxon. Sch. 1853, B.A. 1855, M.A. 1857; Deac. 1858, Pr. 1859, both by Bp of Salis; Fell. and Tut. of Trin. Coll. Oxon. 1860; formerly Asst. Mast. at Marlborough Coll. Wilts. 1858-60.

DUDDING, John, *Naughton, Bildeston, Suffolk.*— Trin. Ha. Camb. LL.B. 1859; Deac. 1860, by Bp of Ely; C. of Naughton, 1860.

DUDLEY, Joseph, *Sarnesfield rectory, Kington, Herefordshire.*—Worc. Coll. Oxon. B.A. 1830; Deac. 1832, by Bp of Worc; Pr. 1833, by Bp of Heref; R. of Sarnesfield, Dio. Heref. 1846 (Patrons, the representatives of Thos. Monington Weston, Esq; Tithe—R. 180l; Glebe, 50 acres; R.'s Gross Inc. 250l and Ho; Pop. 120); formerly C. of Broadwas, Worcestershire, 1832-33; C. of Edwin-Ralph, Herefordshire, 1833-37; P.C. of Marston, Hereford, 1837-43; C. of Cubert, Cornwall, 1843-46.

DUDLEY, Samuel George, *Winchester.*—Jesus Coll. Oxon. B.A. 1837, M.A. 1840; Deac. 1838, Pr. 1839, both by Bp of Oxon; C. of St. John's, Winch.

DUDLEY, William Charles, *Over, Winsford, Cheshire.*—Qu. Coll. Camb. B.A. 1838, M.A. 1851; Deac. 1838, Pr. 1839, both by Bp of Chest; C. of Over; formerly C. of Tarvin, Cheshire.

DUKE, Robert Richard, ... —Caius Coll. Camb. LL.B. 1859; Deac. 1859, Pr. 1860, both by Bp of Chich.

DUKE, William, *St. Mary's vale, Brompton, Chatham, Kent.*—Asst. Chap. of H.M. Prison, Chatham, 1860; formerly Asst. Chap. of Millbank, Lond; previously C. of Stoke-on-Trent.

DUMBLETON, Edgar Norris, *Ryde, Isle of Wight.*—Exon. Coll. Oxon. B.A. 1853; Deac. 1854, by Bp of Oxon. Pr. 1855, by Bp of B. and W; Asst. C. of St Thomas', Ryde, 1860; formerly C. of St Mary the Virgin, Oxford, 1854-56; P.C. of St Edmund's, Wells, Somerset, 1856-57; C. of Chislehurst, Kent, 1858-60; Author, *A Plea for Religious Societies in Parishes* (a pamphlet), 1857; *Five Sermons on the Daily Services,* J. H. Parker, 1859.

DUNCOMBE, William Duncombe Van der Horst, *47 York crescent, Clifton, Bristol, and Belgrave house, Grosmont, Hereford.*—Brasen. Coll. Oxon. B.A. 1856, M.A. 1857; Deac. 1858, Pr. 1859, both by Bp of Heref; C. of Kentchurch, Herefordshire, 1859; formerly C. of Bishopstone-cum-Yazor, Herefordshire, 1858-59.

DUNKLEY, John, *Wesley street, Toxteth park, Liverpool.*—Literate; Deac. 1848, Pr. 1849; Chap. of the Workhouse, Toxteth park, Liverpool (Stipend, 130l); formerly Chap. of the General Hospital, Birmingham.

DUNN, Arthur, *St Andrew's parsonage, Manchester.*—Chr. Coll. Camb. B.A. 1857; Deac. 1859, Pr. 1860, both by Bp of Manch; C. of St Andrew's, Manchester, 1859.

DU PORT, Charles Durell, *10 Portland road, Marylebone, London.*—Caius Coll. Camb. B.A. 1859; Deac. 1860, by Bp of Lond; C. of Holy Trin. Marylebone, 1860.

DUPUIS, Theodore Crane, *Tiverton, Devon.*— Pemb. Coll. Oxon. B.A. 1858, M.A. 1860; Deac. 1860, by Bp of B. and W; C. of Tiverton, 1860.

DURHAM, The Hon. and Right Rev. Henry Montagu VILLIERS, Lord Bishop of Durham, *Upper Portland-place, London, and Auckland Castle, Bishop's Auckland, Durham.*—Ch. Ch. Oxon. B.A. 1834, M.A. 1837, B.D. and D.D. 1856; Deac. 1836, by Bp of Chest; Pr. 1857, by Bp of Worc.; Consecrated by Bp of Carlisle, 1856; translated to Durham, 1860 (Episcopal Jurisdiction, the counties of Durham, Northumland and Hexhamshire; Gross Inc. of See, 8000l; Pop. 701,381; Acres, 1,906,835; Deaneries, 13; Benefices, 245; Curates, 106; Church Sittings, 126,099); his Lordship was formerly C. of Deane, Lancashire, 1836-37; V. of Kenilworth, Warwickshire, 1837-41; R. of St George, Bloomsbury, Lond. 1841-56; Can. Res. of St Paul's CathL 1847-56; Author, *Parochial Sermons,* 12mo. Nisbet, 5s; *Sermons on the Importance and Power of the Word of God,* 12mo. ib. 5s; *Religion no Fiction,* 18mo. ib. 1s 6d, 3 edits; *The Young Professor,* 18mo. ib. 1s 6d; *Principle and Practice,* 18mo. ib. 1s 6d; *Family Prayers,* 12mo ib. 2 edits; various *Sermons, Tracts,* and *Episcopal Charges.*

DUVAL, Philip Snaith, ... —Corpus Coll. Oxon. B.A., 1860; Deac. 1860, by Bp of Lond; C. of St James's, Piccadilly, Lond. 1860.

————◆————

FARNSHAW, John William, *Birstal, Leeds.* St Cath. Coll. Camb. B.A. 1857; Deac. 1859, Pr. 1860, both by Bp of Rip; C. of Birstal, 1859; formerly 2nd Mast. of Qu. Elizabeth's Gram. Sch. Halifax, 1857-58.

EARNSHAW, Samuel Walter, *140, Bathrow, Birmingham.*—St. John's Coll. Camb. B.A. 1857; Deac. 1857, Pr. 1858, both by Bp of Lond; Sen. C. of St Thomas, Birmingham, 1860; late Jun. C. of St Thomas's, 1859-60; formerly C. of Bromley St Leonard's, Middlesex, 1857-59.

EASTMAN, William Samuel, *Stafford.*— King's Coll. Lond. Theol. Assoc; Deac. 1859, Pr. 1860, both by Bp of Lich; C. of Christ Ch. Stafford, 1859.

EATON, Charles Pemberton, ... —St. John's Coll. Camb. B.A. 1860; Deac. 1860, by Bp of B. and W.

EDDOWES, Edmund, *Stockport, Cheshire.*— Jesus Coll. Camb. B.A. 1858; Deac. 1859, Pr. 1860; C. of St Thomas, Stockport, 1859.

EDGAR, Joseph Haythorne, *Clarendon-road, Putney, Surrey.*—Wadh. Coll. Oxon. B.A. 1856, M.A. 1858; Deac. 1860, by Bp of Lond; Asst. C. of Putney, 1860; formerly a Lieutenant in the Royal Artillery; Author, *Descriptions of Old Cannon in the Tower of London; The Royal Military Repository, Woolwich;* and *The Arsenal, Woolwich,* pub. at the R. A. Institution, 1860.

EDWARDS, Charles, *Low Moor, Bradford, Yorkshire.*—Caius Coll. Camb. B.A. 1860; Deac. 1860, by Bp of Rip; C. of Holy Trinity, Low Moor, 1860.

EDWARDS, Charles Smallwood, *Penarth, near Cardiff.*—Literate; Deac. 1859, Pr. 1860, both Bp of Lland; C. of Penarth, 1860; formerly C. of Radir, Glamorganshire, 1859-60.

EDWARDS, Thomas Carnvaldwyn, *Clydach, near Swansea.*—St. David's Coll. Lamp; Deac. 1860, by Bp of St David's; C. of Clydach. 1860.

EDWARDS, William Walter, *18A, Wigmore-street, Cavendish-square, London.*—St. Peter's Coll. Camb. B.A. 1859; Deac. 1860, by Bp of Lond; C. of St. George, Hanover-square, Lond. 1860.

EGLES, Edward Henry, *Enfield, Middlesex.*—Emman. Coll. Camb. B.A. 1857; Deac. 1857, Pr. 1858, both by Bp of Ely; C. of St. Andrew's, Enfield, 1859; formerly C. of Litlington, Cambs, 1857.

ELIOT, Edward, *Sibford Gower, Banbury, Oxfordshire.*—New Coll. Oxon. S.C.L. 1848, B.C.L. 1853; Deac. 1853, Pr. 1854; P.C. of Sibford Gower, Dio. Oxon. 1860 (Patron, New Coll. Oxon; Glebe, 13 acres; P.C.'s Gross Inc. 240*l*.; Pop. 900); formerly Fell. of New Coll. Oxon. and C. of Sutton-under-Brailes, Gloucestershire.

ELIOT, Richard, *Tadmarton, Banbury, Oxfordshire.*—Ch. Ch. Oxon. B.A. 1856, M.A. 1859; C. of Tadmarton, 1858.

ELLERBECK, Jonathan, ... —St. Bees' Theol. Coll; Deac. 1860, by Bp of Lich.

ELLERSHAW, Robert, *Mexborough vicarage, Rotherham, Yorks.*—Bp Hat. Ha. Dur. B.A. 1858; Deac. 1858, P. 1860, both by Bp of Dur; V. of Mexborough, Dio. York, 1860 (Patron, Archd. of York; Tithe—App. 677*l*; Glebe, 39¼ acres; V.'s Gross Inc. 145*l*. and Ho; Pop. 2000); formerly Asst. C. of Berwick-upon-Tweed, 1858-60.

ELLIOT, Robert William, *Bridlington Quay, Bridlington, Yorks.*—Corpus Coll. Camb. B.A. 1853, M.A. 1856; Deac. 1857, Pr. 1858, both by Archbp. of York; C. of Bridlington Quay, 1860; formerly C. of Barton-le-Street, Yorks.

ELLIOTT, Ebenezer, 16, *Lansdowne-crescent, Glasgow.*—St. Peter's Coll. Camb. B.A. 1829; Deac. 1829, by Archbp of York, Pr. 1830, by Bp of Ripon.

ELLIOTT, Robert John, *Cowper, near Morpeth, Northumberland.*—Bp Hat. Ha. Dur. Theol. Licen. 1859; Deac. 1859, Pr. 1860, both by Bp of Dur; C. of Horton, Northumberland, 1859.

ELLIS, George, *Stainton-by-Langworth, Lincoln.*—St. Cath. Ha. Camb. B.A. 1821; Deac. 1824, Pr. 1827, both by Bp of Linc; R. of Snelland, near Wragby, Dio. Linc. 1859 (Patron, Earl Brownlow; Tithe—R. 258*l* 2*s*; Glebe, 43 acres; R.'s Gross Inc. 310*l*; Pop. 127); C. of Stainton-by-Langworth and Snelland.

ELLIS, The Hon. William Charles, *Prestwich, Lancashire.*—Balliol Coll. Oxon. B.A. 1858, M.A. 1860; Deac. 1859, Pr. 1860, both by Bp of Manch; C. of Prestwich, 1859.

ELLISS, Henry Christopher, *Thorganby, near York.*—St. Aidan's Theol. Coll; Deac. 1859, Pr. 1860, both by Archbp of York; C. of Thorganby, 1859.

ESPIN, William, *Glen Magna, near Leicester.*—Qu. Theol. Coll. Birmingham; Deac. 1860, by Bp of Peterb; C. of Glen Magna w Great Stretton, 1860.

ETHERIDGE, Sanders, *Kettering, Northamptonshire.*—Gon. and Cai. Coll. Camb. B.A. 1859; Deac. 1859, Pr. 1860, both by Bp of Peterb; C. of Kettering, 1859.

EUSTACE, George, *The Triangle, Halifax.*—Literate; Deac. 1859, Pr. 1860; C. of St. Peter's, Sowerby, Halifax, 1859.

EVANS, Henry Jones, *Gellyfaelog, Dowlais.*—Abergavenny Theol. Coll; Deac. 1859, by Bp of Land; C. of Gellyfaelog, 1860.

EVANS, John Myddelton, *Ilminster, Somerset.*—Exon. Coll. Oxon. B.A. 1860; Deac. 1860, by Bp of B. and W; C. of Ilminster, 1860.

EVANS, John William, *Cowbridge, Glamorganshire.*—Jesus Coll. Oxon. B.A. 1860; Deac. 1860, by Bp of Lland; C. of Cowbridge and Llanblethian, 1860.

EVANS, Thomas Howe, *Cadeby, Hinckley, Leicestershire.*—St. Aidan's Coll; Deac. 1856, Pr. 1857, both by Bp of Peterb; C. of Cadeby, 1859; late C. of Little Missenden, Bucks; formerly C. of Packington, Leicestershire.

EVANS, Thomas Saunders, *Rugby, Warwickshire.*—St. John's Coll. Camb. Porson Prizeman, 1838, B.A. 1839, M.A. 1845; Deac. 1844, Pr. 1846; Asst. Mast. in Rugby Sch.

EVERETT, Arthur Joseph, *Wells, Somersetshire.*—Clare Coll. Camb. B.A. 1860; Deac. 1860, by Bp of B. and W; C. of St. Cuthbert, Wells, 1860.

FAITHFULL, Valentine Grantham, 23 *Royal Circus, Edinburgh.*—Corpus Coll. Camb. B.A. 1842, M.A. 1845; Deac. 1845, Pr. 1846; Incumb. of Trinity Chapel, Dean Bridge, Edinburgh, Dio. Edinb. 1853 (Patrons, Trustees; Pop. 600); formerly C. of Hatfield, Herts.

FALKNER, Francis Bancks, *Brackley, Northants.*—St John's Coll. Camb. B.A. 1854, M.A. 1859; Deac. 1857, Pr. 1858; Head Mast. of Brackley Gram. Sch; formerly C. of Aldenham, and Second Mast. of Aldenham Gram. Sch. Herts.

FARMAN, Samuel, *Layer-Marney, Kelvedon, Essex.*—St. John's Coll. Camb. B.A. 1859; Deac. 1860, by Bp. of Roch; C. of Layer-Marney, 1860.

FARRAR, Frederic William, *Harrow-on-the-Hill, Middlesex.*—Trin. Coll. Camb. Chancel. Engl. Medal 1852, Le Bas Prize 1856, Norrisian Prize 1857, B.A. 1855, M.A. 1857; Deac. 1854, by Bp of Salis; Pr. 1855, by Bp of Ely; Asst. Master of Harrow Sch; Fell. of Trin. Coll. Camb; Author, *The Arctic Regions* (Prize Poem); *Christian Doctrine of the Atonement*, 1857; *Eric, or Little by Little, a Tale of School Life*, 1857; *Julian Home*, A. and C. Black, 1859; *Lyrics of Life*, Camb. 1859; *The Origin of Language*, Murray, 1860.

FARRAR, James, *St John's parsonage, near Halifax, Yorks.*—Trin. Coll. Camb. B.A. 1854; Deac. 1856, Pr. 1857, both by Bp of Peterb; P.C. of St John's in the Wilderness, Dio. Rip. 1859 (Patron, V. of Halifax; P.C.'s Gross Inc. 135*l*. and Ho; Pop. 1791.)

FARRINGTON, John Curry, *Cornwood, Ivybridge, Devon.*—Exon. Coll. Oxon. B.A. 1859; Deac. 1860, by Bp of Exon; C. of Cornwood, 1860.

FAWCETT, Henry, *Stanwix, Carlisle.*—Clare Coll. Camb. B.A. 1859; Deac. 1859, Pr. 1860, both by Bp of Carl; C. of Stanwix, 1859.

FEARON, Henry, *Loughborough rectory, Leicestershire.*—Emman. Coll. Camb. B.A. 1824, M.A. 1827; Deac. 1826, Pr. 1827, both by Bp of Chich; R. of Loughborough, Dio. Peterb. 1848 (Patrons, Emman. Coll. Camb; Tithe—R. 22*l*; Glebe, 300 acres; R.'s Gross Inc. 1050*l*. and Ho; Pop. 6674); Hon. Can. of Peterb. Cathl. 1849; formerly Fell. of Emman. Coll. Camb; Author, *What to Learn and What to Unlearn; Sermons on Public Occasions*, 1 vol.

FIELDING, the Hon. Charles William Alexander, *Newham Paddox, Lutterworth, Leicestershire.*—Trin. Coll. Camb. M.A. 1856; Deac. 1858, Pr. 1859, both by Bp of Chich; formerly C. of Clayton-cum-Keymer, Sussex, 1858-59; C. of Kirkby Mallory, Leicestershire, 1859-60.

FENDALL, Charles Bathurst, ... —Jesus Coll. Camb. B.A. 1859; Deac. 1859, Pr. 1860, both by Bp of Winch.

FENN, Anthony Cox, *Ilchester, Somerset.*—St John's Coll. Camb. B.A. 1858; Deac. 1859, Pr. 1860, both by Bp of B. and W; C. of Ilchester, 1859.

FENN, Joseph Finch, *Cheltenham.*—Trin. Coll. Camb. B.A. 1842, M.A. 1845; Deac. 1845, Pr. 1846; P.C. of Christ Ch. Lansdown, Cheltenham, Dio. G. and B. 1860 (Patrons, Trustees; P.C.'s Gross Inc. 450*l*; Pop. 5000); late V. of Stotfield, Beds, 1847-60; formerly Fell. of Trin. Coll. Camb. 1844-47.

FENNELL, George Keith, *Paris.*—Trin. Coll. Camb. Deac. 1840, Pr. 1840; formerly Head Mast. of the Temple Gram. Sch. Brighton, 1836-46; R. of Chalvington, Sussex, 1850-54; Author, *The Rule of Church Charity*, London and Paris, 1856.

FERGUSON, Douglas, *Walkington rectory, Beverley, Yorks.*—R. of Walkington, Dio. York, 1860 (Patron, the present R; Tithe—R. 537*l*; Glebe, 237 acres; R.'s Gross Inc. 785*l* and Ho; Pop. 699); Dom. Chap. to the Duke of Cleveland.

FERGUSON, Richard, *Smethwick, near Birmingham.*—Pemb. Coll. Camb. B.A. 1839, M.A. 1842; P.C. of St Matthew's, Smethwick, Dio. Lich. 1859 (Patron, Incumb. of Smethwick; P.C.'s Gross Inc. 170*l*; Pop. 2000*l*); late Fell. of Pemb. Coll. Camb.

FESTING, John Wogan, 19A, *Queen-square, Westminster, London.*—Trin. Coll. Camb. B.A. 1860; Deac. 1860, by Bp of Lond; C. of Christ Ch. Broadway, Westminster, 1860.

FICE, Edwin, *Canton, Llandaff, Glamorganshire.*—Literate; Deac. 1855, Pr. 1857, both by Bp of Lland; P.C. of Canton, Dio. Lland. 1858 (Patron, Bp of Lland; P.C.'s Gross Inc. 150*l*; Pop. 3000.)

FIELD, Arthur Thomas ... ...—St John's Coll. Camb. B.A. 1859; Deac. 1859, by Bp of Norw. Pr. 1860, by Archbp of York; formerly C. of Holbrook, near Ipswich, 1859-60.

FINCH, George, *West Dereham, Stoke Ferry, Norfolk.*—Univ. Coll. Oxon. B.A. 1857; Deac. 1859, Pr. 1860, both by Bp of Norw; C. of West Dereham, Norfolk, 1859.

FINLAY, Edward Bullock, *Gazeley, New-market, Suffolk.*—Worc. Coll. Oxon. 2nd Cl. Lit. Hum. and B.A. 1849, M.A. 1854; Deac. 1854, by Bp of Down and Connor, Pr. 1855, by Bp of Norw; C. of Gazeley w Kentford, 1859; late C. of Frittenden, Kent, 1857-59; formerly 2nd Mast. of Qu. Elizabeth's Gram. Sch. Dedham, 1853-54; C. of Stratford St Mary, Suffolk, 1854-57.

FLAMSTEAD, Alvery Richard Dodsley, *Birstall, near Leicester.*—Exon. Coll. Oxon. B.A. 1859; Deac. 1860, by Bp of Linc; C. of Belgrave-cum-Birstall, 1860.

FORMBY, Richard Edward, *Latchingdon rectory, Maldon, Essex.*—Brasen. Coll. Oxon. B.A. 1846; Deac. 1846, Pr. 1847, both by Bp of Lich; R. of Latchingdon, Dio. Roch. 1859 (Patron, Archbp of Cant; Glebe, 49 acres; R.'s Gross Inc. 710*l* and Ho; Pop. 400); late P.C. of Hythe, Kent, 1854-59.

FORSHAW, Thurston, *Newchapel parsonage, Tunstall, Staffs.*—St Bees' Theol. Coll; Deac. and Pr. 1836; P.C. of Newchapel, Dio. Lich. 1841 (Patrons, Ralph Sneyd, Esq. John Lawton, Esq. and Mr. Thomas Heaton; P.C.'s Gross Inc. 110*l* and Ho; Pop. 3000).

FOSTER, Joseph, *Lydney, Gloucestershire.*—Chr. Coll. Camb. B.A. 1858, M.A. 1860; Deac. 1860, by Bp of G. and B; C. of Lydney, 1860.

FOSTER, Joseph, *Ullesthorpe House, Lutterworth, Leicestershire.*—Trin. Coll. Dub. B.A. 1858; Deac. 1859, Pr. 1860, both by Bp of Peterb; C. of Ashby Magna, Leicestershire, 1859.

FOSTER, Richard, *Hanley, Staffs.*—Bp Hat. Ha. Dur. Theol. Licen; Deac. 1859, Pr. 1860; C. of St Luke's, Wellington, Hanley, 1859.

FOTHERGILL, Ernest Henry, *Clevedon, Somerset.*—Trin. Coll. Dub. B.A. 1853; Deac. 1854, Pr. 1855, both by Bp of Roch; C. of Clevedon, 1858; formerly Chap. of R. N.

FOTHERGILL, Percival Alfred, *South Heighton, Newhaven, Sussex.*—Trin. Coll. Dub. B.A. 1853; Deac. 1858, Pr. 1859, both by Bp of Chich; C. of South Heighton and Tarring-Neville, 1859; formerly Chap. and Naval Instructor, R.N.

FOWLE, Thomas Welbank, *Staines, Middlesex.*—Oriel Coll. Oxon. B.A. 1858; Deac. 1859, Pr. 1860; C. of Staines, 1859

FOWLER, William, *Cleckheaton, Leeds.*—Chr. Coll. Camb. B.A. 1857, M.A. 1860; Deac. 1859, Pr. 1860, both by Bp of Rip; C. of St John's, Cleckheaton, 1859.

FOX, Joseph Hamilton, *Over-Silton, near York.*—King's Coll. Lond. and Queen's Coll. Birmingham; Deac. 1859, Pr. 1860, both by Archbp of York; C. of Over-Silton, 1859.

FRASER, William Francis, *Stisted, Braintree, Essex.*—Emman. Coll. Camb. B.A. 1856; Deac. 1857, Pr. 1858; C. of Stisted, 1860; formerly C. of Coggeshall, Essex.

FREEMAN, Francis Elton, *Southwick, near Sunderland.*—Trin. Coll. Dub. B.A. 1857, M.A. 1860; Deac. 1858, Pr. 1859, both by Bp of Dur; C. of Southwick, 1858.

FREEMAN, Robert Marriott, *Stevenage, Herts.*—Ch. Ch. Oxon. B.A. 1859; Deac. 1860, by Bp of Roch; C. of Stevenage, 1860.

FREER, William Haughton, *Marchington, near Uttoxeter.*—Trin. Coll. Camb. B.A. 1853; Deac. 1853, Pr. 1854; P.C. of Marchington, Dio. Lich. 1860 (Patron, V. of Hanbury; Tithe—App. 11*s*; Glebe, 19 acres; P.C.'s Gross Inc. 90*l*; Pop. 480); formerly C. of Cubley w Marston-Montgomery, Derbyshire.

FRESHFIELD, John Minet, *Great Yarmouth.*—Balliol Coll. Oxon. B.A. 1857; Deac. 1858, by Bp of Norw; Asst. C. of St Nicholas, Great Yarmouth, 1859.

FRESHNEY, Frederick, *Scalby, near Scarborough.*—Ch. Coll. Camb. B.A. 1859; Deac. 1859, Pr. 1860, both by Archbp of York; C. of Scalby, 1859.

FURNEAUX, William Duckworth, *Berkley rectory, Frome, Somerset.*—Exon. Coll. Oxon. Sch. 1835, B.A. 1837, M.A. 1840; Deac. 1840, Pr. 1841, both by Archbp. of Cant; R of Berkley, Dio. B. and W. 1860 (Patron, Sir Chas. Mordaunt, Bart, M.P. Walton, Warwick; Tithe—R. 350*l*; Glebe 56 acres; R.'s Gross Inc. 410*l*. and Ho; Pop. 495); formerly Incumb. of Walton, Warwickshire, 1842-60; Author, *Single Sermons,* Rivingtons.

GALL, Francis Herbert, *Cottesbrooke, Northampton.*—Trin. Coll. Camb. B.A. 1846, M.A. 1849; Deac. 1846, Pr. 1847, both by Bp of Roch; C. of Cottesbrooke, 1860; formerly C. of Rushden, Herts, 1846-59; R. of Letchworth, Herts, 1858-59; C. of Wallington, Herts, 1859-60.

GAPE, Charles, *Ellesmere Port, near Chester.*—Corpus Coll. Camb. B.A. 1859; Deac. 1860, by Bp of Chest; C. of Ellesmere Port, 1860.

GARDINER, Alexander, *Union House, Salford, Manchester.*—Trin. Coll. Dub. B.A. 1847; Deac. 1847, Pr. 1848, both by Bp of Rip; C. of the Salford Union; formerly C. of Hartshead, Yorks; Author, *An Ode to the Queen,* 1837.

GARDNER, Hilton, 30, *Bewsey-street, Warrington.*—Gon. and Cai. Coll. Camb. B.A. 1859; Deac. 1860, by Bp of Chest; C. of St Paul's, Warrington, 1860.

GARDNER, John Ludford, 3, *Surrey-place, Lower-road, Rotherhithe, London.*—C. of St Mary's, Rotherhithe, London.

GARDNER, Tobias Edward, *Effra-road, Brixton, London.*—St John's Coll. Oxon. B.A. 1859; Deac. 1860, by Bp of Winch; C. of St Matthew's, Brixton, 1860.

GARLAND, Thomas Bloom, *Netherton, Dudley, Worcestershire.*—Magd. Coll. Camb. B.A. 1859; Deac. 1859, by Bp of Worc. Pr. 1860, by Bp of Lond; C. of Netherton, 1859.

GARNIER, The Very Rev. Thomas, *The Deanery, Winchester.*—All Souls Coll. Oxon. B.C.L. 1800, D.C.L. 1850; Dean of Winchester, 1840 (Dean's Gross Inc. 1515*l* and Res); R. of Bishopstoke, near Winchester, Dio. Winch. 1807 (Patron, Bp of Winch; Tithe—R. 617*l* 10*s*; Glebe, 21 acres; R.'s Gross Inc. 645*l* and Ho; Pop. 1249).

GARNIER, The Very Rev. Thomas, *The Deanery, Lincoln.*—Worc. Coll. Oxon. B.A. 1830, B.C.L. 1833, Fell. of All Souls Coll. Oxon. 1830; Deac. 1833, Pr. 1834, both by Bp of Oxon; Dean of Lincoln, 1860 (Dean's Gross Inc. 1805*l* and Res); late Dean of Ripon, 1859-60; formerly R. of Trinity, St Marylebone, Lond. 1850-59; previously Chap. to the House of Commons, 1849-50; Author, *Plain Remarks on the Poor Law,* 1835; *Assize Sermon,* Winchester, 1835; *Visitation Sermon,* Lichfield, 1841; *Domestic Duties,* a Series of Sermons, 1851; and various occasional *Sermons.*

GARRETT, Frank, *Carmarthen,* Worc. Coll. Oxon. B.A. 1858; Deac. 1860, by Bp of St David's; Asst. C. of St. David's, Carmarthen, 1860; second Mast. of Carmarthen Gr. Sch; Hon. Chap. to the 2nd Carmarthenshire Rifle Volunteers.

GARRETT, James Perkins, *Kellistown rectory, Carlow, Leinster, Ireland.*—Trin. Ha. Camb. and Trin. Coll. Dub. B.A. 1834, M.A. 1837 ; Deac. and Pr. 1835 ; R. of Kellistown, Dio. Leighlin, 1856 (Patrons, the Crown two turns, and the Bp one turn ; Tithe—R. 269*l* ; Glebe, 37 acres ; R.'s Gross Inc. 320*l* and Ho ; Pop. 340) ; Chap. to the Earl of Annesley, and Hon. Secretary to the Leighlin Diocesan Society for the Scriptural Instruction and Conversion of Roman Catholics.

GARVEN, Edward Dakin, *Runcorn, Cheshire.*—Brasen. Coll. Oxon. B.A. 1858 ; Deac. 1859, Pr. 1860, both by Bp of Chest ; Chap. to the Earl of Ellesmere's Floating Chapel, Runcorn, 1860 ; formerly C. of Runcorn, 1859-60.

GARWOOD, William, *Cottingham, near Hull.*—Worc. Coll. Oxon. B.A. 1858, M.A. 1860 ; Deac. 1859, Pr. 1860, both by Archbp of York ; C. of Cottingham, 1859.

GASCOIGNE, Thomas, *Weybread vicarage, Harleston, Suffolk.*—St Cath. Coll. Camb. B.A. 1843 ; Deac. 1844, Pr. 1845, both by Bp of Linc ; V. of Weybread, Dio. Norw. 1859 (Patrons, Trustees ; Tithe—App. 90*l*, V. 27*l* ; Glebe, 9 acres ; V.'s Gross Inc. 140*l* and Ho ; Pop. 750) ; formerly C. of Carlton, Notts, 1844-46 ; Mast. of Derby Gram. Sch. 1846-48 ; Lect. of St Peter's, Nottingham, 1848-59 ; Author, various *Sermons.*

GATTY, Robert Henry, *Clapton, near Bristol.*—Trin. Coll. Oxon. B.A. 1850, M.A. 1853 ; Deac. 1851, Pr. 1852, both by Bp of Norw ; C. of Clapton, 1859 ; formerly C. of Abbot's Kerswell, Devon.

GAY, Alfred, *Folkestone, Kent.*—Trin. Coll. Camb. B.A. 1858 ; Deac. 1859, Pr. 1860, both by Archbp of Cant ; C. of Christ Ch. Folkestone, 1859.

GEAKE, Augustine, *Willington, near Newcastle-on-Tyne.* — Trin. Coll. Dub. B.A. 1856 ; Deac. 1857, Pr. 1858, both by Bp of Chest ; R. of Willington, Dio. Dur. 1859 (Patrons, the Crown and Bp of Dur. alternately ; Tithe—R. 197*l* 9*s* 2*d* ; R.'s Gross Inc. 220*l* ; Pop. 650).

GEGG, Joseph, *Wandsworth-common, Surrey.*—Literate ; Deac. 1845, Pr. 1847, both by Bp of Jamaica ; Asst.-Chap. to the House of Correction, Wandsworth Common, 1857 (Stipend, 210*l*) ; formerly Chap. to H.M. troops in Br. Honduras, 1847-55 ; C. of Old Weston, Hunts, 1855-57.

GELDART, James William, *Wheatley, near Oxford.*—Trin. Ha. Camb. LL.B. 1859 ; Deac. 1860, by Bp of Oxon ; C. of Wheatley, 1860 (Stipend, 40*l*).

GENNYS, Edmund John Henn, *Idehill, Edenbridge, Kent.*—St Aidan's Theol. Coll ; Deac. 1860, by Archbp. of Cant ; C. of Idehill, 1860.

GEPP, Henry John, *New College, Oxford.*—New Coll. Oxon. B.A. 1857, M.A. 1860 ; Deac. 1860, by Bp of Oxon ; Fell. of New Coll. Oxon.

GIBBENS, William, *Sourton, Oakhampton, Devon.*—Corpus Coll. Camb ; Deac. 1847, Pr. 1848, both by Bp of Lich ; C. of Bridestowe and Sourton, Devon.

GIBBS, John Lomax, *Collina, Torquay.*—Exon. Coll. Oxon. B.A. 1853, M.A. 1856 ; Deac. 1859, Pr. 1860 ; C. of St Mark's, Torwood, Torquay, 1859.

GIBSON, Henry Atkinson, *Clare Villa, Cainscross, Stroud, Gloucestershire.*—Wadh. Coll. Oxon. B.A. 1857, M.A. 1859 ; Deac. 1857, Pr. 1859 ; Travelling Deputation Secretary to the Christian Vernacular Education Society for India, 1860 (Stipend, 250*l*) ; late C. of Bibury, Gloucestershire, 1857-60.

GILBERT, John Bellamy, *Cantley rectory, near Norwich.* — Emman. Coll. Camb. B.A. 1857 ; Deac. 1859, Pr. 1860, both by Bp of Ely ; R. of Cantley, Dio. Norw. 1860 (Patron, W. A. Gilbert, Esq ; Tithe—R. 300*l* ; Glebe, 43½ acres ; R.'s Gross Inc. 336*l* and Ho ; Pop. 277) ; formerly C. of Hadleigh, Suffolk, 1859-60.

GILL, Francis Turner, *Warfield, Bracknell, Berks.*—Downing Coll. Camb. B.A. 1852 ; Deac. 1854, Pr. 1855, both by Bp of Worc ; V. of Warfield, Dio. Oxon. 1860 (Patrons, Exors. of the late Rev. R. Faithfull ; Tithe—Imp. 668*l* 12*s*, V. 200*l* ; Glebe, 16 acres ; V.'s Gross Inc. 250*l* ; Pop. 1317) ; late C. of Warfield, 1859-60 ; formerly C. of St James-the-Great, Stratford-on-Avon.

GILL, Thomas Howard, *Ballasalla, Isle of Man.*—Trin. Coll. Camb. B.A. 1859 ; Deac. 1859, by Bp of S. and M ; C. of Malew, Isle of Man, 1859.

GILLAM, Edmund Carver, *Mungrisdale, near Penrith.*—Literate ; Deac. 1860, by Bp of Carl ; C. of Mungrisdale, 1860.

GILLETT, Hugh Hodgson, *Wantage, Berks.*—Exon. Coll. Oxon, B.A. 1857, M.A. 1860 ; Deac. 1859, Pr. 1860, both by Bp of Oxon ; C. of Wantage *w* Charlton, 1859.

GIRDLESTONE, Robert Baker, *Worthing, Sussex.*— Ch. Ch. Oxon. B.A. 1859 ; Deac. 1860, by Bp of Chich ; C. of Worthing, 1860.

GLEDHILL, Joseph, *Ripponden, Halifax.*—Bp Hat. Ha. Dur. Theol. Licen. 1859 ; Deac. 1859, by Bp of Rip ; C. of Ripponden, 1859.

GLOVER, Frederick Blundell, *Cheetham Hill, Manchester.*—St John's Coll. Camb. B.A. 1856, M.A. 1859 ; Deac. 1857, Pr. 1858, both by Bp of Manch ; C. of St Mark's, Cheetham Hill, 1857.

GOBAT, Samuel Benoni, *Romsey, Hants.*—Trin. Coll. Oxon. B.A. 1860 ; Deac. 1860, by Bp of Winch ; C. of Romsey, 1860.

GOODACRE, Francis Burges, *Lutterworth, Leicestershire.*—St John's Coll. Camb. M.B. 1852, L.M. 1858, M.D. 1860 ; Deac. 1858, Pr. 1859, both by Bp of Exon ; formerly Assist. C. of . Penzance, Cornwall, 1858-60.

GOODACRE, Frederick William, *Little Ashby, Lutterworth, Leicestershire.*—Emman. Coll. Camb. B.A. 1858 ; Deac. 1859, by Bp of Manch. Pr. 1860, by Bp of Peterb ; C. of Little Ashby, 1859.

GOODE, William, *The Deanery, Ripon.*—Trin. Coll. Camb. 1st Cl. 1822, B.A. 1825, M.A. 1828 ; Deac. and Pr. 1825 ; Dean of Ripon, 1860 (Dean's Gross Inc. 1000*l*. and Res) ; late R. of St Margaret Lothbury *w* St Christopher-le-Stocks and St Bartholomew Exchange, London, 1856-60 ; formerly R. of Allhallows the Great *w* Allhallows the Less, London, 1849-56 ; Warburtonian Lect. 1853-57. For list of books published see *Crockford's Clerical Directory* of 1860.

GOODHART, Edward Skelton, *Harrington rectory, Cumberland.*—Trin. Coll. Camb. B.A. 1856 ; Deac. 1857, Pr. 1858, both by Bp of Dur ; C. of Harrington, 1860 ; formerly C. of Wetheral, Cumberland, 1857-59 ; Incumb. of St George's, Battersea, Surrey, 1859-60 ; Author, *Grape Gleanings of the Vintage,* Nisbet and Co. 1859, 2*d*.

GORE, Charles Frederick, *Edenbridge parsonage, Kent.*—St John's Coll. Oxon. B.A. 1853, M.A. 1857 ; Deac. 1853, Pr. 1854, both by Bp of Lond ; P.C. of Edenbridge, Dio. Cant. 1859 (Patron, Fred. Robt. Gore, Esq ; Tithe—Imp. 787*l*, V. 335*l*. 5*s* ; V.'s Gross Inc. 430*l*. and Ho ; Pop. 1718) ; late C. of Edenbridge ; formerly C. of Hampstead, Middlesex.

GOTT, John, *Great Yarmouth, Norfolk.*—Brasen. Coll. Oxon. B.A. 1853, M.A. 1854 ; Deac. 1857, Pr. 1858, both by Bp of Norw ; C. of St Nicholas' and Chap. of St Andrew's, Yarmouth.

GOULD, Joseph, *Repton (Derbyshire), near Burton-on-Trent, Staffs.*—Caius Coll. Camb. B.A. 1857, M.A. 1860 ; Deac. 1858, Pr. 1859, both by Bp of Lich ; Asst. Mast. at Repton School, 1858.

GOWER, John, *Ystradyfodwg, Pontypridd, Glamorgan.*—Qu. Theol. Coll. Birmingham ; Deac. 1860, by Bp of Lland ; C. of Ystradyfodwg, 1860.

GRACE, Oliver James, *Lacey Green, Risborough, Tring, Herts.*—Jesus Coll. Camb. B.A. 1856, M.A. 1859 ; Deac. 1856, Pr. 1858, both by Bp of Oxon ; C. of Sanderton, and Chap. of the Wycombe Union, Bucks, 1859.

GRANT, Henry Carmichael, *Bollington, Macclesfield, Cheshire.*—Jesus Coll. Camb. B.A. 1858 ; Deac. 1860, by Bp of Chest ; C. of Bollington, 1860.

GREEN, Charles, *Seaham Harbour, Durham.*—Literate ; Deac. 1860, by Bp of Dur ; C. of St John's, Seaham Harbour, 1860.

GREEN, Charles Edward Maddison, *Tydd St Mary, Wisbeach, Cambs.*—Emman. Coll. Camb. B.A. 1859 ; Deac. 1859, Pr. 1860 ; C. of Tydd St Mary, 1859.

C

GREEN, George Clark, *Modbury vicarage, Devon.*—King's Coll. Camb. B.A. 1852, M.A. 1856; Deac. 1854, by Bp of Linc. Pr. 1855, by Bp of Peterb; V. of Modbury, Dio. Exon. 1859 (Patron, Eton College; Tithe—Imp. 780*l*; V. 406*l* 15*s*; Glebe, 9 acres;' V.'s Gross Inc. 440*l* and Ho; Pop. 1858); late P.C. of Hamworthy, Dorset, 1858–59; formerly C. of Everdon, Northampton; previously Fell. of Eton Coll. and Fell. of King's Coll. Camb.

GREEN, James Wastie, *Kington, Herefordshire.*—Balliol Coll. Oxon. 2nd Cl. Lit. Hum. and B.A. 1846, M.A. 1851; Deac. 1850, Pr. 1851, both by Bp of Lond; C. of Kington, 1859; late Head Mast. of the Camberwell Coll. Sch. Lond. 1854–59.

GREEN, John Horner, *Ilkeston, Nottingham.*—C. of Ilkeston.

GREEN, John Richard, ...—Jesus Coll. Oxon. B.A. 1860; Deac. 1860, by Bp of Lond; C. of St Barnabas, King's-square, Lond. 1860.

GREER, Frederick, ...—Trin. Coll. Dub. B.A. 1860; Deac. 1859, Pr. 1860, both by Bp of Lich.

GREET, Alexander, *Stoke St Gregory, Taunton, Somerset.*—Caius Coll. Camb. B.A. 1859; Deac. 1859, Pr. 1860, both by Bp of B. and W; C. of Stoke St Gregory, 1859.

GREGORY, Edmund Ironside, *South Lynn, Norfolk.*—Emman. Coll. Camb. B.A. 1858; Deac. 1859, Pr. 1860, both by Bp of Norw; C. of All Saints, South Lynn, 1859.

GREGORY, John George, *Highland-house, Nechells, Birmingham.*—Caius Coll. Camb. B.A. 1853, M.A. 1856; Deac. 1853, Pr. 1854, both by Bp of Worces; Incumb. of St Clement's, Nechells, Dio. Worces. 1860 (Patron, Incumb. of St Matthew's, Birmingham; Incumb.'s Gross Inc. 100*l*; Pop. 8000); formerly C. of Holy Trinity, Coventry, 1853–56; C. of All Saints, Lambeth Lond. 1856–57; C. of Holy Trinity, Islington, Lond. 1857–59.

GRESLEY, Nigel, *Nether Seale, Ashby-de-la-Zouch, Leicestershire.*—Trin. Coll. Camb. B.A. 1858; Deac. 1859, Pr. 1860, both by Bp of B. and W; R. of Nether Seale and Over Seale, Dio. Peterb. 1860 (Patron, Sir Thomas Gresley, Bart. Tithe—R. 950*l*; Glebe, 72 acres; R.'s Gross Inc. 1082*l*; Pop. 1119); formerly Asst. C. of Chewton - Mendip, Somerset, 1859–60.)

GREY, William Hewett Charles, *Wilford, near Nottingham.*—St John's Coll. Camb. B.A. 1822, M.A. 1825; Deac. 1822, Pr. 1823, both by Archbp of York; formerly C. of Kirton, near Tuxford, Notts, 1822–25.

GRIER, Frederick, *Hault Hucknall, Chesterfield, Derbyshire.*—Trin. Coll. Dub. B.A. 1859; Deac. 1859; C. of Heath and Hault Hucknall, 1859.

GRIFFITH, Richard Williams, *Llanfairisgaer, near Carnarvon.*—Jesus Coll. Oxon. B.A. 1854, M.A. 1856; Deac. 1855, by Bp of Chest. Pr. 1856, by Bp of Bang; P.C. of Llanfairisgaer, Dio. Bang. 1860 (Patron, Bp of Bang; P.C.'s Gross Inc. 115*l*; Pop. 687); formerly C. of Holyhead, 1855-58; C. of Llanfairisgaer, 1858-60.

GRIFFITHS, Alban, *New Tredegar, Monmouthshire.*—Literate; Deac. 1859, Pr. 1860, both by Bp of Lland; Home Church Missionary for Dio. Lland. 1860; formerly C. of Ebb Vale, Tredegar, Monmouthshire, 1859-60.

GRIMALDI, Henry Beaufort, *Nonington, Wingham, Kent.*—St John's Coll. Oxon. and King's Coll. Lond. Theol. Assoc. 1858; Deac. 1858, Pr. 1859, both by Bp of Lich; C. of Nonington, 1860; formerly C. of Darlaston, Staffs. 1858-60

GRINSTEAD, Charles, *2 Barn Park-terrace, Teignmouth.*—Literate; Deac. 1860, by Bp of Exon; C. of St Nicholas, East Teignmouth, 1860.

GROVER, John, *Atherstone, Warwickshire.*—Emman. Coll. Camb. B.A. 1856, M.A. 1859; Deac. 1857, Pr. 1858, both by Bp of Worc; C. of St. Mary's, Atherstone, 1857.

GRUNDY, William James, *St James the Less parsonage, Victoria-park, Bethnal-green, London.*—Literate; Deac. 1851, Pr. 1852; Incumb. of St James the Less, Dio. Lond. 1859 (Patron, Bp of Lond; Incumb.'s Gross Inc. 200*l*; Pop. 6000); formerly R. of Kilvington, Notts; Author, various *Sermons*.

GUEST, James Merrick, *St George's-terrace, Birmingham.*—Pemb. Coll. Oxon. B.A. 1856, M.A. 1859; Deac. 1859, Pr. 1860, by Bp of Worc; Assist. Mast. in King Edward's Sch. Birmingham.

GUILLEMARD, William Henry, *Royal College, Armagh, Ireland.*—Pemb. Coll. Camb. Crosse Sch. 1838, B.A. 1838, Tyrwhit Hebrew Sch. 1841, M.A. 1842, B.D. 1849; Deac. 1841, by Bp of Ely, Pr. 1843, by Bp of Bristol; Head Mast. of the Royal Coll. Armagh, 1848 (Patron, Archbp of Armagh); Fell. of Pemb. Coll. Camb.

———◆———

HALL, Edward Duncan, *Foss Bridge, Northleach, Gloucestershire.*—Pemb. Coll. Oxon. B.A. 1848, M.A. 1851; Deac. 1849, Pr. 1850; R. of Coln St. Denis, near Northleach, Dio. G. and B. 1860 (Patron, Pemb. Coll. Oxon; Tithe—R. 298*l*; Glebe, 73 acres; R.'s Gross Inc. 400*l*; Pop. 229); Fell. of Pemb. Coll. Oxon. 1848.

HALLWARD, John William, *Wandsworth, Surrey.*—King's Coll. Lond; Deac. 1851, Pr. 1852; Chap. to the House of Correction, Wandsworth, 1860 (Patron, Secretary of State for the Home Office; Chap's Gross Inc. 250*l*); formerly C. of St Stephen's, Hammersmith, Middlesex, 1853-60.

HALY, John Billing, *20, Oxford-place, Plymouth.*—St John's Coll. Camb. B.A. 1859; Deac. 1859, Pr. 1860, both by Bp of Exon; Asst. C. of Christ Ch. Plymouth, 1859.

HAMMOND, Henry, *Stetchworth vicarage, Cambridgeshire.*—Clare Coll. Camb. LL.B. 1854; Deac. 1851, Pr. 1852, both by Bp of Ely; V. of Stetchworth, Dio. Ely 1859 (Patrons, Trustees of R. Eaton, Esq; V.'s Gross Inc. 186*l*. and Ho; Pop. 700).

HAMMOND, Robert Henry, *Sheffield, Yorkshire.*—King's Coll. Lond; Deac. 1860, by Archbp of York; C. of St Paul's, Sheffield, 1860.

HAMPSHIRE, William Knowlton, ... —Pemb. Coll. Camb. B.A. 1860; Deac. 1860, by Bp of Chich.

HANBURY, John Capel, *Hereford.*—Wadh. Coll. Oxon. B.A. 1857, M.A. 1859; Deac. 1858, Pr. 1859, both by Bp of Heref; C. of Pipe, near Hereford; Second Class Mast. in Heref. Cathl. Sch.

HANDCOCK, John Harward Jessop, *Woodlands parsonage, Sevenoaks, Kent.*—St Aidan's Theol. Coll; Deac. 1858, Pr. 1859; P.C. of Woodlands, Dio. Cant. 1860 (Patron, Rev R. Vincent; Glebe, 3 acres; P.C.'s Gross Inc. 165*l* and Ho; Pop. 267); formerly C. of St Helen's, Lancashire, 1858-1860.

HARDMAN, Charles Leonard, *Sturry, near Canterbury.*—Caius Coll. Camb. B.A. 1859; Deac. 1860, by Archbp of Cant; C. of Sturry, 1860.

HARDMAN, Richard Peers, *Spring Bank, Hull.*—King's Coll. Lond. Theol. Assoc. 1859; Deac. 1859, Pr. 1860, both by Archbp of York; C. of St Stephen's, Hull, 1859.

HARDINGHAM, Charles Hugh, *32 Trinity-square, Southwark, London.*—Trin. Coll. Camb. B.A. 1854; Deac. 1859, Pr. 1860, both by Bp of Winch; Second Mast. of Qu. Elizabeth's Grammar School, St. Olave's, Southwark, Lond.

HARFORD, Edward John, *Henbury, near Bristol.*—Oriel Coll. Oxon. B.A. 1854; Deac. 1857, by Bp of Winch. Pr. 1860, by Bp of G. and B; C. of Henbury, 1860; formerly C. of Deal, Kent.

HARRIES, Thomas Seth Jones, ... —Jesus Coll. Camb. B.A. 1860; Deac. 1860, by Bp of Winch.

HARRIS, William, *Bedford.*—St John's Coll. Camb. B.A. 1859; Deac. 1859, by Bp of Chich.

HARRISON, William, *Pontesbury rectory, near Shrewsbury.*—Brasen. Coll. Oxon. B.A. 1846, M.A. 1849; Deac. 1846, Pr. 1847, both by Bp of Chest; R. of Pontesbury, First Portion, Dio. Heref. 1847 (Patron, the present R; Tithe—R. 785*l* 6*s*; Glebe, 22 acres; R.'s Gross Inc. 835*l* and Ho; Pop. 1657); Surrog. for Dio. of Herf; formerly C. of Christ Ch. Macclesfield, 1846-47.

HART, Robert Paley, *Waltham Abbey, Essex.* —Trin. Coll. Camb. B.A. 1858; Deac. 1859, Pr. 1860, both by Bp of Roch; C. of Waltham Abbey, 1859.

HART, Edgar Oswald, 13, *Popple-street, Hedon-road, Hull.*—St Aidan's Theol. Coll; Deac. 1860, by Archbp of York; C. of Drypool, Hull, 1860.

HARVEY, Charles Musgrave, *Halstead, Essex.*—Ch. Ch. Oxon. B.A. 1859; Deac. 1860, by Bp of Roch; C. of Halstead, 1860.

HARWARD, Edwin Cuthbert, *Minster-yard, Lincoln.*—Trin. Coll. Oxon. B.A. 1857, M.A. 1860; Deac. 1858, Pr. 1859, both by Bp of Linc; C. of St Nicholas, Lincoln, 1858.

HARWOOD, Reynold, *Chichester.*—Theol. Coll. Chich; Deac. and Pr. 1859; C. of Appledram, near Chichester, 1859.

HATHWAITE, Thomas Walter, *Coven, near Wolverhampton.*—Univ. Coll. Dur. B.A. 1859; Deac. 1860, by Bp of Lich; C. of Coven, 1860.

HATTON, John Leigh Smeathman, *Orston, Newark, Notts.*—Worces. Coll. Oxon. B.A. 1859; Deac. 1860, by Bp of Linc; C. of Orston *w* Scarrington and Thoroton, 1860.

HAVART, William James, *Watford, Herts.*— St John's Coll. Camb. B.A. 1858; Deac. 1859, Pr. 1860, both by Bp of Roch; C. of St Andrew's, Watford, 1859.

HAWKER, Isaac, 17 *Lay-gate-terrace, South Shields, Durham.*—St Aidan's Theol. Coll.; Deac. 1859, Pr. 1860; C. of Holy Trinity, South Shields, 1859.

HAYWARD, Frederick Lawson, ... —Corpus Coll. Camb. S.C.L. 1859; Deac. 1859, Pr. 1860, both by Bp of Chich.

HAZELL, James Henry, *Olney, Bucks.*—Corpus Coll. Camb. B.A. 1859; Deac. 1859, Pr. 1860, both by Bp of Oxon; C. of Olney, 1859.

HEBERDEN, George, *Ranmore parsonage, Leatherhead, Surrey.*—Oriel Coll. Oxon. B.A. 1856, M.A. 1859; P. C. of St Barnabas, Ranmore, Dio. Winch. 1860; (Patron—Geo. Cubitt, Esq; P. C.'s Gross Inc. 150*l* and Ho; Pop. 500); formerly C. of Wraxall, Somerset, 1857-58: C. of Great Bookham, Surrey, 1858-60.

HEBERDEN, John, 20 *Oxford-street, Southampton.*—Jesus Coll. Camb. B.A. 1859; Deac. 1859, Pr. 1860, both by Bp of Winch; C. of St Mary, Southampton, 1859.

HELLICAR, Arthur Gresley, *Wraxall, near Bristol.*—Wadh. Coll. Oxon. B.A. 1858; Deac. 1859, Pr. 1860, both by Bp of B. and W.; C. of Wraxall, 1859.

HEMMANS, Fielder, *Tetney vicarage, Grimsby, Lincolnshire.*—St. Peter's Coll. Camb. 29th Wrang. and B.A. 1851, M.A. 1854; Deac. 1851, Pr. 1852, both by Bp of Linc; V. of Tetney, Dio. Linc. 1860 (Patron, Bp of Linc; Tithe—V. 12*l*; Glebe, 144 acres; V.'s Gross Inc. 300*l* and Ho; Pop. 869); late C. of All Saints, Wragby, Lincolnshire; formerly Bye Fell. of St Peter's Coll. Camb.

HENDERSON, Thomas Julius, *South Benfleet vicarage, Rayleigh, Essex.*—Wadh. Coll. Oxon. B.A. 1849, M.A. 1852; Deac. 1850, Pr. 1851, both by Bp of Roch; V. of South Benfleet, Dio. Roch. 1859 (Patrons, D. and C. of Westminster; V.'s Gross Inc. 260*l* and Ho; Pop. 570); late Min. of St Swithin's Chapel, Kennington, Berks, 1856-59; formerly C. of Leigh, Rochford, Essex.

HENHAM, James Larkin, *Scalby, Scarborough, Yorkshire.*—Christ Coll. Camb. B.A. 1859; Deac. 1860, by Archbp. of York; C. of Scalby, 1860.

HENSLEY, Augustus De Morgan, ...—Trin. Coll. Camb. B.A. 1857, M.A. 1860; Deac. 1860 by Bp of G. and B.

HEPPENSTALL, Frederic, 50, *Lee-crescent, Lee-bank-road, Birmingham.*—St John's Coll. Camb. B.A. 1858; Deac. 1860, by Bp of Lond; Asst. Mast. in King Edward's Sch, Birmingham, 1859; formerly Asst. Mast. in Univ. Coll. Sch. Lond. 1858-59.

HEREFORD, Robert, *Ledbury, Herefordshire.* —St John's Coll. Oxon. B.A. 1857, M.A. 1860; Deac. 1860, by Bp of Heref; C. of Ledbury, 1860.

HEWISON, George Henry, *Archbishop Holgate's School, York.*—St John's Coll. Camb. B.A. 1859; Deac. 1859, Pr. 1860; both by Archbp. of York; Math. Mast. of Archbp. Holgate's School, 1859; C. of Osbaldwick, near York, 1859.

HICKS, George Grisdale, *Coberley, near Cheltenham.*—Exon. Coll. Oxon. B.A. 1859; Deac. 1859, Pr. 1860, both by Bp of G. and B; C. of Coberley, 1859.

HILL, Charles Croft, *Manningham, Bradford, Yorkshire.*—Qu. Coll. Oxon. B.A. 1857, M.A. 1860; Deac. 1858, Pr. 1859, both by Bp of Rip; C. of Manningham, 1859; formerly C. of Otley, Yorkshire, 1858-59.

HILL, Francis Thomas, *Terling vicarage, Witham, Essex.*—Trin. Coll. Dub. B.A. 1826, M.A. 1832; Deac. 1846, Pr. 1847, both by Bp of Worces; V. of Terling, Dio. Roch. 1860 (Patron, Lord Rayleigh; V.'s Gross Inc. 310*l* and Ho; Pop. 900); formerly C. of Clifton, Bristol; Author, *Lectures on the Holy Spirit*; *Lectures on the Evil Spirit*; *Letter to the Laity on the Sabbath*; occasional *Sermons.*

HILL, James, 27, *Mecklenburgh-square, London.* —Gon. and Caius. Camb. B.A. 1859; Deac. 1859, Pr 1860, both by Bp of Lond; C. of St. George's, Bloomsbury, London, 1859.

HILLIARD, Joseph Stephen, *Ealing, Middlesex.*—Brasen. Coll. Oxon. B.A. 1848, M.A. 1852; Deac. and Pr. 1850; P.C. of Christ Church, Ealing. Dio. Lond. 1860 (Patroness, Miss R. F. Lewis; P.C.'s Gross Inc. 120*l*; Pop. 1867); late C. of Boughton Malherse, Kent; formerly C. of Ramsden-Bellhouse and Stock, Essex.

HIND, William Marsden, *Harrow, Middlesex.* —Trin. Coll. Dub. B.A. 1836, M.A. 1839; Deac. and Pr. 1839, both by Bp of Down and Connor; formerly C. of Stoneyford, Derryaghy, Ireland, 1839-42; C. of Stapenhill, Derbyshire, 1843-54; Asst. Chap. to the dock Hospital, Paddington, London, 1855-58.

HIRON, Samuel Franklin, *Bugley-road, near Edgbaston, Birmingham.*—Trin. Coll. Dub. B.A. 1859; Deac. 1859, Pr. 1860, both by Bp of Worc; Prin. of the Junior Department of the Proprietary School, Edgbaston, and C. of St. Philip's, Birmingham.

HITCHCOCK, William Maunder, *Bussage parsonage, Stroud, Gloucestershire.*—Wadh. Coll. Oxon. B.A. 1858; Deac. 1858, by Archbp. of Cant; P.C. of Bussage. Dio. G. and B. 1860 (Patron, Bp of G. and B; P.C.'s Gross Inc. 50*l* and Ho; Pop. 311); formerly C. of St James's, Cheltenham, 1858-60.

HOARE, Edward Thomas, *Seavington St Mary, Ilminster, Somerset.*—Gon. and Cai. Coll. Camb. B.A. 1855, M.A. 1858; Deac. 1858, Pr. 1859; C. of Seavington St Michael *w* Dinnington, 1858; formerly Asst. C. of Crewkerne, Somerset, 1858.

HOARE, Richard, *Nottingham.*—St Bees Theol. Coll; Deac. 1857, Pr. 1858, both by Bp of Carl; C. of St Mary's, Nottingham, 1859; formerly C. of Beckermet, Cumberland.

HODD, Albert Harry, *Chesterton, Newcastle, Staffs.*—Univ. Coll. Dur. Sch. 1854, B.A. 1857, Fell. 1858, M.A. 1860; Deac. 1858, Pr. 1859, both by Bp of Lich; C. of Chesterton, 1858.

HODGES, George, 5 *St James's-gardens, Haverstock-hill, London.*—King's Coll. Lond. Theol. Assoc; Deac. 1858, Pr. 1859, both by Bp of Lond; C. of St Andrew's, St Pancras, London, 1858.

HODGES, James, *Lane-end parsonage, High Wycombe, Bucks.*—Trin. Coll. Camb. B.A. 1849, M.A. 1852; Deac. 1849, Pr. 1850, P.C. of Lane-end, Dio. Oxon. 1859 (Patron, R. of Hambledon, Bucks; P.C.'s Gross Inc. 115*l* and Ho; Pop. 955); late P.C. of St Mary's Middleton, Leeds, 1853-58.

HODGSON, Iles John, *The Rectory, Wolverhampton.*—Linc. Coll. Oxon. B.A. 1849, M.A. 1852; Deac. 1852, by Bp of G. and B.; Pr. 1853, by Bp of Worces; R. of St Peter's Coll. Ch. Wolverhampton, Dio. Lich. 1860 (Patron, Bp of Lich; R.'s Gross Inc. 750*l* and Ho; Pop. 9000); Surrog. Dio. Lich.

HOLDERNESS, James, *Saffron Walden, Essex.*—St Cath. Coll. Camb. B.A. 1859; Deac. 1581, by Bp of Victoria, Pr. 1860, by Bp of Roch; C. of Saffron Walden, 1859; formerly Missionary to Seamen at Hong-Kong, 1849-55.

HOLME, Arthur Phidias, *Great Yarmouth, Norfolk.*—Trin. Coll. Camb. B.A. 1859; Deac. 1859, Pr. 1860, both by Bp of Norw; C. of St Nicholas, Great Yarmouth, 1859.

HOLME, Edward, *Northallerton, Yorkshire.*—St Bees Theol. Coll; Deac. 1854, Pr. 1855, both by Bp of Rip; Chap. of the Ho. of Correction for the N. Riding of Yorkshire, 1860; formerly C. of Cleckheaton, Yorkshire, 1854-57; C. of East Cowton, Yorkshire, 1857-59.

HOLMES, Samuel, *Burton-upon-Trent, Staffs.*—St John's Coll. Camb. B.A. 1858; Deac. 1859, Pr. 1860, both by Bp of Lich; C. of Burton-upon-Trent, 1859.

HONE, Evelyn Joseph, *Doncaster, Yorkshire.*—Wadh. Coll. Oxon. B.A. 1859; Deac. 1860, by Archbp of York; C. of Doncaster, 1860.

HOOKE, Alfred, *Chipping-Warden (Northants), near Banbury, Oxfordshire.*—Worc. Coll. Oxon. B.A. 1857, M.A. 1859; Deac. 1859, Pr. 1860, both by Bp of Peterb; C. of Chipping-Warden, 1859.

HOOPPELL, Robert Eli, *Newcastle-on-Tyne.*—St John's Coll. Camb. B.A. 1855, M.A. 1858; Deac. 1857, Pr. 1859, both by Bp of Barg; Head Mast. of the Marine Sch. South Shields, 1861; 2nd Mast. of Beaumaris Gram. Sch. 1855-61; formerly C. of Llandesilio Ch. Menai Bridge, 1859-61; Author, *British Dealings with China,* 8vo. Bennett, Lond. 1859, 2*d.*

HOPE, John, ... —New Coll. Oxon. B.A. 1858, M.A. 1860; Deac. 1860, by Bp of Roch.

HOPKINS, John, *Beaufort, Monmouthshire.*—Theol. Coll. Abergavenny; Deac. 1859, Pr. 1860, both by Bp of Lland; C. of Beanfort, 1859.

HORDERN, Joseph Calveley, H.M.S. "Diadem."—St Aidan's Theol. Coll; Deac. 1855. Pr. 1856, both by Archbp of York; Chap. in the Royal Navy, 1858; Author, *Sermons preached to Seafaring Men,* 1860.

HORNBY, James John, *Bishop Cosin's Hall, Durham.*—Brasen. Coll. Oxon. B.A. 1849, M.A. 1852; Deac. 1854; Prin. of Bp Cosin's Hall, Vice-Mast. of Univ. Coll, and Tutor of Univ. of Durham; Fell of Brasen. Coll. Oxon.

HORNE, Edward Larkin, *Great Dunmow, Essex.*—Clare Coll. Camb. B.A. 1858; Deac. 1858, Pr. 1859, both by Bp of Roch; C. of Great Dunmow, 1858.

HORNE, William, 38 *Southampton-row, Russell-square, London.*—Caius Coll. Camb. B.A. 1859; Deac. 1860, by Bp of Lond; C. of Trinity Ch. St Giles-in-the Fields, London, 1860.

HORROCKS, George, *Sidbury, Sidmouth, Devon.*—Magd. Ha. Oxon. B.A. 1859; Deac. 1860, by Bp of Exon; C. of Sidbury, 1860.

HOSE, John Christian, 62 *Camden-square, Kentish-town, London.*—King's Coll. Lond. B.A. 1854, Theol. Assoc. 1857; Deac. 1857, Pr. 1859, both by Bp of Lond; C. of St Saviour's, South Hampstead, Middlesex, 1857.

HOSE, Thomas Charles, *Harpenden, St Albans, Herts.*—Literate; Deac. 1858, Pr. 1859, both by Bp of Peterb; C. of Harpenden, 1860; formerly C. of Sapcote, Leicestershire, 1838-60.

HOSKING, Henry John, *Rock-park, Rock Ferry, Cheshire.*—Brasen. Coll. Oxon. B.A. 1857, M.A. 1860; Deac. 1858, Pr. 1859, both by Bp of Chest; R. of Thorpe-in-Glebis, Notts, Dio. Linc. 1859 (Patron, the present R; Tithe—R. 119*l*; R.'s Gross Inc. 150*l*; Pop. 40); formerly C. of Rock Ferry, Cheshire, 1858-50.

HOUGH, George D'Urban John, *Wychbold, Droitwich, Worcestershire.*—Pemb. Coll. Oxon. B.A. 1858; Deac. 1858, Pr. 1859, both by Bp of Wore; C. of Dodderhill w Chapelry of Elmbridge, Worcestershire, 1859.

HOUGHTON, Edward James, *Twyford, near Winchester.*—Chr. Ch. Oxon. B.A. 1859; Deac. 1860, by Bp of Winch; C. of Twyford, 1860.

HOWARD, Robert, *Uttoxeter, Staffs.*—Trin. Coll. Oxon. B.A. 1859; Deac. 1860; C. of St Mary's, Uttoxeter, 1859.

HOWELL, Howell, *Appledore, Tenterden, Kent.*—St Aidan's Theol. Coll; Deac. 1859, Pr. 1860, both by Archbp of Cant; C. of Snargate w Snave, Kent, 1859.

HOWELL, John, *Llangattock rectory, Crickhowell, Brecon.*—St Bees Theol. Coll; Deac. 1855, Pr. 1857, both by Bp of Rip; C. of Llangattock cum Llangenney, 1859; formerly C. of St Bartholomew's, Meltham, Huddersfield, 1855-59.

HUDSON, Charles, *Skillington vicarage, Grantham, Lincolnshire.*—St John's Coll. Camb. Sen. Opt. B.A. 1851, M.A. 1854; Deac. 1853, Pr. 1854, both by Bp of Rip; V. of Skillington, Dio. Linc. 1860 (Patron, C. Turner, Esq. Stoke Rochford; Tithe—V. 64*l*; Glebe, 28 acres; V.'s Gross Inc. 120*l* and Ho; Pop. 490); late C. of St Mary's, Bridgnorth; formerly Chap. in the Crimea; Author, *Ascent of Mont Blanc and Monte Rosa without Guides,* Longmans, 2 edits.

HUGHES, Albert, *Market Rasen, Lincolnshire.*—St John's Coll. Oxon. B.A. 1859; Deac. 1859, Pr. 1860, both by Bp of Linc; C. of Market Rasen, 1859.

HUGHES, John Bickley, *Tiverton, Devon.*—Magd. Coll. Oxon. B.A. 1838, M.A. 1841; Deac. 1840, Pr. 1841, both by Bp of Oxon; C. of St. Thomas, Tiverton, 1847; Head Mast. of Blundell's Sch. Tiverton; Local Sec. to the Exon. Dio. Architectural Society; Sec. to the Tiverton Local Board of Education; formerly Asst. Mast. of Marlborough Coll; Author, *Many Papers on Archæological and Architectural Subjects.*

HUGHES, Morgan, *Cyfarthfa, Glamorganshire.*—St David's Theol. Coll. Lamp; Deac. 1859, by Bp of Lland; C. of Cyfarthfa, 1859.

HUMBLE, Henry, *St. Ninian's, Perth, Scotland.*—Univ. Coll. Dur. B.A. 1837, M.A. 1842; Deac. 1843, Pr. 1844; C. of Newburn, Northumberland, 1843; Dom. Chap. to Lord Forbes, 1844; Can. and Precentor of St. Ninian's, Perth; Author, *various Pamphlets.*

HUNT, John William, *Cheltenham.* — St Aidan's Theol. Coll; Deac. 1859, Pr. 1860, both by Bp of Lich; C. of St. Paul's, and Asst. Lect. in the Ch. of Engl. Training Coll. Cheltenham, 1860; formerly C. of Ripley, Derbyshire.

HUNT, William Cornish, ... —Ch. Ch. Oxon. B.A. 1859; Deac. 1859, Pr. 1860, both by Bp of Lich

HUNTER, Evan Haynes, *Little Drayton, Market Drayton, Shropshire.*—Trin. Coll. Camb. B.A. 1839, M.A. 1844; Deac. 1841, Pr. 1842; C. of Christ's Ch, Little Drayton, 1860; formerly C. of St John's, Charlotte-street, Fitzroy-square, Lond. 1848-52; C. of St Thomas, Stamford-hill, Lond. 1852-57; C. of Lymm, Cheshire, 1857-60.

HUNTER, Joseph William, *Dundee, Scotland.*—Trin. Coll. Glenalmond, Theol. Licen; Deac. 1860, by Bp of Oxon; C. of St Mary Magdalen, Dundee, 1860.

HURCOMB, Francis Burdett, 37, *Cecil-street, Carlisle.*—King's Coll. Lond; Deac. 1859, Pr. 1860, both by Bp of Carl; C. of Christ Ch. Carlisle, 1860; formerly C. of St. Paul's, Lindale-in-Cartmel, Lancashire, 1859-60; Author, *various Tracts* for the Relig. Tract Soc.

HURON, The Right Rev. Benjamin CRONYN, Lord Bishop of Huron, *London, Canada West.*—Trin. Coll. Dub. D.D; Consecrated Bp of Huron, 1857 (Episcopal Jurisdiction, the province of Huron, Canada West; Extent, 12,200 sq. miles; Pop. 277,505; No. of Clergy, 43).

HUTCHINS, Charles, *Bridgnorth, Shropshire.*—Magd. Ha. Oxon. B.A. 1860; Deac. 1860, by Bp of Chest; C. of St Mary Magdalen, Bridgnorth, 1860.

HUTCHINSON, Robert Westmorland, *Doddington, Northants.*—Bp Hat. Ha. Dur. Theol. Licen. 1859; Deac. 1859, by Bp of Winch. Pr. 1860, by Bp of Peterb; C. of Doddington, 1859; Second Mast. of Wellingborough Gram. Sch.

HUTCHINSON, Thomas Neville, *King Edward's School, Birmingham.*—St John's Coll. Camb. B.A. 1854, M.A. 1859; Second Mast. of King Edward's Sch. Birmingham, 1860; formerly Vice-Prin. of the Diocesan Training Coll, Chester.

HUTCHINSON, William Henry, *Leckhampton, near Cheltenham.*—Pemb. Coll. Camb. B.A. 1860; Deac. 1860, by Bp of G. and B; C. of Leckhampton, 1860.

HUTTON, Henry Wollaston, *Southwell, Notts.*—Trin. Coll. Oxon. B.A. 1857, M.A. 1860; Deac. 1859, Pr. 1860, both by Bp of Southwell, 1860.

HUTTON, Thomas, *Stilton rectory, Hunts.*—Trin. Coll. Dub. B.A. 1843, M.A. 1849; Deac. 1844, Pr. 1845, both by Bp of L. and C; R. of Stilton, Dio. Ely, 1859 (Patron, Bp of Peterb; Glebe, 265 acres; R.'s Gross Inc. 450l and Ho; Pop. 803); formerly Chap. to the Northampton County Gaol, 1850-9; Author, occasional *Sermons* and *Lectures.*

HYNDE, William, *Ebberston, Heslerton, Yorks.*—Clare Coll. Camb. B.A. 1859; Deac. 1860; C. of Ebberston cum Allerston, 1860.

JAGO, William, *Church-street, Bridgwater, Somerset.*—St John's Coll. B.A. 1859; Deac. 1859; C. of St Mary's cum Chilton, Bridgwater.

IBBOTSON, Thomas Rudd, *Crakehall, Bedale, Yorkshire.*—St John's Coll. Camb. B.A. 1834; Deac. and Pr. 1834, both by Archbp of York; P.C. of Crakehall, Dio. Rip. 1840 (Patron, R. of Bedale; P.C.'s Gross Inc. 100l. and Ho; Pop. 832).

INGE, William, *Crayke, near York.*—Worc. Coll. Oxon. B.A. 1853, M.A. 1856; Deac. 1857, Pr. 1858, both by Archbp of York; C. of Crayke.

INGRAM, William Clavell, *Cosham, near Portsmouth.*—Jesus Coll. Camb. B.A. 1857; Deac. 1859, Pr. 1860, both by Bp of Chich; Head Mast. of St. Paul's Sch. Portsmouth, 1860; formerly Math. Mast. of St Nicholas College, Lancing, Sussex.

JACKSON, Edward Downes, *Carlecotes parsonage, Dunford Bridge, Yorkshire.*—Brasen. Coll. Oxon. Sch. 1849, B.A. 1851, M.A. 1854; Deac. 1852, Pr. 1853, both by Bp of Chest; Incumb. of Carlecotes, Dio. Rip. 1857 (Patron, John Chapman, Esq. Mottram, Cheshire; Incumb.'s Gross Inc. 150l. and Ho; Pop. 700); formerly C. of Over, Cheshire, 1852-56; Author, *A Sermon on the Opening of Carlecotes Church,* 1857; *A Sermon on the Indian Mutiny,* 1858.

JACKSON, Robert Hall, *Swindon, near Cheltenham.*—Litton's Ha. Oxon. B.A. 1860; Deac. 1860, by Bp of G. and B; C. of Swindon, 1860.

JACKSON, Samuel, *Magdalene College, Cambridge.*—Magd. Coll. Camb, B.A. 1854, M.A. 1857; Deac. 1857, Pr. 1858, both by Bp of Ely; Sen. Fell. of Magd. Coll. Camb.

JACOB, The Ven. Philip, *Crawley rectory, Winchester.*—Corpus Coll. Oxon. B.A. 1825, M.A. 1828; Deac. 1827, Pr. 1828, both by Bp of Lland; Archdeac. of Winch. 1860 (Archdeac.'s Gross Inc. 200l.); R. of Crawley w Hunton C. Dio. Winch. 1831 (Patron, Bp of Winch; Tithe—R. 660l; Hunton, 190l; Glebe, 8 acres; R.'s Gross Inc. 850l and Ho; Pop. 507); Can. Res. of Winch. Cathl. 1834 (Value, 650l and Res); Rur. D. of the Deanery of Winch; Chap. to the Bp of Winch; Sec. to the Winch. Diocesan Board of Education; Author, occasional *Sermons.*

JAMES, Theodore William, *West Cottage, Lincoln.*—Pemb. Coll. Oxon. Sch. 1853, B.A. 1857, M.A. 1860; Deac. 1859, Pr. 1860, both by Bp of Linc; C. of St Mary Magdalen, Lincoln, 1859.

JARBO, Peter John, *Calcutta, East Indies.*—Deac. 1852, Pr. 1853, both by Bp of Madras; Chap. of the East India Government in Bengal, 1859; late Chap. of the Sailors' Home, North Shields; formerly Chap. to the Railway Labourers, Rochester, and Morning Preacher at Gillingham, Kent; previously Missionary of the S.P.G. in India; Author, *Sermons,* in Tamil and English.

JECKELL, Joseph John, *Bath.*—St John's Coll. Camb. B.A. 1851; Deac. 1853, Pr. 1854, both by Bp of Norw; C. of the Abbey Ch. Bath, 1860; formerly C. of Southelmham and Flixtan, Suffolk, 1854-56; C. of St Helen's, Ipswich, 1856-60.

JEFFCOATT, Tom, *Bollington, Altrincham, Cheshire.*—Trin. Coll. Camb. B.A. 1856, M.A. 1859; Deac. 1855, Pr. 1856; C. of Rostherne, Cheshire, 1860.

JELF, George Edward, *Clapton, Middlesex.*—Ch. Ch. Oxon. B.A. 1856, M.A. 1859; Deac. 1858, Pr. 1859, both by Bp of Oxon; Asst. C. of St. James's, Clapton, 1860; formerly Asst. C. of St Michael's, Highgate, Middlesex, 1858-60.

JENKINS, James, *Billinge, Wigan, Lancashire.*—St Aidan's Theol. Coll; Deac. 1860, by Bp of Chest; C. of Billinge, 1860.

JENKINS, John Card, *Brussels, Belgium.*—Magd. Coll. Camb. B.A. 1859; Deac. 1859, Pr. 1860, both by Bp of Lond; Asst. C. of the Chapel Royal, Brussels, 1860.

JICKLING, Francis, *Bathford, near Bath.*—Emman. Coll. Camb. B.A. 1860; Deac. 1860, by Bp of B. and W; C. of Bathford, 1860.

JOHN, Ebenezer, *Nantyglo, Tredegar, Monmouthshire.*—Literate; Deac. 1859, by Bp of Lland; C. of Nantyglo, 1859.

JOHNSON, Henry Frank, *Sawbridgeworth, Herts.*—Trin. Coll. Camb. S.C.L. 1857; Deac. 1856, Pr. 1860; C. of Sawbridgeworth, 1860; formerly Asst. C. of Richmond, Surrey, 1858-60.

JOHNSON, Henry Isaac, 59 *York-road, Brighton.*—Chr. Coll. Camb. B.A. 1853, M.A. 1857; Deac. 1853, Pr. 1854, both by Bp of Chich; Asst. Mast. at Brighton Coll.

JOHNSON, John Edward, *Beaulieu, near Southampton.*—Sid.-Suss. Coll. Camb. B.A. 1859; Deac. 1859, Pr. 1860, both by Bp of Winch; C. of Beaulieu, 1859.

JOHNSTON, William Downes, *Milton rectory, Gravesend, Kent.*—St John's Coll. Oxon. B.A. 1826, M.A. 1829; Deac. 1827, by Bp of Lond; Pr. 1829, by Bp of Bristol; R. of Milton-next-Gravesend, Dio. Roch. 1860 (Patrons, Ld. Chan. two turns, and Bp of Roch. one turn; Tithe—R. 325l. 11s; R.'s Gross Inc. 350l. and Ho; Pop. 2110); formerly R. of Ifield, near Gravesend, 1838-60; Author, *The Blessings of Baptism,* S.P.C.K. 1842; *An Order for Family Prayer, on the Plan of a Liturgy,* Caddel, Gravesend, 1844, 1s; *A Short Family Liturgy,* Hughes, 1851, 6d.

JONES, Charles, *Cardigan.*—St David's Coll. Lamp; Deac. 1860, by Bp of St David's; C. of St Mary's, Cardigan, 1860.

JONES, Charles, *Abersychan, Pontypool, Monmouthshire.*—Literate; Deac. 1860, by Bp of Lland; C. of Abersychan, 1860.

JONES, David, *Corwen, Merionethshire.*—St Bees Theol. Coll; Deac. 1853, Pr. 1854, both by Bp of St Asaph; C. of Corwen, 1860; late C. of Castle-Caereinion, Montgomeryshire, 1859-60; formerly Asst. C. of Llanfair, Montgomeryshire.

JONES, Evan, *Bryncock, Neath, Glamorganshire.*—St Bees Theol. Coll; Deac. 1860, by Bp of Lland; C. of Bryncock and Dwrfelin, 1860.

JONES, Francis Innes, *Darley Abbey parsonage, near Derby.*—St Bees Theol. Coll; Deac. 1851, Pr. 1852; Incumb. of Darley Abbey, Dio. Lich. 1854 (Patrons, T. W. Evans, Esq. M.P. and Samuel Evans, Esq; Glebe, 2 acres; Incumb.'s Gross Inc. 150l and Ho; Pop. 950); formerly C. of Elland, Yorkshire, 1851-53; C. of St Michael's, Stockwell, Lond. 1853-54; Author, various *Pamphlets* and *Sermons.*

JONES, Frederick Foster, *Little Bardfield, Braintree, Essex.*—Pemb. Coll. Camb. B.A. 1859 ; Deac. 1860, by Bp of Roch ; C. of Little Bardfield, 1860.

JONES, Henry, *St Bride's, Carleon, Monmouthshire.*—St David's Coll. Lamp ; Deac. 1860, by Bp of Lland ; C. of Caerwent and Llanvair-Discoed, Monmouthshire, 1860.

JONES, Hubert Francis, 131, *Walton-street, Oxford.*—Qu. Coll. Oxon. B.A. 1857, M.A. 1860 ; Deac. 1857, Pr. 1858 ; C. of St Thomas the Martyr, Oxford, 1860 ; formerly C. of Cheddar, Somerset, 1857-60.

JONES, John, *Dowlais, Glamorganshire.*—King's Coll. Lond. B.A. 1858 ; Deac. 1860, by Bp of Lland ; C. of Dowlais, 1860.

JONES, Joshua, *Training College, York.*—Linc. Coll. Oxon. B.A. 1852, M.A. 1855 ; Deac. 1854, Pr. 1855, both by Bp of Chest ; Vice-Prin. of the Training Coll. York, 1860 ; formerly Sen. C. of Holy Trinity, Hulme, Manchester.

JONES, Owen Williams, *Holyhead, Anglesey.*—Trin. Coll. Dub. B.A. 1855 ; Deac. 1856, Pr. 1857 ; C. of Holyhead, 1859 ; formerly C. of Llanfihangel-yn-howyn, 1856-59.

JONES, Thomas, *Woodville, near Burton-on Trent.*—St Aidan's Theol. Coll ; Deac. 1859, Pr. 1860, both by Bp of Peterb ; C. of Woodville, 1859.

JONES, William, *Undy vicarage, Chepstow, Monmouthshire.*—Literate ; Deac. 1824, by Bp of Bristol, Pr. 1825, by Bp of Lland ; V. of Undy, Dio. Lland. 1836 (Patron, Chapter of Lland ; Tithe—V. 141*l* ; Glebe, 34 acres ; V.'s Gross Inc. 200*l* and Ho ; Pop. 370) ; formerly C. of St Bride's, Netherwent, Monmouthshire, 1824-36.

JOSE, Stephen, *Weston-super-Mare, Somersetshire.*—Pemb. Coll. Oxon. B.A. 1854, M.A. 1857 ; Deac. 1856, Pr. 1857, both by Bp of Winch ; C. of Emmanuel Ch. Weston-super-Mare, 1859 ; late C. of Heckfield and Rotherwick, Hants.

JOY, Samuel, *Bramley parsonage, near Leeds.*—Worc. Coll. Oxon. B.A. 1856, M.A. 1859 ; Deac. 1857, Pr. 1858 ; P.C. of Bramley, Dio. Rip. 1859 (Patron, V. of Leeds ; P.C.'s Gross Inc. 240*l* and Ho ; Pop. 10,000) ; formerly C. and Lect. of Parish Ch. Leeds, 1857-59.

———

KANE, Richard Nathaniel, *Bryn Aur villa, St Woolos, Newport, Monmouthshire.*—Oriel Coll. Oxon. B.A. 1859 ; Deac. 1860, by Bp of Lland ; C. of the Chapel of Ease, St Woolos, 1860.

KARNEY, Gilbert Sparshott, *East Mount road, York.*—Trin. Coll. Camb. B.A. 1858 ; Deac. 1859, Pr. 1860, both by Archbp of York ; C. of St John's, York, 1859.

KAYSS, John Morrison, *Urswick, Ulverstone, Lancashire.*—Trin. Coll. Dub. B.A. 1860 ; Deac. 1860, by Bp of Carl ; C. of Urswick, 1860.

KEELING, Richard, *Windhill, Shiples, Leeds.*—Literate ; Deac. 1857, Pr. 1858, both by Bp of Rip ; C. of Idle, near Leeds, 1857.

KEER, William Brown, 3 *Trinity-place, St Ann's-street, Liverpool*—St Bees Theol. Coll. 1856-57 ; Deac. 1858, Pr. 1859, both by Bp of Chest ; Vice-Chap. of the Liverpool Workhouse, Brownlow Hill, 1860 ; formerly C. of Liverpool, 1858-59 ; C. of Wilsden, Yorkshire, 1859-60.

KEIGWIN, James Philip, *The College, Isle of Cumbrae, Greenock, Scotland.*—Wadh. College, Oxon. B.A. 1832, M.A. 1838 ; Deac. 1835, Pr. 1836, both by Bp of Exon ; Incumb. of St Andrew's, Cumbrae, Dio. Argyll and the Isles ; Can. of the Coll. Ch. Cumbrae.

KELLY, James Butler, *Kirk-Michael vicarage, Isle of Man.*—Clare Coll. Camb. Sch. 1851, B.A. 1854, M.A. 1858 ; Deac. 1855, Pr. 1856, both by Bp of Peterb ; V. of St. Michael, Dio. S. and M. 1860 (Patron, the Crown ; Tithe — V. 141*l* 8*s* ; Glebe, 25 acres ; V.'s Gross Inc. 170*l* and Ho ; Pop. 1416) ; formerly C. of Abington, Northants, 1855-56 ; Dio. Inspector of Schools, 1857 ; Dom. Chap. to Bp of S. and M. 1856-60.

KELSALL, Henry, *Smallthorne, near Newcastle-under-Lyne, Staffs.*—King's Coll. Lond. Theol. Assoc. 1850 ; Deac. 1850, Pr. 1851, both by Bp of Heref ; P.C. or Smallthorne, Dio. Lich. 1859 (Patron, R. of Norton-on-the-Moors ; P.C.'s Gross Inc. 100*l* ; Pop. 1700).

KEMP, Thomas Cooke, *Arnesby, Market Harborough, Leicestershire.*—St. Aidan's Theol. Coll. 1859 ; Deac. 1859, Pr. 1860, both by Bp. of Peterb ; C. of Arnesby, 1860 ; formerly C. of Kegworth, near Derby, 1859-60 ; Author, *Sermon on Relinquishing the Curacy of Kegworth, Spencer, Leicester,* 1860, 6*d.*

KENDALL, Herbert Peter, *Batley, Dewsbury, Yorks.*—St. John's Coll. Camb. B.A. 1859 ; Deac. 1860, by Bp of Rip ; Head Mast. of Batley Free Gram. Sch. (Stipend, 150*l.*) ; C. of Batley.

KERSHAW, Edmund Dickie, *Hampton-Lucy, near Warwick.*—Trin. Coll. Camb. B.A. 1851, M.A. 1854, ad eund. Oxon. 1859 ; Deac. 1854, Pr. 1855, both by Bp of Worc ; C. of Hampton-Lucy ; Dom. Chap. to A. W. B. Baillie Cochrane, Esq, M.P.

KETCHLEY, Walter Guy, *Bempton parsonage, Bridlington, Yorkshire.*—Literate ; Deac. 1859, Pr. 1860, both by Archbp. of York ; Incumb. of Bempton, Dio. York, 1860 (Patroness, Miss Broadley, Wilton House, Bempton ; Tithe—Imp. 117*l* and 116 acres of Glebe, Incumb. 13*l*. 6*s*. 8*d*, Glebe, 37 acres ; Incumb.'s Gross Inc. 160*l*. and Ho ; Pop. 350*l*.) ; P.C. of Spelton, near Bridlington, Dio. York, 1860 (Patron, Lord Londesborough ; Glebe, 38 acres ; P.C.'s Gross Inc. 50*l*. ; Pop. 150) ; formerly C. of Lythe, Yorkshire, 1859-60.

KETT, Charles William, ...—Magd. Ha. Oxon. B.A. 1859 ; Deac. 1859, Pr. 1860, both by Bp of Lond ; C. of St. Peter's, Notting Hill, Lond. 1859.

KILLICK, John Henry, *East Leake (Notts), near Loughborough, Leicestershire.* — St John's Coll. Camb. B.A. 1858 ; Deac. 1859, Pr. 1860, both by Bp of Linc ; C. of East Leake w West Leake, 1859.

KING, Edward, *Cuddesdon College, Wheatley, Oxfordshire.*—Oriel Coll. Oxon ; Chap. and Asst. Lect. at Cuddesdon Theol. Coll ; C. of Wheatley.

KING, Robert Turner, *Oakham, Rutland.*—Emman. Coll. Camb. B.A. 1849 ; Deac. 1851, Pr. 1852, both by Bp of Heref ; C. of Langham and Egleton, Rutland, 1855 ; formerly C. of Ledbury, Herefordshire, 1851-55.

KING, Walker, *Leigh rectory, Rochford, Essex.*—Oriel Coll. Oxon. B.A. 1850, M.A. 1853 ; Deac. 1850, Pr. 1851 ; R. of Leigh, Dio. Roch. 1859 (Patron, R. of Roch ; Tithe—R. 500*l* ; Glebe, 4 acres ; R.'s Gross Inc. 510*l*. and Ho ; Pop. 1800) ; Surrog. of Dio. Roch ; formerly C. of Stone, near Dartford, Kent, 1850-59.

KINGDON, Hollingworth Tully, *Sturminster-Marshall, Wimborne, Dorset.*—Trin. Coll. Camb. B.A. 1858 ; Deac. 1859, by Bp of Oxon ; Pr. 1860, by Bp of Salis ; C. of Sturminster-Marshall, 1859.

KINGSFORD, Brenchley, *Hythe, Kent.*—Exon. Coll. Oxon. 3rd Cl. Lit. Hum. and B.A. 1843, M.A. 1849 ; Deac. 1846, Pr. 1847, both by Archbp. of Cant ; P.C. of Hythe, Dio. Cant. 1859 (Patron, R. of Saltwood ; P.C.'s Gross Inc. 200*l* ; Pop. 2675) ; late C. of Bishop's Bourne, near Canterbury, 1852-59.

KINGSFORD, Hamilton, *Chartham, Canterbury.*—Worc. Coll. Oxon. 3rd Cl. Lit. Hum. B.A. 1855 ; Deac. 1856, Pr. 1857, both by Bp of B. and W ; C. of Chartham, 1859 ; late C. of Hentland w Little Dewchurch, Herefordshire ; formerly C. of Chillington, Somerset.

KINGSFORD, Sampson, *Faversham, Kent.*—Trin. Coll. Camb. B.A. 1814 ; Deac. 1816, Pr. 1817 ; Head Mast. of Faversham Gram. Sch, 1828.

KINGSLEY, William Towler, *South Kilvington rectory, Thirsk, Yorkshire.*—Sid.-Suss. Coll. Camb. Wrang. and B.A. 1838, M.A. 1841, B.D. 1848 ; Deac. and Pr. 1842, both by Ely ; R. of South Kilvington, Dio. York, 1859 (Patrons, Sid.-Suss. Coll. Camb ; R.'s Gross Inc. 550*l*. and Ho ; Pop. 389) ; formerly Fell. and Tut. of Sid.-Suss. Coll. Camb.

KINGSTON, The Right Rev. Reginald COURTENAY, Lord Bp of Kingston, *Kingston, Jamaica.*—Mag. Ha. Oxon. B.A. 1835, M.A. 1838, D.D. 1843 ; Consecrated Bp of Kingston, 1856 (Episcopal Jurisdiction—Part of the Island of Jamaica; Gross Inc. of See, 2000*l.* of which 1600*l.* from the Bp of Jamaica, and 400*l.* as Archd. of Middlesex) ; his Lordship was formerly R. of Thornton-Watliss, Yorks, 1842–56.

KINGSTON, John, *Cattistock rectory, Dorchester.*—Bp Cos. Ha. Dur. Licen. Theol. 1855 ; Deac. 1855, by Bp of Manch ; R. of Cattistock, Dio. Salis. 1859 (Patron, the present R ; R.'s Gross Inc. 520*l.* and Ho ; Pop. 594) ; late C. of St Oswald's, Collyhurst, Manchester ; formerly C. of St Andrew's, Deptford, Sunderland ; Author, various *Pamphlets* and short *Papers* in several Periodicals.

KIRK, Thomas, *Glandford, Brigg, Lincolnshire.*—St John's Coll. Camb. B.A. 1859 ; Deac. 1859, Pr. 1860, both by Bp of Linc ; C. of Wragby *w.* Brigg, 1860 ; formerly Asst. Mast. in Repton Sch. Derbyshire.

KIRK, William Boyton, *Bleak Hill, Burslem, Staffs.*—Trin. Goll. Dub. and St Aidan's Theol. Coll ; Deac. 1860 ; C. of Sneyd Ch. Burslem, 1860.

KIRKBY, William, *Wandsworth-common, Surrey.*—Jesus Coll. Camb. B.A. 1850, M.A. 1853 ; Deac. 1851, Pr. 1852, both by Bp of Linc ; Chap of the R. V. Patriotic Asylum, Wandsworth-common, 1858.

KIRKMAN, Joshua, 1 *Caroline-street, Bedford-square, Lond. W.C.*—Qu. Coll. Camb. B.A. 1851, M.A. 1855 ; Deac. 1852, Pr. 1853, both by Bp of Peterb ; C. of St Giles-in-the-Fields, Lond. 1859 ; formerly V. of Field Dalling, Norfolk, 1855–59.

KIRWAN, Richard, *Gittisham rectory, Honiton, Devon.*—Emman. Coll. Camb. B.A. 1853, M.A. 1856 ; Deac. 1855, Pr. 1856, both by Bp of Roch ; R. of Gittisham, Dio. Exon. 1860 (Patron, Rev. H. Marker; Tithe — R. 320*l.* ; Glebe, 40 acres ; R.'s Gross Inc. 380*l.* and Ho ; Pop. 380) ; formerly C. of Little Bardfield, Essex, 1855–57 ; C. of Gosfield, Essex, 1857–60.

KITCHEN, Joseph Laxton, *Loughborough, Leicestershire.*—St. John's Coll. Camb. B.A. 1858 ; Deac 1859, Pr. 1860, both by Bp of Peterb ; Second Mast. of Loughborough Gram. Sch. 1859.

KNAPTON, Augustus James Brine, *Boldre, Lymington, Hants.*—Exon. Coll. Oxon. B.A. 1826, M.A. 1829 ; Deac. 1828, Pr. 1829.

KNAPTON, Henry Pearce, *Wilton-place, Regent's-park, London.*—Qu. Coll. Camb. Sch. 1855, B.A. 1858 ; Deac. 1859, Pr. 1860, both by Bp of Lond ; C. of St Michael's, Burleigh-street, Strand, Lond. 1859.

KNIGHT, Charles ... ... —Gon. and Cai. Coll. Camb. B.A. 1859 ; Deac. 1860, by Archbp. of York.

KNIGHT, Edward Bridges, *Fordcomb, Tunbridge Wells, Kent.*—Exon. Coll. Oxon. B.A. 1852 ; Deac. 1852, by Bp of G. and B ; Pr. 1855, by Bp of Chich ; C. of Fordcomb, 1859.

KNOWLTON, William ... ,... ... ... —Pemb. Coll. Camb. B.A. 1859 ; Deac. 1860, by Bp of Chich.

KYFFIN, Thomas Lloyd, *Bodedern, Bangor.*—Jesus Coll. Camb. B.A. 1859 ; Deac. 1859, Pr. 1860, both by Bp of Bang ; C. of Llanfihangel-yn-howyn and Llanfigael, 1859.

———

ADBROOKE, John Arthur, *Moulton, Long Stratton, Norfolk.*—Bp Hat. Ha. Dur. B.A. 1860 ; Deac. 1860, by Bp. of Norw ; C. of Moulton, 1860.

LAIDMAN, Samuel Lancaster, *Longwood, near Huddersfield.*—Bp Hat. Ha. Dur. Theol. Licen. 1859 ; Deac. 1859, by Bp of Rip ; C. of St Mark's, Longwood, 1859.

LANCE, William Henry, *Thurlbear, Taunton, Somerset.*—King's Coll. Lond. Theol. Assoc. 1858 ; Deac. 1858, by Bp of B. and W ; C. of Thurlbear *w* Stoke St Mary, 1859 ; late C. of Bishops Lydeard, Somerset, 1858–59.

LANE, Edward Aldous, *Stroud, Gloucestershire.*—St John's Coll. Camb. B.A. 1860 ; Deac. 1860, by Bp of G. and B ; C. of Stroud, 1860.

LANFORD, Thomas, *Oxhill rectory, Kineton, Warwickshire.*—Worc. Coll. Oxon. B.A. 1855, M.A. 1858 ; Deac. 1856, by Bp of B. and W. Pr. 1857, by Bp of G. and B ; R. of Oxhill, Dio. Worc. 1859 (Patron, Rev. W. D. Bromley ; Tithe—R. 16*s* ; Glebe, 275 acres ; R.'s Gross Inc. 400*l.* and Ho ; Pop. 319) ; formerly C. of Tormarton and West Littleton, Gloucestershire, 1856–58 ; C. of Wolverton, Hants, 1858–59.

LANGSTAFF, George William, *Filey, near York.*—Madg. Ha. Oxon, B.A. 1859 ; Deac. 1852, by Bp of S. and M, Pr. 1859, by Archbp. of York ; Incumb. of the Iron Ch. Filey, Dio. York, 1860 ; formerly C. of Filey.

LANPHIER, Joseph, *Kirklington, near Ripon.*—Trin. Coll. Dub. B.A. 1852 ; Deac. 1852, Pr. 1853 ; C. of Kirklington, 1857 ; formerly C. of Kilcoe and Missionary to Roman Catholics on Cape Clear, co. Cork, Ireland, 1852–57.

LASCELLES, The Hon. James Walter, *Goldsborough rectory, Knaresborough, Yorkshire.*—Exon. Coll. Oxon. B.A. 1857 ; Deac. 1855, by Bp of G. and B, Pr. 1857, by Bp of Rip ; R. of Goldsborough, Dio. Rip. 1858 (Patron, Earl of Harewood ; Tithe—R. 291*l* ; R.'s Gross Inc. 500*l* and Ho , Pop. 480) ; formerly C. of Cirencester, 1856–58

LATHAM, Edward, *Repton, near Burton-on-Trent.*—Trin. Coll. Camb. B.A. 1856, M.A. 1859 ; Deac. 1856, Pr. 1857 ; Asst. Mast. at Repton Gram. Sch. 1856.

LATHAM, John Larking, *East Malling, Maidstone, Kent.*—Worc. Coll. Oxon. B.A. 1850, M.A. 1853 ; Deac. 1852, Pr. 1853 ; C. of East Malling, 1857.

LATHAM, Samuel, ... —Emman. Coll. Camb. B.A. 1860 ; Deac. 1860, by Bp of Chich.

LAURENCE, George, *Tickenhall, Derby.*—Emman. Coll. Camb. B.A. 1856, M.A. 1859 ; Deac. 1857, by Bp of Worc. Pr. 1858, by Bp of Exon ; C. of Tickenhall, Derby, 1860 ; formerly C. of Loxbear, near Tiverton, 1857–59 ; C. of Ickham, Kent, 1859–60.

LAURENCE, Richard, *Chigwell, Essex.*—Trin. Coll. Dub. B.A. 1845, M.A. 1849 ; Deac. 1847, by Bp of Worc, Pr. 1848, by Bp of Chest ; Incumb. of Chigwell Row, Dio. Roch. 1860 (Patrons, the Crown and Bp of Roch. Altern ; Incumb's Gross Inc. 200*l* ; Pop. 550) ; formerly C. of the Par. Ch. Tunbridge.

LAW, Henry, *Askern, Doncaster.*—Literate ; Deac. 1860 ; C. of Fenwick, near Doncaster, 1860.

LAW, James Edmund, *Little Shelford rectory, Cambridge.*—St John's Coll. Camb. B.A. 1850, M.A. 1853 ; Deac. 1851, Pr. 1852, both by Bp of Ely ; R. of Little Shelford, Dio. Ely, 1852 (Patron, Jas. Edmund Law, Esq ; R.'s Gross Inc. 390*l* and Ho ; Pop. 581) ; formerly C. of All Saints, Sawtry, Hunts, 1851–52.

LAWRENCE, Richard Gwynne, *West Chinnock, Ilminster, Somerset.*—St. John's Coll. Camb. B.A, 1858 ; Deac. 1859, Pr. 1860, both by Bp of B. and W ; C. of West Chinnock *w* Chisleborough, 1859.

LAWSON, Edward, *Longhirst-hall, Morpeth, Northumberland.*—Trin. Coll. Camb. B.A. 1847, M.A. 1852 ; Deac. 1853, Pr. 1854 ; R. of Bothal *w* Shipwash R. and Hebburn C. Northumberland, Dio. Dur. 1859 (Patron, Duke of Portland ; Tithe—R. 1480*l* ; Glebe, 134 acres ; R.'s Gross Inc. 1614*l* ; Pop. 1900) ; formerly C. of Little Barford, Beds, 1853–58.

LEACH, Henry, 11, *Somerset-street, Portman-square, London.*—Emman. Coll. Camb. B.A. 1852, M.A. 1856 ; Deac. 1853, Pr. 1854, both by Bp. of Norw ; C. of St Thomas, Portman-square, Lond. 1858.

LEACHMAN, Edmund, 8 *Oakley-villas, Adelaide-road, Haverstock-hill. London.*—St John's Coll. Camb. B.A. 1847, M.A. 1850 ; Deac. 1848, by Bp of Norw. Pr. 1849, by Bp of Manch ; Chap. of St Luke's Lunatic Asylum, Lond. 1854 ; formerly C. of Sandiacre, Derbyshire, 1848–49 ; C. of St Paul's, Blackburn, Lancashire, 1849–50 ; C. of Mellor, near Blackburn, 1850–51 ; C. of St Barnabas, King's-square, Lond. 1851–52 ; C. of St Simon Zelotes, Bethnal-green, Lond. 1852–53 ; C. of St Mary's, Plaistow, Essex, 1853–54.

LEACROFT, Charles Holcombe, *Dethwick, Chesterfield, Derbyshire.*—Trin. Coll. Camb. B.A. 1847, M.A. 1851; Deac. 1847, Pr. 1848; P.C. of Dethwick, Dio. Lich. 1860 (Patron, Thomas Hallowes, Esq; P. C.'s Gross Inc. 110*l*; Pop. 866); formerly P.C. of Brackenfield, Derbyshire, 1857-60.

LEACHMAN, Francis Joseph, *Fordwick rectory, near Canterbury, and Park-place, Margate, Kent.* —Trin. Coll. Camb. B.A. 1854, M.A. 1857; Deac. 1859, Pr. 1860, both by Archbp of Cant; C. of Fordwich, 1860; formerly Asst. Mast. of Bedford Gram. Sch. 1854-59; Author, Articles in the *British Controversialist.*

LEE, Frederick George, *Aberdeen, N.B.*—St Edm. Ha. Oxon. S.C.L. 1854; Deac. 1854, Pr. 1856, both by Bp of Oxon; Incumb. of St John's Episcopal Ch. Aberdeen, 1860; late Dom. Chap. to the Duke of Leeds, 1858-60; formerly C. of Sunningwell and Kennington, Berks, 1854-56; Author, *Lays of the Church,* 12mo. Masters, 1851; *A Form for the Admission of a Chorister,* ib. 1854; *Poems,* 8vo. 2nd edit. ib. 3*s.* 6*d.;* *The Martyr of Vienne and Lyons* (a Prize Poem), Shrimpton, Oxford, 1854; *Our Village and its Story,* Masters, 1855; *Petronilla* and other *Poems,* 8vo. Bosworth and Harris, 1858, 3*s.*

LEE, John Robinson, *Magdalen College, Cambridge.*—Magd. Coll. Camb. B.A. 1857; Deac. 1859, Pr. 1860; C. of Bardsea, Ulverstone, Lancashire, 1860; Fell. of Magd. Coll. Camb.; Author, *History of Market Drayton; Translator of Antigone.*

LEE, Roger, *Gunton, Lowestoft, Suffolk.*—Trin. Coll. Camb. B.A. 1853, M.A. 1856; C. of Gunton, 1860; late Dom. Chap. to the Earl of Gosford.

LEES, James Chadwick, *Farnworth, Warrington, Lancashire.*—Qu. Coll. Camb. B.A. 1860; Deac. 1860; C. of Farnworth, 1860.

LEGG, William, *Orton-Longueville, near Peterborough.*—St Mary Magd. Ha. Oxon. B.A. 1859; Deac. 1859, by Bp of Manch. Pr. 1860, by Bp of Ely; C. of Orton-Longueville, 1859.

LEGGATT, George Bethune, ... —Theol. Coll. Lich; Deac. 1859, Pr. 1860, both by Bp of Lich.

LENDRUM, Alexander, *Crieff, Scotland.*—King's Coll. Aberdeen; Deac. and Pr. 1832; Incumb. of St Michael's Ch. Crieff, and Principal of St Margaret's Coll; formerly Min. of St James's, Muthill, 1853-54.

LENNY, Henry Stokes Noel, *Ramsgate, Kent.*—Trin. Coll. Camb. B.A. 1857; Deac. 1859, Pr. 1860, both by Archbp of Cant; C. of St Peter's, Isle of Thanet, 1859.

L'ESTRANGE, Alfred Guy Kingham, *Maidstone, Kent.*—Exon. Coll. Oxon. B.A. 1856; Deac. 1859, Pr. 1860, both by Archbp of Cant; C. of Trinity Ch. Maidstone, 1859.

LETCHWORTH, Henry Howard, ...—Oriel Coll. Oxon. B.A. 1859; Deac. 1859, Pr. 1860, both by Bp of G. and B.

LEVESON, Charles Augustus, *Aigburth Vale, near Liverpool.*—Univ. Coll. Dur. B.A. 1859; Deac. 1858, by Bp of Lich. Pr 1860, by Bp of Chest; C. of St Anne's, Aigburth, 1860; formerly C. of St Mary's, Wolverhampton, 1858-60.

LEWES, John Meredith, *Hascomb rectory, Godalming, Surrey.*—Trin Coll. Camb. B.A. 1843; Deac. 1844, Pr. 1855, both by Bp of Heref; R. of Hascomb, Dio. Winch. 1859 (Patron, E. F. M. Lewes, Esq; Tithe—R. 256*l* 10*s*; Glebe, 104 acres; R.'s Gross Inc. 326*l* and Ho; Pop. 400; formerly Chap. to H.M's Forces in the East, 1854-56.

LEWINGTON, Arthur Lord, *Lamborne, Hungerford, Berks.*—Literate; Deac. 1858, Pr. 1860, both by Bp of Oxon; C. of Lamborne, 1858; Head Mast. of St Michael's Gram. Sch. Lamborne.

LEWIS, David, *Llangefni, Anglesey.*—St Aidan's Theol. Coll; Deac. 1855, Pr. 1856, both by Bp of Chest; C. of Llangefni and Tregaion, 1857; formerly C. of Holy Trinity, Birkenhead, Cheshire.

LEWIS, John Tomkins, ...—Trin. Coll. Dub. B.A. 1859; Deac. 1859, Pr. 1860, both by Bp of G. and B.

LEWIS, William Howell, *St Mellons, near Cardiff.*—St Dav. Coll. Lamp. Sch. 1858; Deac. 1859, by Bp of Lland; C. of St Mellons, 1860; formerly C. of Aberystruth, Monmouth, 1859-60.

LEWTHWAITE, Joseph, *Barrow-on-Humber, Ulceby, Lincolnshire.*—Chr. Coll. Camb. B.A. 1859; Deac. 1859, by Bp of Linc; C. of Barrow-on-Humber, 1859.

LIDDON, Henry Parry, *St Edmund Hall, Oxford.* — Ch. Ch. Oxon. 2nd Lit. Hum. and B.A. 1850, Johnson Theol. Sch. 1851, M.A. 1853; Deac. 1852, Pr. 1853, both by Bp of Oxon; Vice-Prin. of St Edm. Ha. 1859; late Stud. of Chr. Ch. Oxon; formerly Vice-Prin. of Cuddesdon Theol. Coll. for the Dio. of Oxon. 1854-59; Author, *Lenten Sermons,* Oxford, 1858.

LIGHTFOOT, Reginald Prideaux, *Shutlanger, Towcester, Northamptonshire.*—Balliol Coll. Oxon. B.A. 1859; Deac. 1859, by Bp of Manch, Pr. 1860, by Bp of Peterb; C. of Preston Deanery, Northants, 1859.

LILLINGSTON, Frederick Arthur Cecil, *Upper Lewisham-road, Deptford, Kent.*—Trin. Coll. Dub. B.A. 1860; Deac. 1860, by Bp of Lond; C. of St John's, Deptford, 1860.

LILLEY, Charles, *Ware, Herts.*—Literate; Deac. 1848, Pr. 1850; Head Mast. of Ware Gram. Sch; formerly C. of Harlow, and Mast. of Harlow Gram. Sch. Essex; Author, various *School Books* and other *Educational Works.*

LITTLEHALES, Walter Gough, *Chieveley, Newbury, Berks.*—New Coll. Oxon. B.A. 1839; Deac. 1860, by Bp of Oxon; C. of Chieveley w Oare, 1860 (stipend 60*l*).

LIGHTFOOT, Nicholas Francis, *Islip rectory, Thrapstone, Northamptonshire.*—Exon. Coll. Oxon. B.A. 1833, M.A. 1836; Deac. 1834, Pr. 1836; R. of Islip, Dio. Peterb. 1855 (Patroness, Mrs Wm. Stopford; R.'s Gross Inc. 400*l* and Ho; Pop. 594); formerly V. of Cadbury, Devon, 1846-55.

LINCOLN, William, *Camberwell-grove, Surrey*—King's Coll. Lond; Deac. 1849, Pr. 1850, both by Bp of Manch; Min. of Beresford Chapel, Walworth, Surrey; Author, various *Sermons.*

LITTLER, The Very Rev. John, *The Deanery, Battle, Sussex.*—St Peter's Coll. Camb. B.A. 1817, M.A. 1822; Deac. 1826, Pr. 1827; D. and V. of Battle, Dio. Chich. 1836 (Patron, Lord Harry Vane; Glebe, 16 acres; D. and V.'s Gross Inc. 643*l* and Ho; Pop. 3849; the Deanery is a Peculiar, having the power of granting Marriage Licences); Surrog. for Dio. Chich; Author, *A Sermon for National Schools; a Visitation Sermon.*

LLOYD, William, *Worcester.*—Magd. Coll. Oxon. B.A. 1856, M.A. 1859; Deac. 1857, Pr. 1859, both by Bp of Oxon; C. of St Clement's, Worcester, 1859; formerly C. of Claydon, Bucks.

LLOYD, Charles, *Sherwood villa, Cobham-road.*—Trin. Coll. Camb. B.A. 1823; Deac. 1825, Pr. 1826, both by Bp of B. and W; C. of Christ Ch. Bristol, 1859 (Stipend, 80*l*); formerly C. of Bideford, North Devon, 1825-26; C. of Witheridge, Devon, 1826-30; of Buckland Brewer, Devon, 1830-32; C. of Abbotsham, Devon, 1832-36; Missionary R. of George Town, Prince Edward's Island, 1836-41; Missionary R. of Milton and Rustico, Prince Edward's Island, 1841-44; Missionary R. of Charlotte Town, Prince Edward's Island, 1844-52; Eccles. Commissary to Bp of Nova Scotia, 1852-57; C. of St John's, Clifton, Bristol (not licensed by the Bp), Nov. 1857-59.

LOFT, James Edmund Wallis, *Healing, Ulceby, Lincolnshire.*—Corpus Coll. Camb. B.A. 1854, M.A. 1858; Deac. 1855, Pr. 1857, both by Bp of Linc; R. of Healing, Dio. Linc. 1860 (Patrons, various Landholders; Tithe—R. 270*l*; Glebe, 24 acres; R.'s Gross Inc. 320*l*; Pop. 92); formerly C. of Healing, 1857-60.

LOFTY, Fitzroy Fuller, *Kingclere (Hants), near Newbury, Berks.*—St John's Coll. Camb. B.A. 1850, M.A. 1854; Deac. 1853, Pr. 1854, both by Bp of Ely; C. of Kingclere, 1859; formerly C. of Stretham-cum-Thetford, Isle of Ely, 1853-55; C. of Rotherfield-Greys, Oxfordshire, 1855-58

LOGAN, Crawford, *Liverpool.*—Chr. Coll. Camb B.A. 1855, M.A. 1858 ; Deac. 1858, Pr. 1859, both by Bp of Chest ; C. of St Philip's, Liverpool, 1858.

LONGHURST, Alfred Augustus, *Fotheringhay vicarage, Oundle, Northants.*—Qu. Coll. Camb. B.A. 1850, M.A. 1854 ; Deac. 1852, Pr. 1853 ; V. of Fotheringhay, Dio. Peterb. 1859 (Patron, Lord Overstone ; Tithe —V. 1*l* 10*s* ; Glebe, 93 acres ; V.'s Gross Inc. 200*l* and Ho ; Pop. 261) ; formerly C. of Bygrave, Herts.

LOVE, Robert, *Egremont, Cheshire.*—Trin. Coll. Dub. B.A. 1860 ; Deac. 1860, by Bp of Chest ; C. of St Paul's, Seacombe, near Egremont, 1860.

LORAINE, Nevison, ... —Literate ; Deac. 1859, Pr. 1860, both by Bp of Lond ; C. of St Giles in the Fields, Lond. 1859 ; Author, *The Lord's Prayer*, Nisbet and Co. 1860, 2*s* 6*d*.

LORD, Thomas Ebenezer, *Howden-Panns, near Newcastle-on-Tyne.*—St Bees' Theol. Coll ; Deac. 1850, Pr. 1851, both by Bp of Lich ; R. of Howden-Panns, Dio. Dur. 1860 (Patrons, The Crown and Bp of Dur. alternately ; Tithe—R. 196*l* 3*s* 8*d* ; R.'s Gross Inc. 218*l* ; Pop. 2284) ; formerly C. of West Rainton, Durham.

LOWTHER, William St. George Penruddocke, *Woodborough, Marlborough, Wilts.*—Trin. Coll. Dub. and Theol. Coll. Chich ; Deac. 1858, Pr. 1860 ; C. of Woodborough, 1858.

LOVE, Edward Hough, 3 *College Precincts, Worcester.*—Sid.-Suss. Coll. Camb. B.A. 1860 ; Deac. 1860, by Bp of Worc ; Math. Mast. at Worcester Catholic School.

LUARD, Henry Richard, *Trinity College, Cambridge.*—Trin. Coll. Camb. B.A. 1847, M.A. 1850 ; Deac. and Pr. 1855 ; P.C. of St Mary the Great, Cambridge, Dio. Ely, 1860 (Patrons, Trin. Coll. Camb ; P.C.'s Gross Inc. 104*l* ; Pop. 700) ; Fell. and Asst. Tut. of Trin. Coll. Camb ; Author, *Life of Porson*, in the "Cambridge Essays" for 1857 ; *Lives of Edward the Confessor*, in the Government Series of Mediæval Chronicles, 1858 ; *Catalogue of the MSS. in the Cambridge University Library—the Theological Portion* ; *Remarks on the Cambridge University Commissioners' New Statutes for Trinity College*, 1858, &c ; *Bartholomæi de Cotton Historia Anglicana*, in the same series, 1859 ; *Reed's Diary*, 1860.

LUBBOCK, Henry Hammond, *Suffield, North Walsham, Norfolk.*—Caius Coll. Camb. B.A. 1858 ; Deac. 1859, Pr. 1860 ; C. of Gunton and Suffield, 1860 ; formerly C. of Stow-cum-Quy, Cambridge, 1859-60.

LUMBY, Joseph Rawson, 33 *Jesus-lane, Cambridge.*—Magd. Coll. Camb. B.A. 1858 ; Deac. and Pr. 1858, both by Bp of Ely ; C. of Girton, Cambs. 1860 ; late Fell. of Magd. Coll. Camb.

LUPTON, Joseph Hirst, *City of London School, Milk-street, Cheapside, Lond.*—St John's Coll. Camb. B.A. 1858 ; Deac. 1859, Pr. 1860, both by Bp of Lond ; C. of St Paul's, Avenue-road, Hampstead, Middlesex, 1859 ; Second Class. Mast. in the City of Lond. Sch. 1859.

LYNE, Joseph Leycester ... ... —Literate ; Deac. 1860, by Bp of B. and W.

LYNES, Robert Francis, *Boulton Villa, Wyke Regis, Weymouth.*—St John's Coll. Oxon. B.A. 1859 ; Deac. 1860, by Bp of Salis ; C. of Fleet, Dorset, 1860.

LYS, Frank George, *Gainsborough, Lincolnshire.* —St John's Coll. Camb. B.A. 1858 ; Deac. 1859, by Bp of Linc ; C. of Holy Trinity, Gainsborough, 1860 ; formerly C. of Warsop, Notts, 1859-60.

M'CAUL, Alexander Israel, *St Magnus the Martyr rectory, London-bridge, London.*— St John's Coll. Oxon. B.A. 1858, M.A. 1860 ; Deac. 1859, Pr. 1860 ; C. of St Magnus the Martyr, Lond. 1859 ; Lect. in Divinity at King's Coll. Lond.

M'CORMICK, William Thomas, *Nechells Park-road, Birmingham.*—King's Coll. Lond. Theol. Assoc.; Deac. 1860, by Bp of Worc. ; C. of St Clement, Nechells, 1860.

MAC ADAM, Wilberforce Hastings ... ... —St. Aidan's Theol. Coll ; Deac. 1860, by Bp of Winch ; C. of St·Andrew's, Lambeth, Lond. 1860.

MACDONALD, Douglas, *West Alvington, Kingsbridge, Devon.*—V. of West Alvington *w* South Huish C. Marlborough C. and South Milton C. Dio. Exon. 1835 (Patrons, D. and C. of Salis ; Tithe—West Alvington ; App. 555*l* 8*s* 3*d*, V. 330*l* 2*s* ; South Huish, App. 170*l*, V. 90*l* ; Marlborough, App. 482*l* 6*s*, Imp. 99*l* 10*s*, V. 340*l* 3*s* ; South Milton, App. 219*l* 1*s*, V. 128*l* 4*s* 4*d* ; V.'s Gross Inc. 889*l* and Ho ; Pop. West Alvington, 1008 ; South Huish, 382, Marlborough, 698, South Milton, 414) ; Rur. D.

MAC GACHEN, John Drummond, 16 *Norfolk-street, Strand, London.*—Pemb. Coll. Oxon. B.A. 1848, M.A. 1855 ; Deac. 1848, Pr. 1850, both by Archbp of York ; P. C. of St. Bartholomew, Bethnal Green, Dio. Lond. 1860 ; Patron—Bp of Lond ; P. C.'s Gross Inc. 200*l* ; Pop. 10,016) ; formerly C. of Wistow, near Selby, Yorkshire.

M'GUINNESS, William Nesbitt, *Preston, Lancashire.*—Trin. Coll. Dub. B.A. 1858, LL.B. 1861 ; Deac. 1859, Pr. 1860, both by Bp of Manch ; C. of St Mary's, Preston, 1859.

M'HUTCHIN, Mark Wilks, *Talk-on-the-Hill parsonage, Stoke-upon-Trent.*—St Bees' Theol. Coll. 1858 ; Deac. 1858, Pr. 1859, both by Bp of Lich ; Incumb. of Talk-on-the-Hill, Dio. Lich. 1859 (Patron, V. of Audley ; Glebe, 5 acres ; Incumb.'s Gross Inc. 200*l*. and Ho ; Pop. 2500) ; formerly C. of Audley, Staffs. 1858-59.

MACILWAIN, George Bower, *Chorley, Lancashire.*— C. of St. George's, Chorley, 1860 ; late C. of Bathford, Somerset.

M'KAY, Charles Elvington, *Inver rectory, Larne, Co. Antrim, Ireland.*—Trin. Coll. Dub. B.A. 1855, M.A. 1859 ; Deac. 1856, Pr. 1857, both by Archbp of Dub. ; R. of Inver, Dio. Connor, 1860 (Patron, the Crown ; Tithe—R. 115*l* 6*s* 8½*d* ; Glebe, 3 acres ; R.'s Gross Inc. 125*l* and Ho ; Pop. 4135) ; formerly C. of Sandymount, Donnybrook, Leinster, 1856-57 ; Head Mast. of Dub. Diocesan Sch. 1857-60.

MACKAY, Sween Macdonald, *Langton, Wragby, Lincolnshire.*—Worc. Coll. Oxon. B.A. 1847, M.A. 1850 ; Deac. 1847, Pr. 1848, both by Bp of Linc ; V. of Langton, Dio. Linc. 1859 (Patron, Earl Manvers and C. Turnor, Esq. altern ; Tithe—Imp. 1900*l* ; Glebe, 47 acres ; V. 290*l* ; V.'s Gross Inc. 330*l* ; Pop. 287*l*) ; formerly V. of Skillington, Lincolnshire. 1850-59.

MACKENZIE, Roderick Bain, *Frampton house, Well street, South Hackney, London.*—Exon. Coll. Oxon. B.A. 1858, M.A. 1860 ; Deac. 1858, Pr. 1859, both by Bp of Lond ; C. of St Philip, Bethnal-green, Lond. 1858.

MACKEY, Clement William, *Pilton, Shapton, Somerset.*—Worc. Coll. Oxon. B.A. 1858 ; Deac. 1859, Pr. 1860, both by Bp of B. and W ; C. of Pilton, 1859.

M'LEOD, Nicholas Kenneth, *Wiston, Colchester, Essex.*—Bp Hat. Ha. Dur. Theol. Licen. 1859 ; Deac. 1859, Pr. 1860, both by Bp of Roch ; C. of Little Horkesley, Essex, 1859.

MACKNESS, George, *Stonham-Aspal, Stonham, Suffolk.*—Linc. Coll. Oxon. B.A. 1856, M.A. 1859 ; Deac. 1858, by Archbp of Cant, Pr. 1858, by Bp of Lich ; C. of Stonham-Aspal, 1860 ; late Asst. C. of Hinstock, Shropshire, 1858-60.

MACNAMARA, Richard, *Portsmouth, Hants.* —King's Coll. Lond ; Chap. to the Royal Sailors' Home, Portsmouth, 1860.

M'NEILL, Hugh, *Burbage, Hinckley, Leicestershire.*—Literate ; Deac. 1860, by Bp of Peterb ; C. of Burbage-cum-Aston Flamville, 1860.

MACRORIE, William Kenneth, *Wingates, Westhoughton, Bolton-le-Moors.*—Brasen. Coll. Oxon. B.A. 1852, M.A. 1855 ; Deac. 1855, Pr. 1857, both by Bp of Oxon ; P.C. of St John's, Wingates, Dio. Manch. 1860 (Patron, V. of Deane ; P.C.'s Gross Inc. 90*l* ; Pop. 2000) ; formerly Fell. of St Peter's Coll. Radley, 1855-58 ; C. of Deane, near Bolton-le-Moors, 1858-60.

M'SORLEY, Hugh, *St Jude's parsonage, Chel-sea, London, S.W.*—Trin. Coll. Dub. B.A. 1850; Deac. 1850, by Archbp of Dub. Pr. 1852, by Bp of Down and Connor; C. of St Jude's, Chelsea; Author, *Last Words of Christ on the Cross,* 7 Sermons, Lond. Lumley; *The Temptation,* 6 Sermons, Lond. Shaw; *Thoughts on Popery,* Lond. Shaw; *Thoughts on Christian Sabbath,* ib; *Thanks-giving Sermon,* ib; various other *Sermons* and *Tracts.*

MALLORY, George, *Moulsham, Chelmsford, Essex.*—St Mary's Ha. Oxon. B.A. 1857, M.A. 1858; Deac. 1860, by Bp of Roch; Asst. C. of St. John's Moulsham, 1860.

MANDALE, Blain, *Staveley, Chesterfield, Derby-shire.*—Trin. Coll. Camb. B.A. 1847, M.A. 1849; Deac. 1848, Pr. 1849; C. of Staveley, 1851.

MANSFIELD, George, *Finchingfield vicarage, Braintree, Essex.*—Trin. Coll. Dub. Premium and Mode-rator, 1832, B.A. 1833; Deac. 1838, Pr. 1839, both by Archbp of Cant; V. of Finchingfield, Dio. Roch. 1860 (Patron, Rev. John Stock, Earl's-terrace, Kensington, Lond; Tithe—Imp. 1506*l.* 5*s* and 38 acres of glebe, V. 719*l*; V.'s Gross Inc. 750*l.* and Ho; Pop. 2700); late R. of Allhallows the Great and the Less, Lond. 1856-60; formerly P.C. of St Peter's, Saffron-hill, London, 1851-56; Author, *Spiritual Conservatism* (A Sermon), Nisbet, 1840; *Look to your Children* (a Pamphlet), Wertheim and Mack-intosh, 1849; *Picture of Grace,* 8vo. ib. 1854, 1*s.*

MANTELL, Edward Reginald, *Greatford rectory, Market Deeping, Lincolnshire.*—Emman. Coll. Camb. B.A. 1821, M.A. 1825; Deac. 1822, by Bp of Bristol, Pr. 1823, by Bp of Chest; R. of Greatford *w* Wils-thorpe, Dio. Linc. 1859 (Patron, Ld. Chan; Tithe—R. 211*l.* 2*s*; Glebe, 183 acres; R.'s Gross Inc. 510*l.* and Ho; Pop. 271); Surrog. for the Dio. of Linc. 1832; Hon. Preb. of Louth in Linc. Cathl. 1845; Rur. Dean, 1855; late V. of Louth, and also V. of Tetney, Lincolnshire, 1831-59.

MARRETT, Edward Lawrence, *Lesbury vicarage, Alnwick, Northumberland.*—St Mary Ha. Oxon. B.A. 1850, M.A. 1855; Deac. 1851, Pr. 1852, both by Bp of Dur; V. of Lesbury, Dio. Dur. 1859 (Patron, Ld. Chan; Tithe—V. 308*l*; Glebe, 3 acres; V.'s Gross Inc. 312*l* and Ho; Pop. 1238); formerly C. of Holy Trinity, Stockton-on-Tees, 1851-53; C. of St Michael, St Albans, Herts, 1853-54; R. of Morborne, Hunts, 1854-59.

MARRIOTT, Harvey, *Loddiswell vicarage, Kingsbridge, Devon.*—Bp Hat. Ha. Dur; B.A. 1852, M.A. 1854; Deac. 1857, Pr. 1859, both by Bp of Worc; Fell. of Bp Hat. Ha. Dur. 1854; formerly C. of St Helen's and St Alban's, Worcester.

MARRIOTT, Randolph Charles, *Loddiswell vicarage, Kingsbridge, Devon.*—C. of Loddiswell.

MARSDEN, William, *Tranmere, Birkenhead, Cheshire.*—Trin. Coll. Dub. B.A. 1859; Deac. 1860, by Bp of Chest; C. of St Catharine's, Tranmere, 1860.

MARSHALL, William Knox, *Wragby vicarage, Lincolnshire.*—Trin. Coll. Dub. B.A. 1832, M.A. and B.D. 1855; Deac. 1832, Pr. 1834, both by Bp of Lich; V. of Wragby *w* East Torrington, Dio. Linc. 1860 (Patron, C. Turnor, Esq; Tithe—V. 264*l*; V.'s Gross Inc. 300*l.* and Ho; Pop. Wragby, 610, East Torrington, 113); R. of Panton, near Wragby, Dio. Linc. 1860 (Patron, C. Turnor, Esq; Tithe—R. 421*l* 18*s*; R.'s Gross Inc. 450*l*; Pop. 182); Preb. of Pratum Majus in Heref. Cathl. 1856; formerly R. of St. Mary Magdalene, Bridgnorth, Shropshire, 1833-60.

MARSHALL, William, *Sheffield, Yorks.*—St Bees Theol. Coll; Deac. 1860, by Archbp of York; C. of St Philip's, Sheffield, 1860.

MARTIN, Edward Brace, *Alderbury, near Salisbury.*—Exon. Coll. Oxon. B.A. 1859; Deac. 1860; C. of Alderbury, 1860.

MARTIN, Henry, *Bristol.*—V. of St Nicholas *w* St Leonard, Bristol, Dio. G. and B. 1858 (Patron, D. and C); V.'s Gross Inc. 300*l*; Pop. 2199).

MARTIN, Henry John, *Exwick, Exeter.*—Trin. Coll. Camb. B.A. 1852; Deac. 1853, Pr. 1854, both by Bp of Oxon; C. of St Thomas the Apostle, Exeter, 1860; formerly C. of Morebath, Devon, 1854-56; C. of Holy Trinity, Exeter, 1856-60.

MARTIN, Hezekiah, *25 William-street, Ro-deswell road, Limehouse, London.*—Corp. Coll. Camb. B.A. 1857; Deac. 1858, Pr. 1859, both by Bp of Chich; C. of St Paul's, Stepney, Lond. 1859; formerly C. of East Guldeford *w* Playden, Sussex, 1858-59.

MASTERS, George, *Swingfield, Folkestone, Kent.*—Magd. Ha. Oxon. B.A. 1816, M.A. 1818, B.D. and D.D. 1827; Deac. 1811, Pr. 1812; P.C. of Swingfield, Dio. Cant. 1858 (Patron, Ld. Chan; P.C.'s Gross Inc. 54*l*; Pop. 421); formerly V. of Compton-Chamberlain, Wilts, 1849-54.

MARTYN, Charles John, *Palgrave Priory, Diss, Norfolk.*—Ch. Ch. Oxon. B.A. 1838; Deac. 1859, Pr. 1860, both by Bp of Norw; C. of Palgrave, 1859.

MATHER, Edward, *Alton, Cheadle, Staffs.*—Brasen. Coll. Oxon. B.A. 1858; Deac. 1859, Pr. 1860, both by Bp of Lich; C. of Alton, 1859.

MATSON, Robert, *Adstock, near Buckingham.*—Literate; Deac. 1849, by Bp of Exon. Pr. 1851. by Bp of Linc; C. of Adstock, 1860; formerly Inc. of Tortola, Virgin Islands, West Indies, 1854-59.

MATTHEWS, Thomas, *Penclawdd, near Swansea, Glamorgan.*—St Dav. Coll. Lamp. 1849; Deac. 1852, Pr. 1853; V. of Llanrhidian *w* Penclawdd C. Dio. St Dav. 1860 (Patrons, Trusts. of G. Morgan, Esq; Tithe—Imp. 696*l* 13*s*; V.'s Gross Inc. 100*l*; Pop. 2006); formerly Stip. C. of Llanrhidian and Penclawdd, 1853-60.

MATTHEY, Alphonso, *Ruswarp, Whitby, Yorks.*—King's Coll. Lond. Theol. Assoc; Deac. 1856, by Bp of Oxon. Pr. 1857, by Bp of Lond; C. of Ruswarp, 1860; formerly C. of St Thomas's, Stepney, Lond; Author, *A Musical Version of the Evening Service;* Various other Pieces of *Ecclesiastical Music.*

MAUD, John, *Tranmere, Birkenhead, Cheshire.*—Trin. Ha. Camb. LL.B. 1860; Deac. 1860, by Bp of Chest; C. of St Paul's, Tranmere.

MAUGHAN, Joseph, *St Blazey, Cornwall.*—King's Coll. Lond; Deac. 1860, by Bp of Exon; C. of St Blazey, 1860.

MEAD, George ... ... St John's Coll. Oxon. B.A. 1859; Deac. 1859, Pr. 1860, both by Bp of Lich.

MEDLAND, William, *The Mount, York.*—Christ Coll. Camb. B.A. 1859; Deac. 1859, Pr. 1860, both by Archbp. of York; C. of St Paul's, York, 1859.

MEEKINS, Reuben William, *Grove-road, St John's Wood, Lond.*—Trin. Coll. Dub. B.A. 1857; Deac. 1857, Pr. 1858, both by Bp of Lond; C. of St Matthew, Marylebone, Lond. 1859; formerly C. of St Michael, Pimlico. Lond. 1857-59.

MELHUISH, George Edward, *Bradford-on-Avon, Wilts.*—Merton Coll. Oxon. B.A. 1858, M.A. 1860; Deac. 1858, Pr. 1859, both by Bp of Salis; C. of Brad-ford-on-Avon. 1858.

MENGE, John Peter, ...—Literate; Deac. 1859, Pr. 1860, both by Bp of Winch.

MEREDITH, James, *The Vicarage, Abergele, Denbighshire.*—Trin. Coll. Dub. B.A. 1824; Deac. 1824, Pr. 1825; V. of Abergele, Dio. St Asaph, 1848 (Patron, Bp of St Asaph; Tithe—App. 1487*l*, V. 490*l*; Glebe, 1 acre, with a house; V.'s Gross Inc. 500*l.* and Ho; Pop. 2855); Hon. Can. of St. Asaph, 1860; Rur. D. of the Deanery of Denbigh, 1844; Surrog. for Dio. of St Asaph.

MEREWEATHER, John Davies, *Lamplugh rectory, Cockermouth, Cumberland.*—St. Edm. Ha. Oxon. B.A. 1842; Deac. 1843, Pr. 1844; formerly Governm. Chap. in N. S. Wales; previously Chap. at Venice; Author, *The Type and the Antitype, or Circumcision and Baptism; Diary on board an Emigrant Ship; Diary of a Working Clergyman in Australia and Tasmania.*

MERRY, William Walter, *Lincoln College, Oxford.*—Balliol Coll. Oxon. B.A. 1857, M.A. 1859; Deac. 1860; Fell. and Tutor of Lincoln Coll. Oxon.

MERIDYTH, John, *Greek-street, Stockport, Cheshire.*—Trin. Coll. Dub. B.A. 1826, M.A. 1832, *ad eund.* Oxon. 1853; Deac. 1833, Pr. 1835; C. of St Peter's, Stockport, 1844.

METCALFE, Frederick, *Great Chesterford, Essex.*—Corpus Coll. Camb. B.A. 1847, M.A. 1850; Deac. 1848, Pr. 1849, both by Bp of Manch; C. of Great Chesterford, 1858; formerly C. of Little Shelford, Cambs. 1850-58.

METCALFE, George Morehouse, *Urishay Castle, Peterchurch, Hereford.*—Worc. Coll. Oxon. B.A. 1860; Deac. 1860, by Bp of Heref; C. of St Margaret, 1860.

MIDDLETON, John Douglas, *2 James-street, Westbourne-terrace, Lond.*—Corpus Coll. Oxon. B.A. 1855, M.A. 1858; Deac. 1858, Pr. 1859, both by Bp of Winch; C. of St James, Paddington, Lond. 1860; formerly C. of Carisbrook, Isle of Wight, 1858-60.

MILLARD, Charles Sutton, *Costock rectory, Loughborough, Leicestershire.*—St John's Coll. Camb. B.A. 1858; Deac. 1858, Pr. 1859; R. of Costock, Dio. Linc. 1859 (Patron, the present R; R.'s Gross Inc. 395l and Ho; Pop, 493).

MILLARD, Frederick Maule, *St Andrew's College, Bradfield, near Reading.*—Magd. Coll. Oxon. B.A. 1858, M.A. 1860; Deac. 1859, Pr. 1860, both by Bp of Oxon.

MILLER, John Robert Charlesworth, *Winkfield, Trowbridge, Wilts.*—Corpus Coll. Oxon. B.A. 1859; Deac. 1860, by Bp of Oxon; C. of Winkfield, 1860.

MILLER, Joseph Augustus, *New Windsor, Berks.*—Literate; Deac. 1856, Pr. 1857, both by Bp of Oxon; C. of Windsor, 1856; Chap. of Windsor Union, 1860.

MINNS, George William Walter, *Charney, Wantage, Berks.*—St Cath. Coll. Camb. LL.B. 1859; Deac. 1860, by Bp of Oxon; C. of Charney, 1860.

MITCHELL, John, *Barrowby, Grantham, Lincolnshire.*—Oriel Coll. Oxon. B.A. 1858; Deac. 1859, by Bp of Linc; C. of Barrowby, 1859.

MITCHELL, John Butler, *Medbourne, Market Harborough, Leicestershire.*—Corpus Coll. Camb. B.A. 1860; Deac. 1859, by Bp of Manch; Pr. 1860, by Bp of Peterb; C. of Medbourne w Holt, 1859.

MITCHINSON, John, *The King's School, Canterbury.*—Pemb. Coll. Oxon. B.A. 1854, M.A. 1857; Deac. 1858, by Bp of Lond; Pr. 1860, by Archbp of Cant; Head Mast. of the King's Sch. Canterbury, 1859; late Class. Mast. of Merchant Taylors' Sch. Lond; and C. of St Philip's, Clerkenwell,

MITTON, Henry Arthur, *Heaton, Bradford, Yorks.*—Christ Coll. Camb. B.A. 1858; Deac. 1860; C. of Shipley-cum-Heaton, 1860.

MOBERLY, Frederick Showers, ... —Trin. Coll. Camb. B.A. 1853, M.A. 1856; Deac. 1860, by Bp of B. and W.

MONCKTON, Inglis George, *Coven parsonage, near Wolverhampton.*—Wadh. Coll. Oxon. B.A. 1856, M.A. 1858; Deac. 1856, by Bp of Oxon; Pr. 1857, by Bp of Lich; Incumb. of Coven, Dio. Lich. 1857 (Patron, V. of Brewood; Tithe—Incumb. 50l; Incumb.'s Gross Inc. 146l and Ho; Pop. 800); formerly C. of Woodstock, Oxfordshire, 1856-57.

MONKHOUSE, Henry Clarke, *Culverthorpe, Sleaford, Lincolnshire.*—Trin. Coll. Camb. B.A. 1853, M.A. 1859; Deac. 1856, by Bp of Lond; Pr. 1858, by Bp of Linc; C. of Haydor, Lincolnshire, 1858; formerly C. of St Luke's, Berwick-street, Lond. 1856-57.

MONRO, Edward, *St John's vicarage, Leeds, Yorks.*—Oriel Coll. Oxon. B.A. 1836, M.A. 1839; Deac. 1837, Pr. 1838; V. of St John the Evangelist, Leeds, Dio. Rip. 1860 (Patrons, V. of Leeds, Mayor, and three Aldermen; Glebe, 80 acres; V.'s Gross Inc. 460l and Ho; Pop. 4321); formerly P.C. of Harrow-Weald, Middlesex, 1842-60. For list of books published, see " Crockford's Clerical Directory " for 1860.

MONTAGU, George, *Epwell, Banbury, Oxfordshire.*—Worc. Coll. Oxon. B.A. 1857; C. of Epwell, 1857.

MOORE, Denis Times, *Chipping-Ongar, Essex.* —Exon. Coll. Oxon. B.A. 1859; Deac. 1859, Pr. 1860, both by Bp of Roch; C. of Chipping-Ongar, 1859.

MOORE, James, *Hoby, near Leicester.*—Worc. Coll. Oxon. B.A. 1859; Deac. 1859, Pr. 1860, both by Bp of Peterb; C. of Hoby w Rotherby, 1859.

MORANT, Henry John, *Wonersh Lodge, Guildford.*—Trin. Coll. Camb. B.A. 1840, M.A. 1844; Deac. 1845, Pr. 1846, both by Bp of Lland; C. of Whiston, Northants, 1859; formerly P.C. of King's Walden, Herts. 1854-58.

MORGAN, Charles James, *Leamington, Warwickshire.*—Linc. Coll. Oxon. B.A. 1844, M.A. 1846; Deac. 1846, Pr. 1847, both by Bp of Lland; formerly C. of Matherne, Monmouth, 1846-51.

MORGAN, Hugh Hanmer, ... —Ch. Ch. Oxon. B.A. 1804, M.A. 1807, B.D. 1814.

MORGAN, John, *8 Victoria-terrace, Lee, Kent.*— Trin. Coll. Dub. B.A. 1859; Deac. 1859, Pr. 1860; Asst. C. of St. Nicholas, Plumstead, Kent, 1859.

MORGAN, Morgan, *Flangoedmore, Cardigan.*— Jesus Coll. Oxon. B.A. 1859; Deac. and Pr. 1860, both by Bp of St Dav; C. of St Cynllo, Llangoedmore, 1860; formerly C. of Llanedi, Carmarthenshire.

MORGAN, Samuel Christopher, *Chepstow vicarage, Monmouthshire,*—Wadh. Coll. Oxon. B.A. 1859; Deac. 1860, by Bp of Lland; C. of Chepstow, 1860

MORISON, John Hall James, *Chingford, Essex*—Worc. Coll. Oxon. B.A. 1850, M.A. 1853; Deac. 1851, Pr. 1852; C. of Chingford, 1859; formerly C. of Tormarton and Acton Turville, Gloucestershire, 1851-58; C. of Bredon, Worcestershire, 1858-59.

MORLEY, David Benjamin, *Marham, Downham Market, Norfolk.*—King's Coll. Lond; Deac. 1860, by Bp of Norw; C. of Marham, 1860.

MORRES, Arthur Philip, *Bishop's Lydeard, Taunton, Somerset.*—Wadh. Coll. Oxon. B.A. 1859; Deac. 1859, Pr. 1860, both by Bp of B. and W; C. of Bishop's Lydeard, 1859.

MORRISON, William Robert, *St James's parsonage, Halifax.*—Trin. Coll. Dub. B.A. 1846, M.A. 1856; Deac. 1852, Pr. 1853, both by Archbp of York; P.C. of St James, Halifax, Dio. Rip. 1859 (Patron, V. of Halifax; P.C.'s Gross Inc. 300l and Ho; Pop. 16,000; Surrog. for Dio. Rip; formerly C. of Brighouse, Yorkshire; Author, *The Plenary Inspiration of Scripture proved both by External and Internal Evidence* (a Sermon) 3d; *The Yoke of Bondage* (a Sermon), 3d; *Addresses to Young Men,* 5 Parts, 2d each; *New Years' Addresses*; numerous other *Sermons* and *Tracts*.

MORTIMER, Christian, ... —Clare Coll. Camb. B.A. 1859; Deac. 1859, Pr. 1860, both by Bp of Heref.

MOUNT, Francis John, *Horsham, Sussex* — Oriel Coll. Oxon. B.A. 1855, M.A. 1858; Deac. 1855, Pr. 1857, both by Bp of Chich; C. of Horsham, 1855.

MOUNTAIN, Jacob Jehoshaphat Salter, *Milston rectory, Amesbury, Wilts.*—King's Coll. Univ. of Windsor, Nova Scotia; B.A. 1845, M.A. 1855, B.C.L. and D.C.L. 1858; Deac. 1847, Pr. 1849, both by Bp of Quebec; C. of Milston, 1858 (Stipend, 80l); formerly Travelling Missionary in the Canadian Backwoods, 1847-49; Incumb. of Coteau du Lac, Dio. Montreal, Canada, 1849-57.

MOWATT, James, *Ipswich, Suffolk.*--Sid.-Suss. Coll. Camb. B.A. 1858, M.A. 1861; Deac. 1859, Pr. 1860, both Bp of Ely; Head Mast. of Qu. Eliz. Sch. Ipswich; Fell. of Sid.-Suss. Coll. Camb.

MULES, John Hawkes, *Payhembury vicarage, Ottery St. Mary, Devon.*—Trin. Coll. Camb. B.A. 1839; Deac. 1838, Pr. 1839; V. of Payhembury, Dio. Exon. 1860 (Patron, G. Messiter, Esq; Tithe—Imp. 150l; V. 147l; Glebe, 80 acres; V.'s Gross Inc. 287l and Ho; Pop. 540); formerly C. of Payhembury.

MUNBY, George Frederick Woodhouse, *Church Missionary College, Islington, London.*—Trin. Coll. Camb. B.A. 1856, M.A. 1859, ad eund. Oxon. 1860; Deac. 1856, Pr. 1857, both by Bp of Lond; Tut. at the Ch. Miss. Coll. Islington, 1856.

MURIEL, Hugh Evans, *Benwick (Cambridgeshire), near Ramsey, Hunts.*—St. Peter's Coll. Camb. Sch. 13th Sen. Opt. and B.A. 1855, M.A. 1858; Deac. 1857, Pr. 1858, both by Bp. of Roch C. of Benwick, 1859.

NICHOLAS, George Davenport, 13 Keppel-terrace, Windsor, Berks.—Pemb. Coll. Oxon. B.A. 1859; Deac. 1860, by Bp of Oxon; Asst. C. of Holy Trinity, Windsor, 1860 (Stipend, 40l and Ho).

NAPIER, John Warren, Stretton parsonage, Penkridge, Staffs.—Trin. Coll. Camb. B.A. 1855; Deac. 1856, by Bp of B. and W; P.C. of Stretton, Dio. Lich. 1857 (Patron, Lord Hatherton; P.C.'s Gross Inc. 100l and Ho; Pop. 303); formerly Asst. C. of Holy Trinity, Taunton.

NASH, Thomas Augustus, 11 St. John-street, Oxford.—Worc. Coll. Oxon. B.A. 1859; Deac. 1860, by Bp of Oxon; C. of St. Aldate, Oxford, 1860 (Stipend, 100l).

NATERS, Charles John, North Pickenham, near Swaffham, Norfolk.—Univ. Coll. Dur. Licen. Theol. 1859; Deac. 1859, by Bp of Lich. Pr. 1860, by Bp of Rip; C. of North Pickenham, 1860; formerly C. of Burley, Yorkshire, 1859; C. of High Ercall, Shropshire, 1859-60.

NEWTON, William Shackfield, Canton, near Llandaff.—Chr. Coll. Camb. B.A. 1859; Deac. 1860; C. of St. John, Canton, 1860.

NICHOLAS, Tressilian George, Lower Halstow, Sittingbourne, Kent.—Wadh. Coll. Oxon. Hon. Double 4th Cl. 1842, B.A. 1843, M.A. 1846; Deac. 1845, Pr. 1846, both by Bp of Oxon; V. of Lower Halstow, Dio. Cant. 1859 (Patrons, D. and C. of Cant; V.'s Gross Inc. 300l; Pop. 344); formerly P.C. of West Molesey, Surrey, 1846-59; Author, Poems, 1851; occasional Sermons.

NICHOLLS, Henry, Shirley, Southampton.—Wadh. Coll. Oxon. B.A. 1859; Deac. 1859, Pr. 1860, both by Bp. of Winch; C. of Shirley, 1860 (Stipend, 80l).

NICOLAS, Percy, Great Oakley, Harwich, Essex.—Chr. Coll. Camb. B.A. 1858; Deac. 1859, Pr. 1860, both by Bp of Worc; C. of Great Oakley, 1859.

NEPEAN, Evan Yorke, Bucknall rectory, Horncastle, Lincolnshire.—Qu. Coll. Oxon. B.A. 1848, M.A. 1851; Deac. 1849, Pr. 1850, both by Bp of Salis; R. of Bucknall, Dio. Linc. 1859 (Patron, Lord Monson; R.'s Gross Inc. 250l and Ho; Pop. 339); late C. of Midgham, and Even. Lect. of Thatcham, Berks.

NEVILLE, Nigel, Badminster, Chippenham, Gloucestershire.—St John's Coll. Camb. B.A. 1857, M.A. 1860; Deac. 1859, Pr. 1860; both by Bp of Ely; C. of Sopworth and Badminster, 1860; formerly C. of Withersfield, Suffolk, 1859-60.

NEVILLE, William Latimer, Falangia, Rio Pongar, Sierra Leone, West Africa.—Qu. Coll. Oxon. 2nd Cl. Lit. Hum. 1825, B.A. 1826, M.A. 1828; Deac. 1826, Pr. 1828, both by Bp of Winch; Chief Missionary of the Sösö Mission, W. Africa, 1860; formerly Asst. C. of Holy Trinity, Brompton, Lond. 1850-57; Missionary in Western Africa, 1858-60; Author, The Necessity of Christ's Suffering (a Sermon for Good Friday), 8vo. Shaftesbury, 1836; A Catholic's Reply to some "Dissenters by Birth, Education, and Conviction," 8vo. ib. 1836; An Answer to the Rev. G. H. Stodart's "Reasons for Secession from the Church of England," 8vo. ib. 1836; Certain Questions and Answers extracted from "St. Augustine's Dissertation on the Trinity," 12mo. Honiton, 1837; Apostolical Succession Proved (in Reply to the Rev. H. E. Head, who maintains the Negative), 8vo. ib. 1839; A Treatise, Demonstrating from Internal Evidence the Divine Origin of the Holy Scripture, 8vo. Birmingham, 1844; Journal of a Voyage from Plymouth to Sierra Leone, with Notices of Madeira, Teneriffe, Bathurst, &c. 8vo. Bell and Daldy, 1858; Journal of a Residence at Falangia in the Soso country, printed for the S.P.G. ib. 1859.

NEVILLE, Seymour, Wraysbury vicarage (Bucks), near Staines, Middlesex.—Magd. Coll. Camb. Jun. Opt. and B.A. 1845; Deac. 1846, Pr. 1848; V. of Wyrardisbury alias Wraysbury, Dio. Oxon. 1856 (Patrons, D. and C. of Windsor; V.'s Gross Inc. 500l and Ho; Pop. 701); formerly Fell. of Magd. Coll. Camb. 1845-48; Min. Can. of St George's Coll. Ch. Windsor, 1845-56.

NEVINS, Archibald, St Nicholas College, Hurstpierpoint, Sussex.—Univ. Coll. Dur. B.A. 1854, M.A. 1857; Deac. 1860, by Bp of Chich.

NEW, John, Duncton, Petworth, Sussex.—St John's Coll. Oxon. B.A. 1851; Deac. 1852, Pr. 1853; R. of Duncton, Dio. Chich. 1859 (Patron, Lord Leconfield; R.'s Gross Inc. 420l; Pop. 272); late C. of Duncton.

NEWBOLT, Henry Francis, St Mary's vicarage, Bilston, Staffs.—St John's Coll. Camb. B.A. 1849, M.A. 1853; Deac. 1849, Pr. 1850; V. of St Mary's, Bilston, Dio. Lich. 1860 (Patron, Bp of Lich; Tithe—V. 300l; V.'s Gross Inc. 350l and Ho; Pop. 11,000); formerly C. of Walsall, Staffs. 1853-60.

NEWBY, Alfred Ryle, ... —St. Bees Theol. Coll; Deac. 1860, by Bp of Lich.

NEWENHAM, Bagenal Burdett, Gateforth, Selby, Yorks.—King's Coll. Lond. Theol. Assoc. 1848; P.C. of Gateforth, Dio. York, 1859 (Patron, H. Osbaldeston, Esq; P.C.'s Gross Inc. 120l; Pop. 192); late C. of West Farleigh, Kent; formerly C. of Teffont-Magna, near Salisbury.

NEWINGTON, Frank, Coombe-Keyner, Wareham, Dorset.—Deac. 1845, Pr. 1846; V. of Coombe-Keyner, Dio. Salis. 1859 (Patron, J. Weld, Esq; V.'s Gross Inc. 110l; Pop. 154); late C. of Broad-Chalke, near Salisbury; formerly C. of Breamore, Hants.

NEWMAN, Frederick Samuel, Clifford, Tadcaster, Yorks.—Qu. Coll. Oxon. B.A. 1858; Deac. 1859, Pr. 1860, both by Archbp of York; C. of Clifford, 1859.

NEWMAN, William, ... —Trin. Coll. Dub. B.A. 1858; Deac. 1859, Pr. 1860, both by Bp of Winch.

NEWTON, Charles, Hope, Shelton, Hanley, Staffs.—St Bees Theol. Coll. 1859; Deac. 1859, Pr. 1860, both by Bp of Lich; C. of Hope, 1859.

NEWTON, Joseph, The College, Brighton.—St John's Coll. Camb. B.A. 1847, M.A. 1850; Deac. 1847, Pr. 1851; Vice-Prin. of Brighton Coll.

NICHOLLS, William Harman, ... —Trin. Coll. Camb. B.A. 1860; Deac. 1860, by Bp of Chich.

NICHOLSON, Octavius, ...—St Aidan's Theol. Coll; Deac. 1860, by Bp of Lich.

NICHOLSON, Rhodes, Roundhay Park, near Leeds.—Literate; Deac. 1859, Pr. 1860, both by Bp of Rip; C. of St George's, Leeds, 1860; formerly C. of St Andrew's, Leeds, 1859-60.

NIX, Charles Devas, St John's parsonage, Hatfield-Broad-Oak, Harlow, Essex.—Trin. Coll. Camb. B.A. 1854, M.A. 1857; Deac. 1854, Pr. 1855, both by Bp of Chich; P.C. of St. John's, Hatfield-Broad-Oak, Dio. Roch. 1860 (Patron, V. of Hatfield; P.C.'s Gross Inc. 75l and Ho; Pop. 347); formerly C. of Worth, Sussex.

NIXSON, Joseph Mayer, Shale, Newport, Isle of Wight.—Clare Coll. Camb. B.A. 1851; Deac. 1851, Pr. 1852, both by Bp of Oxon; C. of Shale.

NOBLE, John Padmore, Ampthill, Beds.—Chr. Coll. Camb. B.A. 1858; Deac. 1860, by Bp of Ely; C. of Ampthill, 1860.

NOOTT, John Frederick, Frostenden, near Wangford, Suffolk.—Qu. Coll. Camb. B.A. 1844; Deac. 1844, Pr. 1845, both by Bp of Norw; Incumb. of the Donative R. of Blyford, near Wangford, Dio. Norw. 1860 (Patron, Rev. J. Day; Pop. 194); late C. of Wangford and Reydon, and Chap. of the Blything Union, Suffolk; formerly C. of Westhall.

NORTH, The Venerable William, St David's College, Lampeter.—Jesus Coll. Oxon. B.A. 1829, M.A. 1832; Archdeacon of Cardigan w Preb. of Llandyfriog, Dio. St Dav. 1860 (Value 50l); R. of Llangoedmore, Cardiganshire, Dio. St David's, 1845 (Patron, St Dav. Coll. Lampeter; Tithe—R. 440l; R.'s Gross Inc. 400l; Pop. 990); Rur. Dean of Lower Sub Ayron, Cardiganshire; formerly Prof. of Latin in St Dav. Coll. Lamp.

NORTON, Hector, Southampton.—Magd. Coll. Camb. B.A. 1850; Deac. 1850, Pr. 1851; C. of St Mary's, Southampton; formerly C. of Ecclesfield, near Sheffield.

NORVAL, William, *Brighton.*—Trin. Coll. Dub. B.A. 1829, M.A. 1831; Deac. and Pr. 1840 ; formerly R. of Ickleford, Herts, 1851-59.

NUNN, Joseph, 57 *Gloucester-place, Portman-square, London.*—St John's Coll. Camb. B.A. 1857, M.A. 1860 ; Deac. 1857, Pr. 1858, both by Bp of Chest; C. of St Mary's, Bryanston-square, Lond. 1859.

NUTTING, George Horatio, *Sherfield-on-Loddon rectory, Basingstoke, Hants.*—R. of Sherfield-on-Loddon, Dio. Winch. 1859 (Patron, Rev. W. Eyre; Tithe —R. 674*l*; Glebe, 36 acres; R.'s Gross Inc. 720*l* and Ho ; Pop. 615).

OAKLEY, Edwin, *South Lopham, East Harling, Norfolk.*—Bp Hat. Ha. Dur. B.A. 1858 ; Deac. 1859, Pr. 1860, both by Bp of Norw ; C. of North and South Lopham, 1859.

OATES, John William, *Bedworth, near Coventry.*—Chr. Ch. Oxon. B.A. 1859 ; Deac. 1860, by Bp of Worc ; C. of Bedworth, 1860.

O'BRIEN, James, *Hove, near Brighton.*—Min. of St James's, Hove.

O'BRIEN, James, *Cleever, Windsor, Berks.*—Sid.-Suss. Coll. Camb. B.A. 1853 ; Deac. 1854, Pr. 1855, both by Bp of Oxon; Asst. C. of Cleever, 1860; formerly C. of St John's, Rownham, near Southampton, 1855-60.

OLDFIELD, Charles, *The Quinton, near Birmingham.*—Trin. Coll. Camb. B.A. 1857 ; Deac. 1857, Pr. 1858, both by Bp of Worc ; P.C. of The Quinton, Dio. Worc. 1857 (Patron, V. of Hales Owen ; P.C.'s Gross Inc. 160*l*; Pop. 2274); C. of Hales Owen, 1858.

OLIVER, Charles Norwood, *Willington, Durham.*—Qu. Coll. Camb. B.A. 1858 ; Deac. 1859, Pr. 1860; C. of St Stephen's, Willington, 1859.

ONSLOW, Alexander Lee, *Marston-Biggott, Frome, Somerset.*—Trin. Coll. Camb. B.A. 1858 ; Deac. 1859, Pr. 1860, both by Bp of B. and W ; C. of Marston-Biggott, 1859.

ONSLOW, Phipps, *Upper Sapey rectory, Bromyard, Herefordshire.*—Exon. Coll. Oxon. B.A. 1846 ; Deac. 1847, Pr. 1848, both by Bp of Worc ; R. of Upper Sapey, Dio. Heref. 1859 (Patron, Sir T. E. Winnington, Bart ; R.'s Gross Inc. 300*l* and Ho ; Pop. 351); late C. of March, Camba. 1858-59.

ORAM, Henry Austin, *Macclesfield, Cheshire.*—St John's Coll. Camb. B.A. 1839 ; Deac. 1846, Pr. 1848, both by Bp of Chest; Chap. to the Union Workhouse, Macclesfield, 1860; formerly Head Mast. of the Modern Free School, Macclesfield ; Author, *Examples in Arithmetic,* Hamilton and Adams ; *Examples in Algebra,* ib ; *Latin Derivation,* ib.

ORDE, Leonard Shafto, *Edinburgh.*—Qu. Coll. Camb. B.A. 1830, M.A. 1842; Min. of St Paul's, Edinburgh, 1859 ; Dom. Chap. to the Duke of Northumberland ; late P.C. of Alnwick, Northumberland, 1854-59.

O'REGAN, Thomas, *Donnington-Wood parsonage, Newport, Shropshire.*—Trin. Coll. Dub. B.A. 1845; Deac. 1845, Pr. 1846, both by Bp of Lich ; P.C. of St Matthew's, Donnington-Wood, Dio. Lich. 1850 (Patron, Duke of Sutherland ; Tithe—R. 200*l*; Glebe, 257 acres; P.C.'s Gross Inc. 665*l*. and Ho ; Pop. 2000).

ORMOND, John, *Great Hampden, Great Missenden, Bucks.*—Pemb. Coll. Oxon. B.A. 1850, M.A. 1853 ; Deac. 1851, Pr. 1852 ; V. of Great Kmble, near Wendover, Dio. Oxon. 1857 (Patron, Rev. W. Browne; V.'s Gross Inc. 120*l*; Pop. 501); C. of Great Hampden, Bucks ; Fell. of Pemb. Coll. Oxon.

ORR, William Holmes, *Sneyd, Newcastle, Staffs.*—St. Bees Theol. Coll ; Deac. 1859, Pr. 1860, both by Bp of Lich ; C. of Sneyd, 1859.

ORTON, John Swaffield, *Shalfleet vicarage, Isle of Wight.*—King's Coll. Lond. Theol. Assoc ; Deac. 1860, by Bp of Winch ; C. of Shalfleet, 1860.

OSMAN, Joseph Wheeler, *Albion-terrace, Dudley-road, Wolverhampton.*—Deac. 1858, Pr. 1859, both by Bp of Lich ; C. of St George's, Wolverhampton, 1860; formerly C. of St John's, Tipton, Staffs.

OSWALD, Henry Murray, *Alnwick, Northumberland.*—Ch. Ch. Oxon. B.A. 1855, M.A. 1860 ; Deac. 1856, Pr. 1857, both by Bp of Linc ; C. of Alnwick, 1859.

OTTER, George, *Whaplode-Drove, Crowland, Lincolnshire.*—Jesus Coll. Camb. M.A ; C. of Whaplode-Drove, 1859.

OTTLEY, George Lethbridge, *Thurlaston, Hinckley, Leicestershire.*—St Bees Theol. Coll ; Deac. 1857, Pr. 1858, both by Bp of Peterb; C. of Thurlaston, 1859 ; formerly C. of Houghton-on-the-Hill, Leicestershire, 1857-59.

OWGAN, Joseph Bullen, 62 *Grove-street, Liverpool.*—Trin. Coll. Dub. B.A. 1847 ; Deac. 1860, by Bp of Chest; C. of St Thomas, Park-lane, Liverpool, 1860 ; formerly Res. Tut. of Trin. Coll. Dub; Author, various *Translations of the Classics,* Kelly, Dublin.

PACKER, Isaac George, *New Walk, Leicester.*—Worc. Coll. Oxon. B.A. 1859 ; Deac. 1859, Pr. 1860, both by Bp of Peterb; C. of St. Mary's, Leicester, 1860.

PAGE, James Robert, 1, *Hobury-street, Chelsea,* and *Athenæum Club, Pall Mall, London.*—Trin. Coll. Dub. B.A. 1825, and incorp. Qu. Coll. Camb. M.A. 1837 ; Deac. 1829, by Bp of Elphin, Pr. 1829, by Bp of Kildare ; formerly Deputy Chap. of the Chapel Royal, Hampton Court ; Author, *Letters in reply to a Priest of the Church of Rome ; The Condition of the Poor under the Roman Priesthood ; Examination of the Government System of Education for Ireland ; Strictures on the Doctrine of the "Sinful Flesh of Christ ; " Catholic Truth not Assailed, and Popery not Vindicated ; Anatomy of a Protest entitled "Is the Church of England not Apostate ?" Sermon on the Coronation of Queen Victoria ; The Rule of Faith ; The Anti-Catholicity of the Papal Church ; Ireland—its Coils traced to their Source ; The true Wisdom of Man ; Questions on History ; A Warning to England in an Exposition of the Papal Apostacy and Policy ; The Qualifications of the Christian Ministry ; Apology for the Roman Priests in Ireland, or their Conduct not Inconsistent with their System ; The House of God ; The History and Nature of Consecrated Places of Worship ; The Position of the Church of England in the Catholic World ; Quid Romæ Faciam ? Reasons for refusing an Invitation to join the Communion of the Papal Church ;* various smaller *Works, Pamphlets,* and *Magazine Articles ;* Editor of Burnet's "Exposition of the Thirty-nine Articles."

PALEY, John, *Godsall, near Wolverhampton.*—St Peter's Coll. Camb. B.A. 1838 ; Deac. 1840, Pr. 1841, both by Bp of G. and B ; P. C. of Godsall, Dio. Lich. 1859 (Patron, Lord Wrottesley ; P. C's. Gross Inc. 160*l* ; Pop. 1195); late P. C. of Hook, Yorkshire, 1843-59.

PALMER, Henry Vaughan, 7, *Trinity-lane, York.*—Literate ; Deac. 1860, by Archbp of York ; C. of St. Mary's, Bishophill Junior, York, 1860; formerly a Dissenting Minister, 1848-60.

PARDOE, Arthur, *Hook, Beaminster, Dorset.*—Jesus Coll. Camb. B.A. 1843 ; R. of Hook, Dio. Salis. 1859 (Patron, Earl of Sandwich ; R.'s Gross Inc. 120*l*; Pop 261); formerly V. of Sidmouth, Devon, 1856-58.

PARDOE, George, *Wolverley, near Kidderminster.*—St. John's Coll. Oxon. B.A. 1845, M.A. 1850 ; C. of Wolverley.

PARISH, William Douglas, *Tirle, Lewes, Sussex.*—Trin. Coll. Oxon. S.C.L. 1858 ; Deac. 1858, Pr. 1860; C. of Beddingham *w* Tirle, 1858.

PARK, John, *Rampside parsonage, Ulverstone, Lancashire.*—Emman. Coll. Camb. B.A. 1853 ; Deac. 1853, Pr. 1854 ; P. C. of Rampside, Dio. Carl. 1859 (Patron, V. of Dalton-in-Furness ; P. C.'s Gross Inc. 16*l*. and Ho ; Pop. 75) ; formerly C. of Petham, Kent, 185.-55 ; C. of St. John's, Lancaster, 1855-58 ; C. of Glentworth, Lincolnshire, 1858-59.

PARKER, Charles William, *Lockeridge, Marlborough, Wilts.*—Wadh. Coll. Oxon. B.A. 1856, M.A. 1859; Deac. 1858, Pr. 1859 ; C. of Overton cum Tyfield, 1859.

PARKER, Christopher, *Skirwith, near Penrith.*—Emman. Coll. Camb. B.A. 1840, M.A. 1845; Deac. 1842, Pr. 1843; P. C. of Skirwith, Dio. York, 1859 (Patron, the present P. C; P. C.'s Gross Inc. 190*l*; Rural Dean; late R. of Ormside, Westmoreland, 1855-58.

PARKER, James Dunne, 6, *Saville-row, Newcastle-on-Tyne.*—Qu. Univ. Ireland B.A. 1854, LL.B. 1857, and St. Aidan's Theol. Coll; Deac. 1859, by Bp of Chester, Pr. 1860, by Bp of Dur; C. of All Saints, Newcastle-on-Tyne, 1859.

PARKER, John, *Aston-on-Trent, Derby.*—Bp Hat. Ha. Dur. Sch. and B.A. 1853, M.A. 1856; Deac. 1855, Pr. 1856, both by Bp of Lich; C. of Aston-on-Trent, 1860; formerly C. of Long Eaton, Derby, 1855-60.

PARKYN, Jonathan Clouter, *Woolborough, Newton-Abbot, Devon.*—St John's Coll Camb. B.A. 1859; Deac. 1859, by Bp of Exon, Pr. 1860, by Bp of G. and B; C. of Woolborough, 1859.

PARMITER, John, *Eastnor, Ledbury, Herefordshire.*—Christ Coll. Camb. B.A. 1859; Deac. 1860, by Bp of Eastnor cum Pixley, 1860.

PARRY, Morris, *Criccieth, Portmadoc, Carnarvonshire.*—St. David's Theol Coll. Lamp; Deac. 1842, Pr. 1843, both by Bp of St David's; C. of Llanuhangel-y-pennant, 1843; formerly C. of Rhostie, Cardiganshire, 1842-1843.

PARRY, Thomas William, *Hereford.*—St. Mary Ha. Oxon, B.A. 1854, M.A. 1857; Deac. 1856, Pr. 1857, both by Bp of Ely; R. of St. Nicholas, city and Dio. Heref. 1859 (Patron, Ld. Chan; Tithe—R. 150*l*, Glebe, 20 acres; R.'s Gross Inc. 200*l*; Pop. 1600); formerly C. of Luton, Beds.

PARRY, William Warner, *St. Mary's rectory, Hulme, Manchester.*—Worces. Coll. Oxon, B.A. 1857, M.A. 1859; Deac. 1859, Pr. 1860, both by Bp of Chest; C. of St. Mary's, Hulme, 1859.

PARSONS, Augustus James, ...—Trin. Coll. Camb. B. A. 1859; Deac. 1859, Pr. 1860, both by Bp. of Chich.

PAUL, Frederick Bateman, *Ottery, St. Mary, Devon.*—Univ. Coll. Dur, Theol. Licen. 1859; Deac. 1859, Pr. 1860, both by Bp. of Exon; Asst. C. of Ottery, St. Mary, 1859.

PAVEY, Alfred, *Bingham, Notts.*—Qu. Coll. Oxon. B.A. 1854, M.A. 1857; Deac. 1854, Pr. 1856, both by Bp of Manch; C. of Bingham, 1859; late C. of Holy Trinity, Bolton; formerly C. of St James, Heywood, near Manchester.

PAYNE, Alfred Dalrymple, *Bicester, Oxfordshire.*—Caius Coll. Camb. Sch. 1855, B.A. 1856, M.A. 1860; Deac. 1858, Pr. 1859, both by Bp of Norw; C. of Bicester, 1860; formerly C. of Burgh Apton, Norfolk, 1858-60.

PEACHE, Alfred, *Mangotsfield, near Bristol.*—Wadh. Coll. Oxon. B.A. 1842, M.A. 1845; Deac. 1842, Pr. 1843; P.C. of Mangotsfield *w* Downsend, Dio. G. and B. 1859 (Patron, the present P.C; P.C.'s Gross Inc. 150*l*; Pop. 3967); late C. of Heckfield-cum-Mattingley, Hants.

PEACOCK, William James, *Upton, Southwell, Notts.*—Trin. Coll. Dub. B.A. 1848; Deac. 1849, Pr. 1850, both by Bp of Linc; V. of Upton, Dio. Linc. 1859 (Patron, Chapter of Southwell; Glebe, 41 acres; V.'s Gross. Inc. 117*l.* and Ho; Pop. 601).

PEARSE, Henry Thornton, *Ovington, Halstead, Essex.*—Chr. Ch. Oxon. B.A. 1859; Deac. 1860, by Bp of Roch; C. of Ovington-cum-Tilbury, 1860.

PEARSE, Vincent, *Barcheston rectory, Shipston-on-Stour, Warwickshire.*—Linc. Coll. 1856, M.A. 1859; Deac. 1859, by Bp of Peterb, Pr. 1860, by Bp of Worc; C. of Barcheston, 1859.

PEARSON, Charles Richardson Jervis, *Bromley St Leonards, Bow, Middlesex.*—King's Coll. Lond; Deac. 1860, by Bp of Lond; C. of Bromley St Leonards, 1860.

PEARSON, Christopher Ridley, *High Cross, Ware, Herts.*—Qu. Coll. Camb. B.A. 1849, M.A. 1852; Deac. 1849, Pr. 1850; V. of Standon, Herts, Dio. Roch. 1860 (Patroness, Lady G. Pullen; Tithe—Imp. 1311*l*, V. 520*l.* 15*s*, Glebe, 6 acres; V.'s Gross Inc. 540*l*; Pop. 629); formerly P.C. of Mark, Somerset, 1853-60.

PEARSON, Frederick, *Sutton, near Potton, St. Neot's, Hunts.*—Trin. Ha. Camb. B.A. 1855, M.A. 1858; Deac. 1856, Pr. 1857, both by Bp of Ely; C. of Sutton, 1856.

PEARSON, Frederick Thorpe, *Loughborough, Leicestershire.*—Qu. Coll. Oxon. B.A. 1844, M.A. 1847; C. of Loughborough, 1860; formerly Min. of St Peter's Chapel, Pimlico, Lond. 1852-58; C. of Dawlish, Devon, 1858-60.

PEEL, Charles Steers, *Rousham rectory, Woodstock, Oxfordshire.*—Worc. Coll. Oxon. B.A. 1843, M.A. 1847; Deac. 1845, Pr. 1846, both by Bp of Lich; R. of Rousham, Dio. Oxon. 1859 (Patron, C. C. Dormer, Esq; R.'s Gross Inc. 260*l.* and Ho; Pop. 134); late R. of Syresham, Northants, 1850-59.

PEILE, Arthur Lewis Babington, *Wimbledon, Surrey.*—Jesus Coll. Camb. B.A. 1852; Deac. 1853, Pr. 1854, both by Bp of Roch; C. of Wimbledon, 1859; formerly C. of Bishop's Hatfield, Herts.

PENNETHORNE, Gregory Walton, *Beeston, near Nottingham.*—Jesus Coll. Cam. B.A. 1860; Deac. 1860, by Bp of Linc; C. of Beeston, 1860.

PENNEY, John William Watkin, *Drigg, Whitehaven, Cumberland.*—Univ. Coll. Dur. B.A. 1859; Deac. 1860, by Bp of Carl; C. of Drigg, 1860.

PENNY, Edward Lewton, *Wentworth-terrace, St. Philip's, Sheffield.*—Pem. Coll. Oxon. B.A. 1859; Deac. 1859, Pr. 1860, both by Archbp of York; C. of St. Jude, Moorfield, Sheffield, 1859.

PENTREATH, Frederick Richard, *South-street, Epsom, Surrey.*—Worces. Coll. Oxon. B.A. 1857, M.A. 1859; Deac. 1857; Second Mast. and Asst. Chap. at the Royal Medical College, Epsom.

PERCY, Philip Henry, *East Retford, Notts.*—King's Coll. Lond; Deac. 1854, Pr. 1856; C. of East-Retford, 1859; late C. of Eastchurch, Kent; formerly C. of St. Leonard's, Deal.

PERCY, William John, *Silton rectory, Bourton, Dorset.*—St. John's Coll. Camb. B.A. 1839, M.A. 1842; Deac. 1839, Pr. 1840, both by Bp of B. and W.; Patron, and late R. of Silton, Dorset, 1851-59; Member of the Senate of the Univ. of Camb. formerly Provincial Grand Chap. to the Freemasons for Dorset; Author, *Masonic Sermons*, Spencer, 8vo. 1844, 3*s*.

PETERS, Thomas Henry, 6, *Melbourne-street, Plymouth.*—Trin. Coll. Dub B.A. 1856; Deac. 1857, Pr. 1859, both by Bp of Exon; C. of Suton-on-Plym, near Plymouth, 1857.

PETTITT, John, *Wortley, near Leeds.*— St John's Coll. Camb. B.A. 1855; Deac. 1855, Pr. 1856. both by Bp of Chest; P.C. of Wortley, Dio. Rip. 1859 (Patrons, Trustees; P.C.'s Gross Inc. 160*l*; Pop. 7896); late C. of Wybunbury, Cheshire.

PHELP, Philip Henry, 36, *Gloucester-crescent, Regent's-park, London.*—St John's Coll. Camb. B.A. 1857, M.A. 1860; Deac. 1857, Pr. 1858, both by Bp of Norw; C. of St. Mark's, St. Pancras, London, 1859.

PHELPS, Arthur Whitmarsh, *Hindon, Wilts.*—Worc. Coll. Oxon. B.A. 1858; Deac. 1858; Pr. 1859, both by Bp of Salis; C. of Berwick St. Leouard, near Hindon, 1858; R. of Upper Pertwood, near Hindon, Dio. Salis. 1859 (Patroness, Mrs. Seymour, Knoyle-house, Wilts; R.'s Gross Inc. 56*l*; Pop. 29).

PHELPS, John, 18, *Royal-terrace, Ramsgate, Kent.*—All Souls Coll. Oxon. B.A. 1857, M.A. 1859; Deac. 1860, by Archbp of Cant; C. of Christchurch, Ramsgate, 1860.

PHILLIPS, George, *Forest School, Walthamstow, Essex.*—Qu. Coll. Camb. B.A. 1855, M.A. 1858; Deac. 1855, Pr. 1856, both by Bp of Roch; Asst. Mast. of Forest Sch. Walthamstow, 1857; formerly C. of West and South Hanningfield, Essex, 1855-57.

PHILLIPS, James, *Abington House, Northampton.*—Trin. Coll. Dub. B.A. 1860; Deac. 1860, by Bp of Peterb; C. of St. Sepulchre's, Northampton, 1860.

PHILLIPS, Spencer William, *Romford, Essex.*—Univ. Coll. Oxon. B.A. 1856, M.A. 1859; Deac. 1857, Pr. 1858, both by Bp of Roch; C. of Romford, 1860; formerly C. of Ifield, Kent, 1857-60.

PHILLIPS, Thomas Lloyd, *Beckenham, Kent.*—Univ. Coll. Lond. B.A. 1856; Deac. 1856, Pr. 1859, both by Archbp of Cant; C. of Beckenham; late Sec. to the Editorial Department of the Brit. and For. Bible Soc.

PHILPOT, Benjamin, *Lydney vicarage, Gloucestershire.*—Chr. Coll. Camb. Sen. Opt. M.A. 1812; Deac. 1815, Pr. 1817; V. of Lydney w Aylburton and St Briavel's C. Dio. G. and B. 1859 (Patrons, D. and C. of Heref; Tithe—App. 420l, V. 680l 10s); Glebe, 11 acres; V.'s Gross Inc. 700l and Ho; Pop. Lydney, 800, Aylburton, 400, St. Briavel's, 567); late ... ... Norfolk, 1839-59; R. of Great Cressingham w Bodney R; formerly Archd. of Sodor and Man. and R. of Kirk Andrews; previously Foundation Fell. of Chr. Coll. Camb; Author, *Sermons on Prophetic Subjects; Four Sermons at Visitations and Ordination; Essay on Religious Revivals,* 1854; *Lectures on Ruth* (preached at All Souls, Langham-place), Nisbet 1854; various *Tracts.*

PHIPPS, Pownoll William, *Shepperton (Middlesex), near Chertsey, Surrey.*—Pemb. Coll. Oxon. B.A. 1858; Deac. 1859, Pr. 1860, both by Bp of Lond; C. of Shepperton, 1859.

PICKFORD, James John, *Bright-Waltham, Wantage, Berks.*—St Mary Ha. Oxon. B.A. 1857, M.A. 1860; Deac. 1859, Pr. 1860, both by Bp of Oxon; C. of Bright-Waltham, 1859.

PICKLES, Joseph Samuel, *St Saviour's, Liverpool.*—St John's Coll. Camb. B.A. 1859; Deac. 1859, Pr. 1860, both by Bp of Chest; C. of St Saviour's, Liverpool.

PIERPOINT, Matthew, *Laxey, Douglas, Isle of Man.*—P.C. of Laxey, Dio. S. and M. 1859 (Patron, Bp of S. and M; P.C.'s Gross Inc. 100l.); Chap. to the Laxey Mining Company, 1859; late C. of St Stephen's, Westminster, Lond; formerly C. of Steeple, Essex.

PILKINGTON, Charles Henry, *Bishopstoke, Hants.*—New Coll. Oxon. B.A. 1860; Deac. 1860, by Bp of Winch; C. of Bishopstoke, 1860.

PILKINGTON, Richard, 2 *Brandford-terrace, Bermondsey, London.*—Qu. Coll. Camb. B.A. 1850, M.A. 1853; Deac. 1850, Pr. 1851, both by Bp of Chest; C. of Christ Ch. Bermondsey, 1860; late C. of Bedale, Yorks. Author, *Six Sermons preached at Rochdale,* Smith, Liverpool, 1851; *A Few Words on the Present State of the Patronage, Public and Private, of the Church of England,* London, Batty, 1860.

PINHORNE, George Stanley, *Beckermet, Egremont, Cumberland.*—St John's Coll. Camb; Deac. 1850, Pr. 1851, both by Bp of Lich; P.C. of St John's, Beckermet, Dio. Carl. 1859 (Patron, H. Gaitskell, Esq; P.C.'s Gross Inc 70l; Pop. 541); late C. of Eskdale, Cumberland.

PIRIE, Henry George, *Dunoon, Scotland.*—Univ. of Edinb; Deac. 1846, Pr. 1847; Incumb. of Holy Trinity Ch. Dunoon, Dio. Argyll and the Isles, 1848 (Patron, Bp of Argyll and the Isles; Gross Inc. 120l); Author, occasional *Letters.*

PITCHER, Amos William, *Broughton, Manchester.*—Literate; Deac. 1858, Pr. 1859, both by Bp of Rip; C. of Holy Trinity, Salford, Manchester, 1860 (Stipend, 120l); formerly C. of Low Harrogate, Yorks. 1850-60; Author, *Le Jugement futur,* Paris, 1857; *Das zukünftige Gericht,* Bonn, 1861.

PITMAN, Edward John Timmings, *Bristol-road, Birmingham.*—Qu. Theol. Coll. Birmingham; Deac. 1860, by Bp of Worc; C. of St Luke's, Birmingham, 1860.

PIX, George Banastre, *Acaster-Selby, Tadcaster, Yorks.*—Linc. Coll. Oxon. B.A. 1846, M.A. 1850; Deac. 1849, Pr. 1851, both by Bp of Worc; P.C. of Acaster-Selby, Dio. York, 1859 (Patron, Sir W. M. Milner, Bart; P.C.'s Gross Inc. 50l; Pop. 184l; late Vice-Prin. of York Training Coll; formerly Head Mast. of Gram. Sch. Trinidad, West Indies, 1853-56.

PLATT, George Moreton, *Masham, Bedale, Yorks.*—Trin. Coll. Camb. Bell's Sch. B.A. 1857, M.A. 1860; Deac. 1860, by Bp of Rip; C. of Masham, 1860.

PLOW, Anthony John, *Wickham, Fareham, Hants.*—Qu. Coll. Camb. B.A. 1855; Deac. 1855, Pr. 1856; C. of Wickham, 1859; formerly C. of Staines, Middlesex.

PLUMMER, William Henry, *Fleetpond, Winchfield, Hants.*—Trin. Coll. Camb. B.A. 1851; Deac. 1852, Pr. 1857; formerly C. of Griston, Norfolk.

POCOCK, John Carne, *Angle vicarage, near Pembroke.*—Cuddesdon Theol. Coll; Deac. 1856, Pr. 1857, both by Bp of Oxon; V. of Angle, Dio. St. Dav. 1859 (Patron, Bp of St. Dav; V.'s Gross Inc. 84l. and Ho; Pop. 450).

PODMORE, William Henry, *Northall, Edlesborough, Dunstable, Beds.*—Trin. Coll. Dub. B.A. 1859; Deac. 1859, Pr. 1860, both by Bp of Oxon; C. of Edlesborough, 1859.

POLEHAMPTON, Edward Thomas William, *Hartfield rectory, near Tunbridge Wells.*—Pemb. Coll. Oxon. B.A. 1847, M.A. 1850; Deac. 1849, Pr. 1851, both by Bp of Oxon; R. and V. of Hartfield, Dio. Chich. 1859 (Patron, Earl Delawarr; Tithe—R. and V. 900l; Glebe, 1½ acres; R. and V.'s Gross Inc. 920l and Ho; Pop. 1573); Chap. to Earl Powlett; late P.C. of Great Bricet, Suffolk, 1855-59; Co-Editor, with the Rev T. S. Polehampton, of "Memoir, Letters, and Diary, of the late Rev S. Polehampton, Chaplain at Lucknow," Bentley, 1858.

POLEHAMPTON, Thomas Stedman, *Hartfield rectory, near Tunbridge Wells.*—Pemb. Coll. Oxon. 1846, 2nd Cl. Math. et. Phy. and B.A. 1850, M.A. 1852; Deac. 1850, by Bp of Oxon, Pr. 1851, by Bp of Salis; C. of Hartfield, 1859; late Asst. C. of Ross, Herefordshire; formerly C. of Betteshanger, Kent; Author, *Three Assize Sermons* (at Maidstone), Rivingtons, 1855; Co-Editor, with the Rev. E. T. W. Polehampton, of "Memoirs, Letters, and Diary of the late Rev Henry S. Polehampton, Chaplain at Lucknow," Bentley, 1858.

POLLARD, Henry Smith, *Coombe-Bissett vicarage, near Salisbury.*—Linc. Coll. Oxon. B.A. 1833, M.A. 1837; V. of Coombe-Bissett w West Harnham C. Dio. Salis. 1857 (Patron, Preb. of Coombe and West Harnham; Tithe—App. 381l 8s; Glebe, 200 acres; V.'s Gross Inc. 260l and Ho; Pop. Coombe-Bissett, 415; West Harnham, 275); P.C. of Homington, near Salisbury, Dio. Salis. 1857 (Patrons, D. and C. of Salis; P.C.'s Gross Inc. 65l; Pop. 176); formerly V. of Edlington, Lincolnshire, 1852-57.

POLLOCK, William James, 8 *Panmure-terrace, Montrose, Scotland.*—Trin. Coll. Dub. B.A. 1853; Deac. 1854, Pr. 1855, both by Bp of Chest; Incumb. of St Peter's, Engl. Episcop. Ch. Montrose, 1860; formerly C. of Bootle, near Liverpool, 1854-56; C. of St. Mattias, Salford, 1856-57; Sen. C. of St Mary's, Cheltenham, 1857-60.

POOLEY, John George, *Bristol.*—Corpus Coll. Camb. B.A. 1859; Deac. 1859, Pr. 1860, both by Bp of G. and B; C. of St. Peter's, Bristol, 1859.

POPE, Alexander, *Frogmore, Kingsbridge, Devon.*—Qu. Coll. Camb. B.A. 1840; Deac. 1841, Pr. 1842, both by Bp of Exon; C. of Sherford, Devon, 1857.

PORTER, John Leech, *St John's parsonage, Trowbridge, Wilts.*—Trin. Coll. Dub. B.A. 1857; Deac. 1857, by Bp of Rip; Pr. 1859, by Bp of Salis; P.C. of St John's, Upper Studley, Trowbridge, Dio. Salis. 1860 (Patron, R. of Trowbridge); formerly C. of St Paul's, Shipley, Yorks. 1857-58; C. of Trowbridge, 1858-60.

PORTER, Richard Ibbetson, *Stewkley, Winslow, Bucks.*—Corpus Coll. Camb. B.A. 1858; Deac. 1860, by Bp of Oxon; C. of Stewkley, 1860 (Stipend, 50l).

POTTER, Alfred, *Keyworth rectory, near Nottingham.*—St John's Coll. Camb. B.A. 1851; Deac. 1850, Pr. 1851, both by Bp of Linc; R. of Keyworth, Dio. Linc. 1860 (Patron, T. Dodson, Esq; R.'s Gross Inc. 500l and Ho; Pop. 667); late C. of Ropsley, Lincolnshire, 1859-60; formerly C. of Skirbeck, Lincolnshire.

POTTER, Thomas Johnson, *Christ's Hospital, Newgate, London.*—Trin. Coll. Camb. B.A. 1850, M.A. 1853; Deac. 1853, Pr. 1854, both by Archbp of York; Asst. Math. Mast. of Christ's Hosp. Sch.

POWELL, Edward Henry, *Weston-super-Mare, Somerset.*—St. John's Coll. Oxon. B.A. 1848, M.A. 1851; Deac. 1849, Pr. 1850, both by Bp of Exon; C. of Locking, Somerset, 1857; formerly C of Lynton, Devon, 1849-51; C. of Wellington, Somerset, 1851-54; R. of Ludchurch, Pembrokeshire, 1854-56.

POWER, John, *Wrexham-house, George-street, Ryde, Isle of Wight.*—St Edm. Ha. B.A. 1847, M.A. 1853; Deac. 1847, Pr. 1848, both by Bp of Rip; Chap. of Missions to Seamen; formerly Incumb. of Shelf, near Halifax, 1848-53.

POWLEY, Matthew, *Malaga, Spain.*—Qu. Coll. Oxon. 4th Cl. Class. and B.A. 1849, M.A. 1853; Deac. 1850, Pr. 1851; British Chap. of Malaga, 1859; late C. of Wallasey, Cheshire, 1850-59.

POWNALL, Alfred, *Trowse vicarage, near Norwich.*—St. Cath. Coll. Camb. B.A. 1852, M.A. 1856; Deac. 1856, Pr. 1857, both by Bp of Ely; V. of Trowse w Lakenham, Dio. Norw. 1860 (Patron, D. and C. of Norw; Tithe — Trowse, App. 92l 5s 8d, V. 178l 4s 6d, Glebe, 11 acres; Lakenham, App. 44l 14s, V. 183l 7s; V 's Gross. Inc. 400l and Ho; Pop. Trowse, 1363, Lakenham, 2079); formerly Chap. of St Cath. Coll. Cambridge, 1856-60; C. of Conington, Hunts, 1857-60.

PRATT, Philip Edgar, *5 Canning-place, Leicester.*—Exon. Coll. Oxon. B.A. 1859; Deac. 1859; Pr. 1860, both by Bp of Peterb; Sen. C. of St. Margaret's, Leicester, 1859.

PRESTON, Joseph, *10 Stanley-street, Pimlico, London.*—Trin. Coll. Camb. B.A. 1849, M.A. 1852; Deac. 1860; C. of St Michael, Chester-square, Pimlico, 1860.

PRICE, Edmund, ... —Univ. Coll. Oxon. B.A. 1859; Deac. 1859, Pr. 1860, both by Bp of B. and W.

PRICE, Henry Mitchinson Coverly, *122 Cheetham-hill, Manchester.*—St John's Coll. Camb. B.A. 1859; Deac. 1860, by Bp of Manch; C. of St Luke's, Cheetham-hill, Manchester, 1860.

PRICE, Richard Edward, *Berriew, near Shrewsbury.*—Jesus Coll. Oxon. B.A. 1858, M.A. 1860; Deac. 1859, Pr. 1860; C. of Berriew, 1859.

PRIESTLY, Richard Edwards, *Lleiniog, Beaumaris, Anglesey.*—Trin. Coll. Oxon. B.A. 1859; Deac. 1859, Pr. 1860, both by Bp of Bang; C. of Llanffinan, Anglesey, 1859.

PRIOR, John, *Sidney Proprietary College, Bath.* —Univ. Coll. Dur. 1st Cl. Class. B.A. 1846, M.A. 1850; Deac. 1849, Pr. 1850; Class. Mast. of Sidney Proprietary Coll. 1859; late Head Mast. of Audlem Sch. Namptwich, Cheshire, 1852-57.

PROCTER, George Allen, *1 Upper Belle-vue-terrace, Southampton.*—Trin. Coll. Dub. B.A. 1852, M.A. 1858; Deac. 1856, Pr. 1857, both by Bp of Lich; C. of Christ's Ch. Northam, Southampton, 1859; formerly C. of Woore, Shropshire.

PROCTER, John Mathias, *North Rode parsonage, Congleton, Cheshire.*—Trin. Coll. Oxon. B.A. 1858; Deac. 1859, Pr. 1860, both by Bp of Oxon; C. of North Rode, 1859; Fell. of Jesus Coll. Oxon.

PROCTOR, William Addy, *Milton-next-Gravesend, Kent.*—St John's Coll. Camb. B.A. 1859; Deac. 1859, Pr. 1860, both by Bp of Roch; C. of Christ's Ch. Milton-next Gravesend, 1859.

PROUD, George, *Aislaby, Whitby, Yorkshire.*—St John's Coll. Camb. B.A. 1859; Deac. 1859, Pr. 1860, both by Archbp of York; C. of Aislaby, 1859.

PRYOR, John Eade, *Shenley, Barnet, Herts.*—C. of Shenley.

PUCKLE, Edwin, *Blisworth, near Northampton.*—Magd. Ha. Oxon. B.A. 1859; Deac. 1859, Pr. 1860, both by Bp of Peterb; C. of Blisworth, 1859.

PULLEN, Henry William, *St Andrew's College, Bradfield, near Reading.*—Clare Coll. Camb. B.A. 1859; Deac. 1859, Pr. 1860, both by Bp of Oxon; Asst. C. of Bradfield, 1859; Asst. Mast. in St Andrew's Coll. Bradfield.

PULLING, Frederick William, *Traine, Modbury, Devon.*—Corpus Coll. Camb. B.A. 1845; Deac. 1847, Pr. 1848; Asst. C. of Modbury; formerly C. of Revelstoke, Devon, 1847-49; C. of Tywardreath, Cornwall, 1850-51.

PURCHAS, William Henry, *Cqulk, near Ashby-de-la-Zouch.*—Univ. Coll. Dur. Theol. Licen. 1857; Deac. 1857, Pr. 1859, both by Bp of Lich; C. of Tickenhall, Derbyshire.

PURSELL, John Reeves, *Rossall, Fleetwood, Lancashire.*—St John's Coll. Oxon. B.A. 1855; Deac. 1856, by Bp of Winch. Pr.1858, by Bp of Chich; Mast. of the Preparatory Sch. Rossall, 1860; formerly 2nd Mast. of the Gram. Sch. and C. of St Anne's, Lewes, Sussex.

PURSER, Samuel Powell, *2 Shorndene-villas, Hastings.*—Trin. Col. Dul. B.A. 1848, M.A. 1851; Deac. 1852, Pr. 1855, both by Bp of Chest; C. of Curzon Chap. Mayfair, Lond. 1860; late C. of Nantwich, Cheshire; formerly Asst. C. of Beighton, Derbyshire; previously Member of the Irish Bar.

PURTON, Walter O'Nions, *Petworth, Sussex.*—St Cath. Coll. Camb. B.A. 1859; Deac. 1859, Pr. 1860, both by B. of Chich; C. of Petworth, 1859.

PUXLEY, Herbert Lavallan, *Cockermouth, Cumberland.*—Brasen. Coll. Oxon. B.A. 1858; Deac. 1859, Pr. 1860, both by Bp of Carl; C. of All Saints, Cockermouth, 1859; Dom. Chap. to the Earl of Bantry, 1860.

——————

QUICK, Adrian Gustavus, *Steeple-Morden, Royston, Camb.*—Corpus Coll. Camb. B.A. 1859; Deac. 1859, Pr. 1860, both by Bp of Ely; C. of Steeple-Morden, 1860.

QUICKE, George Andrew, *New College, Oxford.*—New Coll. Oxon. B.C.L. 1845; Deac. 1845, Pr. 1847; Fell. of New Col. Oxon; formerly C. of Buttermere, Wilts, 1845-46; Asst. C. of Kintbury, Berks, 1846-48; C. of East Hendred, Berks. 1849-51; R. of Ashbrittle, Somerset, 1855-59.

——————

RABY, John, *Exmouth, Devon.*—Clare Coll. Camb. B.A. 1856; Deac. 1857, Pr. 1858; C. of Littleham-cum-Exmouth, 1859.

RABY, William, *Vale-cottage, Lancaster.*—Trin. Coll. Camb. B.A. 1858; Deac. 1859, by Bp of Manch; C. of Halton, Lancashire, 1859.

RADCLIFFE, Henry Eliot Delme, *Oakley, Beds.*—Qu. Coll. Oxon. B.A. 1855, M.A. 1858; Deac. 1856, by Bp of Oxon. Pr. 1858, by Bp of Ely; C. of Oakley and Bromham, Beds, 1859; Michel. Fell. of Qu. Coll. Oxon; formerly C. of Riseley and Melchbourne, Beds, 1857-58.

RAIKES, Frederick Thornton, *Milnthorpe-parsonage, Westmoreland.*—Lit; Deac. 1859, Pr. 1860; P.C. of Milnthorpe, Dio. Carl. 1860 (Patron, V. of Heversham; Glebe, 7 acres; P. C.'s Gross Inc. 110l and Ho; Pop. 1221); formerly C. of St George's, Kend l. Westmoreland, 1859-60; previously Lieutenant in H. M. 62nd Regt.

RAIKES, Henry Puget, *Barton, near Penrith.*—Lit; Deac. 1860, by Bp of Carl; C. of Barton, 1860.

RAM, Stopford James, *Pavenham, near Bedford.*—St John's Coll. Camb. B.A. 1849, M.A. 1852; Deac. 1849, by Archbp of Dublin, Pr. 1851, by Bp of Peter; Incumb. of Pavenham, Dio. of Ely, 1860 (Patron Trin. Coll. Camb.; Incumb.'s Gro. In. 100l.; Pop. 556); late Assoc. Sec. for Irish Ch. Missions, 1858-60, formerly P. C. of Christ Ch. Stratford, Essex, 1854-58; Author, *The Temperance Movement, its Importance and Christian Character*, Oakey; *The Great Evil of the Day*, and other Tracts.

RAMSDEN, Frederick John, *Stratford-on-Avon, Warwickshire.*—Ch. Ch. Oxon. B.A. 1859; Deac. 1860, by Bp of Lond; C. of Stratford-on-Avon, 1860.

RANDALL, The Ven. James, *Binfield, near Bracknell, Berks.*—Trin. Coll. Oxon. B.A.1813, M.A.1816; Deac. 1828, Pr. 1829; Chap. to the Bp of Oxon. 1845; Archd of Berks, 1855; formerly Fell. of Trin. Col. Oxon. 1818-30; R. of Binfield, Berks, 1831-59; Author, *Sermons*, Rivingtons, 1843; *Ordination Sermon*, 1848; *Letter on Court of Appeal in Causes Ecclesiastical*, 1850.

RANDALL, William, *Hayes, Uxbridge, Middlesex.*—C. of Hayes.

RANDOLPH, Herbert, *Tolbury-house, Bruton, Somerset.*—Chap. to the Marquis of Devonshire, 1850; formerly V. of Abbotsley, Hants, 1839-49; Editor of Sir R. Wilson's *Journal of the French Invasion of Russia in 1812,* Murray, 1860.

RANKER, William Henry, *East Retford, Notts.*—Corpus Coll. Camb. B.A. 1854, M.A. 1857; Deac. 1856, Pr. 1858, both by Bp of Oxon; C. of East Retford, 1860; formerly Mast. at St Peter's Coll. Radley, 1855-60.

RAVEN, Thomas, *North Villa, St Leonards, Sussex.*—Corpus Coll. Camb. Wrang. and B.A. 1822, M.A. 1826; Deac. and Pr. 1822, both by Bp of Norw; formerly Min. of Trinity Church, Preston, 1824-49; Author, *A Monthly Series of Family Prayers,* Seeleys; *A Family Commentary,* J. Blackwood.

RAVEN, Berney Wodehouse, 63 *Southwark-bridge-road, Southwark, London.*—St John's Coll. Camb. B.A. 1858; Deac. 1860, by Bp of Winch; C. of St Peter's, Southwark, 1860.

RAWDON, William Frederic, *Ardleigh, Colchester, Essex.*—Wadham Coll. Oxon. B.A. 1858, M.A. 1860; Deac. 1860, by Bp of Roch; C. of Ardleigh, 1860.

RAYMOND, Oliver Edward, *Bulmer (Essex), near Sudbury, Suffolk.*—Clare Coll. Camb. B.A. 1849, M.A. 1852; Deac. 1850, Pr. 1851; C. of Bulmer, 1858; formerly C. of Monks-Eleigh, Suffolk.

RAYNES, William, *Witham, Essex.*—Clare Coll. Camb. B.A. 1852, M.A. 1855; Deac. 1854, Pr. 1856, both by Bp of Ely; C. of Witham, 1859; Fell of Clare Coll. Camb.

READ, William, *Ollerton, Notts.*—St Cath. Coll. Camb. B.A. 1844, M.A. 1847; Deac. 1844, Pr. 1845, both by Bp of Linc; C. of Ollerton, 1859; formerly C. of Great Catworth, Hants, 1852-58.

REDIFER, Alfred, *Hurst Pierpoint, Sussex.*—St Mary Ha. Oxon. B.A. 1853, M.A. 1854, Theol. Coll. Wells; Deac. 1853, Pr. 1854; C. of Hurst Pierpoint; late Asst. C. of Daventry, Northants.

REDKNAP, William Henry, *Milton-parsonage, Portsea, Hants.*—Deac. 1850, Pr. 1852, both by Bp of Chich; P.C. of Milton, Dio. Winch. 1859 (Patron, V. of Portsea; P.C.'s Gross Inc. 120*l* and Ho; Pop. 2547); late C. of Portsea; Author, *Advent Lectures.*

REMINGTON, Frederick Hardy, ... —Magd. Coll. Camb. B.A. 1860; Deac. 1860, by Bp of B. and W.

RENAUD, George, *Clandown-parsonage, near Bath.*—Corpus Coll. Oxon. 2nd Cl. Lit. Hum. and B.A. 1834, M.A. 1837; Deac. 1838, Pr. 1839; P.C. of Clandown, Dio. B. and W. 1858 (Patron, V. of Midsomer Norton; P.C.'s Gross Inc. 125*l*; Pop. 1034.)

REW, Charles, *Cranham rectory, Romford, Essex.* —St John's Coll. Oxon. B.A. 1834, M.A. 1838, B.D. 1843; R. of Cranham, Dio. Roch. 1860 (Patron, St John's Coll. Oxon; Tithe—R. 560*l*, Glebe, 36 acres; R.'s Gross Inc. 670*l* and Ho; Pop. 331); late Fell. of St John's Coll. Oxon.

REYNELL, George Carew, 1 *Sheffield-gardens, Kensington, London.*—Trin. Ha. Camb. B.A. 1859; Deac. 1859, Pr. 1860, both by Bp of Lond; C. of St Mary's, Kensington, 1859.

REYNOLDS, Samuel Harvey, *Brasenose College, Oxford.*—Brasen. Coll. Oxon. B.A. 1857, M.A. 1860; Deac. 1860, by Bp of Oxon; Fell. Brasen Coll. Oxon.

REYNOLDS, William Ferris, ... —Magd. Oxon. B.A. 1859; Deac. 1859, Pr. 1860, both by Bp of Lich.

RHODES, Edward James, *Rugby, Warwickshire.*—Pemb. Coll. Oxon. B.A. 1857, M.A. 1859; Deac. 1859, by Bp of Worces; Deac. 1860, by Bp of Lond; Asst. C. of Rugby, 1859.

RICE, Francis William, *Fairford vicarage, Gloucestershire.*—Ch. Ch. Oxon. B.A. 1826, M.A. 1847; Deac. 1828, Pr. 1829, both by Bp of Gloucester; V. of Fairford, Dio. G. and B. 1828 (Patrons, D. and C. of Gloucester; Tithe—V. 395*l*, Glebe, 30 acres; V.'s Gross Inc. 485*l* and Ho; Pop. 1700.)

RICHARDS, John Brinley, *Clifton-road, Shefford, Bedfordshire.*—St Dav. Coll. Lamp. B.D. 1860; Deac. 1849, by Bp of Heref. Pr. 1850, by Bp of St David's; C. of Clifton, Beds, 1860; formerly C. of New Church, Radnor, 1849-53; C. of Gladestry, Radnor, 1853-57; C. of Wareham and Arne, Dorset, 1857-59.

RICHARDS, Joseph, *Shawbury, Shropshire.*— Trin. Coll. Camb. B.A. 1858; Deac. 1859, by Bp of Chest. Pr. 1860, by Bp of Lich; C. of Shawbury, 1860.

RICHARDS, Richard, *High Halden, Tenterden, Kent.*—St Aidan's Theol. Coll; Deac. 1860, by Archbp of Cant; C. of High Halden, 1860.

RICHARDS, Theodore Edward Maurice, *Hastings, Sussex.*—Jesus Coll. Camb. B.A. 1858; Deac. 1859, Pr. 1860, both by Bp of Chich; C. of Holy Trinity, Hastings, 1859.

RICHARDS, William Henry, *Broughton, Preston, Lancashire.*—Jesus Coll. Camb. B.A. 1855; Deac. 1856, by Bp of Salis; C. of St John's, Broughton, 1859; late C. of Knutsford, Cheshire; formerly C. of Bishop Thornton, Yorks.

RICHARDSON, Edmund Augustine, 2, *Warwick-place, Leeds.*—Qu. Coll. Oxon. B.A. 1858; Deac. 1859, by Bp of Rip; Asst. Mast. of Leeds Gram. Sch, and C. of Roundhay, near Leeds.

RICHARDSON, Francis, *Kersal, near Manchester.*—Cai. Coll. Camb. B.A. 1852, M.A. 1855; Deac. 1852, Pr. 1853; C. of Kersal, 1858; formerly C. of Great Budworth, Cheshire, 1852-53; C. of St Thomas's English Episcopal Chapel, Edinburgh, 1854-58.

RICHARDSON, Herbert Henley, *Isle of Cumbrae, Greenock, N.B.*—St Mary's Ha. Oxon. B.A. 1858; Deac. 1859, Pr. 1860, both by Archbp of Cant; Dom. Chap to the Countess Dowager of Glasgow, 1859.

RICHMOND, Thomas Knyvett, *Great Yarmouth.*—Exon. Coll. Oxon. B.A. 1857, M.A. 1859; Deac. 1858, Pr. 1859, both by Bp of Norw; Asst. C. of St Nicholas, Great Yarmouth, and Even. Lect. at St. George's Chapel of Ease, 1859.

RIGG, William, *Kingston-on-Thames.*—Pemb. Coll. Camb. Sch. 1842, B.A. 1844, M.A. 1847; Deac. 1845, Pr. 1847, both by Bp of Peterb; Head Mast. to Queen Elizabeth's Gram. Sch. Kingston-on-Thames, 1848; Aft. Lect. at New Malden, Surrey, 1858; formerly Mast. of Oundle Gram. Sch. Northants, 1844-48; C. of Lutton, near Oundle, 1845-48.

RIGGE, William Postlethwaite, *Peak-forest parsonage, Tideswell, Derbyshire.*—Trin. Coll. Dub. B.A. 1848; Deac. 1848. Pr. 1849; Incumb. of Peak-forest, Dio. Lich. 1859 (Patron, Duke of Devon; Incumb.'s Gross Inc. 130*l* and Ho; Pop. 596); late C. of Lee, Northumberland; formerly C. of Eglingham, Northumberland.

RILEY, Richard, 21 *Clarence-square, Cheltenham.*—St Bees' Theol. Coll; Deac. 1851, by Bp of Chest. Pr. 1852, by Bp of Winch; C. of St Peter's, Cheltenham, 1859; formerly C. of Ashton-in-Makerfield, 1851-52; C. of St Peter's, Southwark, Lond. 1852-54; C. of Mangotsfield, near Bristol, 1854-59; Author of *A Sermon on Thunderstorms,* Cheltenham, 1859.

RIPLEY, William Nottidge, *Earlham, near Norwich.*—Caius Coll. Camb. Wrang. and B.A. 1848, M.A. 1851; Deac. 1849, Pr. 1850; P.C. of St. Giles's, City and Dio. Norw. 1859 (Patrons, D. and C. of Norw; P.C.'s Gross Inc. 80*l*; Pop. 1611); formerly C. of Lowestoft, Suffolk.

RISK, John Erskine, 29 *Oxford-place, Plymouth.* —Trin. Coll. Dub. B.A. 1847, M.A. 1860; Deac. 1853, by Bp of Meath, Pr. 1854, by Bp of Killaloe; Sen. C. of St Andrew's, Plymouth; Author, *King David the Warrior, with Remarks on the Light in which the New Testament regards War* (a Lecture, 1855); *Sermon Notes on the Old and New Year,* 1858.

ROBARTS, Charles Nathaniel, *Newbury, Berkshire.*—Chr. Coll. Camb. B.A. 1858; Deac. 1858; Pr. 1859, both by Bp of Roch; C. of St John the Evangelist, Newbury, 1860; formerly C. of Halstead, Essex, 1858-60.

D

ROBERTS, Charles Ingram, *Swabey, Lincolnshire.*—Deac. 1856, by Bp of Worc; C. of Swabey, 1859; formerly C. of Hill, Warwickshire.

ROBERTS, Charles Manley, *Monmouth.*—St John's Camb. B.A. 1857, M.A. 1860; Deac. 1860, by Bp of Heref; C. of Whitchurch, Herefordshire, 1860; Head Mast. of the Gram. Sch. Monmouth; formerly Second Mast. of Christ Coll. Brecon.

ROBERTS, Gabriel Lloyd, *Cefn-cock, near Ruthin, Denbighshire.*—St John's Coll. Camb. B.A. 1848, M.A. 1847; Deac. 1846, Pr. 1847, both by Bp of Bang; formerly C. of St Asaph.

ROBERTS, James Barry, *Chorlton-cottage, Malpas, Cheshire.*—Trin. Coll. Dub. B.A. 1860; Deac. 1860, by Bp of Chest; C. of Malpas, Lower Mediety, 1860.

ROBERTS, William, *Milton-next-Gravesend, Kent.*—Emman. Coll. Camb. B.A. 1856; Deac. 1856, Pr. 1857, both by Bp of Roch; C. of Holy Trinity, Milton-next-Gravesend, 1856.

ROBERTSON, Patrick Frederick William, *Windsor, near Liverpool.*—Cai. Coll. Camb. B.A. 1859; Deac. 1859, Pr 1860, both by Bp of Chest; C. of St Clement's, Windsor, 1859.

ROBERTSON, William Archibald Scott, *Sutton-Montis, Ilchester, Somerset.*—Chr. Coll. Camb. B.A. 1859; Deac. 1859, Pr. 1860, both by Bp of B. and W; R. of Sutton-Montis, Dio. B. and W. 1860 (Patroness, Mrs Burton Leach; Tithe—R. 152l, Glebe, 37 acres; R.'s Gross Inc. 302l; Pop. 180); formerly C. of Chilthorne Dorner, Somerset, 1859-60.

ROBINSON, Arthur Edward, *Highworth, Wilts.*—New Coll. Oxon. B.A. 1857, M.A. 1860; Deac. 1860, by Bp of Oxon; C. of Highworth w Marston, 1860; Fell. of New Coll. Oxon.

ROBINSON, Edward, *Oswestry, Shropshire.*—Trin. Coll. Dub. B.A. 1858; Deac. 1858, Pr. 1859; Head Mast. of the Deytheur Gram. Sch. Oswestry.

ROBINSON, Frederic Sidney, *The Priory, Leeds.*—St John's Coll. Camb. B.A. 1859; Deac. 1859, Pr. 1860, both by Bp of Rip; C. of the Parish Ch. Leeds, 1859.

ROBINSON, Isaac Banks, *Long Melford, Sudbury, Suffolk.*—Trin. Coll. Camb. B.A. 1823, M.A. 1827; Deac. 1829, Pr. 1830, both by Bp of Norw; V. of Little Waldingfield, Suffolk, Dio. Ely, 1850 (Patroness, Mrs Wilkinson; Tithe—Imp. 245l, V. 164l 14s; Glebe, 1 acre; V.'s Gross Inc. 165l; Pop. 404); Author, *English Homes, an Essay on the Dwellings of the Agricultural Poor,* King, Sudbury; various *Sermons.*

ROBINSON, Leighton, ...—Qu. Coll. Birmingham; Deac. 1860, by Bp of Lich.

ROCHESTER, The Right Rev. Joseph Cotton Wigram, Lord Bishop of Rochester.—77 *Chester-square, London, W.* and *Danbury Palace, Chelmsford, Essex.*—Trin. Coll. Camb. 6th Wrang. and B.A. 1819, M.A. 1822; Deac. 1822, by Bp of Ely, Pr. 1823, by Bp of Lond; Consecrated Bp of Rochester, 1860 (Episcopal Jurisdiction—the City and Deanery of Rochester, the Co. of Hertford, and the Co. of Essex, excepting ten Parishes in the latter; Gross Inc. of See, 5000l; Pop. 577,298; Acres, 1,535,450; Deaneries, 36; Benefices, 564; Curates, 240; Church Sittings, 203,643); his Lordship was formerly Archd. of Winchester, 1847-60; R. of St. Mary's, Southampton, 1851-60; Author, various *Tracts,* and single *Sermons.*

RODD, Frederick Arthur, *High Wycombe, Bucks.*—St Aidan's Theol. Coll; Deac. 1857, Pr. 1858, both by Bp of Chest; C. of High Wycombe, 1860; formerly C. of Hurdsfield, Cheshire, 1857-59; C. of Holbrook, Suffolk, 1859-60.

ROFE, John, *Calcutta, East Indies.*—St. John's Coll. Camb. B.A. 1850, M.A. 1853; Deac. 1852, Pr. 1853, both by Bp of Chest; Chap. at Calcutta, 1859; late C. of Upwell, Cambs.

ROOKE, Thomas, *New Windsor, Berkshire.*—Trin. Coll. Dub. and ad. eund. Ch. Ch. Oxon. B.A. 1848, M.A. 1851; Deac. 1848, Pr. 1849; C. of New Windsor, 1859; formerly C. of Carateel, co. Tyrone, Ireland, 1848-50; C. of Monkstown, co. Dublin, 1850-59; Author, *Biblical Catechist,* 12mo; *Questions on Bible,* 1848; *Address to Monkstown Sunday Schools* in "*Sunday-school Magazine;*" *Farewell Sermon on Leaving Monkstown Parish,* 1859; *Sermon on Psalm* xci. 1, 2, 1859; occasional contributions to *Sunday (Irish) Magazine.*

ROOKER, John, *Runcorn, Cheshire.*—Chr. Coll. Camb. B.A. 1853, M.A. 1856; Deac. 1853, Pr. 1854; P.C. of Trinity Church, Runcorn, Dio. Chest. 1859 (Patrons, John Johnson, Esq. and Thomas Johnson, Esq; P.C.'s Gross Inc. 235l; Pop. 3042); late Sen. C. of St George's, Leeds; formerly C. of St Mary's, Cheltenham; previously C. of The Lye, Stourbridge.

ROSENTHAL, Samuel, *Uppingham, Rutland.*—Ch. Coll. Camb. B.A. 1857; Deac. 1859, Pr. 1860, both by Bp of Peterb; C. of Uppingham, 1859.

ROUCH, Frederick, *The Precincts, Canterbury.*—St John's Coll. Oxon. B.A. 1820, M.A. 1824; Min. Can. of Canterbury Cathl. 1827 (Value, 150l. and Res.); V. of Littlebourn, Kent, Dio. Cant. 1859 (Patrons, D. and C. of Cant; V.'s Gross Inc. 300l and Ho; Pop. 745); formerly V. of Lower Halstow, Kent, 1840-59.

ROUSE, Rolla Charles Meadows, *Christ Church parsonage, Carlisle.*—Trin. Coll. Camb. 10th Wrang. and B.A. 1856, M.A. 1859; Deac. 1856, Pr. 1857, both by Bp of Roch; P.C. of Christ Ch. City and Dio. Carl. 1860 (Patrons, D. and C. of Carl; P.C.'s Gross Inc. 130l and Ho; Pop. 8500); formerly C. of Kendal, and Chap. to Kendal Gaol.

ROWDEN, George Croke, *Chichester.*—New Coll. Oxon. B.C.L. 1842, D.C.L. 1848; Precentor and Preb. of Chich. Cathl. 1859; Chap. to the Royal Society of Musicians; late Fell. of New Coll. Oxon.

ROWE, Richard Marrack, *Queen's College, Birmingham.*—Exon. Coll. Oxon. 3rd Cl. Lit. Hum. and B.A. 1851, M.A. 1854; Deac. 1852, Pr. 1853; Asst. Mast. in the Theol. Department of Qu. Coll. Birmingham; Fell. of Exon.Coll. Oxon.

ROWE, Theophilus Barton, *Grosvenor College, Bath.*—St John's Coll. Camb. Chancellor's Medallist, B.A. 1856, M.A. 1859; Deac. 1859, by Bp of B. and W; Vice-Prin. and Divin. Lect. of Grosvenor Coll. Bath; C. of Bathampton, near Bath, 1859; Fell of St John's Coll. Camb.

ROWLAND, Charles, *Great Witley, Stourport, Worcestershire.*—St John's Coll. Oxon. B.A. 1859, M.A. 1859; Deac. 1859, by Bp of Worc; Pr. 1860, by Bp of Lond; C. of Great Witley, 1859.

ROWLAND, Evan, 34, *Wellington-street, Merthyr Tydfil.*—Literate; Deac. 1860; C. of Merthyr-Tydfil. 1860.

ROWLAND, Lewis Thomas, *Thomas Town, Merthyr Tydfil, Glamorgan.*—St David's Theol. Coll. Lamp; Deac. 1859; C. of St David's, Merthyr Tydfil, 1859.

ROWLEY, Richard, *Pattingham, near Wolverhampton.*—Ch. Ch. Oxon. B.A. 1856, M.A. 1858; Deac. 1859, Pr. 1860; C. of Pattingham, 1860.

ROWSELL, Evan Edward, *Hambledon rectory, Godalming, Surrey.*—St John's Coll. Camb. B.A. 1827, M.A. 1830; Deac. 1827, Pr. 1828, both by Bp of Lond; R. of Hambledon, Dio. Winch. 1859 (Patron, Earl of Radnor; R.'s Gross Inc. 235l and Ho; Pop. 586); late C. of Brinkley, near Newmarket; formerly Fell. of St John's Coll. Camb.

RUDGE, Frederick, *Lawshall, Bury St Edmunds, Suffolk.*—Trin. Coll. Camb. B.A. 1853, M A. 1857; Deac. and Pr. 1854; C. of Stanningfield, Suffolk, 1857.

RUMBOLL, Abraham Henry, *Cambridge.*—Corpus Coll. Camb. B.A. 1857, M.A. 1860; Deac. 1857, Pr. 1858, both by Bp of Ely; C. of Trin. Ch. Cambridge, 1857.

RUMPF, John, *Bluntisham rectory, St Ives, Hunts.*—Trin. Coll. Oxon. B.A 1835, M.A. 1841;

Deac. 1836, by Bp of Linc. Pr. 1837, by Bp of Norw; R. of Bluntisham, Dio. Ely, 1859 (Patron, Bp of Peterb—Tithe, R. 1070*l*, Glebe, 61 acres; R.'s Gross Inc. 1190*l* and Ho; Pop. 1350); late R. of Pakefield, Suffolk, 1856-59; formerly C. of Pakefield and Kirkley, Suffolk, 1837-56.

RUSSELL, Thomas, *Laurel-cottage, Banbury.* —St John's Coll. Oxon. B.A. 1852, M.A. 1854; Deac. 1853, Pr. 1855, both by Bp of Oxon; Mast. of Banbury Gram. Sch. 1860; C. of Drayton, near Banbury, 1860; formerly C. of Shotteswell, Warwickshire.

RYLEY, Edward, *Sarratt vicarage, Rickmansworth, Herts.*—Trin. Coll. Oxon. B.A. 1853, M.A. 1856; Deac. 1853, Pr. 1854; V. of Sarratt, Dio. Roch. 1859 (Patron, J. A. Gordon, Esq; V.'s Gross Inc. 275*l* and Ho; Pop. 613); late C. of Plaxtol, Kent.

RYVES, George Thomas, ...— Brasen. Coll. Oxon. B.A. 1857, M.A. 1859; Deac. 1859, Pr. 1860, both by Bp of Lich.

————♦————

SADLER, Henry, *St James's parsonage, Ratcliff, London.*—Chr. Coll. Camb. B.A. 1847; Deac. 1856, Pr. 1858; C. of St James's, Ratcliff, 1858; formerly Head Mast. of the Malta Protestant Coll. 1855-58.

ST. GEORGE, Leonard Henry, *Hong Kong, China.*—Chap. to the Forces at Hong Kong, 1859; late Asst. Chap. to the Forces, Mauritius; formerly Military Chap. at Parkhurst Depôt; previously C. of Semley, Wilts.

ST HILL, Thomas, *St Pierre, Calais, France.* —Deac. 1848, Pr. 1850; British Chap. at St Pierre, 1858; formerly C. of St Matthew's, Birmingham, 1856-58.

SALE, Charles Hanson, *Kirby-on-the-Moor, Boroughbridge, Yorks.*—Brasen. Coll. Oxon. B.A. 1840, M.A. 1843; Deac. 1842, Pr. 1843, both by Bp of Worc; V. of Kirby-on-the-Moor, Dio. Chest. 1859 (Patron, Ld. Chan; Tithe—App. 72*l*; Imp. 364*l* 15*s*; Glebe, 100 acres; V.'s Gross Inc. 365*l*; Pop. 637); late C. of Newton Regis, Warwickshire, 1842-59.

SALE, Thomas Walker, *Boston, Lincolnshire.* —Wadh. Coll. Oxon. B.A. 1858; Deac. 1859, Pr. 1860, both by Bp of Linc; C. of Boston, 1859.

SALISBURY, Edward, *Leamington.*—Magd. Coll. Camb. Sch. 1849, B.A. 1852, M.A. 1855; Deac. 1856.

SALMON, Edwin Arthur, *Martock vicarage, Somerset.*—Wadh. Coll. Oxon. B.A. 1854, M.A. 1857; Deac. 1855, by Bp of B. and W. Pr. 1856, by Bp of G. and B; V. of Martock w Long Load C. Dio. B. and W. 1859 (Patron, Treasurer of Wells Cathl; Tithe—App. 799*l* 15*s*; Imp. 182*l* 11*s*; V. 316*l*; Glebe, 81 acres; V.'s Gross Inc. 500*l* and Ho; Pop. 2574); late C. of Christian-Malford, Wilts, 1856-59.

SALMON, Henry Wilson, *Oldberrow rectory, Henley-in-Arden, Worcestershire.*—St John's Coll. Camb. B.A. 1812, M.A. 1815; Deac. 1813, Pr. 1814; R. of Oldberrow, Dio. Worc. 1859 (Patron, Rev. S. Peshall; Tithe—R. 208*l*; Glebe, 12 acres; R.'s Gross Inc. 230*l*. and Ho; Pop. 56); late C. of Long Compton, Warwickshire.

SALTER, Edward, *Penzance, Cornwall.*—Literate; Deac. 1852, Pr. 1854, both by Bp of Chest; Chap. to the Borough Gaol, and Head Mast. of the Gram. Sch. Penzance.

SALTER, William Charles, *Balliol College, Oxford.*—Balliol Coll. Oxon. B.A. 1846, M.A. 1851; Deac. 1849, Pr. 1860, both by Bp of Oxon; Fell. of Balliol Coll. Oxon.

SANDERS, Henry Martyn, *Skidby parsonage, Beverley, Yorks.*—Emman. Coll. Camb. Sen. Opt. B.A. 1855, M.A. 1858; Deac. 1856, Pr. 1857, both by Archbp of Cant; P.C. of Skidby, Dio. York, 1860 (Patron, V. of Cottingham; P.C.'s Gross Inc. 105*l* and Ho; Pop. 361); formerly C. of Bexley, Kent, 1856-57

SANDERS, William, *Christ Church, Oxford, and Woodstock, Oxfordshire.*—Magd. Coll. Oxon. B.A. 1856, M.A. 1857; Deac. 1857, Pr. 1858. both by Bp of Oxon; Chap. of Ch. Ch. Cathl. Oxon. 1857; Head Mast. of Woodstock Gram. Sch. Chap. to the Woodstock Union, and C. of Bletchingdon, Oxfordshire, 1860.

SANDWITH, Henry, *Norley, Frodsham, Cheshire.*—St Cath. Coll. Camb. Div. Prizeman, 1849, B.A. 1851; Deac. 1852, by Archbp of York, Pr. 1853, by Bp of Oxon; P.C. of Norley, Dio. Chest. 1859 (Patron, S. Woodhouse, Esq; P.C.'s Gross Inc. 150*l*; Pop. 698); late C. of Harthill, Yorks.

SANGAR, James Mortimer, *Brislington House, near Bristol.*—Caius Coll. Camb. B.A. 1856; Deac. 1856, Pr. 1857, both by Bp of B. and W; Chap. of Brislington House Asylum; late Asst. C. of Shepton-Mallet, Somerset.

SANKEY, William Thompson, *Stony-Stratford parsonage, Bucks.*—Exon. Coll. Oxon. B.A. 1852, M.A. 1854; Deac. 1853, Pr. 1855, both by Bp of Roch; P.C. of Stony-Stratford, Dio. Oxon. 1859 (Patron, Bp of Oxon; P.C.'s Gross Inc. 150*l* and Ho; Pop. 1757); late C. of St Stephen's, near St Albans.

SARJANT, Samuel Crusha, ...— Univ. Glasgow, B.A. 1858; Deac. 1859, Pr. 1860, both by Bp of Norw.

SATTERTHWAITE, Charles James, *Disley, Stockport, Cheshire.*—Jesus Coll. Camb. B.A. 1857, M.A. 1860; Deac. 1858, Pr. 1859, both by Bp of Chest; P.C. of Disley, Dio. Chest. 1859 (Patron, W. J. Legh, Esq; P.C.'s Gross Inc. 117*l*; Pop. 2222).

SAUNDERS, John Goulding, *Stowmarket vicarage, Suffolk.*—V. of Stowmarket w Stowupland V. Dio. Norw. 1859 (Patron, Rev. A. Hollingsworth; Tithe—Stowmarket, Imp. 93*l*, V. 186*l*; Glebe, 5 acres; Stowupland, Imp. 287*l* and 29 acres of Glebe, V. 175*l*; V.'s Gross Inc. 400*l* and Ho; Pop. Stowmarket, 3306, Stowupland, 284); formerly C. of Stowmarket, 1850-59.

SAVELL, William James, *Saltley, near Birmingham.*—St. John's Coll. Camb. B.A. 1858; Deac. 1860, by Bp of Lond; Math. Lect. of Worc. Dio. Training Coll. Saltley.

SAXBY, Stephen Henry, *Monk's-Kirby, Lutterworth, Leicestershire.*—Caius Coll. Camb. B.A. 1855; Deac. 1856, by Bp of Lond; C. of Monk's-Kirby, 1859; Dom. Chap. to the Earl of Carnwath; late C. of Harrow, Middlesex.

SAYER, William Carlisle, *Thaxsted, Chelmsford, Essex.*—Trin. Coll. Camb. B.A. 1859; Deac. 1860, by Bp of Roch; C. of Thaxted, 1860.

SCALE, John, *Woodford, Daventry, Northants.*— St Aidan's Theol. Coll; Deac. 1860, by Bp of Peterb; C. of Woodford-cum-Membris, 1860.

SCARR, Grover, *Caistor, Lincolnshire.*— Bp Cosin's Ha. Dur. B.A. 1860; Deac. 1860, by Bp of Linc; C. of Caistor, 1860.

SCARSDALE, The Right Hon. Alfred Nathaniel Holden Curzon, Baron Scarsdale, *Kedleston Hall, near Derby.*—Merton Coll. Oxon. M.A. 1853; Deac. 1854, Pr. 1855; R. of Kedleston, Dio. Lich. 1856 (Patron, the present R; R.'s Gross Inc. 180*l*; Pop. 105); Patron of Mickleover V. and of Quardon P.C. Derbyshire. and of Worthington P.C. Leicestershire.

SCHOFIELD, James, *Felling, near Gateshead.*— St Bees Theol. Coll; Deac. 1853, Pr. 1854, both by Bp of Chest; C. of Felling, 1858; formerly C. of St Paul, Portwood, Cheshire, 1853-57, C. of St Matthias, Salford, Manchester, 1857-58.

SCHOLFIELD, Charles Richard, *Aldborough Boroughbridge, Yorks.*— Trin. Coll. Camb. B.A. 1855, M.A. 1858; Deac. 1857, Pr. 1858; Incumb. of Low Dunsforth, near Boroughbridge, Dio. Rip. 1859 (Patron, V. of Aldborough; Glebe, 52 acres; Incumb.'s Gross Inc. 62*l*; Pop. 303); formerly C. of Harrowden, Northants, 1857-59.

SCHLOCHOW, Emmanuel Moritz, ... —Literate; Deac. 1860, by Bp of Lond.

SCOTT, John Haigh, *26 Canterbury-street, Liverpool.*—Wadham Coll. Oxon. B.A. 1849, M.A. 1851; Deac. 1850, by Bp of Chest. Pr. 1851, by Bp of Peterb;

Chap. of the Workhouse, Liverpool, 1851; formerly C. of Kirby Muxloe, Leicestershire, 1852-59; Organising Sec. to Additional Curates Soc. for Dio. of Peterb. 1857-59; Author, *Hymns for the Public Worship of the Church*, 1853, 1s 6d.

SCOTT, Richard Folliott, *Fradswell, Stone, Staffs.*—Emman. Coll. Camb. B.A. 1858; Deac. and Pr. 1859, both by Bp of Lich; C. of Fradswell, 1859.

SCOTT, William, *Forest house, Llandovery, Carmarthenshire.*—Worc. Coll. Oxon. B.A. 1855; Deac. 1860, by Bp of St Dav; C. of Cledfwah, Llandilo, 1860.

SCOTT, William Richard, *St Mary Magdalene parsonage, Harlow, Essex.*—Trin. Coll. Dub. Hebrew Prem. B.A. 1847; Deac. 1848, Pr. 1849, both by Bp of Manch; P.C. of St Mary Magdalene, Harlow, Dio. Roch. 1859 (Patron, V. of Harlow; P.C.'s Gross Inc. 120l and Ho.); late C. of Compton-Dando, Somerset; Author, *Apostolic Succession, proved from Holy Scripture and the Tradition of the Church, with especial reference to the Ordinal of the English Church, and Canon LV. in reference to the Church in Scotland,* Masters, 1852, 1s 6d; *Parochial Tracts.*

SCRAGG, William, *Kirk Ireton, Wirksworth, Derbyshire.*—Literate; Deac. 1857, Pr. 1858, both by Bp of Rip; C. of Kirk Ireton, 1860; formerly C. of Sandal Magna, Yorks. 1857-60.

SEALY, William Guidott, *West Hill, Winchester.*—St John's Coll. Camb. B.A. 1823, M.A. 1827; Deac. 1823, Pr. 1824; R. of St Lawrence, City and Dio. Winch. 1857 (Patron, Lord Chan; R.'s Gross Inc. 70l; Pop. 324).

SEDDON, William, *Grantham, Lincolnshire.*—Emman. Coll. Camb. B.A. 1859; Deac. 1859, Pr. 1860, both by Bp of Linc; C. of St John, Spittlegate, Grantham, 1859.

SEGGINS, William Henry, ...—St Cath. Coll. Camb. B.A. 1859; Deac. 1859, Pr. 1860, both by Bp of Lond; C. of Holy Trinity, Newington, Lond. 1859.

SEPPINGS, Dillingham William, *Bridgwater, Somerset.*—Caius Coll. Camb. B.A. 1859; Deac. 1859, Pr. 1860, both by Bp of B. and W; C. of Bridgwater, 1859.

SERJEANTSON, James Jordan, *Stoke-upon-Trent.*—Trin. Coll. Camb. B.A. 1858; Deac. 1859, Pr. 1860; C. of Stoke-upon-Trent.

SEVERNE, William, *Whitstone Priory, near Shrewsbury.*—Qu. Coll. Oxon. B.A. 1828, M.A. 1831; formerly R. of Rochford, Herefordshire, 1854-57.

SEWELL, Thomas Wilder, *Sternfield, Saxmundham, Suffolk.*—Trin. Coll. Camb. B.A. 1856, M.A. 1859; Deac. 1858, Pr. 1859, both by Bp of Ely; C. of Sternfield, 1860; formerly C. of Swineshead, Hunts.

SEWELL, William Henry, *Halstead, Essex.* Trin. Coll. Camb. B.A. 1858; Deac. 1859, by Bp of Roch; C. of Holy Trinity, Halstead, 1859.

SEWELL, William Henry, ... —Trin. Coll. Camb. B.A. 1859; Deac. 1859, Pr. 1860, both by Bp of Roch.

SEYMOUR, William Scorer, ... —King's Coll. Lond. Theol Assoc; Deac. 1860, by Bp of Winch; C. of St Paul's, Southwark, Lond. 1860.

SHARP, Theophilus, *Richmond, Surrey.*—St Cath. Coll Camb. B.A. 1847, M.A. 1851; Deac. 1847, by Bp of Chest. Pr. 1848, by Bp of Manch; Chap. to Hickey's Almshouses, Richmond, 1860; late C. of the Abbey Ch. Bath; formerly Sen. C. of St Martin's, Birmingham.

SHARPE, Robert Napier, *St Mary's parsonage, Rochdale, Lancashire.*—Qu. Coll. Oxon. B.A. 1847, M.A. 1851; Deac. 1849, Pr. 1850, both by Bp. of Chest; P.C. of St Mary's, Rochdale, Dio. Manch. 1857 (Patron, V. of Rochdale; Endowment, 65l; P.C.'s Gross Inc. 100l and Ho; Pop. 10,000); formerly C. of St Mark's, Dukinfield, Cheshire, 1849-52: Sen. C. of Parish Ch. Rochdale, 1852-57.

SHARPE, Thomas Wethererd, *Chapel-Allerton, near Leeds.*—Trin. Coll. Camb. Bell's Univ. Sch. 12th Wrang. 1st Cl. Class. and B.A. 1852; Deac. 1853, Pr. 1854, both by Bp of Ely; Inspector of Schools, 1859; late Fell. of Chr. Coll. Camb. 1852.

SHARPE, William Charles, *St John's College, Cambridge.*—St John's Coll. Camb. Wrang. and B.A. 1837, M.A. 1840, B.D. 1850; V. of All Saints, Cambridge, Dio. Ely, 1856 (Patron, Jesus Coll. Camb; V.'s Gross Inc. 150l; Pop. 1503); Fell. of St John's Coll. Camb.

SHARROCK, James, *Biddulph, Congleton, Cheshire.*—St Bees Theol. Coll; Deac. 1857, Pr. 1858, both by Bp of Lich; C. of Biddulph, 1857.

SHAW, Thomas Head, *12 Soley terrace, Pentonville, London.*—Univ. Coll. Dur. B.A. 1857; Deac. 1858, Pr. 1859, both by Bp of Lich; C. of St James's, Clerkenwell, Lond. 1860; formerly C. of Tamworth, Staffs.

SHAW, Charles, *Waltham, Melton Mowbray, Leicestershire.*—Chr. Coll. Camb. B.A. 1857; Deac. 1858, Pr. 1859, both by Bp of Lond; formerly C. of Christ Ch. Marylebone, Lond. 1858-60.

SHEAN, Harry Shum, *Westbourne (Sussex), near Emsworth, Hants.*—Literate; Deac. 1844; Pr. 1850, both by Bp of Chich; C. of Westbourne, 1860; formerly C. of Westbourne, Sussex, 1844-58; C. of Bolney, Sussex, 1858-60.

SHEFFIELD, John, *The Refuge, Manor House, Dalston, London.*—Late C. of Christ Ch. West Bromwich, Staffs.

SHELDON, Robert William, *Fawley, near Southampton.*—Trin. Coll. Camb. B.A. 1842, M.A. 1845; C. of Fawley.

SHEPHEARD, Henry, *Casterton parsonage, Kirkby Lonsdale, Westmoreland.*—Worc. Coll. Oxon. B.A. 1835, and Oriel Coll. Oxon. M.A. 1838; Deac. 1838, Pr. 1839, both by Bp of Oxon; P.C. of Casterton, Dio. Carl. 1856 (Patrons, Trustees; P.C.'s Gross Inc. 83l and Ho; Pop. 576): late Head Mast. of Cheam Sch. Surrey, 1846-56; formerly V. of Thornton-Steward, Yorks. 1843-46; previously Fell. Dean, and Tut. of Oriel Coll. Oxon. 1836-43.

SHEPHERD, Robert, *Newcastle-upon-Tyne.*—Deac. 1854, Pr. 1854; Chap. of the Newcastle Borough Gaol and House of Correction; formerly C. of All Saints, and Chap. of the Union, Newcastle; Author, *The Succession of the Christian Ministry,* 1858; *An Address on Confirmation,* 1859.

SHEPHERD, Thomas Dowker, *Heywood, Manchester.*—Qu. Coll. Oxon. B.A. 1858; Deac. 1859, Pr. 1860, both by Bp of Manch; C. of St. James, Heywood, 1859.

SHEPHERD, William Bradley, *Walton-le-Dale, Preston, Lancashire.*—Qu. Coll. Oxon. B.A. 1856, M.A. 1859; Deac. 1857, Pr. 1858, both by Bp of Manch; C. of Walton-le-Dale, 1857.

SHEPPARD, Henry Fleetwood, *Kilnhurst parsonage, Rotherham, Yorks.*—Trin. Ha. Camb. B.A. 1855, M.A. 1858; Deac. 1856, Pr. 1857, both by Bp of Chest: Min. of Kilnhurst (Stipend, 125l).

SHERRARD, Hugh, *Stourbridge, Worcestershire.*—Trin. Coll. Dub. B.A. 1850, M.A. 1859; Deac. 1856, by Archbp of Dub; Pr. 1857, by Bp of Worc; P.C. of St Thomas's, Stourbridge, Dio. Worc. 1858 (Patrons, Householders; P.C.'s Gross Inc. 130l; Pop. 4000); formerly C. of St Luke's. Dublin.

SHERWEN, William, *Brayfield, Olney, Bucks.*—Qu. Coll. Oxon. B.A. 1854, M.A. 1860; Deac. 1860, by Bp of Oxon; C. of Brayfield, 1860.

SHIPMAN, Thomas Trafford, *20 Spencer-street, Carlisle.*—St Cath. Coll. Camb. B.A. 1855, M.A. 1859; Deac. 1856, Pr. 1857; R. of Scaleby, near Carlisle, Dio. Carl. 1859 (Patron, Bp of Carl; Tithe—R. 30l; R.'s Gross Inc. 124l; Pop. 600); formerly C. of Barbon, Westmoreland, 1856-58; C. of Christ Ch. Carlisle, 1858-59.

SHIRLEY, Walter Waddington, *Wadham College, Oxford.*—Wadh. Coll. Oxon. B.A. 1851, M.A. 1854; Deac. 1855, Pr. 1859; Tut. of Wadh. Coll; late Fell. of Wadh. Coll; Author, *Fasciculi Zizaniorum Magistri Johannis Wyclif,* edited for H. M. Government, under the direction of the Mast. of the Rolls, 8vo. 1858, 8s. 6d.

SHORLAND, William Henry, *Silton rectory, Wincanton, Dorset.*—Wadh. Coll. Oxon. B.A. 1856, M.A. 1859; Deac. 1857, Pr. 1859, both by Bp of B. and W; R. of Silton, Dio. Salis. 1859 (Patron, Rev. W. J. Percy; Tithe—R. 380*l* 11*s*; Glebe, 64½ acres; R.'s Gross Inc. 464*l* and Ho; Pop. 368); formerly Asst. C. of Drayton and Muchelney, Somerset.

SHORT, Henry Hassard, *York.*—Trin. Ha. Camb. M.A. 1840; Deac. 1835, Pr. 1837, both by Archbp of York; Chap. to York County Hospital; Hon. Chap. to Lord Denman; formerly C. of Christ Ch. Bradford, Yorks. 1835-36; C. of Bury St Edmunds, Suffolk, 1838-45; Incumb. of Bleasdale, Lancaster, 1845-52; Author, *Family Prayers for a Week; On Baptism; On the Churching of Women;* and various other *Tracts.*

SHUTTE, Albert Shadwell, *St Mary's parsonage, Rochdale, Lancashire.*—Clare Coll. Camb. Sch. 1857, B.A.|1859; Deac. 1859,-Pr. 1860, both by Bp of Manch; C. of St Mary's, Rochdale, 1859.

SIDEBOTTOM, Frederick Radclyffe, *Chippenham, Wilts.*—Bp Cos. Ha. Dur. B.A. 1855; Deac. 1856, Pr. 1858, both by Bp of Lich; C. of Chippenham, 1859.

SILVER, Edgar, *Holy Trinity parsonage, West Cowes, Isle of Wight.*—Oriel Coll. Oxon. B.A. 1852, M.A. 1854; Deac. 1853, Pr. 1854, both by Bp of Winch; Incumb. of Holy Trinity, West Cowes, Dio. Winch. 1860 (Patrons, Trustees of the late Mrs. Goodwin; Incumb.'s Gross Inc. 130*l* and Ho; Pop. 1300); formerly C. of Shirley, near Southampton, 1853-55; C. of Bitterne, near Southampton, 1855-60.

SIMPSON, George, *Northbourne vicarage, Deal, Kent.*—Chr. Coll. Camb. B.A. 1830, M.A. 1833; Deac. 1832, Pr. 1833, both by Archbp of Cant; V. of Northbourne, Dio. Cant. 1859 (Patron, Archbp of Cant; V.'s Gross Inc. 190*l* and Ho; Pop. 880); late C. of Sutton-Valence, Kent.

SIMPSON, James, *Shap vicarage, near Penrith, Westmorland.*—Univ. Coll. Dur. Licen. Theol. 1843; Deac. 1843, Pr. 1844; V. of Shap, Dio. Carl. 1857 (Patron, Earl of Lonsdale; V.'s Gross Inc. 95*l* and Ho; Pop. 1009); formerly C. of Morland, near Penrith.

SINDEN, Henry, *Honley, Almondbury, Huddersfield.*—King's Coll. Lond; Deac. 1859, Pr. 1860, both by Bp of Rip; C. of Honley, 1859.

SIRNEV, George, *Ely.*—Univ. Coll. Dur. B.A. 1851, Theol. Licen. 1852, Deac. 1852, Pr. 1853, both by Bp of Dur; Sen. C. of Holy Trinity, Ely, 1858; Author, *single Sermons.*

SLIGHT, John Bullivant, *The College, Brighton.*—St John's Coll. Camb. Sch. 1857, B.A. 1859; Deac. 1859, Pr. 1860, both by Bp of Chich; Asst. Mast. of Brighton Coll.

SMELT, Henry, *Wilcot vicarage, Marlborough, Wilts.*—Jesus Coll. Camb. B.A. 1849, M.A. 1852; Deac. 1849, Pr. 1850; V. of Wilcot *w* Oare C. Dio. Salis. 1856 (Patron, Lieut.-Col. Geo. W. Broughton; V.'s Gross Inc. 176*l* and Ho; Pop. 702).

SMITH, Albert, *King Edward's School, Birmingham.*—Linc. Coll. Oxon. B.A. 1856, M A. 1859; Deac. 1857, Pr. 1858, both by Bp of Worc; Asst. Mast. in King Edw. Sch. Birmingham.

SMITH, Alfred Fowler, *Grammar School house, Thetford, Norfolk.*—Pemb. Coll. Camb. B.A. 1855, M.A. 1858; Deac. 1856, Pr. 1857, both by Bp of Manch; Head Mast. of Thetford Gram. Sch. 1860; Lect. of St Mary's and St Cuthbert's, Thetford, 1860.

SMITH, Christopher, *Preston, Lancashire.*—Literate; Deac. 1859, Pr. 1860, both by Bp of Manch; 2nd Mast. of the Preston Gram. Sch. 1859.

SMITH, Daniel, *Hartshead, Dewsbury, Yorks.*—King's Coll. Lond. B.A. 1849, LL.B. 1850; Deac. 1855, by Bp of Chest. Pr. 1856, by Bp of Carl; C. of Hartshead-cum-Clifton, 1859; formerly C. of the Episcopal Chap. Great Horton, Bradford.

SMITH, Edward Braithwaite, *Gresford, Denbighshire.*—Brasen. Coll. Oxon. B.A. 1851, M.A. 1855; Deac. 1853, Pr. 1854; C. of Gresford, 1858; formerly C. of Huntley, Gloucestershire, 1853-56; C. of Thruxton and Kingstoo, Herefordshire, 1856-58.

SMITH, Edwin Trevelyan, *St Paul's parsonage, Warwick.*—St John's Coll. Camb. Sch. 1838, B.A. 1839, M.A. 1860; Deac. 1841, Pr. 1842; P.C. of St Paul's, Warwick, Dio. Worc. 1849 (Patron, V. of St Mary's, Warwick; P.C.'s Gross Inc. 175*l* and Ho; Pop. 2702); Surrog. for Dio. Worc.

SMITH, Frederick Jeremiah, *Wells, Somerset.*—Balliol Coll. Oxon. B.A. 1830, M.A. 1836; Preb. of Whitchurch in Wells Cathl. 1848; Surrog. for the Dio. of B. and W; formerly P.C. of Holy Trinity, Taunton, and Chap. of the Taunton Union, 1842-56.

SMITH, Henry Fielding, *Lancaster.*—Pemb. Coll. Camb. B.A. 1852; Deac. 1853, Pr. 1854, both by Bp of Manch; Chap. of Lancaster Castle, 1858; formerly Min. of Dolphinholme, Lancashire, 1853-57.

SMITH, Herbert Clementi, *Shrewsbury.*—St John's Coll. Camb. B.A. 1859; Deac. 1859, Pr. 1860, both by Bp of Lich; Chap. and Asst. Mast. of the Gram. Sch. Shrewsbury, 1859.

SMITH, Isaac, *Bridge, near Canterbury.*—Ch. Miss. Coll. Islington; Deac. 1843, Pr. 1844, both by Bp of Lond; C. of Patrixbourne *w* Bridge, 1859; formerly Miss. to Sierra Leone and Abbeokutu, Africa.

SMITH, James Newland, *Carshalton, Surrey.*—St John's Coll. Camb. B.A. 1851, M.A. 1854; Deac. 1858, Pr. 1859, both by Bp of Oxon; Head Mast. and Chap. of St Edmund's Proprietary Coll. Carshalton, 1859; formerly Asst. C. of Reading, Berks, 1858-59.

SMITH, John Boys, *Warsaw, Russia.*—Trin. Coll. Camb. B.A. 1848; Deac. 1848, Pr. 1849; British Chap. at Warsaw, 1857; formerly C. of Tenby, Pembrokeshire, 1848-57.

SMITH, Joseph, *3 Osborne villas, Lansdowne, Cheltenham.*—Trin. Coll. Oxon. B.A. 1815, M.A. 1818, B.D. 1827; Deac. 1818, by Bp of Glouc. Pr. 1825, by Bp of Oxon; late R. of Rotherfield Greys, near Henley-on-Thames, 1851-60.

SMITH, Kenelm Henry, ...—St John's Coll. Camb. B.A. 1860, Deac. 1860, both by Bp of B. and W.

SMITH, Thomas Ayscough, *Tenbury vicarage, Worcestershire.*—Trin. Coll. Camb. B.A. 1853, M.A. 1856; Deac. and Pr. 1854, both by Archbp of York; V. of Tenbury, Dio. Worc. 1860 (Patron, Ayscough, Smith, Esq. Leesthorpe, near Melton Mowbray; Tithe—Imp. 511*l* 14*s* 5*d*; V. 744*l* 13*s*; V.'s Gross Inc. 750*l* and Ho; Pop. 1700); formerly C. of All Saints, Loughborough, Leicestershire, 1857-60; C. of Skipsea, Yorkshire, 1854-57.

SMITH, William, *2 Salutary Mount, Heavitree, Exeter.*—Jesus Coll. Camb. B.A. 1855; Deac. 1859, Pr. 1860; Asst. C. of Heavitree, 1859.

SMITH, William Saumarez, *Trinity College, Cambridge.*—Trin. Coll. Camb. B.A. 1858, Carus Greek Testament Prize and Scholefield Prize, 1859, M.A. 1860; Deac. 1859, Pr. 1860, both by Bp of Ely; Asst. C. of St Paul's Cambridge, 1859; Fell. of Trin. Coll. Camb. 1860.

SMYTH, Thomas Cartwright, *Wrestlingworth rectory, Potton, Bedfordshire.*—St Cath. Coll. Camb. Skirne Sch. B.A. 1843, M.A. 1846; Deac. and Pr. 1844, both by Bp of Dur; Chap. in H. M. East India Service, Bengal Establishment (Chap.'s Gross Inc. 960*l*); Author, *Freemasonry Represented and Misrepresented;* various *Masonic Tracts* and *Sermons.*

SMYTH, Vere Broughton, *30 Addison-road, Kensington, London.*—Trin. Coll. Camb. B.A. 1856, M.A. 1859; Deac. 1857, Pr. 1858, both by Bp of Lond; C. of St Barnabas, Kensington, 1857.

SMYTHIES, Edward, *Hathern rectory, Loughborough, Leicestershire.*—Emman. Coll. Camb. Prize Essay, 1840, Jun. Opt. and B.A. 1842; Deac. 1843, Pr. 1844; R. of Hathern, Dio. Peterb. 1859 (Patron, C. M. Phillips, Esq; R.'s Gross Inc. 400*l* and Ho; Pop. 1187); late C. of Hathern, Leicestershire.

SNAPE, Robert William, *St Mary's vicarage, Kensington, London.*—St John's Coll. Camb. B.A. 1859; Deac. 1860, by Bp of Lond; C. of St Mary Abbotts, Kensington, Lond. 1860.

SNEATH, Thomas Aikin, 7 *St Catherine's-terrace, Guildford, Surrey*—Gon. and Cai. Coll. Camb. B.A. 1858; Deac. 1858, Pr. 1859, both by Bp of Winch; C. of St Nicholas, Guildford, 1858.

SNELL, Alfred, *Wanstead, Essex.*—Trin. Coll. Camb. B A. 1857, M.A. 1860; Deac. 1859, Pr. 1860, both by Bp of Lond; C. of Wanstead, 1859.

SNOW, Herbert, *Eton College, Windsor.*—St John's Coll. Camb. Porson Sch. Browne's Medal, and Camden Medal, B.A. 1857, M.A. 1860; Deac. 1859, Asst. Mast. at Eton Coll.

SNOWDEN, Edmund, *Huddersfield, Yorks.*—Univ. Coll. Oxon. B.A. 1854; P.C. of St. Thomas, Huddersfield, Dio. Rip. 1859 (Patroness, Mrs. Starkey; P.C.'s Gross Inc. 170*l*); formerly C. of St George's, Hulme, near Manchester.

SNOWDEN, John, 4 *Lower Belgrave-street, Pimlico, London.*—Univ. Coll. Oxon. B.A. 1851, M.A. 1853; C. of St. Peter's, Pimlico, Lond. 1856.

SNOWDON, John, *Ilkley vicarage, Otley, Yorks.*—St. John's Coll. Camb. B.A. 1828, M.A. 1836; Deac. 1829, by Bp of Dur. Pr 1830, by Bp of Bristol; V. of Ilkley, Dio. Rip. 1842 (Patron, L. L. Hartley, Esq: Tithe—V. 275*l*; Glebe, ¾ acre; V.'s Gross Inc. 320*l* and Ho; Pop. 1202); Head Mast. of Ilkley Free Sch; formerly C. of Lockburn, Durham, 1829-31; C. of Grindon, Durham, 1831-33; C. of Crosby-Garrett, 1833-34; C. of Stockton-on-Tees, 1834-36; C. of Greatham, Durham, 1836-40; C. of Middleton-Tyas, Yorks. 1840-42.

SODEN, John Jordan, 3 *Quadrant, Coventry.*—Emman. Coll. Camb. B.A. 1854, M.A. 1857; Deac. 1855, Pr. 1856, both by Bp of Worc; 2nd Mast. of the Gram. Sch. Coventry; formerly C. of Stivichall, Warwickshire.

SOMERSET, Boscawen Thomas George Henry, *Chipping Campden, Gloucestershire.*—Oriel Coll. Oxon. B.A. 1856, M.A. 1858; Deac. 1858, Pr. 1859, both by Bp of G. and B; C. of Chipping Campden.

SOMERVILLE, Dudley, *Shorncliffe, Folkstone, Kent.*—Qu. Coll. Camb. Wrang. and B.A. 1846, M.A. 1847; Deac. 1844, Pr. 1845; Chap. to the Forces, Shorncliffe, 1859; late Asst. Chap. to the Forces, Malta; formerly Chap. to H.M. Army in the East; previously Fell. of Qu. Coll. Camb.

SOUTH, Richard, *Wellgate, Rotherham, Yorks.*—Trin. Coll. Oxon. B.A. 1859; Deac. 1860, by Bp of Rip; C. of Rotherham, 1860.

SPENCER, Almeric Churchill, *Earl-Sterndale parsonage, Bakewell, Derbyshire.*—Deac. 1857, Pr. 1858, both by Archbp of York; P.C. of Earl-Sterndale, Dio. Lich. 1859 (Patron, Duke of Devonshire; P.C.'s Gross Inc. 150*l*. and Ho; Pop. 307).

SPENCER, The Right Rev. George John Trevor, *Edge-Moor, Buxton, Derbyshire.*—Univ. Coll. Oxon. B.A. 1822, D.D. 1847; Deac. 1823, by Bp of Linc; Pr. 1824, by Bp of Salis; Chan. of St Paul's Cath. Lond. 1860; formerly Bp of Madras, 1837-49; P.C. of Buxton, Derbyshire, 1824-29; R. of Leaden-Roothing, Essex, 1829-37; Author, *Journal of a Visitation to the Provinces of Travancore and Tinnevelly, in the Diocese of Madras*, 1840-41, 12mo. Lond. 1842; various *Sermons* and *Charges.*

SPENCER, Henry, *Field Dalling, Holt, Norfolk.*—St Bees Theol. Coll. 1841; Deac. 1845, Pr. 1846, both by Bp of Norw; V. of Field Dalling, Dio. Norw. 1859 (Patron, R. K. Cobbold, Esq; P.C.'s Gross Inc. 150*l*; Pop. 404); late C. of Ilketshall St Andrews; formerly C. of Bagthorpe, Norfolk.

SPENCER, John Scott Ellis, *Honley, near Huddersfield.*—Trin. Coll. Dub. B.A. 1858; Deac. 1858, Pr. 1859, both by Bp of Rip; C. of Honley, 1858.

SPENCER, Leigh, *Renhold vicarage, near Bedford*—Chr. Coll. Camb. B.A. 1839, M A. 1845; V. of Renhold, Dio. Ely, 1859 (Patron, F. C. Polhill Turner, Esq; V.'s Gross Inc. 150*l* and Ho; Pop. 484); formerly P.C. of Little Linford, near Newport-Pagnel, Bucks, 1852-59.

SPOONER, Edward, *Heston vicarage, Hounslow, Middlesex.*—Exon. Coll. Oxon. B.A. 1843, M.A. 1847; Deac. 1846, Pr. 1847, both by Bp of Lich; V. of Heston,

Dio. Lond. 1859 (Patron, Bp of Lond; V.'s Gross Inc. 690*l* and Ho; Pop. 2844); late Incumb. of Holy Trinity, Haverstock-hill, Lond. 1858-59; formerly C. of Elmdon, Essex.

SPOOR, Robert Boyce, *Chirbury, Shropshire.*—C. of Chirbury.

SPOOR, William, *Penshaw rectory, Durham.*—Deac. 1859, Pr. 1860, both by Bp of Dur; C. of Penshaw, 1859.

SPRAGUE, William Saville, *Luton, Beds.*—Clare Coll. Camb. B.A. 1858; Deac. 1859, Pr. 1860, both by Bp of Ely; C. of Luton, 1859.

SPURGEON, John Norris, ...—Corpus Coll. Camb. B.A. 1859; Deac. 1859, Pr. 1860, both by Bp of Norw.

SPURRIER, Horatio, *Sleaford, Lincolnshire.*—Oriel Coll. Oxon. B.A. 1858; Deac. 1858, Pr. 1859; C. of Sleaford, 1858; Author, *Light in Darkness*, J. H. Parker, Oxford, 1*s.*

STAINFORTH, Frederick, 4 *Wycombe-terrace, Hornsey-road, Lond.*—Qu. Coll. Camb. B.A. 1857; Deac. 1858, Pr. 1859; C. of St Barnabas, Holloway, Lond. 1860; formerly C. of Spring Grove, Heston, Middlesex, 1858-60.

STAMMERS, Frederick Halliley, *Cleator, Cumberland.*—Qu. Coll. Oxon. B.A. 1859; Deac. 1859, Pr. 1860; C. of Cleator, 1859.

STANDEN, William, *East Worldham, Alton, Hants.*—Emman. Coll. Camb. B.A. 1851, M.A. 1854; Deac. 1852, Pr. 1856, both by Bp of Salis; C. of East Worldham, and Chap. to the Alton Union, 1859; formerly V. of Tarrant Monkton *or* Tarrant Launceston, Dorset, 1855-58.

STANIFORTH, Thomas, *Storr's Hall, Windermere, Westmoreland.*—Ch. Ch. Oxon. B.A. 1830, A.M. 1833; Deac. 1830, Pr. 1831, both by Archbp of York; formerly R. of Bolton-by-Bolland, Yorks. 1831-59.

STANLEY, Robert Rainy Pennington, *Felstead vicarage, Chelmsford, Essex.*—Emman. Coll. Camb. B.A. 1848, M.A. 1851; Deac. 1849, Pr. 1850, both by Bp of Lond; V. of Felstead, Dio. Roch. 1859 (Patron, Earl of Mornington; Tithe—Imp. 1265*l*, V. 636*l*; V.'s Gross Inc. 700*l* and Ho; Pop. 1715); formerly C. of Banstead, Surrey.

STANTON, Joseph John, *Taunton, Somerset.*—St John's Coll. Oxon. B.A. 1856, M.A. 1858; Deac. 1859, Pr. 1860; C. of Holy Trinity, Taunton, 1859.

STANTON, Vincent John, ...—St John's Coll. Camb. B.A. 1842, M.A. 1850; Deac. 1842, Pr. 1843, both by Bp of Lond.; formerly Colonial Chap. at Hong Kong, 1843-51; Incumb. of Southgate, Middlesex, 1851-55; Author, *Jesus First and Last*, Wertheim, 6*d.*

STAPLETON, Eliot Henry, *Mereworth, Maidstone, Kent.*—Ch. Ch. Oxon. B.A. 1859; Deac. 1859, Pr. 1860, both by Archbp of Cant; C. of Mereworth, 1859.

STAPLETON, Frederick George, *Eversley, Winchfield, Hants.*—Trin. Ha. Camb. B.A. 1859; Deac. 1860, by Bp of Winch; C. of Eversley, 1860.

STARKEY, Arthur Brydon, Cross, *St John's College, Oxford*—St John's Coll. Oxon. 2nd Cl. Lit. Hum. and B.A. 1839, M.A. 1843, B.D. 1848; Deac. 1840, Pr. 1841, both by Bp of Oxon; R. of Bygrave, Herts, Dio. Roch. 1858 (Patron, Marquis of Salisbury; R.'s Gross Inc. 400*l*; Pop. 221); formerly P.C. of Northmoor, Oxfordshire, 1855-58; Fell. of St John's Coll. Oxon.

STARRATT, Moses, *Alton, Cheadle, Staffs.*—Trin. Coll. Dub. B.A. 1824, M.A. 1827; Deac. and Pr. 1830; P.C. of Cotton, near Cheadle, Dio. Lich. 1855 (Patron, Duke of Norfolk; P.C.'s Gross Inc. 44*l* 10*s*; Pop. 502); formerly C. of Eaton-Locon, Beds, 1837-40; Asst. C. of St Martin's, Birmingham, 1840-43; C. of Alton, Staffs. 1843-55.

STAYNER, Thomas Lawrence, *Newbold, Ashby-de-la-Zouch, Leicestershire.*—Trin. Coll. Camb. B.A. 1859; Deac. 1860, by Bp of Peterb; C. of Worthington, near Ashby-de-la-Zouch, 1860.

STEERE, Edward, *Little Steeping, Spilsby, Lincolnshire.*—Univ. of Lond. B.A. 1847, LL.B. 1848, LL.D. 1850; Deac. 1856, by Bp of Exon. Pr. 1858, by Bp of Linc; R. of Little Steeping, Dio. Linc 1859 (Patron,

Lord Willoughby d'Eresby; R.'s Gross Inc. 200*l*; Pop. 326) ; late C. of Skegness, Linc ; formerly C. of King's-Kerswell, Devon; Author, *An Essay on the Being of God*, 8vo. Bell and Daldy, 1856; *Some Unpublished Remains of Bp Butler*, 8vo. Rivingtons, 1853 ; *An Historical Sketch of the English Brotherhoods which existed at the beginning of the Eighteenth Century*, 24mo. Masters, 1856; Editor of an Edition of "Butler's Analogy," 8vo. Bell and Daldy, 1857.

STEEL, John, *Welby, Grantham, Lincolnshire.*—Balliol Coll. Oxon. B.A. 1859; Deac. 1860, by Bp of Linc; C. of Welby, 1860.

STEELE, George, *Bladon, Woodstock, Oxfordshire.*—Worc. Coll. Oxon. B.A. 1857, M.A. 1858; Deac. 1857, Pr. 1858; C. of Bladon, 1857 ; Chap. at Blenheim Palace, Woodstock, 1859.

STEPHENS, Lawrence Johnstone, *Howick, Alnwick, Northumberland*—Caius Coll Camb. B.A. 1851, M A. 1855 ; Deac. 1852, Pr. 1853, both by Bp of Worc ; C. of Howick, 1859 ; late C. of Lesbury, Northumberland; formerly C. of Shawbury, Shropshire.

STEVENS, Thomas, *Hathersage vicarage, Bakewell, Derbyshire.*—V. of Hathersage, Dio. Lich. 1859 (Patron, Duke of Devonhire; V.'s Gross Inc. 145*l* and Ho; Pop. 1376).

STILES, George Edward Carter, *The Abbey, Daventry, Northants.*—St Edm. Ha. Oxon B.A. 1859 ; Deac. 1859, Pr. 1860, both by Bp of Peterb; C. of Daventry, 1859.

STILLINGFLEET, Henry James William, *Clehonger, Hereford.*—Brasen. Coll. Oxon. B.A. 1848, M.A. 1850 ; Deac. 1851, Pr. 1853, both by Bp of Oxon; C. of Clehonger, 1859.

STOCK, John Russell, 1 *South Grove, Mildmay-park, Islington, London.*—St. John's Coll. Camb. 1839, B.A. 1841, M.A. 1844; Deac. 1841, Pr. 1842; R. of Allhallows the Great *w* Allhallows the Less, City and Dio. Lond. 1860 (Patron, Archbp of Cant ; R.'s Gross Inc. 550*l*; Pop. 900); formerly V. of Finchfield, Essex, 1853–60; Author. occasional *Sermons* and *Lectures.*

STOCKDALE, Jeremiah, *Baslow parsonage, Bakewell, Derbyshire.*—St. Cath. Ha. Camb. Jun. Opt. and B.A. 1853 ; Deac. 1853, Pr. 1854; P.C. of Baslow, Dio. Lich. 1859 (Patron, Duke of Devonshire ; P.C.'s Gross Inc. 140*l* and Ho ; Pop. 2400); formerly C. of St George's, Birmingham, 1853–59.

STOCKER, Edward Seymour, *Titchwell rectory, Lynn, Norfolk.*—Univ. Coll. Dur. B.A. 1850, M.A. 1851; Deac. 1852, Pr. 1853, both by Bp of Oxon; R. of Titchwell, Dio. Norw. 1859 (Patron, Eton Coll; Tithe—R. 408*l*; Glebe, 17 acres; R.'s Gross Inc. 450*l* and Ho; Pop. 146); late Asst. Chap. to the English Congregation at Rome, 1854–59; formerly Fell. of Univ. of Dur.

STOKES, George, *North Leigh rectory, Honiton, Devon.*—Trin. Ha. Camb. LL.B. 1817 ; Deac. 1818, Pr. 1819, both by Bp of Norw ; R. of North Leigh, Dio Exon. 1859 (Patrons, D. and C. of Exon; Tithe—V. 169*l* 12*s*; Glebe, 45 acres; V.'s Gross Inc. 250*l* and Ho; Pop. 290); late V. of St Mary Magdalene, Taunton, 1858–59; formerly Chap. to the Wolverhampton Union, 1840–58; Author, *Poem* on the Death of the Princess Charlotte of Wales, 1817 ; *Syllabuses on Modern and English History.*

STOKOE, Thomas Henry, *Uppingham, Rutland.*—Linc. Coll. Oxon, B.A. 1855, M.A. 1857 ; Deac. 1857, Pr. 1858, both by Archbp of York; Asst. Mast. in Uppingham Sch ; formerly Theol. Tut. in Qu. Coll. Birmingham ; Author, *On the Use and Abuse of the Proverb "Charity Begins at Home"* (Denyer Theol. Essay), J. H. Parker, Oxford.

STONE, Edward Daniel, *Eton College, near Windsor.*—King's Coll. Camb. B.A. 1856, M.A. 1859 ; Deac. 1860, by Bp of Oxon; Asst. Mast. at Eton Coll ; Fell. of King's Coll. Camb.

STONEY, Edward Sadleir, *Lytham, Lancashire.*—Trin. Coll. Dub. B.A. 1854, M.A. 1857 ; *ad eund.* Oxon. M.A. 1859 ; Deac. 1855, Pr. 1856, both by Bp of Cashel ; C. of St John's, Lytham, 1857.

STONEY, Robert Baker, *Bloxwich, Walsall, Staffordshire.*—Trin. Coll. Dub; Deac. 1851, by Bp of Tuam, Pr. 1852, by Bp of Meath ; C. of Bloxwich ; Author, *Church Music, in Tonic Solfa Type.*

STOTT, John, *Branch-road, Blackburn.*—St Bees Theol. Coll ; Deac. 1859, Pr. 1860 ; C. of St Paul's, Blackburn, 1859.

STOWELL, Hugh Ashworth, *Christ Church parsonage, Maughold, Isle of Man.*—Brasen. Coll. Oxon. B.A. 1852, M.A. 1855 ; Deac. 1853, Pr. 1854, both by Archbp of Cant ; P.C. of Christ Ch. Maughold, Dio. S. and M. 1858 (Patrons, Trustees ; Glebe, 3 acres ; P.C.'s Gross Inc. 90*l* and Ho ; Pop. 600); formerly C. of Luddenham, Kent, 1853–57.

STOWELL, Thomas Alfred, *Bradford, Yorks.*—Qu. Coll. Oxon. B.A. 1855, M.A. 1856 ; Deac. 1857, Pr. 1858, both by Bp of Rip ; P.C. of St Stephen's, Bowling, Bradford, Dio. Rip. 1860 (Patron, Chas. Hardy, Esq ; P.C.'s Gross Inc. 100*l* ; Pop. 2000); formerly C. of Bolton, Calverley, Yorks. 1858–60.

STRAFFEN, George Martin, *The Minster-yard, York.*—Chr. Coll. Camb. B.A. 1855, M.A. 1859 ; Deac. 1859, Pr. 1860, both by Archbp of York; C. of St Michael-le-Belfrey, York, 1859.

STRATTON, Freeman Richard, *Romsey, Hants.*—Trin. Coll. Camb. B.A. 1851, M.A. 1856 ; Deac. 1851, Pr. 1853, both by Bp of Winch ; C. of Romsey, 1860.

STREATFIELD, Newton William, *Speldhurst, near Tunbridge Wells.*—Chr Ch. Oxon. B.A. 1850, M.A. 1855 ; Deac. 1854, Pr. 1856, both by Archbp of Cant ; C. of Speldhurst, 1860 ; formerly C. of Chiddingstone, Kent, 1854–58 ; C. of Candover, Hants, 1858–60.

STREETER, George Thomas Piper, 2, *Eaton-grove, Dacre-park, Plumstead, Kent.*—Clare Coll. Camb. B.A. 1856 ; Deac. 1857, Pr. 1858, both by Bp of Lond; C. of Plumstead, 1857 ; Asst. Mast. of the Blackheath Proprietary School, Kent ; Author, *Hints to Candidates for the English Civil Service*, 8vo. Stanford, 1858.

STUART, Alexander George, *Raphoe, co. Donegal, Ireland.*—Trin. Coll. Dub. B.A. 1857 ; Deac. 1860 ; C. of Raphoe, 1860 ; Stipend, 80*l*; Min. Can. of Raphoe Cathl.

STUART, James Orchard, *Sulby, Ramsey, Isle of Man.*—Corpus Coll. Camb. S.C.L. 1851 ; Deac. 1859, by Bp of S. and M ; P.C. of St Stephen's, Sulby, Dio. S. and M. 1859 (Patron, Bp of S. and M ; P.C.'s Gross Inc. 80*l* and Ho; Pop. 1500).

STUBBS, Elias Thackeray, *The Deanery, Raphoe, co. Donegal, Ireland.*—Trin. Coll. Dub. B.A. 1849 ; Deac. 1850, Pr. 1851, both by Archbp of Dub ; P.C. of Raphoe, Dio. Raphoe, 1858 (Patron, Dean of Raphoe ; P.C.'s Gross Inc. 110*l*; Pop. 1007) ; Min. Can. of Raphoe Cathl; Dom. Chap. to the Earl of Castle Stuart.

STUBBS, Warden Flood, *Rocester parsonage (Staffs), near Ashbourne, Derbyshire.*—Trin. Coll. Dub. B.A. 1852 ; Deac. 1853, Pr. 1855 ; P.C. of Rocester, Dio. Lich. 1857 (Patron, W. H. Bainbridge, Esq, Woodseat; P.C.'s Gross Inc. 160*l*. and Ho ; Pop. 1100) ; formerly C. of Rossdroit, co. Wexford, Ireland, 1853–55 ; C. of Ballinasloe, Ireland.1855–57.

STURMAN, Mark Cephas Tutel, 7 *Neckinger-terrace, Lower-road, Bermondsey, London.*—Univ. and King's Coll. Lond. B.A. 1855, A.K.C. 1857 ; Deac. 1857, Pr. 1858, both by Bp of Lond ; C. of St James's, Bermondsey, 1860; late C. of St Simon Zelotes, Bethnal-green, Lond.

STURTON, Jacob, *Ramsbury, Wilts.*—Trin. Coll. Oxon. B.A. 1856, M.A. 1857 ; Deac. 1858, Pr. 1859, both by Bp of Salis ; C. of Ramsbury, 1858.

SUMMERHAYES, Julius, *Ealing, Middlesex.*—Qu. Coll. Camb. B.A. 1859 ; Deac. 1859, Pr. 1860, both by Bp of Lond ; C. of Ealing, 1859.

SUMMERS, Edgar, *Bury St Edmunds, Suffolk.*—Trin. Coll. Camb. B.A. 1857, Scholefield Prizeman 1858, M.A. 1860 ; Deac. 1860, by Bp of Ely ; 2nd Mast. of King Edw. Gram. Sch. Bury St Edmunds.

SUMNER, John Henry Robertson, *Lambeth Palace, London, and Bishopsbourne rectory, near Canterbury.*—Univ. Coll. Dur. B.A. 1843, M.A. 1846; Deac. 1846, by Bp of Dur. Pr. 1847, by Bp of Rip; Dom. Chap. to Archbp of Cant. 1850; R. of Bishopsbourne, Dio. Cant. 1859 (Patron, Archbp of Cant; Tithe—R. 500*l*, Glebe, 1 acre; R.'s Gross Inc. 780*l* and Ho; Pop. 341); late Fell. of Univ. Coll. Dur.

SUMNER, Joseph, 66 *Lamb's Conduit-street, Russell-square, London.*—Bp Hat. Ha. Dur. Theol. Licen. 1856; Deac. 1856, Pr. 1857, both by Bp of Manch; C. of St George the Martyr, Queen-square, Bloomsbury, Lond. 1860.

SUMNER, Oliver, *Milborne Port, Sherborne, Somerset.*—Bp Hat. Ha. Dur. 1851; C. of Milborne Port, 1859; late C. of St Stephen's, Lansdowne, Bath; formerly C. of Bugthorpe, Yorks.

SUTCLIFFE, James Crabtree, *Stapleton, near Bristol.*—Bp Hat. Ha. Dur; Deac. 1859, Pr. 1860, both by Bp of G. and B; C. of Stapleton, 1859.

SUTHERLAND, Charles, 15 *Pembroke-road, Kensington, London.*—Trin. Coll. Camb. B.A. 1856, M.A. 1859; Deac. 1859, Pr. 1860, both by Bp of Lond; Jun. C. of St Philip's, Earl's Court, Kensington, Lond. 1859.

SUTTON, Robert, *Bilsthorpe rectory, Ollerton, Notts.*—Trin. Coll. Camb. B.A. 1835, M.A. 1838; Deac. 1837, by Archbp of York, Pr. 1838, by Bp of Linc; R. of Bilsthorpe, Dio. Linc. 1858 (Patron, Henry Savile, Esq. Rufford Abbey; Tithe—R. 372*l*; Glebe 75 acres; R.'s Gross Inc. 450*l* and Ho; Pop. 220); formerly C. of Averham *w* Kelham, Notts, 1837-44; R. of Averham *w* Kelham, 1844-52.

SUTTON, Thomas, *Sunk-island, near Hull.*—Emman. Coll. Camb. B.A. 1836; Deac. 1836, Pr. 1837; P.C. of Sunk-Island, Dio. York, 1858 (Patron, Ld. Chan; P.C.'s Gross Inc. 250*l*; Pop. 400); formerly Chap. of York Castle, 1842-58.

SWALLOW, Francis Richard, *Hepworth, Kirkburton, Yorkshire.*—St. Aidan's Coll; Deac. and Pr. 1856, both by Bp of S. and M; C. of Hepworth, 1859; formerly P.C. of Foxdale, Isle of Man, 1856-58.

SWANN, Johnson Fowell, *East Donyland, Colchester, Essex.*—Caius Coll. Camb. B.A. 1859; Deac. 1860, by Bp of Roch; C. of East Donyland, 1860.

SWAYNE, William John, *Downton, near Sclisbury.*—Ch. Ch. Oxon B.A. 1854, M.A. 1857; Deac. 1858, Pr. 1859, both by Bp of Salis; C. of Downton.

SWEATMAN, Arthur, 18 *Lonsdale square, Islington, London.*—Chr. Coll. Camb. B.A. 1859; Deac. 1859, Pr. 1860, both by Bp of Lond; C. of Holy Trinity, Islington, Lond. 1859.

SWINBURNE, Frederick Thomas, *Yardley, Worcestershire.*—Trin. Coll. Dub. B.A. 1856, M.A. 1859; Deac. 1857, Pr. 1858, both by Bp of Worc; C. of Yardley, 1857; Head Mast. of the Free Sch. Hall Green, Yardley; Author, *A School and What it should be,* Groombridge and Co. 1857.

SYKES, Edward John, *Basildon vicarage, Reading, Berks.*—Worc. Coll. Oxon. B.A. 1851, M.A. 1854; Deac. 1852, Pr. 1853; V. of Basildon, Dio. Oxon. 1859 (Patrons, Rev. W. Sykes and Simeon's Trustees; V.'s Gross Inc. 220*l*. and Ho; Pop. 798); late C. of Timberscombe, Somerset.

TANCRED, William, *Kilmersdon, near Bath.*—Ch. Ch. Oxon. 2nd Cl. Lit. Hum B.A. 1841, M.A. 1845; Deac. 1842, Pr. 1843, both by Bp of Winch; V. of Kilmersdon, Dio. B. and W. 1859 (Patron, Ld. Chan; V.'s Gross Inc. 245*l* and Ho; Pop. 824); late C. of St Martion, Dorking, Surrey; formerly Colonial Chap. and Archd. of Launceston, Tasmania.

TANDY, Charles Henry, *Roxeth villas, Harrow, Middlesex.*—Trin. Coll. Dub. B.A. 1858; Deac. 1859, Pr. 1860, both by Bp of Lond; C. of Pinner, Middlesex, 1859.

TANNER, William, *Wittersham, Staplehurst, Kent.*—St Peter's Coll. Camb. LL.B. 1859; Deac. 1859, by Bp. of Worc. Pr. 1860, by Archbp of Cant; C. of Wittersham, 1860.

TAPSFIELD, Edward, *St John's School, Hurstpierpoint, Sussex.*—Bp Hat. Ha. Dur. Theol. Licen. 1860; Deac. 1860, by Bp of Chich.

TARLTON, Thomas Henry, *Glebe house, Stroud, Gloucestershire.*—Gon. and Cai. Coll. Camb; Deac. and Pr. 1858; Incumb. of Stroud w. Holy Trinity C. Dio. G. and B. 1858 (Patron, Bp of G. and B; Glebe, 80 acres; Incumb.'s Gross Inc. 250*l* and Ho; Pop. 8500); Surrog. of Dio. G. and B; Hon. Sec. to the Young Men's Christ. Assoc. Lond; Author, *Preface to Lectures on Great Men,* 1855, Nisbet, Lond. 5*s*.

TASKER, John Campbell Wheatley, 1 *Upper Lansdown Villas, Bath.*—Pem. Coll. Camb. B.A. 1846; Deac. 1847, Pr. 1849, both by Bp of Ely; Chap. of Bath United Hospital, 1858 (Patrons, Hospital Committee; Stipend 100*l*); formerly C. of Lawahall, Suffolk, 1847-51; C. of Chapel-of-Ease, Worthing, Sussex, 1851-52; C. of Weston, near Bath, 1852-58.

TATE, Francis Blackburne, *Quebec, Canada.*—Magd. Coll. Camb. B.A. 1831, M.A. 1834; Deac. and Pr. 1833; Chap. to the Forces, Quebec, 1859; V. of Charing, Kent, Dio. Cant. 1838 (Patron, D. and C. of St Paul's Cathl; Tithe—V. 430*l*; V.'s Gross Inc. 460*l* and Ho; Pop. 1321).

TATE, George Edward, *Widcombe, Bath.*—St John's Coll. Camb. Wrang. and B.A. 1841, M.A. 1844; Deac. 1841, Pr. 1842; V. of Widcombe *w* St Matthew's C, Bath. Dio. B. and W. 1856 (Patrons, Simeon's Trustees; V. and C.'s Gross Inc. 320*l*; Pop. 5000; formerly P.C. of St Jude's, Southwark, Lond. 1849-56; Chap. to the Earl of Kintore; Hon. Sec. to Ch. of Eng. Educ. Soc.

TATE, James, *Marsk vicarage, Redcar, Yorkshire.*—Corpus Coll. Oxon. B.A. 1858; Deac. 1859, Pr. 1860, both by Bp of Norw; V. of Marsk, Dio. York, 1860 (Patron, Earl of Zetland; V.'s Gross Inc. 90*l* and Ho; Pop. 1500); formerly C. of Aylsham, Norfolk, 1859-60.

TATLOCK, William, *St Mary's parsonage, Widnes, Warrington, Lancashire.*—Deac. 1848, Pr. 1849; P.C. of St Mary's, Widnes, Dio. Chest. 1859 (Patron, Wm. Wright, Esq; P.C.'s Gross Inc. 190*l* and Ho; Pop. 5000); late C. of Ormskirk, Lancashire, 1857-59; formerly Incumb. of Christ Ch. Barkisland, 1854-56; Author, *The Man of Sorrows,* 12mo. Seeleys, 1850, 1*s* 6*d*; *The Lost One, or the Soul Ruined by Sin,* 12mo. ib. 1850, 3*d*.

TAVERNER, Frederick John, *Great Grimsby, Lincolnshire.*—Oriel Coll. Oxon. B.A. 1854; Deac. 1854, Pr. 1855, both by Bp of Linc; C. of Great Grimsby, 1859; formerly C. of Coddington, Notts.

TAYLER, Henry Carr Archdale, *Orwell, Arrington, Cambs.*—Trin. Coll. Camb. Browne's Medallist, 1848, Members' Prizeman, 1851, 4th in 1st Cl. Class. Trip. 14th Jun. Opt. and B.A. 1849; Deac. 1853, Pr. 1854; R. of Orwell, Dio. Ely, 1859 (Patron, Trin. Coll. Camb; R.'s Gross Inc. 340*l* and Ho; Pop. 662); late P.C. of St Mary-the-Great, Cambridge, 1854-59; formerly Fell. of Trin. Coll. Camb. 1851-54.

TAYLOR, Alfred Lee, *Ruabon, Denbighshire.*—Corpus Coll. Camb. B.A. 1849, M.A. 1853; Deac. 1851, Pr. 1852; Head Mast. of the Gram. Sch. Ruabon.

TAYLOR, Charles, *Great Cressingham rectory, Thetford, Norfolk.*—Brasen. Coll. Oxon. B.A. 1826, M.A. 1831, B.D. 1840; Deac. 1826, Pr. 1827; R. of Great Cressingham *w* Bodney R. Dio. Norw. 1859 (Patron, Lord Chan; Tithe—Great Cressingham R. 519*l*; Glebe, 52 acres, Bodney R. 195*l*; R.'s Gross Inc. 820*l*. and Ho; Pop. Great Cressingham, 583, Bodney, 103; formerly V. of Lydney *w* Aylburton and St Briavel's C.'s, Gloucestershire, 1838-59; Preb. of Moreton Magna in Heref. Cathl. 1836-38.

TAYLOR, Charles Johnson, *Folkstone, Kent.*—St John's Coll. Oxon. B.A. 1858, M.A. 1859; Deac. 1859, Pr. 1860, both by Archbp of Cant; C. of Folkstone, 1860; formerly C. of Ashford, Kent, 1859-60.

TAYLOR, George, *Egham, Surrey.*—Qu. Coll. Oxon. B.A. 1852, M.A. 1856; Deac. 1852, Pr. 1853, both by Bp of Oxon; C. of Wyrardesbury, Bucks. 1857 (Stipend, 40*l*); Chap. and Schoolmaster of Strode's Charity, Egham, 1857 (Patrons, the Coopers' Company, Lond; Chap.'s Gross Inc. 100*l* and Ho); formerly C. of Checkendon, Oxfordshire, 1852-53; C. of Great Marlow, Bucks. 1853-57.

TAYLOR, Henry Walter, *Rowde, near Devizes, Wilts.*—Magd. Ha. Oxon. B.A. 1850 ; C. of Rowde, 1859 ; formerly C. of North Nibley, Gloucestershire.

TAYLOR, James, *Broughton, near Shrewsbury.*—St Bees Theol. Coll; Deac. 1859, Pr. 1860, both by Bp of Lich ; C. of Grinshill, Shropshire, 1859.

TAYLOR, Robert, *Rothbury, Northumberland.*—Trin. Ha. Camb. B.A. 1848, M.A. 1851 ; Deac. 1848, Pr. 1849 ; C. of Brenckburn-cum-Framlington, Northumberland, 1859 ; formerly Incumb. of Thurgoland, Yorkshire ; Author, various *Tracts*.

TEASDALE, Robert Webster, *Barnard Castle, Darlington, Durham.*—Bp Hat. Ha. Dur. Theol. Licen. 1857 ; Deac. 1858, Pr. 1859, both by Bp of Dur ; C. of Barnard Castle, 1858.

TEUTSCHEL, Anthony Sigismund, *Askern, Doncaster, Yorkshire.*—Univ. of Padua, Ph.D. and St Aidan's Theol. Coll ; Deac. 1859, Pr. 1860, both by Archbp of York ; C. of Askern, 1859.

THEED, Edward Reed, *Sampford-Courtenay rectory, Crediton, Devon.*—King's Coll. Camb. B.A. 1835, M.A. 1838 ; R. of Sampford-Courtenay, Dio. Exon. 1859 (Patron, King's Coll. Camb ; Tithe—R. 650*l* ; R.'s Gross Inc. 720*l* and Ho ; Hop. 1084) ; Fell. of King's Coll. Camb.

THEED, Thomas Maylin, *Bishop-Middleham, Ferry-hill, Durham.*—St John's Coll. Camb. LL.B. 1854 ; Deac. 1857, Pr. 1858 ; C. of Bishop-Middleham, 1859.

THELWALL, Algernon Sidney, 43 *Torrington-square, London.*—Trin. Coll. Camb. B.A. 1818, M.A. 1826 ; Deac. 1818, Pr. 1819 ; Lect. on Public Reading at King's Coll. Lond ; formerly Min. of the Engl. Episcop. Chap. Amsterdam, 1819-22 ; Missionary to the Jews, 1822-27 ; C. of Blackford, Somerset, 1828-30 ; Mon. of Bedford Chap. Lond, 1842-43 ; C. of St Matthew's, Pell-street, Lond. 1849-50 ; Author, *Tracts for the Jews* (1823), afterwards collected into a volume, under the title of *Old Testament Gospel*, 1847, 12mo. 1*s* 6*d*, Wertheim and Macintosh ; *Thoughts in Affliction*, 1831. 32mo. 3*s* 6*d*, Seeleys ; 2nd edit. 1834, Seeleys ; *Sermons,* chiefly on Subjects connected with the Present State of the Church and of the World, 1833. 8vo. 12*s*, Seeleys ; *A Scriptural Refutation of Mr Irving's Heresy,* 1834, 12mo. 1*s* 6*d*, Werthiem ; *Letters to a Friend, whose Mind has long been harassed by many Objections against the Church of England,* 1835, sm. 8vo. 5*s* 6*d*, Seeleys ; *Anti-Mammon* (in concert with the Rev. Francis Ellaby), three edits, 1837, 8vo. 5*s* 6*d*, Nisbet and Co ; *Iniquities of the Opium Trade with China,'* 1839, 8vo. 3*s* 6*d*, Wm. H. Allen and Co ; *The Idolatry of the Church of Rome* (a Manual of that part of the controversy), 1844, for the Protestant Association, W. H. Dalton, 12mo, 5*s* ; *A Statement of Facts respecting the Instruction given to the Students for the Romish Priesthood in the Royal College of St Patrick,* Maynooth, 1845, 12mo. 4*d*, Seeleys and Dalton ; *Proceedings of the Anti-Maynooth Conference of* 1845 (Compiled and Edited by A. S. T.), 1845, 8vo. 6*s*, Seeleys, Hamilton, and Adams ; *Evangelical Alliance* (Report of the Proceedings of the Conference held at Freemasons'-hall, London, from Aug. 19 to Sept. 2 inclusive, 1846 ; Edited principally by A. S. T. 1847, 8vo. 6*s*, Partridge and Oakey ; *The Doctrine of the Trinity practically considered, in connexion with our Baptism, as the Foundation of the whole Gospel, and the Basis of Christian Union* (a Sermon), 1848, 8vo. 4*d*, Nisbet and Co ; *The Importance of Elocution in connexion with Ministerial Usefulness* (an Introductory Lecture delivered at King's College, London, on entering upon the duties of Lecturer on Public Reading, Jan. 30, 1850, 8vo. 1*s*, Wertheim and Macintosh ; *Exercises in Elocution, in Verse and Prose,* 1850, 8vo. 5*s* 6*d*, Wertheim and Macintosh ; *The Heidelberg Catechism of the Reformed Christian Religion* (first published in 1563), *with a Preface, containing historical Facts and other Illustrative Matter,* 1850, 12mo. 1*s*, Wertheim and Macintosh ; *The Heidelberg Catechism* (without the Preface), 1851, 12mo. 6*d* ; Wertheim and Macintosh ; *The Romish Doctrine of Justification,* being a Lecture delivered in the Trinity District School-room, Cloudesley-

street, Islington, on Tuesday, Feb. 17, 1852, 12mo. 4*d*, T. Murphy ; "*Open his Grief:*" *the Meaning and Abuse of this expression in the Communion Service,* 1859 (a Tract), 6*d* per dozen, Wertheim, Macintosh and Hunt ; *A Page out of my Ministerial Experience, with reference to the question, Do you wish for a Revival in the Church and Congregation to which you belong?* 1860 (a Tract), 6*d* per dozen, Wertheim, Macintosh and Hunt ; *Hope for Eternity* (a Tract), 2*d*, 1860, Wertheim, Macintosh and Hunt ; *Are you Safe for Eternity?* (a Tract), 2*d*, 1860, Wertheim, Macintosh and Hunt ; *Soul-saving Truth* (a Tract), 1*d*, Wertheim, Macintosh and Hunt.

THOMAS, Benjamin, ...—St Bees Theol. Coll ; Deac. 1859, Pr. 1860, both by Bp of Lich.

THOMAS, Edmund, *Bonvilstone, near Cardiff.* Univ. Coll. Dur. B.A. 1853 ; Deac. 1853, Pr. 1854 ; P.C. of Bonvilstone, Dio. Lland. 1859 (Patron, J. J. Bassett, Esq ; P.C.'s Gross Inc. 100*l* ; Pop. 294) ; late R. of Kingsley, Staffs. 1856-59 ; formerly C. of Alfreton, Derbyshire, 1853-56.

THOMAS, John, *Workington, Cumberland.*—St Bees Theol. Coll ; Deac. 1856, Pr. 1857, both by Bp of Chest ; C. of Workington, 1859 ; formerly C. of Congleton, Cheshire, 1856-59.

THOMAS, Owen Davies, *Penydarren, Merthyr Tydvil, Glamorgan.*—St Dav. Theol. Coll. Lamp ; Deac. 1860 ; C. of Merthyr-Tydvil, 1860.

THOMAS, Samuel, *Margam, Taibach, Glamorganshire.*—Magd. Ha. Oxon. B.A. 1859 ; Deac. 1860 ; C. of Margam, 1860.

THOMAS, Thomas, *Talley, Llandilo, Carmarthenshire.*—St Dav. Coll. Lamp. 1846-49 ; Deac. 1849, Pr. 1851 ; P.C. of Talley, Dio. St Dav. 1854 (Patron, Rev. W. T. Nicholls ; P.C.'s Gross Inc. 148*l* ; Pop. 1000) ; formerly 2nd Mast. of Qu. Eliz. Gram. Sch. Carmarthen, 1849-54.

THOMAS, William Jones, *Newcastle Court, Kington, Herefordshire.*—St Peter's Coll. Camb. B.A. 1835, M.A. 1838 ; Deac. 1836, Pr. 1837, both by Bp of Exon ; R. of Gladestry, near Kington, Dio. St Dav. 1856 (Patron, Ld. Chan ; R.'s Gross Inc. 390*l* ; Pop. 362), formerly P.C. of Llanelwedd, Radnorshire, 1838-56.

THOMAS, William Mathew, *Alvington, Lydney, Gloucestershire.*—St John's Coll. Camb. B.A. 1858 ; Deac. 1859 ; C. of Woolestone and Alvington, 1859.

THOMAS, William Samuel, *Uffculme, Collumpton, Devon.*—Kg. Coll. Lond. Theol. Assoc. 1858 ; Deac. 1858, by Bp of Exon. Pr. 1859, by Bp of B. and W ; 2nd Mast. of Aychford's Gram. Sch. Uffculme, 1858 ; C. of Stamford Arundel, near Wellington, 1859.

THOMPSON, Archibald Douglas Cavendish, *Hildenley Hall, Malton, Yorkshire.*—Bp Hat. Ha. Dur. B.A. 1859 ; Deac. 1859, Pr. 1860, both by Archbp of York ; C. of Appleton-le-Street, near Malton, 1860.

THOMPSON, Arthur Steinkopff, 3 *Upper George-street, Portman-square, London.*— Wadh. Coll. Oxon. B.A. 1858 ; Deac. 1859, Pr. 1860, both by Bp of Lond ; C. of St Mary's, Marylebone, 1859.

THOMPSON, Christopher, *Leicester.*—King's Coll. Lond. Theol. Assoc ; Deac. 1859, Pr. 1860, both by Bp of Peterb ; C. of St. John's, Leicester, 1859.

THOMPSON, Frederick, *Haverland, near Norwich.*—Magd. Ha. Oxon. B.A. 1853 ; Deac. 1855, Pr. 1856, both by Bp of Norw ; P.C. of Haverland, Dio. Norw. 1857 (Patron, H. Fellowes, Esq ; P.C.'s Gross Inc. 75*l* and Ho ; Pop. 143) ; formerly C. of Hackford w Whitwell, Norfolk ; Author, *The Glory and Cost of Victory* (a Sermon on the Fall of Sebastopol), Thew and Son, Lynn, 1855.

THOMSON, William Yalden, ... Literate ; Deac. 1859, Pr. 1860, both by Bp of G. and B.

THORNTON, Henry Woffenden, *Langley, Clavering, Essex.*—St Bees Coll. 1st Cl. 1853 ; Deac. 1853, by Bp of Norw. Pr. 1854, by Archbp of York ; C. of Langley, 1859 ; late C. of Alvington, Gloucestershire ; formerly C. of Whitby, Yorks.

THORNTON, John, *Aston-Abbott vicarage, Aylesbury, Bucks.*—St. Cath. Coll. Camb. Skerne Sch. B.A. 1840, M.A. 1848; Deac. 1840, Pr. 1841, both by Bp of Peterb; V. of Aston-Abbotts, Dio. Oxon. 1853 (Patron, Lord Overstone; Glebe, 99 acres; V.'s Gross Inc. 150*l* and Ho; Pop. 320); formerly Chap. to the General Asylum and Infirmary, Northampton, 1842–47; Head Mast. of the Gram. Sch. Kimbolton, Hunts, 1847–53.

THORNTON, Thomas, *Golborne, Warrington, Lancashire,*—Bp Hat. Ha. Dur. B.A. 1857; Deac. 1860, by Bp. of Chest; C. of Golborne, 1860; formerly 2nd Mast. of Warrington Gram. Sch. 1858–60.

THORNTON, William Henry, *Exmoor parsonage (Somerset), near South Molton, Devon.*—Trin. Coll. Camb. B.A. 1853; Deac. 1853, Pr. 1855; P.C. of Exmoor, Dio. B. and W. 1856 (Patron, the Crown; P.C.'s Gross Inc. 170*l* and Ho; Pop. 500); formerly C. of Lynton and Countisbury, Devon.

THORP, Charles, *Nymphsfield rectory, Stonehouse, Gloucestershire.*—Magd. Ha. Oxon. B.A. 1834, M.A. 1839; Deac. 1835, Pr. 1836, both by Bp of Oxon; R. of Nymphsfield, Dio. G. and B. 1860 (Patron, Ld. Chan; Tithe—R. 258*l*; Glebe, 27 acres; R.'s Gross Inc. 290*l* and Ho; Pop. 417); formerly Chap. of Northleach, Gloucestershire, 1847–56; Chap. of the Horsley House of Correction, Gloucestershire, 1856–60.

THORP, John, *Chirk, Denbighshire.*—Magd. Ha. Oxon, B.A. 1859; Deac. 1860, by Bp of St Asaph; C. of Chirk, 1860.

THORP, Gervase, *Danbury, Essex.*—King's Coll. Lond. Theol. Assoc. 1858; Deac. 1858, Pr. 1859, both by Bp of Norw; C. of Danbury, 1860.; formerly C. of St Margaret's, Ipswich, 1859–60.

THRING, Edward, *2 Rock villas, Rock Ferry, Birkenhead.*—St Bees Theol. Coll; Deac. 1851, Pr. 1852, both by Archbp of York; Chap. on the Mersey.

THURSFIELD, Richard, *3 Clifton villas, South Norwood, Surrey.*—Caius Coll. Camb. B.A. 1854; Deac. 1854, by Bp of Chest, Pr. 1860, by Archbp. of Cant; C. of St Mark's, South-Norwood; formerly C. of Chr. Ch. Everton, Liverpool; Author, *Bethany, a Poem,* Wertheim and Co. Lond. 1859.

THURSFIELD, Richard Periam, *Sidbury rectory, Bridgnorth, Shropshire.*—St John's Coll. Camb. B.A. 1819; Deac. 1820, Pr. 1821; R. of Sidbury, Dio. Heref. 1851 (Patron, Earl of Shrewsbury; Tithe—R. 181*l* 8*s* 6*d*; R.'s Gross Inc. 242*l* and Ho; Pop 61).

TIBBITS, Frederic, ...—St John's Coll. Camb. B.A. 1860; Deac. 1860, by Bp of Norw.

TIBBITS, Newman, *Moulsham, Chelmsford, Essex.*—Sid.-Suss. Coll. Camb. B.A. 1856; Deac. 1858, Pr. 1859, both by Bp of Roch; C. of Moulsham, 1858.

TILBURY, Robert, *Langford, Lechlade, Berks.* —Emman. Coll. Camb. B.A. 1860; Deac. 1860, by Bp of Oxon; C. of Langford w Little Faringdon, Berks, 1860 (Stipend, 100*l*).

TILL, Lawrence William, *Chertsey vicarage, Surrey.*—Pembroke Coll. Oxon. B.A. 1852, M.A. 1856; Deac. 1852, Pr. 1853, both by Bp of Lond; V. of Chertsey, Dio. Winch. 1857 (Patrons, The Haberdashers' Company, Lond. as Trustees; V.'s Gross Inc. 330*l* and Ho; Pop. 2473); late C. of St. Philip's, Dalston, Lond. 1854–57; formerly Asst. C. of St. John's, Westminster, 1852–54.

TINDALL, Richard Abbey, *Brighouse, Yorkshire.*—Bp Hat. Ha. Dur. Licen. Theol. 1859, B.A. 1860; Deac. 1860, by Bp of Rip; C. of Brighouse, 1860.

TIPTON, William, *9 Shaftesbury-crescent, Westminster, Lond.*—St. Mary Ha. Oxon. B.A. 1851; Deac. 1854, Pr. 1855; C. of St. Andrew's, Westminster, 1859; formerly C. of St. Margaret's, Westminster, 1854–59.

TITLEY, Richard, *33 Bedford-street South, Liverpool.*—Trin. Coll. Camb. B.A. 1856, M.A. 1859; Deac. 1856, Pr. 1857, both by Bp. of Lich; C. of St. Nicholas, Liverpool, 1859; formerly C. of Tamworth, Staffs. 1856–59.

TODD, Edward Hallett, *Blackheath, Lee, Kent.*—Worc. Coll. Oxon. B.A. 1859; Deac. 1860, by Bp of Lond; C. of All Saints, Blackheath, 1860.

TODD, Horatio Lovell, *Great Amwell, Ware, Herts.*—Pemb. Coll. Oxon. B.A. 1856, M.A. 1859; Deac. 1857, Pr. 1858, both by Bp of Norw; C. of Great Amwell, 1860; formerly C. of Burstall, Suffolk, 1857–58; C. of Stoke-upon-Trent, Staffordshire, 1858–60.

TOLLEMACHE, Clement Reginald, *7 Crescent-buildings, Leicester.*—Brasen. Coll. Oxon. B.A. 1857; Deac. 1858, Pr. 1859; C. of St. John, Leicester, 1860; formerly C. of All Saints, Wykeham, near Scarborough, 1858–60.

TOMKINS, William Smith, *Crewkerne, Somerset.*—King's Coll. Lond. Theol. Assoc; Deac. 1859, Pr. 1860, both by Bp of B. and W.; Asst. C. of Crewkerne, 1859.

TOMLINSON, Charles Henry, *Worcester College, Oxford, and New-street, Salisbury.*—Worc. Coll. Oxon. B.A. 1857, M.A. 1860; Deac. 1859, Pr. 1860, both by Bp. of Oxon; Fell. of Worc. Coll. Oxon.

TOMLINSON, William Bannister, *Horton-in-Ribblesdale, Settle, Yorkshire.*—Trin. Coll. Dub. B.A. 1857; Deac. 1858; Head Mast. of the Gram. Sch. Horton-in-Ribblesdale (Patrons, Governors of the Gram. Sch; Head Mast.'s Gross Inc. 180*l*).

TOPHAM, Robert, *Biggin parsonage, Ashbourne, Derbyshire.*—P.C. of Biggin, Dio. Lich. 1860 (Patron, Duke of Devonshire; Tithe—P.C. 15*l*; Glebe, 2 acres; P.C.'s Gross Inc. 100*l* and Ho; Pop. 436).

TOWNSEND, John, *Hockley-house, Hockley-heath, Warwickshire.*—King's Coll. Lond. Theol. Assoc; Deac. 1854, Pr. 1856; C. of Nuthurst, Hampton-in-Arden, Warwickshire, 1854.

TOWNSHEND, George Henry, *117 Bath-row, Birmingham.*—King's Coll. Lond. Theol. Assoc; Deac. 1860, by Bp of Worc; C. of St Thomas, Birmingham, 1860.

TREVENEN, Thomas John, *St Barnabas College, Pimlico, London.*—Magd. Ha. Oxon. B.A. 1857, M.A. 1860; Deac. 1858, Pr. 1859, both by Bp of Exon; C. of St Barnabas, Pimlico, 1860; formerly Asst. C. of St Mary Ch. Devon, 1858–60.

TRIMMER, Algernon Arthur, *Putney, Surrey.*—St John's Coll. Oxon. B.A. 1854, M.A. 1859; Deac. 1859, Pr. 1860; C. of St John's, Putney, 1859.

TRINGHAM, William, *Wootton rectory, Charmouth, Dorset.*—St John's Coll. Oxon. B.A. 1856, M.A. 1858; Deac. 1856, Pr. 1857, both by Bp of Winch; R. of Wootton-Fitzpaine, Dio. Salis. 1858 (Patron, Wm. Tringham, Esq; Tithe—R. 245*l*; R.'s Gross Inc. 250*l* and Ho; Pop. 361); formerly C. of Yateley, Hants, 1856–58.

TRUEMAN, Samuel, *Nempnett, near Bristol.*—St John's Coll. Camb. B.A. 1847, M.A. 1850; Deac. 1849, Pr. 1852, both by Bp of Norw; P.C. of Nempnett, Dio. B. and W. 1859 (Patron, the present P.C.; P.C.'s Gross Inc. 290*l*; Pop. 284); late C. of Banningham, Norfolk formerly Head Mast. of the Free Gram. Sch. Ormskirk, Lancashire; previous Asst. Mast. of King Edward VI. Endowed Sch. Bath.

TRUMAN, George William Harrison, *Wythop, Cockermouth, Cumberland.*—Qu. Coll. Camb. B.A. 1860; Deac.1860, by Bp of Carl; C. of Wythop, 1860.

TUCKNISS, William, *Winterbourne Stickland, Blandford, Dorset.*—Magd. Ha. Oxon. B.A. 1858; Deac. 1858, Pr. 1860, both by Bp of Salis; C. of Winterbourne Stickland, 1858; Author, *Infidelity in the Pulpit* (a pamphlet), Longman, 1857; Editor of the *Magdalen's Friend and Female Home's Intelligencer,* a monthly magazine, crown 8vo. Nisbet and Co.

TUDOR, Charles, *Merton, Bicester, Oxfordshire.*—Jesus Coll. Oxon. B.A. 1848, M.A. 1850; Deac. 1849, Pr. 1850, both by Bp of Heref; C. of Merton, 1852.

TUDOR, Summerton, *Ivy cottage, Minster, near Ramsgate.*—St. Edm. Ha. Oxon. B.A. 1826, M.A. 1828; Deac. and Pr. 1827; Chap. of the Isle of Thanet Union, 1860 (Patrons, the Board of Guardians; Chap.'s Gross Inc. 100*l*); formerly C. of Woodham Ferrers, Essex, 1826–57; C. of Hoo St Warburgh, Kent, and Chap. to the Hoo Union, 1856–59.

TURING, John Robert, *Trinity College, Cambridge.*—Trin. Coll. Camb. B.A. 1847, M.A. 1851 ; Deac. 1848, Pr. 1849 ; Chap. of Trin. Coll. Camb. 1859 ; formerly Incumb. of Holy Trinity, Rotherhithe, Lond. 1851-59.

TURNBULL, George, *Longhorsley, Northumberland* —Univ. of Edinb ; Deac. 1859, Pr. 1860 ; C. of Longhorsley, 1859.

TURNER, Edward Tindal, *Brasenose College, Oxford.*—Trin. Coll. Oxon. Sch. 1840, Brasen. Coll. Oxon. B.A. 1844, M.A. 1847 ; Deac. 1852, Pr. 1853 ; Fell. and Tut. of Brasen. Coll. Oxon ; Member of the Hebdomadal Council, and Sen. Proctor of the Univ. 1859.

TURNER, John Richard, *Spalding, Lincolnshire.*—St Peter's Coll. Camb. B.A. 1847, M.A. 1850 ; Deac. 1848, Pr. 1849, both by Bp of Manch ; C. of Spalding, 1860 ; formerly C. of Whaplode-Drove, Lincolnshire.

TURNER, Joseph Kirby, *Lawton, Cheshire.*—Trin. Coll. Camb. B.A 1857 ; Deac. 1859, Pr. 1860 ; C. of Lawton, 1860 ; formerly C. of Prestbury, Cheshire, 1859-60.

TURNER, Rupert, *3 St John's-road, New town, Deptford, Kent.*—St Bees Theol. Coll ; Deac. 1856, Pr. 1857, both by Archbp of York ; C. of St Paul, Deptford, 1860 ; formerly C. of Howden, and Lect. of Barmby-upon-the-Marsh, Yorkshire, 1856-60. •

TURTON, Henry Meysey, *Nelson, New Zealand.*—Trin. Coll. Oxon. B.A. 1846 ; Deac. 1848, Pr. 1849 ; late V. of Great Milton, Oxfordshire, 1856-59 ; formerly Dom. Chap. to Earl Paulett.

TWEDDLE, Thomas, *Banbury, Oxfordshire.*—St John's Coll. Camb. B.A. 1854, M.A. 1857 ; Deac. 1859, Pr. 1860, both by Bp of Oxon ; C. of South Banbury, 1859.

TWELLS, Edward, *Hammersmith, Middlesex.*—St Peter's Coll. Camb. B.A. 1851, M.A. 1854 ; Deac. 1853, Pr. 1854, both by Bp of Rip ; P.C. of St John the Evangelist, Hammersmith, Dio. Lond. 1859 (Patron, V. of Hammersmith) ; P.C.'s Gross Inc. 110*l* ; Pop. 3845) ; late C. of Hammersmith ; formerly Asst. C. of All Saints, Wakefield.

TWISLETON - WYKEHAM - FIENNES, The Hon. Wingfield Stratford, *Ashow, rectory, Kenilworth, Warwickshire.*—New Coll. Oxon. B.A. 1858, M.A. 1859 ; Deac. 1860, by Bp of Worc ; C. of Ashow, 1860 ; Fell. of New Coll. Oxon.

TYACKE, John Sidney, *Marlborough-college, Wilts.*— Exon. Coll. Oxon. B.A. 1857, M.A. 1859 ; Deac. 1858, Pr. 1859 ; Asst. Mast. in Marlborough College.

TYRWHITT, Beauchamp, *Tissington, Ashbourne, Derbyshire.*—Clare Ha. Camb. B.A. 1853, Hebrew Sch. Tyrwhitt's Found. 1856, M.A. 1856 ; Deac. 1855, Pr. 1855, both by Bp of Lich ; P.C. of Tissington, Dio. Lich. 1859 (Patron, Sir Wm. Fitzherbert ; P.C.'s Gross Inc. 105*l* ; Pop. 344 ; formerly C. of Paddington, Lond.

TYRWHITT, Richard St John, *Christ Church, Oxford.*—Ch. Ch. Oxon. 2nd Cl. Lit. Hum. and B.A. 1849 ; Deac. 1851, Pr. 1852 ; V. of St Mary Magdalen *w* St George-the-Martyr V, city and Dio. Oxon, 1858 (Patron, Ch. Ch. Oxon ; V.'s Gross Inc. 170*l* ; Pop. 2476) ; Tut. of Ch. Ch. Oxon.

TYSON, Joshua, *Dissington, Workington, Cumberland.*—St Bees Theol. Coll ; Deac. 1860, by Bp of Carl ; C. of Dissington, 1860.

AN HEMERT, John, *Gautby rectory, Horncastle, Lincolnshire.*—Deac. 1818, Pr. 1819 ; R. of Gautby, Dio. Linc. 1859 (Patron, Ld. Chan ; R.'s Gross Inc. 95*l* and Ho ; Pop. 99) ; formerly C. of Frodingham, Lincolnshire.

VAUGHAN, Charles John, *The vicarage, Doncaster.*—Trin. Coll. Camb. Craven Univ. Sch. Porson Prizeman, 1836 and 1837 ; Browne's Medallist for Greek Ode, Epigrams, and Latin Essay, 1837, Chancellor's Medallist, 1838, B.A. 1838, Fell. of Trin. Coll. 1839, M.A. 1841, D.D. 1845 ; Deac. and Pr. 1841 ; Chap. in Ordinary to the Queen, 1859 (Stipend, 30*l*) ; V. of Doncaster, Dio. York, 1860 (Patron, Archbp of York ; Tithe-App. 1805*l* 2*s* ; V.'s Gross Inc. 460*l* and Ho ; Pop. 7162) ; Hon. Chancellor of York Cathl. 1860 ; formerly V. of St Martin's, Leicester, 1841-44 ; Head Mast. of Harrow Sch. 1844-59 ; Author, *Sermons, preached in the Chapel of Harrow School* (First Series), 8vo. Murray, 1847 ; *Nine Sermons for Advent, Easter, &c.* 12mo. 1849 ; *Two Letters on the late Post-office Agitation,* 1849-50 ; *The Personality of the Tempter, and other Sermons,* 8vo. 1851 ; *Sermons preached in the Parish Church of St Martin's, Leicester,* Rivingtons, 1852 ; *Sermons preached in the Chapel of Harrow School* (Second Series), ib. 1853 ; *Independence and Submission* (Two Addresses), 8vo. ib. 1853 ; *Personality of the Tempter, and other Sermons,* 8vo. ib. 1853 ; *A few Words on the Crystal Palace Question,* 1853 ; *A Letter to Lord Palmerston on the Monitorial System of Harrow School,* 1854 ; *A Discourse on Church Discipline and the Burial Service,* 1854 ; *Passages from the Life of Cicero* (A Lecture delivered in Exeter Hall), 1854 ; *Two Sermons on the War,* 1854 ; *Memorials of Harrow Sundays,* crown 8vo. Macmillan, 1859, 10*s* 6*d* ; *Revision of the Liturgy,* crown 8vo. ib. 4*s* 6*d* ; *Notes for Lectures on Confirmation,* 12mo. ib. 1*s* 6*d* ; *Epistle to the Romans, with English Notes,* 8vo. ib. 7*s* 6*d* ; *Epiphany, Lent, and Easter: Sermons preached in St Michael's Church, Chester-square,* crown 8vo. ib. 1860, 7*s* 6*d*.

VAUGHAN, David James, *St Martin's vicarage, Leicester.*—Trin. Coll. Camb. Bell's Sch. 1845, Browne's Medallist, 1847, Members' Prizeman, 1847 and 1848 ; B.A. 1848, M.A. 1851 ; Deac. 1853, Pr. 1854, both by Bp of Peterb ; V. of St Martin's, Leicester, Dio. Peterb. 1860 (Patron, Ld. Chan ; V.'s Gross Inc. 160*l* and Ho ; Pop. 2863) ; late P.C. of St Mark's, Whitechapel, Lond. 1856-60 ; formerly C. of St John's, Leicester ; previously Fell. of Trin. Coll. Camb ; Author, *The Republic of Plato, Translated into English, with an Introduction, Analysis and Notes,* Macmillans, 1852, 7*s* 6*d* ; *A few Words about Private Tuition, by a Private Tutor,* ib. 1852, 6*d*.

VAUGHAN, Edward Thomas, *Harpenden, near St Albans.*—Chr. Coll. Camb. Bell's Univ. Sch. 1831, Members' Prizeman, 1833 and 1835, 29th Wrang. 7th in 1st Cl. Class. Trip. and B.A. 1834, M.A. 1837 ; Deac. 1836, Pr. 1837, both by Bp of Linc ; P.C. of Harpenden, Dio. Roch. 1859 (Patron, Bp of Peterb ; Tithe—P.C. 810*l*, Glebe, 10 acres ; P.C.'s Gross Inc. 850*l* ; Pop. 1980) ; late V. of St Martin's, Leicester, 1845-59 ; formerly Fell. of Chr. Coll. Camb. 1837-38 ; Author, *Sermons, University and Parochial,* 8vo. Rivingtons, 1850, 6*s* ; several occasional *Sermons,* Cropley, Leicester.

VAUGHAN, Joseph Marychurch, *36 Brunswick-road, Brighton.*—Trin. Ha. Camb. and King's Coll. Lond. Theol. Assoc. 1858 ; Deac. 1859, Pr. 1860 ; formerly C. of Shildon, Durham, 1859-60.

VAUGHAN, Walter William, *Castle Caereinion, Welshpool, Montgomeryshire.*—St Dav. Theol. Coll. Lamp. Sch. 1854 ; Deac. 1856, Pr. 1858, both by Bp. of St Dav ; C. of Castle-Caereinion, 1860 ; formerly C. of Steynton, Pembrokeshire, 1856-59.

VENN, Edward Sherman, *Damerham, near Salisbury.*—Wadh. Coll. Oxon. 2nd Cl. Lit. Hum. and B.A. 1840, M.A. 1842 ; Deac. 1845, by Bp of Lond. Pr. 1848, by Bp of Norw ; C. of Damerham, 1859 ; late C. of Hale, Surrey ; formerly C. of Little Hinton, Wilts ; previously Asst. Min. of Ovington, Norfolk.

VERNON, Henry George, *St Aidan's College, Birkenhead.*—St Aidan's Coll ; Deac. 1853, Pr. 1854, both by Bp of Chest ; Res. Chap. Bursar and Sec. to the Council of St Aidan's Coll ; P.C. of St Stephen's, Liverpool ; Dio. Chest. 1859 (Patron, R. of Liverpool ; P.C.'s Gross Inc. 150*l*) ; late C. of Holy Trinity, Birkenhead.

VERNON, John Richard, *Sellinge, Hythe, Kent.*—Magd. Ha. Oxon. B.A. 1859 ; Deac. 1860, by Archbp of Cant ; C. of Sellinge, 1860.

VERNON, William Henry, *Aintree, near Liverpool.*—Min. of St Stephen's, Aintree, Dio. Chest. 1853 (Patrons, the joint R.'s of Liverpool ; Min.'s Gross Inc. 120*l*).

VERNON, William James, ...— St John's Coll. Camb. B.A. 1860; Deac. 1860, by Bp of B. and W.

VICARS, John, 4 *Nelson-place, Bath.*—Chr. Coll. Camb. B.A. 1854, M.A. 1857; Deac. 1856, Pr. 1858; C. of St Mary's Episcop. Chapel, Walcot, Bath, 1860; Head Mast. of the Bath Rectory Middle School.

VINCENT, James Crawley, *Llanbeblig vicarage, Carnarvon.*—Jesus Coll. Oxon. B.A. 1849, M.A. 1853; Deac. 1852, Pr. 1853, both by Bp of Bang; V. of Llanbeblig, Dio. Bang. 1859 (Patron, Bp of Chest; Tithe—329l; Glebe, 1 acre; V.'s Gross Inc. 330l. and Ho; Pop. 10,000); Chap. of the County Gaol, Carnarvon, 1860; formerly C. of Llantrisaint, 1851-53; C. of Dyserth, Flintshire. 1853-56; C. of St Asaph, 1856-59.

VINCENT, John Charles Frederick, *Morborne rectory, Stilton, Hunts.*—Trin. Coll. Dub. B.A. 1842, M.A. ;1845, LL.D. 1849; Deac. 1842, Pr. 1843; R. of Morborne, Dio. Ely, 1859 (Patron, W. Slingsby, Esq; R.'s Gross Inc. 300l and Ho; Pop. 122); late Head Mast. of the Norwich Sch. 1852-59; formerly Head Mast. of Henry VII.'s Gram. Sch. of St Anastasius, 1842-44; Prin. of the Coll. at Roseau, 1844-45; Min. of St Aubin's and Lect. of St Peter's, Jersey, 1845-52.

VINCENT, Richard, *Crockham Hill, Westerham, near Edinbridge, Kent.*—Brasen. Coll. Oxon. B.A. 1847, M.A. 1849; Deac. 1848, Pr. 1849, both by Bp of Winch; P.C. of Trin. Ch. Crockham Hill, Dio. Cant. 1859 (Patron, C. Warde, Esq; P.C.'s Gross Inc. 100l); formerly P.C. of Woodlands, Kent, 1850-59; Author, *Reality in Religion, and Religion in Practice* (a Sermon on Education), Rivingtons, 1858; *Private Prayers for Children in National Schools*, on card, Bell and Daldy.

VINES, Thomas Hotchkin, *Easingwold, Yorkshire.*—Corpus Coll. Camb. B.A. 1859; Deac. 1860, by Archbp of York; C. of Easingwold, 1860.

VYVYAN, Henry Moyle, *Coatham, Redcar, Yorkshire.*—Pemb. Coll. Oxon; Deac. 1859, by Archbp of York; C. of Coatham, 1860.

VYVYAN-ROBINSON, Henry, *St Giles-in-the-Wood parsonage, Great Torrington, Devon.*—St John's Coll. Camb. B.A. 1845; Deac. 1847, Pr. 1849; P.C. of St Giles-in-the-Wood, Great Torrington, Dio. Exon. 1856 (Patrons, Heirs of Lord Rolle; P.C.'s Gross Inc. 115l. and Ho; Pop. 964); formerly C. of Poughill, Cornwall.

WADDELL, William Dudley, *East Challow, Wantage, Berks.*—Trin. Coll. Camb. and Cuddesdon Theol. Coll; Deac. 1860, by Bp of Oxon; C. of East and West Challow, 1860.

WADDINGHAM, Thomas, *Winterton vicarage, Glandford Brigg, Lincolnshire.*—St John's Coll. Camb; V. of Winterton, Dio. Linc. 1859 (Patron, Ld. Chan; Tithe—Imp. 4l 2s 6d, V. 182l 10s, Glebe, ½ acre; V.'s Gross Inc. 190l and Ho; Pop. 1665); late Fell. of St John's Coll. Camb.

WALDY, John Edward, *Littleborough, Rochdale, Lancashire.*—Univ. Coll. Oxon. R.A. 1847; Deac. 1849, Pr. 1850, both by Bp of B. and W; C. of Littleborough, 1859; formerly C. of Curry Mallet w Curland, Somerset.

WALES, William, *Uppingham rectory, Rutland.*—St Cath. Ha. Camb. B.A. 1827, M.A. 1833; Deac. 1827, Pr. 1828; R. of Uppingham, Dio. Peterb. 1859 (Patron, Bp of Lond; Glebe, 266 acres; R.'s Gross Inc. 600l and Ho; Pop. 2068); Hon. Can. Peterb. Cathl. 1846; Chancellor of the Dio. of Peterb. 1850; late V. of All Saints, Northampton, 1832-59.

WALKER, Samuel Abraham, 7 *Westbourne-place, Clifton, Bristol.*—Trin. Coll. Dub. B.A. 1832, M.A. 1835; Deac. 1832, Pr. 1833, both by Bp of Kildare; R. of St Mary-le-Port, Bristol, Dio. G. and B. 1859 (Patron, Geo. Cooke, Esq. Clifton; R.'s Gross Inc. 320l; Pop. 250); formerly R. of Gallow, co. Meath, Ireland, 1833-36; C. of St Mark's, Dublin, 1836-48; Min. of St Paul's Chap. Aberdeen, 1848-58; Author, *Missions in Africa,*

8vo. 12s, Curry, Dublin, 1845; *Mission in Sierra Leone,* 8vo. 12s, Seeleys, 1847; *Abraham's Bosom,* 8vo. 5s, Kennedy, Edinburgh; *Things New and Old,* 2 vols. 4s, Wertheim and Co; *The Papacy, its Author and Aim,* 1s 6d, ib; *Address to Servants,* 2d, *Address to Masters and Mistresses,* 2d, ib; *Romanising Tendencies,* 2d, ib; *A Few Words of Truth spoken in Love to Religious Liberators and Church Defenders,* 3d, ib; *The Christian Soldier Ready,* 8vo. 5s, ib.

WALKER, Samuel, 7 *Wheeler-terrace, Wheeler-street, Lozello, Birmingham.*—Qu. Theol. Coll. Birmingham; Deac. 1860, by Bp of Worc; C. of St Matthias, Birmingham, 1860.

WALKER, William, ... —King's Coll. Lond; Deac. 1859, Pr. 1860, both by Bp of Lich.

WALKEY, Charles Elliott, *Cusop (Hereford-shire), near Hay, Brecon.*—Linc. Coll. Oxon. B.A. 1857, M.A. 1859; Deac. 1857, Pr. 1858; C. of Cusop, 1860; formerly C. of Mamble and Bayton, Worcestershire, 1857-60.

WALL, William James, *Cloona House, Surbiton, Kingston-on-Thames.*—Trin. Coll. Dub. B.A. 1834, M.A. 1838; Deac. 1836, Pr. 1837; formerly Conductus of Kildare Cathl. Ireland, 1836-38; C. of West Drayton, Notts, 1838-40; C. of Feltham, Middlesex, 1840-48; C. of Westerham, Kent, 1848-56; Author, *Sermons.*

WALLACE, George, *Burghclerc rectory (Hants), near Newbury, Berks.*—Trin. Coll. Camb. B.A. 1831; Deac. 1833, Pr. 1836; R. of Burghclerc w Newtown C. Dio. Winch. 1859 (Patron, Earl of Carnarvon; Tithe—Burghclerc R. 1073l; Glebe, 118¼ acres; Newtown, R. 100l 13s; Glebe, 2 acres; R.'s Gross Inc. 1340l and Ho; Pop. Burghclerc, 809, Newtown, 262); late Head Mast. of the King's School, Canterbury, 1833-59.

WALLACE, John, *Kingswood Lodge, Croydon, Surrey.*—Univ. Coll. Dur. B.A. 1842, M.A. 1845; Deac. 1849, Pr. 1851; C. of Sanderstead, near Croydon, 1859; formerly Chap. of Brisbane and Ipswich, Queen's Land, Australia, 1849-55.

WALLER, Ernest Alfred ... ...—Trin. Coll. Oxon. B.A. 1859; Deac. 1859, Pr. 1860, both by Bp of Lich.

WALLER, Robert Plume, *Stratton vicarage, Cornwall.*—Jesus Coll. Camb. B.A. 1839, M.A. 1842; Deac. 1839, by Archp of Cant. Pr. 1839, by Archbp of York; V. of Stratton, Dio. Exon. 1858 (Patron, Prince of Wales; Glebe, 3 acres; V.'s Gross Inc. 200l and Ho; Pop. 800).

WALMISLEY, Horatio, *St Briavels, Coleford, Gloucestershire.*—Sid.-Suss. Coll. Camb. B.A. 1847, M.A. 1850; Deac. 1848, Pr. 1849, both by Bp of Norw; P.C. of Briavels, Dio. G. and B. 1859 (Patron, Bp of G. and B; P.C.'s Gross Inc. 200l; Pop. 1194); late C. of Hulme, Wakefield; formerly C. of Clehonger, Herefordshire.

WALSH, John Henry Arnold, *Bishopstrow rectory, near Warminster, Wilts.*—Balliol Coll. Oxon. B.A. 1826, M.A. 1829; Deac. 1827, Pr. 1829, both by Bp of Salis; R. of Bishopstrow, Dio. Salis. 1859 (Patron, Sir F. D. Astley; R.'s Gross Inc. 250l and Ho; Pop. 287); late P.C. of Christ Ch. Warminster, Wilts, 1831-59; Author, *Practical Commentary on the Four Gospels, in the Form of Lectures, designed to assist Family Devotion* (privately printed in 1846, since sold in aid of the funds of the Ch. Pastoral Aid Soc.)

WALSH, Thomas Harris, *Ashton-Hayes parsonage, near Chester.*—St Bees Theol. Coll; Deac. 1850, Pr. 1851, both by Bp of Rip; P.C. of Ashton-Hayes, Dio. Chest. 1857 (Patron, W. Atkinson, Esq; P.C.'s Gross Inc. 180l and Ho; Pop. 621); formerly C. of St Peter's, Oldham.

WALSH, William, *Horsell, Ripley, Surrey.*—St Alb. Ha. Oxon. B.A. 1859; Deac. 1860, by Bp of Winch; C. of Horsell, 1860.

WALTER, Arthur, *Fenny-Compton, Southam, Warwickshire.*—Caius Coll. Camb. B.A. 1853; Deac. 1853, Pr. 1854, both by Bp of Worc; C. of Fenny-Compton, 1859; formerly C. of St Thomas's, Stourbridge, 1853-58.

WALTER, James Conway, 3, *Belvedere-terrace, Brighton.*—St Cath. Coll. Camb. B.A. 1853; Deac. 1855, Pr. 1856, both by Bp of Chich; C. of Trinity Chapel, Brighton, 1858; formerly C. of Patcham, Sussex, 1855-57.

WALTERS, John Thomas, *Freystrop, Haverfordwest, Pembrokeshire.*—St John's Coll. Camb. 1st Cl. B.A. 1850; Deac. and Pr. 1850; R. of Freystrop, Dio. St David's, 1859 (Patron, Ld Chan; R.'s Gross Inc. 180*l*; Pop. 679); formerly R. of Stradishall, Suffolk, 1853-59.

WALTERS, William, *Hanley-Castle, Upton-on-Severn, Worcestershire*—Ch. Ch. Oxon. B.A. 1854, M.A. 1857; Deac. 1857, Pr. 1858, both by Bp of Worc; C. of Hanley-Castle, 1860; formerly C. of Pershore, Worcestershire, 1857-60.

WAMBEY, Cornelius Copner, *Upper Holland parsonage, Wigan, Lancashire.*—Magd. Ha. Oxon. B.A. 1859; Deac. 1860, by Bp of Chest; C. of Upper Holland, 1860; formerly Professor of Class. and Divin. Lect. at Gothic House Coll. Clapham.

WANNOP, Thomas Nicholson, *The Parsonage, Haddington, Scotland.*—Bp. Hat. Ha. Dur. Licen. Theol. 1849; Deac. 1849, Pr. 1850, both by Bp of Dur; Incumb. of Haddington, Dio. Edinburgh, 1855 (Patron, the Vestry; Incumb's Gross Inc. 230*l* and Ho; Pop. 300); formerly C of Pittington, Durham, 1849-55; Author, various *Sermons.*

WARD, Benjamin, *West Walls, Carlisle.*—Deac and Pr. 1817; Hon Can. of Carl. Cathl. 1857; R. of Meesden, near Buntingford, Herts, Dio. Roch. 1859 (Patron, Rev. A. Gaussen; R.'s Gross Inc. 250*l* and Ho; Pop. 185); late Incumb. of Chr. Ch. Carlisle, 1831-59; formerly Missionary to Ceylon.

WARD, Charles Cotterill, *Niton, Newport, Isle of Wight.*—Qu. Coll. Camb. B.A. 1854; Deac. 1857, Pr. 1858, both by Bp of Winch; C. of Niton *w* Godshill and Whitwell, Isle of Wight, 1857.

WARD, Henry, *St Barnabas parsonage, King-square, Clerkenwell, London, E.C.*—Qu. Coll. Camb. B.A. 1836, M.A. 1840; Deac. 1838, Pr. 1839, both by Bp of Salis; P.C. of St Barnabas, King-square, City and Dio. Lond. 1859 (Patron, R. of St Luke's; P.C.'s Gross Inc. 350*l* and Ho; Pop.9773); formerly Preacher at the Magdalen, London.

WARD, Horatio James, *Bridgnorth, Shropshire.*—Emman. Coll. Camb. Sen. Opt. and B.A. 1854, M.A. 1857; Deac. 1856, by Bp of Winch. Pr. 1857, by Bp of Lond; Head Mast. of the Gram. Sch. Bridgnorth, 1859; formerly C. of St. Stephen's, Paddington, and Math. Mast. in Westbourne Coll. Bayswater, London.

WARD, John, *Edgbaston, Birmingham.*—Clare Coll. Camb. B.A. 1859; Deac. 1859, Pr. 1860, both by Bp of Worc; C. of Christ Ch. Birmingham, 1859.

WARD, John Henry Kirwan, *Marlborough, Wilts.*—Trin. Coll. Camb. B.A. 1854, M.A. 1857; Deac. 1858, Pr. 1860, both by Bp of Salis; C. of St Mary's, Marlborough, 1850.

WARD, Richard Charles, *Gamston, Retford, Nottinghamshire.*—Emman. Coll. Camb. B.A. 1859; Deac. 1859, Pr. 1860, both by Bp of Linc; C. of Eaton and Gamston, 1859.

WARDELL, Henry John, *Forest School, Walthamstow, Essex.*—Emman. Coll. Camb. Sch. 1850, B.A. 1853, M.A. 1858; Deac. 1853, Pr. 1854, both by Bp of Dur; Precentor and Asst. Class. and Math. Mast. in the Forest Sch. Walthamstow, 1859; formerly C. of Winlaton, Durham, 1853-59; Author, *Church Psalm Tunes,* Ollivier, Pall Mall, 1851.

WARDELL, William Henry, *Bedale, Yorkshire.*—Univ. Coll. Dur. B.A. 1858, Deac. 1860, by Bp of Rip; C. of Bedale, 1860.

WARE, Henry Ryder, *Topsham, near Exeter.*—Corpus Coll. Camb. B.A. 1858; Deac. 1859, Pr. 1860, both by Bp of Exon; C. of Topsham, 1859.

WARE, Wilmot Westmorland, *Adwick-le-Street rectory, near Doncaster, Yorks.*—Jesus Coll. Camb. Rustat Sch. B.A. 1855; Deac. 1855, by Bp of Linc; R. of Adwick-le-Street, Dio. York, 1859 (Patron, J.

Fullerton, Esq; R.'s Gross Inc. 480*l* and Ho; Pop. 480); late C. of Withington, Lancashire; formerly C. of St Peter's, Nottingham.

WARLOW, George, *Lee, Kent.*—St John's Coll. Camb. B.A. 1860, Deac. 1860, by Bp. of Lond; C. of Christ Ch. Lee, 1860.

WARNER, Richard Edward, *Finedon, Higham Ferrers, Northants.*—Exon. Coll. Oxon. B.A. 1858; Deac. 1859, by Bp of Manch. Pr. 1860, by Bp of Peterb; C. of Finedon, 1859.

WARRE, Francis, *Oakleage, Almondsbury, Bristol*—Balliol Coll. Oxon. B.A. 1857, M.A. 1860; Deac. 1858, Pr. 1859; C. of Olveston, near Bristol, 1859.

WASSE, Henry Watson, *Twyford parsonage, Melton Mowbray, Leicestershire.*—Magd. Coll. Camb. B.A. 1856, M.A. 1859; Deac. 1856, Pr. 1857, both by Bp of Peterb; C. of Hungarton *w* Twyford and Thorpe-Satchville, Leicestershire, 1856.

WATERS, Richard, *Navigation-street, Burslem, Staffordshire.*—King's Coll. Lond. Theol. Assoc. 1859; Deac. 1859, Pr. 1860, both by Bp of Lich; C. of St John's, Burslem, 1859.

WATERS, Robert, *Bristol-road, Gloucester.*—King's Coll. Lond. Theol Assoc. 1858; Deac. 1858, Pr. 1859, both by Bp of G. and B; Chap. of the Mariners' Chapel, Gloucester, 1858.

WATKINS, Watkin Morgan, *Llansannan, Rhyl, Denbighshire.*—St David's Theol. Coll. Lamp. S.D.C. 1856-57; Deac. 1857, by Bp of Bang. Pr. 1858, by Bp of St Asaph; C. of Llansannan, 1858.

WATSON, Arthur, *Mostyn House, Parkgate, Chester.*—Caius Coll. Camb. Sch. 1856, B.A. 1858; Deac. 1860; C. of Neston, Cheshire, 1860.

WATSON, Edward Collis, *Meetham-Mills, Huddersfield.*—St Aidan's Theol. Coll; Deac. 1859, Pr. 1860; Asst. C. of Meetham-Mills, 1859.

WATSON, Frederick, *Salcott, near Colchester, Essex.*—Caius Coll. Camb. B.A. 1856; R. of Salcott, Dio. Roch. 1859 (Patron, Bp of Roch; R.'s Gross Inc. 130*l*; Pop. 189); formerly C. of Aslacton, Norfolk.

WATSON, John Watson, *Ringwood, Hants.*—Qu. Coll. Camb. B.A. 1855; Deac. 1856, Pr. 1857, both by Bp of Chest; C. of Harbridge, near Ringwood, 1860.

WATSON, Ralph Francis, *Comberford, near Burton-on-Trent.*—Trin. Coll. Dub. B.A. 1846, M.A. 1853, ad eund. Oxon. 1853; Deac. 1846, Pr. 1847, both by Bp of Lich; C. of Croxall, near Burton-on-Trent; formerly C. of Willesborough and St Nicholas-at-Wade, Kent.

WATTSFORD, Henry James, *Greenwich, Kent.*—Univ. Coll. Dur. B.A. 1853; Deac. 1854, by Bp of Rip; Pr. 1855, by Bp of Manch; formerly C. of South Shields, 1855-59.

WAYLAND, Charles, *Holcombe rectory, Shepton-Mallet, Somerset.*—Wadh. Coll. Oxon. B.A. 1808, M.A. 1811; Deac. 1810, by Bp of Bang. Pr. 1811, by Archbp. of York; R. of Holcombe, Dio. B. and W. 1845 (Patron, Rev. T. R. Joliffe; Tithe—Imp. 2*l*; R. 58*l*; Glebe, 18 acres; R.'s Gross Inc. 99*l* and Ho; Pop. 464); C. of Babington, Somerset.

WEBBER, William Thomas Thornhill, *Chiswick, Middlesex.*—Pemb. Coll. Oxon.B.A. 1859; Deac. 1860, by Bp of Lond . C. of Chiswick, 1860.

WEBSTER, John, 28, *King's-road, Ball's-pond-road, London.*—Gon. and Caius Coll. Camb. B.A. 1859; Deac. 1860, by Bp. of Lond; C. of St. Jude's, Mildmay-park, Islington. London, 1860.

WEDDELL, John Egdell, *Hanslope, Stony Stratford, Bucks.*—St. Bees Theol. Coll; Deac. 1852, P. 1853, both by Bp of Lich; C. of Hanslope, 1860; late C. of Winchendon, Bucks; formerly C. of St. George's, Birmingham; previously C. of Tunstall, Staffs.

WELBY, Walter Hugh Earle, *Strensham rectory, Tewkesbury.*—Corpus Coll. Oxon. B.A. 1855, M.A. 1859; Deac. 1856, Pr. 1857, both by Bp of Linc; R. of Strensham, Dio. Worc. 1860 (Patron, G. A. Taylor, Esq; Glebe, 156 acres; R.'s Gross Inc. 230*l*. and Ho; Pop. 350); formerly C. of Stroxton, Lincolnshire, 1856-60.

WELLDON, Edward Ind, *Tonbridge, Kent.*—Qu. Coll. Camb.B.A.1844,M.A.1847; Deac. 1847, Pr. 1849, both by Archbp. of Cant; 2nd Mast. of Tonbridge School.

WELLS, George Francis, *Chisleden, Swindon, Wilts.*—Chr. Ch. Oxon. B.A. 1860; Deac. 1860, by Bp of Salis; C. of Chisleden, 1860.

WENN, James William, *Broome rectory, Bungay, Norfolk.*—Caius Coll. Camb. B.A. 1820; R. of Broome, Dio. Norw. 1859 (Patron, Sir W. F. F. Middleton; R.'s Gross Inc. 300l. and Ho; Pop. 552); Dom. Chap. to the Duke of Hamilton and Brandon.

WEST, William Henry, *Stogursey, Bridgwater, Somerset.*—Worc. Coll. Oxon. B.A. 1824; C. of Stogursey, 1859; formerly C. of Westbury, Wilts.

WESTALL, William, *Halstead, Essex.*—Qu. Coll. Camb. B.A. 1847, M.A. 1850; Deac. 1848, Pr. 1849; C. of St James the Apostle, Halstead, 1859; formerly C. of St Paul's, Knightsbridge, and Head Mast. of St Paul's Gram. Sch. Knightsbridge, Lond. 1855–59.

WESTBROOK, Francis, *Wall, Hexham, Northumberland.*—Worc. Col. Oxon. B.A. 1859; Deac. 1859, by Archbp of York; C. of St Oswald and St Mary's, Bingfield, Northumberland.

WESTHORP, Sterling Browne, *Earl's-court, Kensington, London, W.*—Chr. Coll. Camb. B.A. 1854; Deac. 1854, Pr. 1855, both by Bp of Norw; C. of St Philip's, Earl's-court, Kensington, 1859; formerly C. of Sternfield, Suffolk.

WESTON, Frederick, *Chargfield, Woodbridge, Suffolk*—St. John's Coll. Camb. B.A. 1849, M.A. 1854; Deac. 1850, Pr. 1851, both by Bp of Salis; P.C. of Charsfield, Dio. Norw. 1859 (Patron, Earl Howe; P. C.'s Gross Inc. 110l; Pop. 511); formerly C. of Biddulph, Cheshire.

WETENHALL, William Henry, *Powerstock, Bridport, Dorset.*—St Peter's Coll. Camb. B.A. 1859; Deac. 1860, by Bp of Salis; C. of Powerstock, 1860.

WETHERELL, William, *Heyford-Warren, Bicester, Oxfordshire.*—New Coll. Oxon. B.C.L. 1843, M.A. 1856; Deac. 1842, Pr. 1843, both by Bp of Oxon; R. of Heyford Warren, Dio. Oxon. 1859 (Patron, New Coll. Oxon; R.'s Gross Inc. 120l; Pop. 399); formerly Fell. and Bursar of New Coll. Oxon.

WHEELER, William Hancock, *Winscombe, Axbridge, Somerset.*—Wadh. Coll. Oxon. B.A. 1860; Deac. 1860, by Bp of B. and W; C. of Winscombe, 1860.

WHITAKER, Robert, *Leconfield parsonage, Beverley, Yorks.*—Trin. Coll. Camb. B.A. 1854, M.A. 1857; Deac. 1854, Pr. 1855, both by Archbp of York; R. of Scorborough w Leconfield P.C. Dio. York, 1859 (Patron, Lord Leconfield; Tithe—Scarborough, R. 306l 18s, Leconfield, Glebe, 27 acres; R.'s Gross Inc. 380l and Ho; Pop. Scarborough, 90, Leconfield, 260); late C. of Cheney-Burton, Yorkshire, 1858–59; formerly C. of Stokesley.

WHITE, Henry, *4 Lancaster-place, Strand, London.*—King's Coll. Lond. Theol. Assoc. 1857; Deac. 1857, by Bp of Lich. Pr. 1858, by Archbp of Cant; Chap. of the Chapel Royal, Savoy-street, Strand, Dio. Lond. 1859 (Patron, the Crown; Chap.'s Gross Inc. 300l); formerly C. of St James's, Dover, 1857–59.

WHITE, Henry Towry, *Wereham, Stoke-Ferry, Norfolk.*—Trin. Coll. Dub. B.A. 1847, Theol. Test. 1849; Deac. 1850, Pr. 1852, both Bp of Oxon; P.C. of Wereham w Wretton P.C. Dio. Norw. 1859 (Patron, E. R. Pratt, Esq; P.C.'s Gross Inc. 150l; Pop. Wereham, 609, Wretton, 538); formerly C. of Newbury and Chap. to the Newbury Union, Berks, 1850–59.

WHITEHEAD, Edward, *Chichester.*—Wadh. Coll. Oxon. B.A. 1836, M.A. 1838; Deac. 1838, Pr. 1839; P.C. of St John the Evangelist, City and Dio. Chich. 1859 (Patrons, Trustees; P.C.'s Gross Inc. 100l); formerly Dom. Chap. to the Bp of Madras, 1839–49; R. of Saltford, Somerset, 1849–53; Min. of Laura Chapel, Bath, 1853–59; Author, *Sketch of the Church in India,* Rivingtons, 1848; various *Sermons.*

WHITEHEAD, Edward, ...—St John's Coll. Oxon. B.A. 1851, M.A. 1858; Deac. 1859, by Bp of Norw. Pr. 1860, by Bp of Winch; formerly C. of Banham, Norfolk.

WHITEHEAD, Henry, *Avington rectory, near Winchester.*—Linc. Coll. Oxon. 2nd Cl. Lit. Hum. and B.A. 1850, M.A. 1854; Deac. 1851, Pr. 1852, both by Bp of Lond; R. of Avington, Dio. Winch. 1860 (Patron, Bp of Winch; Tithe—R. 270l 7s; Glebe, 25 acres; R.'s Gross Inc. 300l and Ho; Pop. 176); late C. of Holy Trinity, Clapham, Surrey; formerly C. of St Luke's, Berwick-street, London; Author, *The Cholera in Berwick-street,* Hope and Co; *The Outcast at Home, a History of the Belvidere-crescent Reformatory,* Hatchards.

WHITELEGG, William, *Threlkeld parsonage, Penrith, Cumberland.*—Qu. Coll. Oxon. B.A. 1837, M.A. 1840; Deac. and Pr. 1850; P.C. of Threlkeld, Dio. Carl. 1858 (Patron, Earl of Lonsdale; Glebe, 14 acres; P.C.'s Gross Inc. 70l and Ho; Pop. 375); formerly P.C. of Tilstock, Shropshire.

WHITESTONE, William Arthur, *Slindon, Arundel, Sussex.*—Trin. Coll. Dub. B.A. 1856; Deac. 1857, by Bp of G. and B. Pr. 1860, by Bp of Chich; C. of Slindon and Binsted, 1860; formerly C. of Holy Trinity, Forest of Dean, Gloucestershire.

WHITFIELD, Frederick, *Otley, Yorks.*—Trin. Coll. Dub. B.A. 1860; Deac. 1859, Pr. 1860; C. of Otley, 1859; Author, *Book of Sacred Poems* and *Prose,* Carey and Co. Dublin; various *Sermons* and *Tracts.*

WHITLEY, Thomas, *Clun, Shropshire.*—Emman. Coll. Camb. B.A.1855, M.A.1858; Deac. 1857, Pr. 1857, both by Bp of Ely; C. of Clun, 1859; formerly C. of Elton, Hunts, 1856–57; C. of Oundle, Northants, 1857–59.

WHITLOCK, John Aston, *Plaxtole, Sevenoaks, Kent*—Brasen. Coll. Oxon.B.A. 1859; Deac. 1859, Pr. 1860, both by Archbp of Cant; C. of Plaxtole, 1859.

WHITMORE, Henry, *Dalton-in-Furness, Ulverstone, Lancashire.*—Trin. Coll. Camp. B.A. 1859; Deac. 1859, Pr. 1860, both by Bp of Carl; C. of Dalton-in-Furness, 1859.

WHITTINGTON, Henry Gambier, *Irthlingborough, Higham-Ferrers, Northants,*—St Peter's Coll. Camb. B.A. 1860; Deac. 1860, by Bp of Peterb; C. of Irthlingborough, 1860.

WHITTLE, Charles, *Stoke-Abbas, Dorset.*—Trin. Coll. Oxon. S.C.L. 1846; Deac. 1848, Pr. 1849, both by Archbp of York; C. of Stoke-Abbas, 1859; P.C. of Greenham, Berks, 1855–59.

WHYTE, James Richard, *Launcells vicarage, Stratton, Cornwall.*—Oriel Coll. Oxon. B.A. 1832; Deac. 1832, Pr. 1833, both by Bp of Exon; V. of Launcells, Dio. Exon. 1844 (Patron, Sir G. S. Stueley, Bart. Hartland Abbey, Devon; Tithe—V. 220l; Glebe, 9 acres; V.'s Gross Inc. 230l. and Ho; Pop. 728); formerly C. of Launcells, 1832–34; C. of Okehampton, Devon, 1834–40; C. of King's-Nympton, Devon, 1840–44.

WICKHAM, Edward Charles, *New College, Oxford.*—New Coll. Oxon. Chan. Prize Lat. Verse, 1856; M.A. 1858; Deac. 1857, Pr. 1858; Fell. and Tutor of New Coll. Oxon.

WICKHAM, Latham, *Twyford, near Winchester.* Ch. Ch. Oxon. B.A.1857; Deac. 1858, Pr. 1859, both by Bp of Worc; C. of Twyford; formerly Asst. Mast. of Leamington Coll.

WIGAN, Septimus, *East Malling, Maidstone, Kent.*—Trin. Coll. Camb. B.A. 1856, M.A. 1858; Deac. 1856, Pr. 1859, both by Archbp of Cant; C. of East Malling, 1859; formerly C. of St Mary's, Dover.

WIGHTWICK, Humphrey Mercer, ...—Literate; Deac. 1859, Pr. 1860, both by Bp of Lond; C. of Chr. Ch. Spitalfields, Lond. 1859.

WIGLESWORTH, James Langton, *Chickerell, Weymouth, Dorset.*—Magd. Coll. Camb. B.A. 1845, M.A. 1849; Deac. 1846, Pr. 1847; C. of West Chickerell, 1859; formerly C. of Elmstead, near Colchester, 1846–48; C. of St John the Evangelist, Westminster, Lond. 1848–59.

WIGRAM, Spencer Robert, *Farnham, Surrey.*—Balliol Coll. Oxon. B.A. 1859; Deac. 1860, by Bp of Winch; C. of Farnham, 1860.

WILBERFORCE, William Francis, *4 Upper Southampton-street, Reading.*—Univ. Coll. Oxon. B.A. 1856, M.A. 1858; Deac. 1857, Pr. 1859, both by Bp of Oxon; C. of St Giles's, Reading, 1859.

WILCOCKS, Horace Stone, *Stone cottage, Devonport.*—St John's Coll. Camb. B.A. 1859; Deac. 1859, by Bp of Manch. Pr. 1860, by Bp of Exon; C. of St. James the Great, Devonport, 1860; formerly Asst. C. of St Luke's, Heywood, Lancashire, 1859-60.

WILD, Robert Louis, *Ashperton, near Ledbury, Herefordshire*—Oriel Coll. Oxon. B.A. 1860; Deac. 1860, by Bp of Heref; C. of Canon Frome, near Ledbury, 1860.

WILDE, Albert Sydney, *The Vicarage, Louth, Lancashire.*—Trin. Coll. Camb. Coll. Prizeman 2nd Sen. Opt. and B.A. 1849; Deac. 1849, Pr. 1850; V. of Louth, Dio. Linc. 1859 (Patron, Bp of Linc; Tithe—V. 48*l*, Glebe, 147 acres; V.'s Gross Inc. 350*l*. and Ho; Pop. 10,553); Chap. to Bp of Linc. 1859; formerly R. of Greatford *w* Wilsthorpe, Lincolnshire, 1850-59.

WILKINSON, George Howard, *Seaham-Harbour. near Sunderland.*—Oriel Coll. Oxon. B.A. 1859; Deac. 1857, Pr. 1858, both by Bp of Lond; P.C. of Seaham-Harbour, Dio. Dur. 1859 (Patroness, Marchioness of Londonderry; P.C.'s Gross Inc. 245*l*; Pop. 6000); formerly C. of Kensington, 1857-59.

WILKINSON, George Pearson, *Harperley-park, Darlington, Durham.*—Univ. Coll. Dur. B.A. 1844, M.A. 1845; Deac. 1857, Pr. 1858, both by Bp of Dur; P.C. of Thornley, Dio. Dur. 1857 (Patron, Bp of Chest; P.C.'s Gross Inc. 100*l*; Pop. 3500).

WILKINSON, Joseph, 3 *Saxon-street, Dover.*—Gon. and Caius Coll. Camb. B.A. 1856, M.A. 1860; Deac. 1857, Pr. 1858, both by Archbp of Cant; C. of Ch. Ch. Dover, 1857.

WILLIAMS, Alfred, *Prior's-Portion rectory, Tiverton, Devon.*—Qu. Coll. Camb. B.A. 1842, M.A. 1845; Deac. 1846, Pr. 1850; R. of Prior's-Portion, Tiverton, Dio. Exon. 1855 (Patron, King's Coll. Camb; R.'s Gross Inc. 490*l*. and Ho; Pop. 2000).

WILLIAMS, Arthur Vaughan, *Christ Church, Oxford.*—Ch. Ch. Oxon. B.A. 1857, M.A. 1860; Deac. 1860, by Bp of Oxon; Student of Ch. Ch. Oxon.

WILLIAMS, Garnon, *St John's parsonage, Brecon.*—Oriel Coll. Oxon. B.A. 1851; Deac. 1852, Pr. 1853; V. of St John's *w* St Mary's C. Brecon, Dio. St David's 1859 (Patron, Dean of Lland; V.'s Gross Inc. 180*l*. and Ho; Pop. 4285); formerly V. of Llowes and P.C. of Llanddewi-Fach, Radnorshire, 1853-59; Author, *The Happy Isles* (Poems), Saunders and Otley, 1858, 5*s*.

WILLIAMS, Isaac, *Stinchcombe, near Dursley, Gloucestershire.*—Trin. Coll. Oxon. B.A. 1826, M.A. 1831, B.D. 1839; formerly Fell. of Trin. Coll. Oxon; Author, Poems—*The Cathedral,* 1838; *Thoughts in Past Years,* 1838; *Hymns from the Breviary,* 1839; *The Baptistry,* 1842; *Ancient Hymns,* 1842; *Hymns on the Catechism,* 1843; *Sacred Verses with Pictures,* 1846; *The Altar,* 1847; *The Christian Scholar,* 1849; *The Creation,* 1850; *The Christian Seasons,* 1854; *In Lyra Apostolica Signature,* 1836; *Commentary on the Gospels,* 8 vols. 1841-50; *The Apocalypse,* 1852; *The Way of Eternal Life,* 1845; Editor of the *Plain Sermons,* 10 vols. 1840-48; *Sermons on the Catechism,* 1851; *Sermons on the Epistle and Gospel,* 3 vols. 1853; *Sermons on the Old Testament Characters,* 1856; *Female Characters of Scripture,* 1859; *Sermon at Llangorwen,* 1841; *Tracts for the Times,* Nos. 80, 87; *On Reserve in Religious Teaching,* No. 86; *On the Prayer-book;* Reviews on the *Epistle to the Hebrews,* Brit. Crit. 1839, No. 26; Reviews on the *Oxford Psalter,* 1840, No. 27.

WILLIAMS, Jeremiah, *Hope vicarage, Mold, Flintshire.*—Qu. Coll. Oxon. B.A. 1843; Deac. 1844, by Bp of St Asaph, Pr. 1845, by Bp of Bang; V. of Hope, *alias* Estyn, Dio. St Asaph, 1859 (Patron, Bp of St Asaph; V.'s Gross Inc. 270*l* and Ho; Pop. 1787); formerly C. of Pontblyddvn, Flintshire.

WILLIAMS, Morris, *Llanrhyddlad rectory, near Holyhead.*—Jesus Coll. Oxon. 2nd Cl. Class. and B.A. 1835, M.A. 1840; Deac. 1836, by Bp of Chest. Pr. 1836, by Bp of St Asaph; R. of Llanrhyddlad *w* Llanvlewin C. and Llanrhwydrus C. Dio. Bang. 1858 (Patron, Bp of Bang; R.'s Gross Inc. 590*l* and Ho; Pop. Llanrhyddlad, 796, Llanvlewin, 121, Llanrhrwydrus, 160); Rur. Dean and Surrog. for the Dio. of Bang; for-

merly P.C. of Amlwch, Anglesey, 1847-58; Author, *Y Flwyddyn Eglwysig,* 16mo. 1843; *A Welsh Translation of Dr. Sutton's "Disce Vivere,"* 1847; *A New Translation of the "Book of Homilies" into Welsh,* 8vo. 1847; *A Welsh Translation of Dr. Sutton's "Disce Mori,"* 12mo. 1848; *A Metrical Version in Welsh of the Psalms,* 2 edits. 1850; several *Sermons;* Editor of the amended folio "Welsh Prayer-book," 1845; Editor of the revised folio "Welsh Bible," 1852.

WILLIAMS, Philip, *Rewe rectory, near Exeter.*—New Coll. Oxon. B.C.L. 1851, M.A. 1859; Deac. 1856, Pr. 1857, both by Bp of Linc; R. of Rewe, Dio. Exon. 1860 (Patrons, Earl of Ilchester and Countess of Egremont, altern; Tithe—R. 350*l*; Glebe, 50 acres; R.'s Gross Inc. 500*l* and Ho; Pop. 380); formerly Asst. C. of Gedling, Notts, 1856-59; Min. Can. of Chester Cathl. 1859-60.

WILLIAMS, William Rice Steuart, *Esher Green, Esher, Surrey.*—Jesus Coll. Oxon. B.A. 1844, M.A. 1851, ad eund. Camb. 1857; Deac. 1846, by Bp of St David's, Pr. 1847, by Bp of St Asaph; C. of Esher, 182; formerly C. of Selattyn, Shropshire.

WILLIAMS, William Venables, *Llangedwyn (Denbighshire), near Oswestry, Shropshire.*—Jesus Coll. Oxon. B.A. 1852, M.A. 1854; Deac. 1852, by Bp of Bang. Pr. 1853, by Bp of St Asaph; P.C. of Llangedwyn, Dio. St Asaph, 1859 (Patron, Sir W. Wm. Wynn, Bart; Tithe—Imp. 3*l*, App 332*l* 2*s*; P.C.'s Gross Inc. 130*l*; Pop. 325); formerly C. of Ruabon, Denbighshire, 1852-59.

WILLIAMSON, Joseph, *Ashton, Oundle, Northants.*—Magd. Ha. Oxon. B.A. 1860; Deac. 1860, by Bp of Peterb; C. of Oundle, 1860.

WILLINK, Arthur, *Tranmere parsonage, Birkenhead, Cheshire.*—St John's Coll. Camb. Sch. 1845, B.A. 1846, M.A. 1849; Deac. 1849, by Bp of Chest. Pr. 1850, by Bp of Oxon; P.C. of St Paul's, Tranmere, Dio. Chest. 1857 (Patron, John Orred, Esq. Ashwicke, Somerset; P.C.'s Gross Inc. 364*l* and Ho; Pop. 4000); formerly C. of Bickerstaffe, Lancashire, 1849-50; P.C. of Linslade, Bucks, 1850-57.

WILLIS, Alfred, *Strood, Rochester, Kent.*—St John's Coll. Oxon. B.A. 1858; Deac. 1859, Pr. 1860, both by Bp of Roch; C. of Strood, 1859.

WILLIS, Frederick Augustus, *Highworth, Wilts.*—Trin. Coll. Dub. and ad eund. Oxon, B.A. 1855, M.A. 1858; Deac. 1855, Pr. 1857, both by Bp of G, and B; C. of Broad Blunsdon, and Even. Lect. of Highworth, Wilts, 1855; formerly Head Mast. of Peckham Coll. Sch. Surrey, 1850-55; Author, *Methode pratique et raisonnée d'enseigner la langue francaise pour la conversation,* C. Bean, Hoxton, Lond. 1860, 2*s*.

WILLIS, Robert Francis, *Bradpole vicarage, Bridport, Dorset.*—Gon. and Cai. Coll. B.A. 1857; Deac. 1860, by Bp of Salis; C. of Bradpole, 1860.

WILLIS, Robert, *Stanhope, Darlington, Durham.*—Magd. Ha. Oxon. B.A. 1853; Deac. 1854, Pr. 1855; C. of Rookhope, near Stanhope, 1858; formerly C. of Edmonbyers, Durham, 1854-55; C. of Benfieldside, Durham, 1856-57; C. of Carham, Northumberland, 1857-58.

WILLMOTT, Henry, *Kirkley, Lowestoft, Suffolk.*—Pemb. Coll. Oxon. B.A. 1856, M.A. 1859; Deac. 1857, Pr. 1858, both by Bp of Norw; R. of Kirkley, Dio. Norw. 1860 (Patron, the present R; Tithe—R. 142*l* 10*s*; Glebe, 21 acres; R.'s Gross Inc. 163*l*; Pop. 1000); formerly C. of Pakefield, near Lowestoft, 1858-60.

WILLS, Edward Cooper, *Southampton.*—Sid.-Suss. Coll. Camb. B.A. 1859; Deac. 1860, by Bp of Winch; C. of St Mary's, Southampton, 1860.

WILLSON, William Wynne, *Farncombe, Godalming, Surrey.*—St John's Coll. Oxon. Pusey and Ellerton Sch. 1855, B.A. 1859; Deac. 1859, by Bp of Oxon. Pr. 1860, by Bp of Winch; C. of Farncombe, 1860.

WILSON, Hill, 37, *Rue Mogador, Havre-de-Grace, France.*—Trin. Coll. Dub. B.A. 1836; Deac. and Pr. 1839, both by Bp of Down and Connor; British Consular Chap. at Havre, 1857; formerly C. of Stoneyford, Derryaghy, Ireland, 1839-40; C. of Forgney and Noughaville, Longford, Ireland, 1840-44; P.C. of Forgney and Noughaville, 1844-57.

WILSON, James, *Trinity parsonage, Trinity-street, Rotherhithe, London.*—Emman. Coll. Camb. B.A. 1848, M.A. 1854; Deac. 1849, Pr. 1851, both by Bp of St Dav; P.C. of Holy Trinity, Rotherhithe, Dio. Winch, 1859 (Patron, R. of Rotherhithe; P.C.'s Gross Inc. 190*l* and Ho; Pop. 3000); formerly Sen. C. of St. Mary, Rotherhithe, 1851–59.

WILSON, Daniel Frederic, *Mitcham vicarage, Surrey.*—Wadh. Coll. Oxon. B.A. 1852, M.A. 1855; Deac. 1853, by Bp of Calcutta, Pr. 1854, by Bp of Salis; V. of Mitcham, Dio. Winch. 1859 (Patron, W. Simpson, Esq.; Tithe—Imps. 355*l*; V. 435*l*; V.'s Gross Inc. 460*l* and Ho; Pop. 4641); late C. of St Mary's, Islington, Lond; formerly C. of Calne, Wilts.

WILSON, Plumpton Stravenson, *Ringstead, Lynn, Norfolk.*—Exon. Coll. Oxon. B.A. 1852, M.A. 1854; Deac. 1854, Pr. 1855; C. of Ringstead, 1860; formerly C. of Roydon, Norfolk.

WILSON, Richard William, *Woodbridge, Suffolk.*—St Cath. Coll. Camb. B.A. 1858; Deac. 1859, Pr. 1860; C. of St Mary's, Woodbridge, 1859.

WILSON, Robert Spedding, *St Peter's College, Radley, Berkshire.*—Brasen Coll. Oxon. B.A. 1852, M.A. 1855; Deac. 1857, Pr. 1858, both by Bp of Oxon; Fell. of St Peter's Coll. Radley, 1856; late Fell. of Brasen Coll. Oxon.

WILSON, Thomas Charles, *Kirkby Fleetham vicarage, Bedale, Yorks.*—Clare Ha. Camb. 3rd Jun. Opt. and B.A. 1835; Deac. 1836, Pr. 1837; V. of Kirkby Fleetham *w* Fencote C. Dio. Rip. 1859 (Patron, Ld. Chan: V.'s Gross Inc. 350*l* and Ho; Pop. 605); formerly C. of Kirkby-Malzeard, near Ripon. 1840–59.

WILTON, Charles Turner, *Ham-green, Pill, Bristol.*—Exon. Coll. Oxon. B.A. 1855, M.A. 1858; Deac. 1856, Pr. 1857; P.C. of Pill, Dio. G. and B. 1860 (Patron, Rev. H. Mirehouse; P.C.'s Gross Inc. 90*l*; Pop. 2000); formerly C. of Hambledon, Hants, 1856–59.

WILTON, Richard, *Kirkby-Wharfe vicarage, Tadcaster, Yorks.*—St Cath. Coll. Camb. B.A. 1851; Deac. 1851, Pr. 1852, both by Bp of Heref; V. of Kirkby-Wharfe, Dio. York, 1857 (Patron, Archbp. of York; V.'s Gross Inc. 345*l* and Ho; Pop. 702); Dom. Chap. to Lord Londesborough. 1860; formerly C. of Broseley, Shropshire, 1851–54, P.C. of St Thomas, York, and Chap. to the York Union, 1854–57.

WINGFIELD, Charles Lee, *All Souls' College, Oxford.*—Exon. Coll. Oxon. B.A. 1854; All Souls' Coll. M.A. 1857; Deac. 1858, Pr. 1859; Fell. of All Souls' Coll. Oxon. 1855; formerly Under Mast. of Westminster Sch. 1856–58.

WINLAW, William, *Preston, Lancashire.*—King's Coll. Lond. Theol. Assoc; Deac. 1855, Pr. 1856, both by Bp of Manch; P.C. of St Luke's, Preston, Dio. Manch. 1859 (Patron, J. Bairstow, Esq; P.C.'s Gross Inc. 230*l*; Pop. 4000); late C. of St Paul's, Preston; formerly C. of St Peter's, Ashton-under-Lyne.

WINTER, John, *Wednesbury, Staffs.*—Jesus Coll. Deac. 1829, Pr. 1830, both by Bp of Bang; P.C. of St John's, Wednesbury, Dio. Lich. 1844 (Patroness, Lady E. Foley; P.C.'s Gross Inc. 29*Cl*; Pop. 2665).

WINTERBOTTOM, Edward. *Carrington (Cheshire), near Manchester.*—Chr. Coll. Camb. B.A. 1855; C. of Carrington; formerly C. of Middleton, near Manchester.

WINTLE, Frederic Thomas William, *St. Albans, Herts.*—Magd. Coll. Oxon. B.A. 1854, M.A. 1858; Deac. 1859, Pr. 1860, both by Bp of Roch; C. of St. Stephen's, St. Albans, 1859.

WINTLE, Ogle Richard, *Rayleigh, Essex.*—Linc. Coll. Oxon. B.A. 1858; Deac. 1859, Pr. 1860, both by Bp of G. and B; C. of Rayleigh, 1860; formerly C. of Lydiard-Tregoze, Wilts, 1859–60.

WINWOOD, Henry Hoyle, *4 Cavendish crescent, Bath.*—Exon. Coll. Oxon. B.A. 1852, M.A. 1855; Deac. 1855, Pr. 1856, both by Bp of Winch; formerly C. of Farlington, Hants, 1855–58.

WITHERS, Joseph, *Chedgrave, Loddon, Norfolk.* Trin. Coll. Dub. B.A. 1859; Deac. 1859, Pr. 1860, both by Bp of Norw; C. of Chedgrave and Langley, 1860.

WODEHOUSE, Philip Cameron, *Teddington, Twickenham, Middlesex.*—Exon. Coll. Oxon. B.A. 1860; Deac. 1860, by Bp of Lond; C. of Teddington, 1860.

WOLLASTON, William Monro, *Exeter College, Oxford.*—Trin. Coll. Oxon. B.A. 1855, M.A. 1857; Deac. 1857, Pr. 1860, both by Bp of Oxon; Fell of Exon. Coll. Oxon. 1855; Tut. *ib.* 1857.

WOLSTON, Charles, *Chittoe, Chippenham, Wilts.*—St. John's Coll. Camb. S.C.L. 1854, LL.B. 1856; Deac. 1859, Pr. 1860, both by Bp of Worc; C. of Chittoe, 1860; formerly C. of Cradley, Worcestershire, 1858–59; C. of Ashbury, Berks, 1859–60.

WOLSTON, Thomas, *11 Higher-terrace, St Leonard's, Exeter.*—Caius Coll. Camb. B.A. 1819; Deac. 1824, Pr. 1825, both by Bp of Exon; Chap. of St Thomas's Union, Exeter, 1857 (stipend, 80*l*); formerly C. of Withycombe, Rawleigh, Devon, 1824–27; C. of Charleton, Devon, 1827–31; C. of Southleigh, near Honiton, 1831–40.

WOOD, Alfred, *Wolverhampton.*—Qu. Theol. Coll. Birmingham, 1857; Deac. 1859, Pr. 1860, both by Bp of Lich; C. of St Matthew's, Wolverhampton, 1859.

WOOD, Andrew, *Blackheath Proprietary School, Lee, Kent.*—Trin. Coll. Camb. B.A. 1855, M.A. 1858; Deac. 1856, Pr. 1857; Asst. Mast. in Blackheath Proprietary Sch. 1858; formerly C. of Droxford, Hants.

WOOD, Charles Claypon, *Newbiggen-by-the-Sea, Morpeth.*—Chr. Coll. Camb. B.A. 1859; Deac. 1860, by Bp of Dur; C. of Woodhorn *w* Newbiggen, 1860.

WOOD, Frederick John, *Little Marcle parsonage, Ledbury, Herefordshire.* — Trin. Coll. Camb. B.A. 1856; Deac. 1857, Pr. 1858, both by Bp of Rip; C. of Little Marcle; late C. of St Peter's, Leeds; formerly Asst. C. of Berwick-on-Tweed.

WOOD, Henry, *Passenham rectory (Northants), near Stony-Stratford, Bucks.*—King's Coll. London Theol. Assoc. 1859; Deac. 1859, by Bp of Manch. Pr. 1860, by Bp of Peterb; R. of Passenham *w* Denshanger C. Dio. Peterb. 1860 (Patron, Viscount Maynard; R.'s Gross Inc. 750*l* and Ho; Pop. 969); formerly C. of Passenham, 1859–60; Author, *Sermons.*

WOOD, Henry Sotheby, *Dinnington vicarage, near Newcastle-on-Tyne.*—St Cath. Ha. Camb. B.A. 1841; Deac. 1841, Pr. 1842; V. of Dinnington, Dio. Dur. 1857 (Patron, M. Bell, Esq; V.'s Gross Inc. 200*l* and Ho; Pop. 668); formerly Mast. of the Diocesan Commercial Sch. Stoke-upon-Trent, 1847–57.

WOOD, James Russell, *Blackheath Proprietary School, Lee, Kent.*—Trin. Coll. Camb. B.A. 1854, M.A. 1857; Deac. 1856, Pr. 1857; Asst. Mast. in Blackheath Proprietary Sch. 1859; formerly 2nd Mast. of the Gram. Sch. Richmond, Yorks, 1854–56; Asst. Mast. in Blackheath Prop. Sch. 1859; formerly 2nd Mast. of Gram. Sch. Richmond, Yorks, 1854–56; Asst. C. of Hemingford-Abbots, Hunts, 1856–57; C. of Holybourne, Hants, 1857–59.

WOOD, Joseph, *Nunney, Frome, Somerset.*—Brasen. Coll. Oxon. B.A. 1856, M.A. 1859; Deac. 1858, Pr 1859, both by Bp of Worc; C. of Nunney.

WOOD, Matthew, *Giggleswick, Settle, Yorkshire.*—St Cath. Coll. Camb. B.A. 1855, M A. 1858; Deac. 1860, by Bp of Rip; 2nd Mast. of Giggleswick Gram. Sch; formerly Asst. Mast. in the Gram. Sch. Lancaster; Editor, "The Persæ of Æschylus," with notes and translations, Johnson, Cambridge, 1855, 4*s* 6*d.*

WOOD, William Hardy, ... —Univ. Coll. Oxon. B.A. 1859; Deac. 1859, Pr. 1860, both by Bp of Lich.

WOODMAN, Ebener Flood, *Haverfordwest, Pembrokeshire.*—Univ. of Göttingen, Hanover; Deac. 1859, Pr. 1860, both by Bp of St David's; R. of Walton-West, Dio. St Dav. 1860 (Patron, the present R; Tithe — R.'s Gross. Inc. 166*l*; Glebe 1½ acres; Pop. 400); late C. of Steynton; Author, *Work or Worship: which? An Argument for the Christian Sabbath;* various *Sermons* and *Tracts.*

WOODGATES, James Richard, *Holme-Lacy, near Hereford.*—Pemb. Coll. Camb. B.A. 1855; Deac. 1858, Pr. 1859, both by Bp of Salis; C. of Holme-Lacy, 1860; formerly C. of Wingfield, Wilts, 1858–60.

WOODWARD, Samuel, *Hanbury, Bromsgrove, Worcestershire.*—Univ. Coll. Dur. B.A. 1859, Theol. Licen. 1860; Deac. 1860, by Bp of Worc; C. of Hanbury, 1860.

WOOLAM, John, *Cathedral Close, Hereford.*—St John's Coll. Oxon. B.A. 1850, M.A. 1853; Deac. 1854, Pr. 1855, both by Bp of Heref; Head Mast. of the Cathl. Sch. Hereford, 1858; formerly C. of Pipe and Lyde, Herefordshire, 1854-58.

WOOLCOMBE, George, *High Hampton, Hatherleigh, Devonshire.*—Ch. Ch. Oxon. B.A. 1841, M.A. 1844; Deac. 1842, Pr. 1843; Author, *Prohibitions in Marriage,* London, Batty, 2d.

WOOLRYCH, William Henry, *Crowle vicarage, Worcestershire.*—Pemb. Coll. Oxon. B.A. 1849; Deac. 1850, Pr. 1851, both by Bp of Manch; V. of Crowle, Dio. Worc. 1860 (Patron, the present V; V.'s Gross Inc. 300*l* and H; Pop. 580); formerly C. of Jesus' Chapel, Enfield, Middlesex.

WORCESTER, The Right Rev. Henry

PHILPOTT, Lord Bishop of Worcester, 24 *Grosvenor-place, London,* and *Hartlebury Castle, Worcestershire.* — St Cath. Coll. Camb. Sen. Wrang. Smith's Prizeman, 1st Cl. Class. Trip. and B.A. 1829, M.A. 1832, B.D. 1839, D.D. 1847; Deac. 1831, Pr. 1833. Consecrated Bp of Worcester, 1861 (Episcopal Jurisdiction—the Counties of Worcester and Warwick, with 1 Par. in Gloucestershire and 3 in Staffordshire; Gross Inc. of See, 5000*l*; Pop. 752,376; Acres, 1,037,451; Deaneries, 13: Benefices, 417; Curates, 199; Church Sittings, 211,021); his Lordship is Co-Visitor with the Bp of Oxford of Worc. Coll. Oxon; was formerly Mast. of St Cath. Coll. *w* a Can. of Norwich annexed, 1845-60; Chap. to H.R.H. Prince Albert, 1854-60.

WORSLEY, Henry, *Norwood parsonage, Southall, Middlesex.*—Exon. Coll. Oxon, 1839; Michel Sch. of Qu. Coll. Oxon. B.A. 1842, M.A. 1845; Deac. 1844, by Bp of Linc. Pr. 1845, by Bp of Oxon; P.C. of Norwood, Dio. Lond. 1860, Patron, the present P.C; Glebe, 34 acres; P. C.'s Gross Inc. 140*l* and Ho; Pop. 1600); formerly R. of Easton, Suffolk, 1847-60; Author, *Prize Essay on Juvenile Depravity,* 1849, 5*s*; *The Life of Martin Luther,* 2 vols. 8vo. 1856, Bell and Daldy, 24*s*.

WORTHINGTON, Thomas, *Fradswell rectory, Stone, Staffs.*—St Bees Theol. Coll; Deac. 1854, Pr. 1855, both by Bp of Lich; R. of Fradswell, Dio. Lich. 1857 (Patron, Bp of Lich; R.'s Gross Inc. 138*l* and Ho; Pop. 240); formerly C. of Sneyd, Staffs. 1854-57.

WRANGHAM, Digby Strangeways, *South Cave, Brough, Yorkshire.* — St John's Coll. Oxon. B.A. 1854, M.A. 1859; Deac. 1854, by Bp of G. and B. Pr. 1855, by Bp of B. and W; V. of South Cave, Dio. York, 1859 (Patron, H. G. Barnard, Esq; V.'s Gross Inc. 180*l*; Pop. 1421); formerly C. of Sopworth, Wilts, and Badminton, Gloucestershire.

WRANGHAM, Richard, *Middleton-on-the-Wolds, near Beverley.*—St. Bees Theol. Coll; Deac. 1856, by Bp of Carl. Pr. 1857, by Archbp of York; C. of Middleton-on-the-Wolds, 1858; formerly C. of Skelton, near Redcar, Yorks. 1856-58.

WREY, Arthur Bourchier, *Buckingham.*—Trin. Coll. Camb. B.A. 1854, M.A. 1857; Deac. 1855, Pr. 1856, both by Bp of Roch; C. of Buckingham, 1859; formerly C. of Great Berkhamsted, 1855-58.

WRIGHT, Francis Harrison, *Worcester College, Oxford.*—Worc. Coll. Oxon. B.A. 1859; Deac. 1860, by Bp of Winch.

WRIGHT, Henry, *Outwell rectory (Norfolk), near Wisbeach, Cambs.*—Ch. Ch. Oxon. B.A. 1843, M.A. 1846; R. of Outwell, Dio. Norw. 1859 (Patron, Bp of Norw; R.'s Gross Inc. 450*l* and Ho; Pop. 1448); formerly R. of Hambledon, Surrey, 1854-59.

WRIGHT, Henry Henton, 17 *Broomhall-place, Sheffield.*—King's Coll. Lond. Theol. Assoc; Deac. 1859, Pr. 1860, both by Archbp of York; C. of St George's, Sheffield, 1859.

WRIGHT, John Pyndar, *West Ham, Leytonstone, Essex.*—King's Coll. Lond. Theol. Assoc. 1848; Chap. of the West Ham Union, 1857; formerly English Chap. at Valence, France, 1854-55.

WRIGHT, Richard Franklin, *Wrangle vicarage, Boston, Lincolnshire.*—St John's Coll. Oxon. B.A. 1842, M.A. 1853; Deac. 1842, Pr. 1843, both by Archbp of York; V. of Wrangle, Dio. Linc. 1858 (Patron, Rev.Thomas B. Wright; Glebe, 12 acres; V.'s Gross Inc. 760*l* and Ho; Pop. 1196); formerly C. of Wrangle. 1848-58.

WRIGHT, Robert Henry, *Ashford, Kent.*—Trin. Coll. Camb. B.A. 1857, M.A. 1860; Deac. 1860, by Archbp of Cant; C. of Ashford, 1860.

WYATT, Lawrence Alexander, *Enfield, Middlesex.*—Trin. Coll. Camb. Sch. 1857, B.A. 1859; Deac. 1860, by Bp of Lond; Asst. C. of St James's, Enfield, 1860.

WYCHE, Cyrill Herbert Eyre, 11 *York-place, Kennington-park, Lond.*—Trin. Coll. Camb. B.A. 1856; Deac. 1857, Pr. 1859; C. of St. Mark's, Kennington, Lond. 1858.

WYNN, Simon Hart, *Burgh-upon-Baine vicarage, Louth, Lincolnshire.*—Magd. Coll. Camb. B.A. 1824; Deac. 1824, by Bp. of Winch. Pr. 1825, by Bp of Linc; V. of Burgh-upon-Baine, Dio. Linc. 1825 (Patron, W. J. Fox, Esq, Girsby, near Louth; Tithe—V. 80*l*; Glebe, 53½ acres; V.'s Gross Inc. 170*l*. and Ho; Pop. 131.)

YONGE, Denys Nelson, *Shottesbrooke, Maidenhead, Berks.*—Chr. Coll. Camb. B.A. 1859; Deac. 1860, by Bp of Oxon; C. of Shottesbrooke *to* White-Waltham, 1860.

YORK, The Right Hon. and Most Rev. Charles Thomas LONGLEY, Lord Archbp of York, Primate of England and Metropolitan, 41 *Belgrave-square, London, S.W.* and *Bishopthorpe Palace, York.* —Ch. Ch. Oxon. B.A. 1815, M.A. 1818, B.D. and D.D. 1829; Deac. 1818, Pr. 1819, both by Bp of Oxon; Consecrated first Bp of Ripon, 1836; Translated to Durham, 1856; Translated to York, 1860 (Episcopal Jurisdiction—Yorkshire, except that portion of it allotted to See of Ripon; Gross Inc. of See, 10,000*l*; Pop. 764,538; Acres, 2,261,493; Deaneries, 10; Benefices, 534; Curates, 205; Church Sittings, 225,614); his Grace is Visitor of Qu. Coll. Oxon; a Governor of the Charterhouse; Governor of King's Coll. Lond; an Elector of St Augustine's Coll. Cant; one of the Lords of her Majesty's Most Hon. Privy Council; his Grace was formerly one of the Examiners in Lit. Hum. at Oxford, 1825, and subsequently Head Mast. of Harrow Sch; Author, *Charges* (to the Clergy of Dio. of Rip.), 8vo. London, 1838, 1841, 1844, 1847, 1850, 1853; *A Sermon* (for the S.P.C.K. printed in the Report), 1842; *A Sermon* (on the Consecration of Holy Trin. Church, Wakefield), 8vo. Lond. 1844; *The Danger of Neglecting Religious Privileges* (a Sermon) 8vo. Ripon, 1845; *A Pastoral Letter to the Clergy of the Diocese of Ripon,* 8vo. Lond. 1850; *A Letter to the Parishioners of St. Saviour's, Leeds, with an Appendix,* 8vo. ib. 1851; various other *Sermons* and *Episcopal Charges.*

YOUNG, Frederick, *The Cottage, Aylesbury, Bucks.*—Qu. Coll. Oxon. B.A. 1848; Deac. 1848, Pr. 1850; P.C. of Walton, near Aylesbury, Dio. Oxon. 1859 (Patron, The Church Patronage Society; Endowment 60*l*; P.C.'s Gross Inc. 110*l*; Pop. 1100); formerly C. of Trinity Ch. Reading, 1848-54; C. of St. Paul's Ball's-pond, Islington, Lond. 1854-56.

YOUNG, Frederick John, *Sherburn, Milford-Junction, Yorks.*—Chr. Coll. Camb. B.A. 1851, M.A. 1854; Deac. 1852, Pr. 1853, both by Archbp of York; P.C. of South Milford, near Milford Junction, Dio. York. 1859 (Patron, Archbp of York; P.C.'s Gross Inc. 135*l*; Pop. 1000); formerly C. of Sherburn.

YOUNG, William Edward Allen ... . —Worc. Coll. Oxon. B.A. 1857, M.A. 1859; Deac. 1859, Pr. 1860, both by Bp of Chich.

E

NAMES TO BE ELIMINATED

FROM

Crockford's Clerical Directory for 1860.

I.—OBITUARY, &c.

	Page		No.
ADDISON, John	3		20
Alder, Edward Thomas	5	—	15
Aldrich, William	6	—	8
Allanson, Thomas	7	—	12
Amphlett, Joseph	10	—	6
Anson, Arthur Henry	12	—	10
Atkins, Walter Baker	17	—	13
Ayres, Thomas	20	—	12
BAGOT, Egerton Arden	22	—	11
Baker, John	24	—	11
Baker, Richard Peace	24	—	19
Bandinel, Bulkeley	26	—	13
Banks, Jabez	26	—	28
Barlow, Joseph Wagstaff	29	—	14
Barnes, Richard Arthur Knowles	30	—	13
Barrett, William	31	—	7
Batten, Henry	35	—	13
Baylee, John Tyrrell	36	—	20
Bayly, William Goodenough	37	—	10
Baynes, Adam	37	—	12
Bell, John Harrison	41	—	22
Bennett, Hugh	43	—	24
Birds, William Taylor	52	—	1
Board, Richard	59	—	18
Bonnett, Charles Shrubsole	61	—	24
Boothby, Cunningham	62	—	25
Bourke, Sackville Gardiner	64	—	20
Bourne, Lutwidge	65	—	6
Bowlby, Edward	67	—	5
Bowness, George	67	—	27
Bradstock, Rowland Thomas	70	—	15
Bransby, William	71	—	17
Brett, William	73	—	8
Brewster, John	73	—	12
Brewster, William	73	—	14
Browning, David Cunningham	82	—	27
Brownlow, John	83	—	5
Bruce, James	83	—	11
Buck, John Parmenter	84	—	17
Buckland, John	84	—	30
Buckwell, William	86	—	4
Bull, Samuel William	87	—	1
Burra, Richard Curteis	91	—	14
Burridge, Richard	91	—	19
CAMPBELL, Colin Alexander	98	—	19
Candy, John William	99	—	27
Canning, William	100	—	5
Carlisle, Henry Montagu Villiers, Bishop of	102	—	6
Carr, John	103	—	13
Carter, George	104	—	4
Chaffers, Thomas	108	—	3
Chambers, William	109	—	5
Chapman, William Emerson	110	—	9
Chenery, Walter	112	—	21

			No.	
Cholmeley, John Montague	Page 114	No.	13	
Christie, John Frederic	— 114	—	27	
Clare, George Boodle	— 115	—	25	
Clark, William	— 116	—	26	
Clarke, John Alexander	— 117	—	19	
Clarke, Joseph	— 117	—	25	
Clarke, Thomas	— 118	—	7	
Clarkson, Isaac	— 118	—	24	
Close, Isaac	— 121	—	21	
Cobbold, Edward	— 123	—	5	
Cobden, Halsted Elwin	— 123	—	10	
Colby, William	— 125	—	15	
Colton, William Charles	— 129	—	16	
Cooke, Francis	— 132	—	1	
Cookson, Francis Thomas	— 132	—	26	
Corbett, Joseph	— 135	—	24	
Cornish, Arthur Athelstan	— 136	—	16	
Craven, Thomas Philip	— 142	—	15	
Croly, George	— 145	—	10	
Crowther, Thomas	— 146	—	24	
DADE, Thomas	— 150	—	8	
Dakeyne, John Osmond	— 150	—	12	
Dale, Joseph	— 150	—	19	
Davies, David Rowland	— 155	—	16	
Davies, George	— 155	—	30	
Davies, Morgan	— 157	—	8	
Davison, George Edward Wood	— 159	—	15	
Dawson, John	— 160	—	12	
Denham Joshua Frederick	— 164	—	10	
Dix, Edward	— 168	—	2	
Donne, James	— 171	—	9	
Drake, Charles Style	— 173	—	27	
Drake, John Tyrwhitt	— 174	—	1	
Durham, Charles Thomas Longley, Bishop of	— 178	—	26	
Dykes, Charles Edward	— 179	—	26	
Dyson, Charles	— 180	—	6	
Evans, William	— 196	—	3	
EDGAR, John Robert	— 182	—	16	
Edgell, Edward	— 183	—	3	
Ensor, Edmund Smith	— 191	—	9	
Evans, Charles William	— 192	—	14	
FARDELL, Thomas	— 200	—	10	
Ferguson, Daniel	— 205	—	3	
Finch, Charles	— 206	—	19	
Fitzherbert, Alleyne	— 209	—	12	
Forrest, Matthias	— 213	—	4	
Fox, John	— 216	—	18	
French, William	— 220	—	10	
Fry, Thomas	— 221	—	4	
GARRARD, Samuel Ellis	— 225	—	8	
Gee, Frederick	— 227	—	7	
Geneste, Maximilian	— 227	—	25	
Gilpin, Edwin	— 233	—	2	

Name	Page	No.
Goodacre, William ... ... Page 238	—	3
Gray, James ... ... — 244	—	21
Greaves, George... ... ... — 245	—	17
Green, George Rowney ... ... — 246	—	13
Greenwood, Robert ... ... — 248	—	26
Guildford, Right Hon. Francis North — 255	—	1
Gully, Samuel Thomas Slade ... ... — 255	—	11
Gunning, William ... ... — 255	—	18
HALL, Samuel William ... ... — 260	—	20
Hamilton, James ... ... — 262	—	18
Hanson, William Henry ... ... — 265	—	2
Harcourt, Leveson Vernon ... ... — 265	—	9
Harries, Howell... ... ... — 268	—	15
Harrison, William ... ... — 272	—	3
Hart, John ... ... — 272	—	17
Hay, Edward ... ... — 278	—	27
Hayward, George Christopher ... ... — 280	—	11
Head, Henry Erskine ... ... — 280	—	22
Henney, Thomas Frederick ... ... — 284	—	27
Hepworth, William ... ... — 285	—	20
Hickin, William ... ... — 289	—	16
Hill, Charles ... ... — 291	—	7
Hillcoat, Henry Brougham William ... — 293	—	9
Hine, Henry Thomas Cooper ... ... — 294	—	17
Holdsworth, Henry ... ... — 300	—	11
Holdsworth, Robert ... ... — 300	—	13
Holmes, William ... ... — 303	—	19
Hunt, John Higgs ... ... — 318	—	22
Hunt, Thomas ... ... — 318	—	26
Hutchins, Edward ... ... — 320	—	20
INMAN, William Charles ... ... — 324	—	26
Ion, John ... ... — 325	—	2
Irving, George Charles ... ... — 325	—	21
JAMES, Edward ... ... — 330	—	4
Jenkins, Joseph ... ... — 334	—	18
Johnson, Frederick William ... ... — 338	—	16
Jones, Henry Prowse ... ... — 343	—	19
Jones, James ... ... — 344	—	10
Julian, Richard Archer ... ... — 350	—	24
KINGSLEY, Charles ... ... — 359	—	17
Kirby, John ... ... — 360	—	9
Kirke, St. George ... ... — 360	—	10
Knollis, James ... ... — 363	—	5
Knox, John Henry ... ... — 363	—	20
LAING, David... ... ... — 364	—	24
Lambe, Thomas Robert ... ... — 365	—	20
Lancaster, Thomas William ... ... — 366	—	13
Lawton, Joseph Thomas ... ... — 371	—	11
Leach, Walter Burton ... ... — 372	—	18
Le Bas, Charles Webb ... ... — 373	—	12
Leventhorpe, Thomas William ... ... — 378	—	10
Lewis, Edward ... ... — 378	—	28
Lloyd, George Wood ... ... — 384	—	17
Lloyd, Robert Watkin ... ... — 385	—	13
Longhurst, Charles ... ... — 387	—	17
Lovell, Edward... ... ... — 388	—	26
Lowe, Thomas ... ... — 389	—	18
Lowe, Thomas Hill ... ... — 389	—	20
Lowndes, Thomas ... ... — 390	—	4
Luxmoore, John Henry Montagu ... — 393	—	15
Lyde, Samuel ... ... — 393	—	22
MABERLEY, Frederick Herbert ... — 394	—	19
Machell, Robert ... ... — 395	—	26
Martin, George ... ... — 410	—	8
Mason, James Holman ... ... — 411	—	24
Mason, Thomas ... ... — 412	—	11
Mason, Thomas Wall... ... ... — 412	—	13
Mayor, Joseph ... ... — 417	—	20
Mence, Samuel ... ... — 420	—	3
Metcalfe, James Wood ... ... — 422	—	1
Mill, Sir John Barker ... ... — 424	—	13
Miller, Charles ... ... — 424	—	18
Mills, John ... ... — 425	—	18
Molony, Francis Wheler ... ... Page 429	—	6
Moon, Samuel ... ... — 431	—	6
Moysey, Charles Abel ... ... — 441	—	3
Murray, Thomas Boyles ... ... — 443	—	1
NAYLOR, Frederick Leeds ... ... — 445	—	6
Neilson, Horatio ... ... — 446	—	5
Newland, Henry ... ... — 449	—	5
Nichols, Henry ... ... — 450	—	21
Nixon, Edward John ... ... — 452	—	13
Nott, Anthony... ... ... — 454	—	17
OAKES, James ... ... — 456	—	2
Osmond, Charles ... ... — 460	—	12
Outhwaite, Thomas ... ... — 460	—	27
PACKE, Augustus ... ... — 464	—	7
Palmer, Charles Archdale ... ... — 466	—	8
Parker, John ... ... — 468	—	23
Parkinson, Abraham Dunlin ... ... — 469	—	19
Partridge, Charles Francis ... ... — 471	—	26
Peachey, John ... ... — 474	—	15
Pearce, Prossor ... ... — 474	—	26
Pearson, George ... ... — 475	—	18
Peel, Frederic ... ... — 477	—	9
Pilling, Charles Richard ... ... — 486	—	25
Pine-Coffin, John Thomas, ... — 487	—	11
Pochin, George... ... ... — 489	—	21
Potenger, Richard ... ... — 493	—	23
Powell, Baden ... ... — 494	—	17
Powell, Morgan ... ... — 495	—	13
Powley, Robert... ... ... — 496	—	21
Price, John Standish ... ... — 500	—	1
Price, Thomas ... ... — 500	—	9
Price, William ... ... — 500	—	13
Pryor, Frederick Bell ... ... — 503	—	11
Pugh, Richard ... ... — 503	—	23
Pulling, William ... ... — 504	—	13
Purbrick, Lewis ... ... — 504	—	17
Purser, Samuel Powell ... ... — 505	—	3
RABETT, Reginald ... ... — 507	—	24
Radclyffe, Henry Clifford ... ... — 508	—	12
Ramsden, William ... ... — 509	—	9
Randolph, Henry Jones ... ... — 510	—	1
Reay, Stephen ... ... — 513	—	29
Rees, William Jennings ... ... — 515	—	4
Repton, Edward ... ... — 515	—	29
Reynolds, John ... ... — 516	—	18
Rice, Henry ... ... — 517	—	9
Richards, Evan ... ... — 517	—	24
Richards, Lewis ... ... — 518	—	15
Richardson, John ... ... — 519	—	10
Roberts, Alfred ... ... — 523	—	7
Roberts, Richard ... ... — 524	—	22
Rochester, George Murray, Bishop of — 528	—	2
Round, James Thomas ... ... — 531	—	19
Rowlandson, Thomas ... ... — 533	—	5
Roxby, Henry Roxby ... ... — 533	—	23
Rutherford, James ... ... — 537	—	2
SANDFORD, Richard ... ... — 542	—	7
Scaife, George ... ... — 545	—	8
Scobell, Edward ... ... — 545	—	26
Scott, Thomas Hobbes ... ... — 547	—	11
Sharpe, John ... ... — 552	—	26
Shore, William Henry ... ... — 556	—	21
Shuckburgh, Robert ... ... — 557	—	12
Shutte, Richard ... ... — 557	—	20
Simpson, John Holt ... ... — 560	—	1
Skelton, Joseph ... ... — 561	—	11
Smith, James Allan ... ... — 567	—	6
Smyth, Benjamin Staples Trapaud ... — 570	—	10
Snape, Richard... ... ... — 571	—	9
Snody, John Morison ... ... — 571	—	19
Soames, Henry ... ... — 572	—	5
Southwell, Marcus Richard ... ... — 573	—	9
Spence, John ... ... — 574	—	11
Sprigg, Henry ... ... — 575	—	13

Spurgeon, John ... ... Page 575 No. 25
Spurrier, George Henry ... ... — 576 — 2
Staunton, William ... ... — 578 — 19
Stead, Samuel ... ... — 578 — 22
Stokes, John ... ... — 583 — 16
Storks, Thomas Trundle ... ... — 584 — 19
Strangways, Henry Fox ... ... — 585 — 10
Streatfield, William ... ... — 585 — 18
Strong, Thomas ... ... — 586 — 13
Suckling, Richard Randal ... ... — 587 — 27
Swire, John ... ... — 591 — 5

TAYLOR, Henry ... ... — 595 — 27
Taylor, Henry ... ... — 596 — 1
Thompson, Edward ... ... — 602 — 15
Thompson, James ... ... — 603 — 12
Thornton, Richard ... ... — 605 — 12
Thorp, William ... ... — 606 — 3
Todd, Thomas ... ... — 608 — 20
Townsend, Abraham Boyle ... ... — 611 — 7
Traherne, John Montgomery ... ... — 612 — 4
Trimmer, Barrington James ... ... — 613 — 21
Trimmer, Henry Scott ... ... — 613 — 23
Tripp, William Owen ... ... — 614 — 11

UNDERWOOD, Thomas ... ... — 622 — 1

VAUGHAN, John ... ... — 624 — 12
Villers, William ... ... — 626 — 25

WALKER, William ... ... — 632 — 22
Walter, Weever ... ... — 635 — 1

Warcup, Thomas Chute Ellis ... ... Page 636 No. 5
Ward, John Giffard ... ... — 636 — 26
Watson, William Grey ... ... — 642 — 1
Webster, George Mountjoy ... ... — 644 — 13
Weight, George ... ... — 645 — 6
Wheler, Henry Trevor ... ... — 649 — 19
Wild, William Taylor ... ... — 657 — 1
Williams, David ... ... — 661 — 2
Williams, Edmund ... ... — 661 — 10
Williams, John James ... ... — 663 — 12
Williams, Morgan ... ... — 663 — 16
Williamson, William ... ... — 667 — 2
Wilson, George ... ... — 668 — 27
Wilson, William ... ... — 670 — 20
Woodward, Frederick ... ... — 678 — 18
Worcester, Henry Pepys, Bishop of ... — 679 — 20
Worsley, Henry ... ... — 680 — 11
Wrench, Jacob George ... ... — 681 — 15
Wyndham, Robert ... ... — 685 — 8
Wynnyatt, Reginald ... ... — 685 — 18

YATE, Charles ... ... — 686 — 8
York, Thomas Musgrave, Archbishop of — 687 — 9
Youlden, Abraham ... ... — 687 — 18
Young, James ... ... — 688 — 5

II.—SECESSIONS FROM THE CHURCH.

Coventry, John ... ... — 139 — 19
Rawes, Henry Augustus ... ... — 511 — 17
Walford, Edward ... ... — 631 — 1

INDEX

TO

Benefices, Curacies, and Schools

IN ENGLAND AND WALES.

ABERGELE	Meredith, J.	Banbury, Gram. School	Russell, T.
Abersychan	Jones, C.	Banchory-Ternan	Barry, W. F.
Aberystruth	Lewis, W. H.	Banstead	Buckle, E. V.
Acaster-Selby	Pix, G. B.	Barbon	Ben-Oliel, M. M.
Adstock	Matson. R.	Barcheston	Pearse, V.
Adwick-le-Street	Ware, W. W.	Bardfield, Little	Jones, F. F.
Aigburth	Leveson, C. A.	Bardsea	Lee, J. R.
Aintree	Vernon, W. H.	Barkwith, West	Archer, E.
Aislaby	Proud, G.	Barnard-Castle	Teasdale, R. W.
Albans, St.	Wintle, F. T. W.	Barnham	Cornwall, A. W.
Alderbury...	Martin, E. B.	Barr, Great	Davy, A.
Alkrington	Davis, W. S.	Barrington	Devon, E. B.
Allerston	Hynde, W.	Barrow-in-Furness	Barrett, T. S.
Alnwick	Oswald, H. M.	Barrowby	Mitchell, J.
Alnwick, St. Paul ...	Charlton, C.	Barrow-on-Humber	Lewthwaite, J.
Althorne	Candy, H. H.	Barton (Westmoreland) ...	Raikes, H. P.
Alton	Mather, F.	Barton-on-Humber	Day, G.
Alvington...	Thomas, W. M.	Basildon	Sykes, E. J.
Alvington, West	Macdonald, D.	Baslow	Stockdale, J.
Altrincham	Barnacle, H.	Baston	Colton, W. C.
Ampthill	Noble, J. P.	Bath, Abbey Church ...	Jeckell, J. J.
Amwell Great	Todd, H. L.	,, St. Matthew ...	Tate, G. E.
Angle	Pocock, J. C.	Bath, Grosvenor College ...	Rowe, T. B.
Appleby, St. Michael ...	Doughty, E. J.	,, King Edward Gram. School	Collyns, C. H.
Appledore...	Davis, J. L.	,, Rectory Middle School ...	Vicars, J.
Appledram...	Harwood, R.	,, Penitentiary ...	Baskerville, C. G.
Appleton-le-Street ...	Thompson, A. D. C.	,, Sidney College ...	Prior, J.
Ardleigh	Rawden, W. F.	,, United Hospital ...	Tasker, J. C. W.
Arlesey, Three-Counties Asylum...	Butt, J. A.	Bathford	Jickling, F.
Armley	Armfield, H. T.	Batley, School	Kendall, H. P.
Arnesby	Kemp, T. C.	Battle	Littler, J.
Arreton	Burland, C. W.	,, ...	Dobree, J. B.
Ashby, Little	Goodacre, S. B.	Bawburgh...	Deacle, T. H.
Ashby Magna	Foster, J.	Beaufort	Hopkins, J.
Ashford	Wright, R. H.	Beaulieu	Johnson, J. E.
Ashford-Carbonel... ...	Armistead, H. S.	Beckenham	Phillips, T. L.
Ashow	Twisleton-Wykeham-Fiennes, W. S.	Beckermet	Pinhorne, G. S.
		Bedale	Wardell, W. H.
Askern	Teutschel, A. S.	Beddingham	Parish, W. D.
Aspatria	Clay, G. H.	Bedworth	Oates, J. W.
Ashperton	Buckle, J.	Beeston	Pennethorne, G. W.
Ashton-Hayes	Walsh, T. H.	Belgrave cum Birstall ...	Flamstead, A. R. D.
Astley-Bridge	Birley, A.	Belper	Danby, S.
Aston-Abbotts	Thornton, J.	Bempton	Ketchley, W. G.
Aston-on-Trent	Parker, J.	Benenden	Drew, A. A. W.
Atherstone, St. Mary ...	Grover, J.	Benfleet, South	Clulee, C.
Audley, Gram. School ...	Darby, T.	,, ...	Henderson, T. J.
Avington	Whitehead, H.	Benton, Long	Blair, J. L.
Awre	Corfe, N. B.	Benwick	Muriel, H. E.
Aylburton...	Philpot, B.	Berkhamstead, Great ...	Barnes, I.
Aylesbury	Bennett, W.	Berkley	Furneaux, W. D.
		,, ...	Crosland, J.
BADMINSTER	Neville, N.	Berriew	Price, R. E.
Banbury	Brathwaite, F. G. C.	Berwick, St. Leonard ...	Phelps, A. W.
Banbury, South	Tweddle, T.	Bicester	Payne, A. D.

Biddulph	Sharrock, J.
Bidford cum Salford	Clutterbuck, L.
Biggin	Topham, R.
Billinge	Jenkins, J.
Bilston	Newbolt, H. F.
Bilstorpe	Sutton, R.
Bingfield	Westbrook, F.
Bingham	Pavey, A.
Binsted	Whitestone, W. A.
Birmingham, Christ church ...	Ward, J.
,, St. Clement, Nechells,	M'Cormick, W. T.
,, St. Luke	Pitman, E. J. T.
,, ,, ...	Davenport, G.
,, St. Matthias ...	Walker, S.
,, St. Philip ...	Hiron, S. F.
,, St. Thomas ...	Earnshaw, S. W.
,, ,, ...	Townshend, G. H.
Birmingham, King Edward School	Guest, J. M.
,, ,,	Heppenstall, F.
,, ,,	Smith, A.
,, ,,	Hutchinson, T. N.
,, Queen's College ...	Rowe, R. M.
Birstal ,, ...	Earnshaw, J. W.
Bishopsbourne	Sumner, J. H. R.
Bishop's-Lydeard	Morris, A. R.
Bishop-Middleham ...	Theed, T. M.
Bishopstoke	Garnier, T.
,, ...	Pilkington, C. H.
Bishopstrow	Walsh, J. H. A.
Blackburn, St. Paul ...	Stott, J.
,, St. Peter ...	Cooper, T.
Blackley	Doria, A.
Blackheath, All Saints ...	Todd, E. H.
Blackheath, Propr. School ...	Wood, A.
,, ,, ...	Wood, J. R.
,, ,, ...	Streeter, G. T. P.
Bladon	Steele, G.
Blazey, St.	Maughan, J.
Blenheim	Steele, G.
Bletchingdon ... • ...	Sanders, W.
Blisworth	Puckle, E.
Bloxwich	Stoney, R. B.
Blunsdon, Broad	Willis, F. A.
Bluntisham	Rumpf.
Blyford	Noott, J. F.
Bodney	Taylor, C.
Bollington	Grant, H. C.
Bonvilstone	Thomas, E.
Bordesley	Baines, J.
Boroughbridge	Scholfield, C. R.
Boston	Sale, T. W.
Bothal	Lawson, E.
Bourton-on-Water ...	Crawfurd, C. W. P.
Bovey, North	Arden, G.
Boxted	Borton, C.
Boxwell	Clutterbuck, J. B.
Brackley, Gram. School ...	Falkner, T. B.
Bradfield, St. Andrew's College ...	Pullen, H. W.
,, ,,	Denning, S. P.
Bradford, Christ Church, ...	Donagan, H. R.
,, St. Stephen, Bowling ...	Stowell, T. A.
Bradford-on-Avon ...	Barter, H.
,, ...	Candy, H.
,, ...	Melhuish, G. E.
Bradpole	Willis, R. F.
Bramley	Joy, S.
Brayfield ,, ...	Sherwen, W.
Breaston	Dawes, G.
Brecon, St. John and St. Mary ...	Williams, G.
,, St. Mary	Baylis, W. W.
,, ,, ...	Clarke, D. G.
Brenckburn	Taylor, R.
Brisvels, St.	Walmisley, H.
Bridekirk	Brierly, E.
Bridestowe	Gibbens, W.
Bridge	Smith, J.
Bridgnorth, St. Mary Magdalene	Hutchins, C.
Bridgnorth, Gram. School ...	Ward, H. J.
Bridgwater	Seppings, D. W.

Bridgwater, St. Mary	Iago, W.
Bridlington-Quay	Elliott, R. W.
Brigg	Kirk, T.
Brighouse	Tindall, R. A.
Brighton, Christ Church ...	Cutler, H. G. G.
,, Trinity Chapel ...	Walter, J. C.
,, St. Stephen ...	Brass, H.
,, ,, ...	Chalmers, J.
Brighton, College	Day, H. G.
,, ,, ...	Newton, J.
,, ,, ...	Johnson, H. S.
,, ,, ...	Slight, J. B.
Bright-Waltham	Pickford, J. J.
Brigstock	Burton, E.
Brinkworth	Brice, E.
Bristol, Christ Church ...	Lloyd, C.
,, St. Leonard ...	Martin, H.
,, St. Mary-le-Port ...	Walker, S. A.
,, St. Nicholas ...	Martin, H.
,, St. Paul ...	Allan, H.
,, St. Peter ...	Pooley, J. G.
Bromham	Radcliffe, H. E. D.
Broome	Wenn, J. W.
Brosely	Cobbold, R. H.
Broughton, St. John ...	Richards, W. H.
Brynoock	Jones, E.
Buckfastleigh	Bullock, G. F.
,, ...	Cudlip, P. H.
Buckingham	Wrey, A. B.
Buckland-Monachorum ...	Buckley, F.
Buckleham	Allnutt, T.
Bucknall	Nepean, E. Y.
Bulmer	Raymond, O. E.
Bulwell	Brewster, H. C.
Burghclere cum Newtown	Wallace, G.
Burgh-upon-Baine ...	Wynn, S. H.
Burslem	Kirk, W. B.
,, St. John ...	Waters, R.
Burton-Agnes	Clough, J.
Burton-on-Trent	Holmes, S.
,, Holy Trinity ...	Banks, W. T.
,, ,, ...	Cochrane, D. C.
Bury St. Edmund's, Gram. Sch. ...	Summers, E.
Bussage	Hitchcock, W. M.
Butterwick, West	Alcroft, W. R.
Buxton	Blick, J. J.
Bygrave	Starke, A. B. C.
CADEBY	Evans, T. H.
Caerwent	Jones, H.
Caistor	Scarr, G.
Camborne	Buckland, W.
Cambridge, Abbey Church ...	Baker, G. B.
,, All Saints ...	Sharp, W. C.
,, St. Andrew-the-Great	Bull, R. C.
,, Christ Church	Baker, G. B.
,, St. Mary the Great ...	Luard, H. L.
,, St. Paul ...	Smith, W. S.
,, Trinity Church ...	Rumboll, A. H.
,, Corpus College	D'Orsey, A. J. D.
,, St. John's College	Bonney, T. G.
,, King's College	Burnaby, H. F.
,, Magdalen College	Clark, J. M.
,, ,,	Jackson, S.
,, Trinity College	Turing, J. R.
,, Trinity Hall	Atkinson, G. B.
Cambridge, Perse Grammar School	Asplen, G. W.
Came	Dawson-Damer, L. D.
Canford Magna	Daniell, E. F.
Canon-Frome	Wild, E. L.
Canterbury, King's School ...	Mitchinson, J.
Cantley	Gilbert, J. B.
Canton	Fice, E.
,, ...	Newton, W. S.
Capenhurst	Avent, J.
Cardigan, St. Mary ...	Jones, C.
Carlecote	Jackson, E. D.
Carlisle, Christ Church ...	Hurcomb, F. B.
,, ,, ...	Rouse, R. C. M.

Carlton, North	...	Dolphin, J. M.
Carmarthen	...	Acock, E. M.
Carmarthen, St. David ...		Garrett, F.
Carrington	...	Collier, H. A.
,, ...	...	Winterbotton, E.
Carshalton, Proprietary School	...	Smith, J. N.
Casterton	...	Shepheard, H.
Casterton, Little ...	...	Byng, F.
Castle Caereinion ...	...	Vaughan, W. W.
Cattistock	...	Kingston, J.
Chalfont St. Giles ...	...	Drake, E. T.
Challow, East and West ...	...	Waddell, W. D.
Charing	...	Tate, F. B.
Charlton	...	Burkitt, W. E.
,, ...	...	Gillett, H. H.
Charlton-Abbots ...	...	Clarke, W. G.
Charney	...	Minns, G. W. W.
Charsfield	...	Weston, F.
Chartham	...	Kingsford, H.
Chedgrave	...	Withers, J.
Cheltenham, Christ Church	...	Fenn, J. F.
,, St. Mary ...	...	Braithwaite, R.
,, St. Paul ...	...	Hunt, J. W.
,, St. Peter ...	...	Riley, R.
Cheltenham, College ...	...	Cox, G. W.
Chepstow	...	Morgan, S. C.
Chertsey	...	Till, L. W.
Chester, St. John ...	...	Cripps, W. R.
Chesterford, Great ...	...	Metcalfe, F.
Chesterton	...	Coetlogon, C. P. de
,, ...	...	Hodd, A. H.
Cheveley	...	Bennett, E. K.
Chevening	...	Cordeaux, H. T.
Chichester, St. John the Evangelist		Whitehead, E.
Chickerell, West		Wiglesworth, J. L.
Chieveley	...	Littlehales, W. G.
Chingford	...	Morison, J. H. J.
Chinnock, West ...	...	Lawrence, R. G.
Chippenham	...	Sidebottom, F. R.
Chipping-Campden ...	...	Somerset, B. T. G. H.
Chipping-Norton		Barwis, W. C.
Chipping-Ongar ...	...	Moore, D. T.
Chipping-Warden ...	...	Hooke, A.
Chirburg	...	Spoor, R. B.
Chiselhurst	...	Binney, J. E.
Chisleborough		Lawrence, R. G.
Chisledon	...	Wells, G. F.
Chiswick	...	Webber, W. T. T.
Chittoe	...	Wolston, C.
Chorley, St. George ...		Macilwain, G. B.
Christchurch	...	Aitkens, A.
Church-Broughton ...	...	Dalton, J.
Church-Fenton		Banff, H. T.
Clandown	...	Renaud, G.
Clapham, All Saints ...		Campbell, W. A.
Clapton	...	Gatty, R. H.
,, St. James ...	...	Jelf, G. E.
Claverley	...	Beedham, M. J.
Clayton cum Keymer ...		Chritchley, J. M.
Cleator	...	Stammers, F. H.
Cleckheaton		Fowler, W.
Cledfwlch	...	Scott, W.
Cleever	...	O'Brien, J.
Clehonger	...	Stillingfleet, H. J. W.
Clevedon	...	Bliss, T.
,, ...	...	Fothergill, E. H.
Clifford	...	Newman, F. S.
Clifton, Beds.		Richards, J. B.
Clitheroe, Grammar School	...	Beaumont, G. R.
Clun	...	Whitley, T.
Coatham	...	Vyvyar, H. M.
Clydach	...	Edwards, T. C.
Coberley	...	Hicks, G. G.
Cockermouth, All Saints ...		Puxley, H. L.
Coddenham	...	Cooper, E. H.
Codsall	...	Paley, J.
Colchester, St. Peter ...		Clements, W. F.
Coldwaltham		Bazely, J.
Coleshill	...	Allsop, R. W.
Coln St. Denis	...	Hall, E. D.
Coombe-Bissett	...	Pollard, H. S.
Coombe-Keynes	...	Newington, F.
Copford	...	Baynes, C. A.
Cornwood	...	Farrington, J. C.
Corwen	...	Jones, D.
Costock	...	Millard, C. S.
Cottesbrooke	...	Gall, F. H.
Cottingham	...	Garwood, W.
Cotton	...	Starratt, M.
Coven	...	Hathwaite, T. W.
Coventry, Grammar School	...	Soden, J. J.
Cowbridge	...	Evans, J. W.
Cowes, Holy Trinity ...	...	Silver, E.
Crakehall	...	Ibbotson, T. R.
Cranham	...	Rew, C.
Crawley	...	Bourne, C. J.
,, ...	...	Castleman, W. H.
Crawley-cum-Hunton ...	...	Jacob, P.
Crayke	...	Inge, W.
Crediton, Collegiate Church	...	Deans, J.
Cressingham, Great ...	...	Taylor, C.
Cressingham, Little ...	...	Bolling, E. J.
Crewkerne	...	Tomkins, W. S.
Crixeth	...	Candy, H. H.
Crockham-Hill	...	Vincent, R.
Crowhurst	...	Cameron, F. M.
Crawle	...	Woolrych, W. H.
Croxall	...	Watson, R. F.
Crux-Easton	...	Bagge, J.
Cuddesdon, College ...	...	King. E.
Cussop	...	Walkey, C. E.
Cyfarthfa	...	Hughes, M.
DALSTON	...	Blake, W.
Dalton-in-Furness ...	...	Whitmore, H
Damerham	...	Venn, E. S.
Darfield	...	Clayforth, H.
Darley	...	Cutler, C. S.
Darley Abbey	...	Jones, F. J.
Darlington, Holy Trinty ...	...	Charlesworth, E. G.
,, St. John ...	...	Castley, E.
Daventry	...	Stiles, G. E. C.
Dean, East	...	De Quetteville, P.
Debenham	...	Cornish, C. J.
Dedham Grammar School	...	Auden, T.
Denshanger	...	Wood, H.
Denton cum Caldecote ...	...	Badley, E.
Deptford, St. John ...	...	Lilingston, F. A. C.
,, St. Paul ...	...	Turner, R.
Derby, West, St. James ...	...	Burgess, W. R.
Dereham, West	...	Finch, G.
Dethwick	...	Leacroft, C. H.
Devonport, St. James-the-Great ...	...	Wilcocke, H. S.
,, St. Paul ...	...	Bellamy, F.
Dinnington	...	Hoare, E. T.
,, ...	...	Wood, H. S.
Disley	...	Satterthwaite, C. J.
Dissington	...	Tyson, J.
Dodderhill	...	Hough, G. D. J.
Doddington	...	Hutchinson, R. W.
Dolphinholme	...	Adam, W. J.
Doncaster	...	Hone, E. J.
,, St. George ...	...	Vaughan, C. J.
Donnington Wood ...	...	O'Regan, T.
Donyland, East ...	...	Swann, J. T.
Dover, Christ Church ...	...	Wilkinson, J.
,, St. Mary ...	...	Collett, A.
Dowlais	...	Jones, J.
Downend	...	Peache, A.
Downton	...	Swayne, W. J.
Drayton, Little ...	...	Hunter, E. H.
Drigg	...	Beckwith, G.
,, ...	...	Penney, J. W. W.
Drypool	...	Hart, E. O.
Duddon	...	Bryans, F. O.
Dudley	...	Browne, J. G. C.
Duncton	...	New, J.
Dunmow, Great ...	...	Horne, E. L.

Dunsforth, Low	Scholfield, C. R.
Durham, Bishop Cosin's Hall	Hornby, J. J.
Dwrfelin	Jones, E.
EALING...	Hilliard, J. S.
„	Summerhayes, J.
Earl Sterndale	Spencer, A. C.
Easingwold	Vines, T. H.
Eastnor cum Pixley	Parmiter, J.
Eaton cum Gamston	Ward, R. C.
Ebberston...	Hynde, W.
Edenbridge	Gore, C. F.
Edgbaston, Proprietary School	Hiron, S. F.
Edlesborough	Podmore, W. H.
Egleton	King, R. T.
Egham	Dampier, A.
Egham, Strode's Charity ...	Taylor, G.
Ellesmere Port	Gape, C.
Elm	Currie, F. H.
Elmbridge	Hough, G. D. J.
Elmley Castle	Bennett, H.
Ely, Holy Trinity...	Sirney, G.
Enfield	Egles, E. H.
„ St. James...	Wyatt, L. A.
Epsom, Medical College ...	Pentreath, F. R.
Epwell	Montagu, G.
Erpinham	Bowles, W.
Esher	Williams, W. R. S.
Estyn	Williams, J.
Eton, College	Day, R.
„	Stone, E. D.
Exmoor	Thornton, W. H.
Eversley	Stapleton, F. G.
Everton, Christ Church ...	Cornall, R.
Exeter, Cathedral...	Browne, E. H.
„ St. Thomas-the-Apostle ...	Martin, H. J.
Exeter, St. John's Hosp. Gram. Sch.	Butcher, J. H.
„ St. Thomas' Union	Wolston, T.
Exhall cum Wixford	Clutterbuck, L.
FAIRFORD	Rice, F. W.
Faringdon	Dawson-Damer, L. D.
Faringdon, Little	Tilbury, R.
Farncombe	Willson, W. W.
Farnham (Hants)...	Baugh, W J.
Farnham (Surrey)	Borradaile, R. H.
„	Wigram, S. R.
Farnworth	Lees, J. C.
Faversham, Grammar School	Kingsford, S
Fawley	Sheldon, R. W.
Felling	Schofield, J.
Felstead	Stanley, R. R. P.
Fencote	Wilson, T. C.
Fenny Compton	Walter, A.
Fenwick	Law, H.
Field Dalling	Spencer, H.
Filey	Langstaff, G. W.
Finchingfield	Mansfield, G.
Finedon	Warner, R. E.
Fingest	Baker, G. A.
Fleet	Lynes, R. F.
Folkstone	Taylor, C. J.
„ Christ Church ...	Gay, A.
Fordcomb...	Knight, E. B.
Fordwick	Leachman, F. J.
Fotheringhay	Longhurst, A. A.
Fradswell	Scott, R. F.
„	Worthington, T.
Framlington	Taylor, R.
Freystrop...	Walters, J. T.
Frome, Christ Church ...	Drake, J.
Frome Selwood	Bedford, H.
Fyfield	Parker, C. W.
GAINSBOROUGH	Clements, J.
Gamston cum Eaton	Ward, R. C.
Gateforth...	Newenham, B. R.
Gantby	Van Hemert, J.
Gazeley cum Kentford ...	Finlay, E. B.

Gellyfaelog	Evans, H. J.
Giggleswick, Grammar School ...	Wood, M.
Girlington	Allen, T. K.
Girton	Lumby, J. R.
Gittisham...	Kirwan, R.
Gladestry	Thomas, W. J.
Glen Magna	Espin, W.
Gloucester, Mariners' Chapel	Waters, R.
Goathurst...	Codrington, H.
Golborne	Thornton, T.
Godshill	Ward, C. C.
Goldsborough	Lascelles, J. W.
Grantham, St. John Spittlegate ...	Seddon, W.
Greatford...	Mantell, E. R.
Gresford	Smith, E. B.
Grimsby, Great	Taverner, F. J.
Grinshill	Taylor, J.
Guildford, St. Nicholas ...	Sneath, T. A.
Guildford, Grammar School	Arthur, P.
Gunton	Lubbock, H. H.
„	Lee, R.
HAIGH	Bryan, W. R.
Halden, High	Richards, R.
Halifax, St. James	Morrison, W R.
„ St. John-in-the-Wilderness	Farrar, J.
Halstead	Harvey, C. M.
„ St. James-the-Apostle ...	Westall, W.
„ Holy Trinity ...	Sewell, W. H.
Halstow, Lower	Nicholas, T. G.
Halton	Raby, W.
Ham, West (Essex)	Wright, J. P.
Hambledon	Daltry, T. W.
„	Rowsell, E. E.
Hambleton	Cholmeley, W.
Hammersmith, St. John-the-Evan.	Twells, E.
„ St. Stephen	Bartlett, A. J.
Hampden, Great	Ormond, J.
Hampton Lucy	Kershaw, E. D.
Hanbury	Woodward, S.
Hanley, St. Luke... ...	Foster, R.
Hanslope	Weddell, J. E.
Harbridge...	Watson, J. W.
Hardham	Bazely, J.
Harlow	Scott, W. R.
Harnham, West	Pollard, H. S.
Harpenden	Hose, T. C.
„	Vaughan, E. T.
Harpham	Clough, J.
Harpsden...	Bagot, F.
Harrington	Goodhart, E. S.
Harrow, Grammar School	Butler, H. M.
„	Farrar, F. W.
Hascomb	Lewes, J. M.
Hartest	Borton, C.
Hartfield	Polehampton, E. T. W.
„	Polehampton, T. S.
Hartshead cum Clifton ...	Smith, D.
Hastings, Holy Trinity ...	Richards, T. E. M.
Hatfield-Broad-Oak ...	Nix, C. D.
Hathern	Smythies, E.
Hathersage	Stevens, T.
Hault-Hucknall	Grier, F.
Haverfordwest, St. Mary...	Chandler, H. C. D.
Haverland	Thompson, F.
Hawes	Cooper, E. J.
Haydor	Monkhouse, H. C.
Hayes	Randall, W.
Hayton cum Bealby ...	Arundell, T.
Healing	Loft, J. E. W.
Heath	Grier, F.
Heavitree...	Smith, W.
Hebburn	Lawson, E.
Heighton, South	Fothergill, P. A.
Helme	Brook, J.
Henbury	Harford, E. J.
Henley	Sinden, H.
„	Spencer, J. S. E.
Henley-Castle	Walters, W.

Hepworth...	Swallow, F. R.
Hereford, St. Nicholas ...	Parry, T. W.
„　　　„　　　...	Dixon, R.
Hereford, Cathedral School	Woollam, J.
Hereford, Little ...	Armistead, H. S.
Hexton	Spooner, E.
Heyford-Warren	Wetherell, W.
Heywood	Shepherd, T. D.
Highworth	Willis, F. A.
Highworth cum Marston ...	Robinson, A. E.
Hildenborough	Creswell, S. F.
Hoby	Moore, J.
Holcombe...	Wayland, C.
Holdenhurst	Barnard, T.
Holland, Upper	Wambey, C. C.
Holloway	Bruce, W. S.
Holme-Lacy	Woodgates, J. R.
Holme-Low	Bone, W.
Holyhead...	Jones, O. W.
Hook (Dorset) ...	Pardoe, A.
Hope (Staffordshire)	Newton, C.
Hope (Flintshire)... ...	Williams, J.
Horbury	Cass, W. A.
Horkesley, Little	M'Leod, N. K.
Hornsea	Browne, S. S.
Horsell	Walsh, W.
Horsham	Mount, F. J.
Horton	Elliott, R. J.
Horton-in-Ribblesdale ...	Tomlinson, W. B.
Houghton-le-Spring ...	Atcheson, R. S. E.
Houghton-on-the-Hill ...	Andrews, W.
Hove	O'Brien, J.
Howden-Panns ...	Lord, T. E.
Howick	Stephens, L. J.
Huddersfield, St. Thomas...	Snowden, E.
Hugglescote	Cave-Browne-Cave, E
Huish, South ...	Macdonald, D.
Hulme, St. Mary	Parry, W. W.
„　　St. Philip ...	Birley, R.
„　　Holy Trinity ...	Buckley, C. F.
Hull, Christ Church ...	Barnett, J. L.
„　　Mariners' Church ...	Dickinson, G. C.
„　　St. Mary ...	Bird, J.
„　　St. Stephen... ...	Hardman, R. P.
Hundleby...	Bacon, F.
Hungarton	Wasse, H. W.
Hurstgreen-Whalley ...	Beaumont, G. R.
Hurstpierpoint	Redifer, A.
Hythe	Kingsford, B.
IBSTONE	Baker, G. A.
Icklesham	Bartlett, P.
Idehill	Gennys, E. J. H.
Idle	Keeling, R.
Ilchester	Fenn, A. C.
Ilford, Great	Branfoot, T. R.
Ilkeston	Green, J. H.
Ilkley	Snowden, J.
Ilminster	Evans, J. M.
Ipswich, St. Margaret ...	Clark, F. S.
Ipswich, Queen Eliz. Gram. School	Barclay, H. A.
„　　　„　　　„	Mowat, J.
Irthlingborough	Whittington, H. G.
Islip	Lightfoot, N. F.
KEDLESTON	Scarsdale, A. N. H. C.
Kenardington	Davies, J. L.
Kentchurch	Duncombe, W. D. H.
Kersal	Richardson, F.
Kettering...	Etheridge, S.
Ketton	Burroughs, R.
Keyworth...	Potter, A.
Kilmersdon	Tancred, W.
Kilnhurst...	Sheppard, H. F.
Kilvington, South... ...	Kingsley, W. T.
Kimble, Great	Ormond, J.
Kingsclere	Lofty, F. F.
Kingston-on-Thames, Qu. Eliz. Sch.	Rigg, W.
Kington	Green, J. W.
Kinoulton...	Darby, E. G.
Kinson	Daniell, E. F.
Kirby-on-the-Moor ...	Sale, C. H.
Kirkburn	Allen, R.
Kirkby	Blyth, F. C.
Kirkby-Fleetham	Wilson, T. C.
Kirkby-Wharfe	Wilton, R.
Kirk-Ireton	Scragg, W.
Kirkley	Bell, J. H.
„　　...	Willmott, H.
Kirklington	Lanphier, J.
Knowl-Hill	Aldridge, R.
LAKENHAM	Pownall, A.
Lamborne...	Bramston, W. M.
„　　...	Lewington, A. L.
Lancaster Castle	Smith, H. F.
Lane-End...	Hodges, J.
Langford	Tilbury, R.
Langham (Essex) ...	Auden, T.
Langham (Rutland) ...	King, R. T.
Langley (Essex)	Thornton, H. W.
Langley (Norfolk) ...	Withers, J.
Langton	Mackay, S. M.
Lapworth...	Burd, C.
Latchingdon	Formby, R. E.
Launcels	Whyte, J. R.
Lavenham	Beck, A.
Lawton	Turner, J. K.
Layer-Marney	Farman, S.
Leake, East and West ...	Killick, J. H.
Leckhampton	Blunt, A. R.
„　　...	Hutchinson, W. H.
Leconfield...	Whitaker, R.
Ledbury	Hereford, R.
Lee	Warlow, G.
Leeds, Parish Church ...	Robinson, F. S.
„　　St. George ...	Nicholson, R.
„　　St. John the Evangelist ...	Monro, E.
„　　St. Saviour ...	Collins, R.
Leeds, Grammar School ...	Richardson, E. A.
Leicester, St. John ...	Thompson, C.
„　　　„　　　...	Tollemache, C. R.
„　　　St. Margaret ...	Bryan, H.
„　　　„	Pratt, P. E.
„　　　St. Martin ...	Vaughan, D. J.
„　　　St. Mary ...	Packer, S. G.
Leigh (Essex)	King, W.
Leigh (Devon)	Stokes, G.
Leighterton	Clutterbuck, J. B.
Lesbury	Marrett, E. L.
Lincoln, Deanery	Garnier, T.
„　　St. Mary Magdalene ...	James, T. W.
„　　St. Nicholas ...	Harward, E. C.
Linton	Batty, R. E.
Litchfield...	Cotes, P.
Littleborough	Waldy, J. E.
Littlebourn	Rouch, F.
Littleham cum Exmouth...	Ruby, J.
Liverpool, St. Bride ...	Bailey, J. A.
„　　St. Luke ...	Bardsley, J. W.
„　　St. Mary, Edghill ...	Balls, O. C.
„　　St. Nicholas ...	Titley, R.
„　　St. Philip ...	Logan, C.
„　　St. Saviour ...	Pickles, J. S.
„　　St. Stephen ...	Vernon, H. G.
„　　St. Thomas, Park Lane	Owgan, J. R.
Liverpool, Union	Dunkley, J.
„　　Workhouse ...	Keer, W. B.
„　　　„　　　...	Scott, J. H.
Llanbeblig	Vincent, J. C.
Llanblethian	Evans, J. W.
Llanfairisgaer	Griffith, R. W.
Llanffinan...	Priestly, R. E.
Llanfiguel...	Kyffin, T. L.
Llanfihangel-yn-howyn ...	Kyffin, T. L.
Llanfihangel-y-pennant ...	Parry, M.
Llangattock	Howell, J.
Llangedwyn	Williams, W. V.

Llangefni ...	...	...	Lewis, D.
Llangenney	...	...	Howell, J.
Llangoedmore	...	..	Morgan, M.
"	...	...	North, W.
Llanrhidian	...	...	Matthews, T.
Llanrhyddlas	...	...	Williams, M.
Llansannan	...	...	Watkins, W. M.
Llanvair-Discoed	...	...	Jones, H.
Llanvanor...	...	...	Bradshaw, J. M.
Llanvlewin	...	...	Williams, M.
Locking ...	...	...	Powell, E. H.

LONDON :—

Allhallows the Great, City		Stock, J. R.
All Souls, Marylebone ...		Bishop, H. H.
St. Andrew, Lambeth ...		MacAdam, W. H.
" "	...	Allen, W.
St. Andrew, St. Pancras		Hodges, G.
St. Andrew, Westminster		Tipton, W.
St. Barnabas, Clerkenwell		Ward, H.
St. Barnabas, Holloway		Stainforth, F.
St. Barnabas, Kensington		Davis, E. J.
" "	...	Smyth, V. B.
St. Barnabas, King-square		Green, J. R.
St. Barnabas, Pimlico ...		Trevenen, T. J.
St. Bartholomew, Bethnal-green		MacGachen, J. D.
Camden Ch., Camberwell		Carrington, R.
Chapel Royal, Savoy ...		White, H.
Christ Ch., Bermondsey		Coombe, A. B.
" "	...	Pilkington, R.
Christ Ch., Spitalfields...		Wightwick, H. M.
Christ Ch., Broadway West.		Testing, J. W.
St. Clement Danes, Strand		Coxhead, J. J.
Curzon Chapel, Mayfair		Purser, S. P.
St. Gabriel, Pimlico ...		Arnold, F.
" "	...	Dawson, A. A.
St. George, Hanover-square		Edwards, W. W.
St. Geo.-the-Martyr, Bloomsbury		Sumner, J.
" "	...	Hill, J.
St. Giles-in-the-Fields...		Kirkman, J.
" "	...	Loraine, N.
St. James, Bermondsey		Sturman, M. C. T.
St. James, Clerkenwell...		Shaw, T. H.
St. James, Paddington...		Boyd, A.
" "	...	Middleton, J. D.
St. James, Piccadilly ...		Duval, P. S.
St. James, Ratcliff ...		Sadler, H.
St. James-the-Less, Vict. Park		Dandsday, J. H.
" "	...	Grundy, W. J.
St. John, Broad-ct., St. Martin-in-the-Fields		D'Oyly, C. J.
St. John the Evan., Fitzroy-sq.		Alder, J.
St. Jude, Chelsea ...		M'Lorley, H.
St. Jude, Mildmay Park		Webster, J.
St. Jude, St. Pancras ...		Andrews, J. M.
St. Jude, Southwark ...		Cruse, F.
St. Luke, Chelsea ...		Blunt, A. G. W.
" "	...	Blunt, R. F. L.
St. Luke's Lunatic Asylum		Leachman, E.
St. Margaret, Lothbury		Crowden, C.
St. Mark, Kennington		Wyche, C. H. E.
St. Mark, St. Pancras ...		Phelp, P. H.
St. Mark, Whitechapel...		Bartlett, R. E.
St. Mary, Bryanston-square		Nunn, J.
St. Mary, Kensington ...		Reynell, G. C.
St. Mary, Marylebone ...		Thompson, A. S.
St. Mary, Rotherhithe ...		Gardner, J. L.
St. Mary Abbott, Kensington ...		Snape, R. W.
St. Mary-the-Less, Lambeth		Blacker, M. J.
St. Matthew, Brixton ...		Gardner, T. E.
St. Matthew, City-road		Baird, W.
St. Matthew, Marylebone		Meekings, R. W.
St. Matt. Chap., Spring-gardens		Carey, A. F.
St. Matthias, Bethnal-green		Chambers, W. H.
St. Michael, Burleigh-street		Knapton, H. P.
St. Michael, Chester-square		Preston, J.
St. Pancras, Parish Ch.		Champneys, W. W.
St. Paul's Cathedral ...		Spencer, G. J . T
St. Paul, Hampstead-road		Lupton, J. H.
St. Paul, Southwark ...		Seymour, W. S.

St. Paul, Stepney ...		Martin, H.
Percy Episcopal Chapel		Baillie, J.
St. Peter, Notting-hill...		Kett, C. W.
St. Peter, Pimlico ...		Snowden, J.
St. Peter, Southwark ...		Raven, B. W.
St. Philip, Bethnal-green		Mackenzie, R. B.
St. Philip, Earl's-ct. Kensington		Sutherland, C.
" "	...	Westhorp, S. B.
Regent-square Ch., St. Pancras		Burrowes, H.
" "	...	Buss, S.
St. Saviour's, South Hampstead		Hose, J. C.
St. Stephen, Camden-town		Cameron, W.
St. Thomas, Bethnal-green		Doran, J.
St. Thomas, Portman-square ...		Leach, H.
Trin. Ch., St. Giles-in-the-Fields		Horne, W.
Trinity Ch., Gray's-inn-road ...		Acland, C. L.
Trinity Ch., Islington ...		Sweatman, A.
Trinity Ch., Marylebone		Bucke, B. W.
" "	...	Du Port, C. D.
" "	...	Cadman, W.
Trinity Ch., Newington...		Seggins, W. H.
Trinity Ch., Rotherhithe		Wilson, J.
London, Christ Hospital School ...		Potter, T. J.
City School	...	Lupton, J. H.
King's College ...	...	Thelwall, A. S.
St. Mark's College, Chelsea		Benham, W.
Merchant Taylors' School		Crowden, C.
Church Miss. Coll. Islington		Munby, G. T. W.
Qu. Eliz. Gram. Sch. Southwark		Hardingham, C. H.
Westminster School ...		Andrews, S.
Loddiswell ...	...	Marriott, R. C.
Longhorsley	...	Turnbull, G.
Longwood...	...	Laidman, S. L.
Lopham, North and South		Oakley, E.
Lopham, South ...		Dix, T. W.
Loughborough ...		Fearon, H.
" ...	...	Pearson, F. T.
Loughborough, Gram. School		Kitchen, J. L.
Lound ...	...	Dowson, C.
Louth ...	...	Wilde, A. S.
Low-Moor ...	...	Edwards, C.
Luton ...	...	Sprague, W. S.
Lydd ...	...	Burton, C. J.
Lydney ...	...	Foster, J.
" ...	...	Philpot, B.
Lyncombe...	...	Colwill, J.
Lynn, South ...		Gregory, E. S.
Lytham, St. John's ...		Stoney, E. S.
MABLETHORPE ...		Denham, A. F.
Macclesfield ...	...	Oram, H. A.
Maddington ...	...	Chamberlain, S.
Maidstone, Trinity Church		L'Estrange, A. G.
Malden, New ...		Rigg, W.
Malew, Isle of Man		Gill, T. H.
Malling, East ...		Latham, J. L.
" "	...	Wigan, S.
Malpas, Lower Mediety ...		Roberts, J. B.
Man, Isle of, Christ Ch., Manghold		Stowel, H. A.
" Laxey, Church		Pierpoint, M.
" St. Michael ...		Bellamy, J.
" "	...	Kelly, J. B.
" St. Stephen, Sulby		Stuart, J. O.
Manchester, St. Andrew ...		Dunn, A.
" St. Luke, Cheetham-hill		Price, H. M. C.
" St Mark, Cheetham-hill		Glover, F. B.
" Holy Trinity, Salford...		Pitcher, A. W.
Manchester Union ...		Bridges, W.
Mangotsfield ...	...	Peache, A.
Manningham ...	...	Hill, C. C.
Mansfield, St. John ...		Craster, T. H.
Marchington ...	...	Freer, W. H.
Marcle, Little ...	...	Wood, F. J.
Margam ...	...	Thomas, S.
Margaret's, St. ...	...	Metcalfe, G. M.
Marham ...	...	Morley, D. B.
Market-Rasen ...		Hughes, A.
Marlborough, St. Mary ...		Ward, J. H. K.
Marlborough College ...		Tyacke, J. S.

Marsk	Tate, J.
Marston-Biggott	Onslow, A. L.
Martock cum Long Load ...	Salmon, E. A.
Masham	Platt, G. M.
Medbourne cum Holt ...	Mitchell, J. B.
Meesden	Ward, B.
Meetham-Mills	Watson, E. C.
Mentmore	Currie, M. W.
Mereworth	Stapleton, E. H.
Merthyr-Tydfil	Rowland, E.
„	Thomas, O. D.
„ St. David	Rowland, L. T.
Merton	Tudor, C.
Mexborough	Ellershaw, R.
Middleton-on-the-Wolds	Wrangham, R.
Milborne-Port	Sumner, O.
Milford, South	Young, F. J.
Milnthorpe	Raikes, F. T.
Milston	Mountain, J. J. S.
Milton, Hants.	Redknap, W. H.
Milton, Devon.	Macdonald, D.
Milton-Abbas	Birch, F.
Milton-next-Gravesend ...	Johnston, W. D.
„	Proctor, W. A.
„ Holy Trinity	Roberts, W.
Mitcham	Wilson, D. F.
Modbury	Green, G. C.
„	Pulling, F. W.
Monk's-Kirby	Saxby, S. H.
Monmouth Grammar School	Roberts, C. M.
Morborne	Vincent, J. C. F.
Moulsham	Mallony, G.
„	Tibbits, N.
Moulton (Lincolnshire) ...	Brooke, W.
Moulton (Norfolk) ...	Ladbrook, J. A.
Muchelney cum Drayton ...	Baker, S. O.
Mungrisdale	Bewsher, T.
„	Gillam, E. C.
NANTYGLO	John, E.
Naseby	Cawley, T.
Naughton	Dudding, J.
Nechell's	Gregory, J. G.
Nempnett	Trueman, S.
Neots, St.	Blagden, H.
„	Cook, C.
Neston	Watson, A.
Netherton	Garland, T. B.
Nettleden	Cautley, G. S.
Newark-upon-Trent ...	Busell, J. G.
Newbiggen	Wood, C. C.
Newburn	Humble, H.
Newburgh	Darby, J. L.
Newbury	Robarts, C. N.
Newcastle-on-Tyne, All Saints	Parker, J. D.
Newcastle, Borough Gaol	Shepherd, R.
Newcastle-under-Lyme, St. George	Collins, T.
Newchapel	Forshaw, T.
Newlyn	Dix, E.
Newton-in-Makerfield ...	Byrth, H. S.
Niton	Ward, C. C.
Nonington	Grimaldi, H. B.
Norley	Sandwith, H.
Northampton, St. Sepulchre	Phillips, J.
„ St. Peter ...	Douglass, T. W.
Northbourne	Simpson, G.
Northfleet	Akers, J.
Norton Grammar School ...	Balshaw, E.
Norwell cum Carlton	Cocke, F. H.
Norwich, Cathedral ...	Bulmer, E.
„ St. Giles ..	Ripley, W. N.
„ St. Peter Mancroft	Burrell, J. F.
Norwood (Middlesex) ...	Worsley, H.
Norwood (Surrey) ...	Thursfield, R.
Nottingham, St. Mary ...	Allen, R.
„ „	Hoare, R.
Nunney	Wood, J.
Nunton	Dingley, S. R.
Nuthurst	Townsend, J.

Nymphsfield	Thorp, C.
OAKLEY (Beds.)	Radcliffe, H. E. D.
Oakley (Essex)	Nicholas, P.
Oare	Littlehales, W. G.
Oby	Barlow, T. D.
Oldberrow	Salmon, H. W.
Ollerton	Reade, W.
Olney	Huzell, J. H.
Olveston	Warre, F.
Orston	Hatton, J. L. S.
Orton-Longueville ...	Legg, W.
Orwell	Tayler, H. C. A.
Oswestry, Deytheur Gram. Sch. ...	Robinson, E.
Otley	Whitfield, F.
Ottery St. Mary	Paul, F. B.
Oundle	Williamson, J.
Outwell	Wright, H.
Over	Dudley, W. C.
Over-Silton	Fox, J. H.
Overton	Parker, C. W.
Ovington	Pearse, H. T.
Oxford, St. Aldate ...	Nash, T. A.
„ Christ Church ...	Bayne, T. V.
„ „ ...	Bristow, W. J.
„ „ ...	Sanders, W.
„ „ ...	Williams, A. V.
„ St. Mary Magdalen cum St. George the Martyr ...	Tyrwhitt, R. S. J.
„ St. Thomas-the-Martyr ...	Jones, H. F.
Oxford, All Soul's College	Wingfield, C. L.
„ Balliol College ...	Salter, W. C.
„ Brasenose College ...	Reynolds, S. H.
„ „ ...	Turner, E. T.
„ St. Edmund Hall ...	Liddon, H. P.
„ Exeter College ...	Wollaston, W. M.
„ Jesus College ...	Chepmell, W. H.
„ Lincoln College ...	Merry, W. W.
„ Magdalen College ...	Deane, C. H.
„ New College ...	Gepp, H. J.
„ „ ...	Quicke, G. A.
„ „ ...	Wickham, E. C.
„ Trinity College ...	Duckworth, R.
„ Wadham College ...	Shirley, W. W.
„ Worcester College ...	Tomlinson, C. H.
Oxford, Industrial Training Sch. ...	Charsley, R. H.
Oxhill	Landford, T.
PALGRAVE	Martyn, C. J.
Panton	Bailey, A. W.
„	Marshall, W. K.
Papworth St. Agnes ...	Bren, R.
Parham	Beck, J.
Passenham	Wood, H.
Patrixbourne	Smith, S.
Pattingham	Rowley, R.
Pavenham	Ram, S. J.
Payhemburg	Mules, J. H.
Peak Forest	Rigge, W. P.
Penarth	Edwards, C. S.
Penclawdd	Matthews, T.
Penistone	Aldom, J. W.
Penshaw	Spoor, W.
Penzance Grammar School	Salter, E.
Peterborough Cathedral ...	Babington, J.
Petworth	Purton, W. O.
Pickenham, North ...	Naters, C. J.
Pill	Wilton, C. T.
Pilton	Mackey, C. W.
Pinner	Tandy, C. H.
Pipe	Hanbury, J. C.
Plaxtole	Whitlock, J. A.
Plumstead	Streeter, G. T. P.
„ St. Nicholas ...	Morgan, J.
Plymouth, Christ Church	Haly, J. B.
Pontesbury, First Portion	Harrison, J.
Portsmouth, St. Paul's School	Ingram, W. C.
„ Sailors' Home	Macnamara, R.
Postwick	Andrews, W.

Powerstock	... Wetenhall, W. H.
Preston, Parish Church ...	... Chapman, D. F.
„ St. Luke ...	... Winlaw, W.
„ St. Mary ...	... M'Guinness, W. N.
Preston Grammar School	... Smith, C.
Preston Deanery	... Brookes, J. H.
„	... Lightfoot, R. P.
Prestwich	... Ellis, W. C.
Prior's Portion ...	... Williams, A.
Preston	... Dowding, C.
Puddletown	... Crichlow, H. M.
Putney	... Edgar, J. H.
„ St. John ...	... Trimmer, A. A.
QUINTON, The	... Oldfield, C.
RADLEY, St. Peter's College	... Wilson, R. S.
Ramsbury...	... Sturton, J.
Rampside...	... Park, J.
Ramsgate, Christ Church	... Phelps, J.
„ St. George ...	... Dodd, H. P.
Ranmore	... Heberden, G.
Ravensden	... Dodwell, H. J.
Rayleigh	... Wintle, O. R.
Reading, St. Giles ...	... Addison, W. F.
„ „ ...	... Wilberforce, W. F.
Renhold	... Spencer, L.
Rennington ...	... Cooley, W. L. J.
Repton, Gram. Sch. ...	... Latham, E.
„ „ ...	... Gould, J.
Retford, East	... Brooke, J. S.
„ „	... Percy, P. H.
„ „	... Ranken, W. H.
Retford East, Gram. School	... Christie, J. J.
Rewe	... Williams, P.
Richmond, Hickey's Almshouses	... Sharp, T.
Ringstead...	... Wilson, P. S.
Ripley	... Armstrong. R.
Ripon, Deanery	... Goode, W.
Rippenden	... Gledhill, J.
Rocester	... Stubbs, W. F.
Rochdale, St. Mary ...	... Sharpe, R. N.
„ „ ...	... Shutte, A. S.
Rochester, St. Margaret ...	... Drawbridge, W. B.
„ St. Nicholas ...	... Adams, A. C.
Rock	... Cooley, W. L. J.
Rode, North	... Procter, J. M.
Romford	... Phillips, S. W.
Romsey	... Gobat, S. B.
„	... Stratton, F. R.
Rookhope	... Willis, R.
Rossall, School ...	... Pursell, J. B.
Rostherne	... Jeffcoatt, T.
„ St. Mary ...	... Davies, H. S.
Rotherby	... Moore, J.
Rotherham	... Barnes, W.
„	... South, R.
Roundhay...	... Richardson, E. A
Rousham	... Peel, C. S.
Rowde	... Taylor, H. W.
Ruabon, Grammar School...	... Taylor, A. L.
Rugby, Trinity Church ...	... Rhoades, E. J.
Rugby, Gram. School ...	... Butler, A. G.
„ „ ...	... Evans, T. S.
„ „ ...	... Smythies, R. B.
Rugeley	... Buckston, H.
Runcorn, Trinity Ch. ...	... Rooker, J.
„ Floating Chapel	... Garven, E. D.
Ruswarp	... Matthey, A.
Ryde, St. Thomas ...	... Dumbleton, E. N.
Rye-Harbour	... Bartlett, P.
SAFFRON-WALDEN ...	... Holderness, J.
Salcott	... Watson, F.
Salford, Union	... Gardiner, A.
Saltley, Training College...	... Savell, W. J.
Sampford-Courtenay ...	... Theed, E. R.
Sanderstead	... Wallace, J.
Sanderton...	... Grace, O. J.

Sandwich	... Bird, R. J.
Sapey, Upper	... Onslow, P.
Sarnesfield	... Dudley, J.
Sarratt	... Ryley, E.
Sawbridgeworth	... Johnson, H. F.
Scalby	... Freshney, F.
„	... Henham, J. L.
Scaleby	... Shipman, T. T.
Scarborough, St. Thomas...	... Bogle, M. J.
Scarrington	... Halton, J. L. S.
Scawby	... Clifford, H. M.
Scorborough	... Whitaker, R.
Scropton	... Dalton, J.
Seacombe	... Love, R.
Seaham-Harbour ...	... Green, C.
„	... Wilkinson, G. H.
Seale, Nether and Over ...	... Gresley, N.
Seasalter	... Dodd, J.
Seavington, St. Michael ...	... Hoare, E. T.
Sefton	... Ball, T. P.
Sellinge	... Vernon, J. R.
Send	... Cancellor, J. H.
Shale	... Nixson, J. M.
Shalfleet	... Orton, J. S.
Shap	... Simpson, J,
Sharrington	... Dollington, J. R.
Shawbury...	... Richards, J.
Sheffield, Parish Church ...	... Camidge, C. E.
„ St. George ...	... Wright, H. H.
„ St. Jude, Moorfield	... Penny, E. I.
„ St. Paul ...	... Hammond, R. H.
„ St. Philip ...	... Marshall, W.
Shefford	... Richards, J. B.
Shelford, Little ...	... Law, J. E.
Shenley	... Pryor, J. E.
Shepperton	... Phipps, P. W.
Shepton-Beauchamp ...	... Devon, E. B.
Shere	... Adams, C. V.
Sherfield	... Barton, J.
Sherfield-on-Loddon ...	... Nutting, G. H.
Sherford	... Pope, A.
Shields, Holy Trinity ...	... Hawker, J.
Shields, South, Marine School	... Hooppell, R. E.
Shillington	... Hudson, C.
Shipley cum Heaton ...	... Milton, H. A.
Shipwash...	... Lawson, F.
Shirley	... Nicholls, H.
Shotterbrook	... Yonge, D. N.
Shrawley	... Carew, J. W.
Shrewsbury, Grammar School	... Smith, H. C.
Sibford-Gower	... Eliot, E.
Sidbury	... Horrocks, G.
Sidmouth	... Crocker, W. F.
Silton	... Shorland, W. H.
Silverstone	... Aske, T.
Skelton-cum-Brotton ...	... Bowen, C. T.
Skidby	... Sanders, H. M.
Skirwith	... Parker, C.
Sleaford	... Spurrier, H.
Slindon	... Whitestone, W. A.
Smallthorne	... Kelsall, H.
Smethwick, St. Matthew ...	... Crook, J.
„ „ ...	... Ferguson, R.
Snargate	... Howell, H.
Snae	... Howell, H.
Snelland	... Ellis. G.
Sneyd	... Orr, W. H.
Solihull, Gram. School ...	... Bennett, J. H.
Sopworth	... Neville, N.
Sonrton	... Gibbens, W.
South-Cave	... Wrangham, D. S.
Southampton, Christ Ch., Northam	Procter, G. A.
„ St. Mary ...	... Heberden, J.
„ „ ...	... Norton, H.
„ „ ...	... Wills, E. C.
„ „ ...	... Cooper, M.
Southsea, St. Paul ...	... Crofton, E.
Southwell...	... Hutton, H. W.
Southwick	... Freeman, F. E.

Sowerby ... ... Eustace, G.
Spalding ... ... Turner, J. R.
Speeton ... ... Ketchley, W. G.
Speldhurst ... ... Streatfield, N. W.
Spennymoor ... ... Carter, A. R.
Stafford, Christ Church ... ... Eastman, W. S.
Staines ... ... Fowle, T. W.
Stainton-by-Langworth ... ... Ellis, G.
Standon ... ... Pearson, C. R.
Stanningfield ... ... Rudge, F.
Stanwix ... ... Fawcett, H.
Stapleton ... ... Cutcliffe, J. C.
Staveley ... ... Mandale, B.
Steeping, Little ... ... Steere, E.
Steeple-Morden ... ... Quick, A. G.
Sternfield ... ... Sewell, T. W.
Stert ... ... Boys, C.
Stetchworth ... ... Hammond, H.
Stevenage... ... ... Freeman, R. M.
Stewkley ... ... Porter, R. S.
Stillingfleet ... ... Cooke, G. R. D.
Stilton ... ... Hutton, T.
Stisted ... ... Fraser, W. F.
Stockport, St. Peter ... ... Meredith, J.
  „ St. Thomas ... ... Eddowes, E.
Stockport, Gram. School ... ... Coombes, J.
Stockwell ... ... Cox, T.
  „ St. Michael ... ... Bousfield, H. N.
Stockwith, West ... ... Burrell, J.
Stogursey... ... ... West, W. H.
Stoke, St. Mary ... ... Lance, W. H.
Stoke-Abbas ... ... Whittle, C.
Stoke-cum-Easton ... ... Blyth, E. H.
Stoke-upon-Trent ... ... Serjeantson, J J
Stoke, St. Gregory ... ... Greet, A.
Stone, Christ Church ... ... Dimont, C. H.
Stonham-Aspal ... ... Mackness, G.
Stony-Stratford ... ... Sankey, W. T.
Stourbridge, St. Thomas ... ... Sherrard, H.
Stowmarket ... ... Saunders, J. G.
Stowupland ... ... Saunders, J. G.
Stratford-on-Avon ... ... Ramsden, F. J.
Stratton (Cornwall) ... ... Waller, R. P.
Strensham ... ... Welby, W. H. E.
Stretford ... ... Airey, J. P.
  „ , ... Brendon, W. E.
Stretton (Staffordshire) ... ... Napier, J. W.
Stretton (Leicestershire) ... ... Espin, W.
Stretton-Grandison ... ... Buckle, J.
Strood ... ... Willis, A.
Stroud ... ... Cornford, E.
  „ ... ... Lane, E. A.
Stroud, Holy Trinity ... ... Tarlton, T. H.
Studley, Upper ... ... Porter, J. L.
Sturminster-Marshall ... ... Kingdon, H. T.
Sturry ... ... Haroman, C. L.
Suffield ... ... Lubbock, H. H.
Summertown ... ... Bayley, W. R.
Sunk-Island ... ... Sutton, T.
Sutton (Beds.) ... ... Pearson, F.
Sutton (Lincolnshire) ... ... Bompas, W. C.
Sutton-Montis ... ... Robertson, W. A. S.
Sutton-on-Plym ... ... Peters, T. H.
Swaby ... ... Roberts, C. S.
Swanscombe ... ... Ashley, J. M.
Swindon ... ... Jackson, R. H.
Swingfield ... ... Masters, G.

TADMARTON ... ... Eliot, R.
Talk-on-the-Hill ... ... M'Hutchin, M. W.
Talley ... ... Thomas, T.
Tarring-Neville ... ... Fothergill, P. A.
Taunton, Holy Trinity ... ... Stanton, J. J.
  „ St. Mary Magdalen ... Clark, W. R.
  „ „ „ Cook, G. F.
Taunton, Bishop's Hull School ... Addison, R.
  „ „ „ Bankes, F.
Teath, St. ... ... Dawson, B. J.
Teddington ... ... Wodehouse, P. C.

Teignmouth, St. Michael ... ... Cartwright, A. W. H.
  „ St. Nicholas ... ... Grinstead, C.
Tenbury ... ... Smith, T. A.
Terling ... ... Hill, F. T.
Tetney ... ... Hemmans, F.
Thanet, St. Peter... ... ... Lenny, H. S. N.
Thanet, Union ... ... Tudor, S.
Thaxted ... ... Sayer, W. C.
Thetford ... ... Smith, A. F.
Thorganby ... ... Elliss, H. C.
Thornley ... ... Wilkinson, G. P.
Thornton ... ... Hatton, J. L. S.
Thorpe-in-Glebis ... ... Hosking, H. J.
Thorpe-Satchville ... ... Wasse, H. W.
Thrapstone ... ... Bagshaw, W. S.
Threlkeld... ... ... Whitelegg, W.
Thurlaston ... ... Ottley, G. L.
Thurlbear... ... ... Lance, W. H.
Thurloxton ... ... Bartlett, R. L.
Tickenhull ... ... Laurence, G.
Tinwell ... ... Christian, F. W.
Tirle ... ... Parish, W. D.
Tissington ... ... Tyrwhitt, B.
Titchwell ... ... Stocker, E. S.
Tiverton ... ... Dupuis, T. C.
  „ St. Thomas ... . Hughes, J. B.
Tiverton, Blundell's School ... Hughes, J. B.
Tixover ... ... Burroughes, R.
Tonge ... ... Davis, W. S.
Topsham ... ... Ware, H. R.
Torquay, St. Mark ... ... Gibbs, J. L.
Tranmere, St. Catherine ... ... Marsden, W.
Torrington, East ... ... Marshall, W. H.
Torrington, Great... ... ... Vyvyan Robinson, H.
Tranmere, St. Paul ... ... Willink, A.
  „ „ ... ... Maud, J.
  „ „ ... ... Lewis, D.
Tregaion ... ... Brigstocke, M. W.
Tretire ... ... Bonus, E.
Tring ... ... Pownall, A.
Trowse ... ... Blissard, J. C.
Tunbridge Wells, St. John ... Welldon, E. S.
Tunbridge, Grammar School ... Curry, H. T.
Tunstall ... ... Houghton, E. J.
Twyford (Hants)... ... ... Wickham, L.
  „ „ ... ... Wa-se, H. W.
Twyford (Leicestershire) ... ... Green, C. E. M.
Tydd St. Mary ... ...

WADDESDON ... ... Burges, R. B.
Waldingfield, Little ... ... Robinson, S. B.
Wantage ... ... Gillett, H. H.
Walker ... ... Drought, H.
Walkington ... ... Ferguson, D.
Walsall ... ... Craven, S.
Waltham Abbey ... ... Hart, R. P.
Walthamstow, Forest School ... Phillips, G.
  „ „ „ Wardell, H. J.
Walton (Bucks) ... ... Young, F.
Walton-le-Dale ... ... Shepherd, W. B.
Walton-West ... ... Woodman, E. F.
Walworth, Beresford Chapel ... Lincoln, W.
Wandsworth, House of Correction ... Gegg, J.
  „ „ „ Hallward, J. W.
  „ Patriotic Asylum ... Kirkby, W.
Wanstead... ... ... Craig, A. T.
  „ ... ... Snell, A.
Ware, Grammar School ... ... Lilley, C.
Warfield ... ... Gill, F. T.
Warminster ... ... Crawley, C. D.
Warminster, Lord Weymouth's Sch. ... Crallan, T. E.
Warrington ... ... Gardner. H.
Warwick ... ... Smith, E. T.
Watford ... ... Havart, W. J.
Wednesbury ... ... Winter, W.
Welby ... ... Steel, J.
Wellingborough ... ... Beasley, T. C.
Wellington ... ... Denny, J.
Wells, St. Cuthbert ... ... Everett, A. J.
Wereham ... ... White, H. T.

Werneth	...	Bourke, T.
Westbourne	...	Shean, H. S.
Westbury cum Priddy	...	Adair, H. J.
Weston-super-Mare	...	Jose, S.
Weybread...	...	Gascoigne, T.
Whaddon	...	Baker, W. J.
Whaplode-Drove ...	...	Otter, G.
Wheatacre-Burgh	...	Boycott, W.
Wheathampstead ...	...	Davys, O. W.
Wheatley	...	King, E.
„	...	Geldart, J. W.
Whiston	...	Morant, H. J.
Whitchurch	...	Chamberlain, F. T.
Whitehaven	...	Douglas, C.
White-Waltham ...	...	Yonge, D. N.
Whitstable	...	Dodd, J.
Whittlebury	...	Ashe, T.
Whitwell	...	Ward, C. C.
Whitworth	...	Carter, A. B.
Wickham	...	Plow, E. J.
Widnes	...	Tatlock, W.
Widcombe	...	Tate, G. E.
Wigan	...	Copeland, G. D.
Wilcot	...	Corser, R. K.
Wilcot cum Oare ...	...	Smelt, H.
Willington	...	Geake, A.
„	...	Oliver, C. N.
Wilsthorpe	...	Mantell, E. R.
Wimbledon	...	Peile, A. L. B.
Wimborne, St. Giles	...	Billington, G. H.
Winchester Deanery	...	Garnier, T.
„ St. John ...	...	Dudley, S. G.
„ St. Lawrence ...	...	Sealy, W. G.
Windsor, Holy Trinity	...	Nicholas, G. D.
„ „ ...	...	Rooke, T.
Windsor, Union	...	Miller, J. A.
Windsor, Cheshire	...	Robertson, P. F. W.
Wing	...	Boys, C.
Wingates	...	Macrorie, W. K.
Winkfield	...	Miller, J. R. C.
Winlaton	...	Clarke, J.
Winscombe	...	Wheeler, W. H.
Winterbourne-Cam ...	...	Dawson-Damer, L. D.
Winterbourne-Stickland ...	...	Tuckniss, W.
Winterton	...	Waddingham, T.
Wisbech	...	Brown, J. S.
Witham	...	Raynes, W.
Withiell-Florey ...	...	Davies, C. R. F.
Witley, Great ...	...	Rowland, C.
Wittersham	...	Tanner, W.
Woburn	...	Barnett, R. L.
Wolverhampton, St. George	...	Osman, J. W.
„ St. Matthew	...	Wood, A.

Wolverhampton, St. Peter	...	Hodgson, S J.
Wolverley	...	Pardoe, G.
Woodborough	...	Lowther, W. S. P.
Woodbrige, St. Mary	...	Wilson, R. W.
Woodford cum Membris ...	...	Scale, J.
Woodhorn	...	Wood, C. C.
Woodlands	...	Handcock, J. H. J.
Woodmansterne	...	Aitken, J.
Woodstock, Grammar School	...	Sanders, W.
„ Union ...	...	Sanders, W.
Woodville	...	Jones, T.
Woolaston	...	Thomas, W. M.
Woolborough	...	Parkyn, J. C.
Woolos, St.	...	Kane, R. N.
Wootton-Fitzpaine ...	...	Tringham, W.
Wooton-Rivers	...	Brodribb, W. J.
Wootton-under-Wood ...	...	Addison, J. C.
Worcester, St. Clement ...	...	Lloyd, W.
Worcester Cathedral School	...	Love, E. H.
Workington	...	Thomas, J.
Worldham, East	...	Standen, W.
Worthing	...	Girdlestone, R. B.
Worthington	...	Stayner, T. L.
Wortley	...	Pettitt, J.
Wragby	...	Kirk, T.
„	...	Marshall, W. K.
Wrangle	...	Wright, R. F.
Wraxall	...	Hellicar, A. G.
Wraysbury	...	Neville, S.
Wretton	...	White, H. T.
Wycombe, High ...	...	Covey, R.
„ „	...	Redd, F. A.
„ Union	...	Grace, O. J.
Wyrasdisbury	...	Neville, S.
Wythop	...	Truman, G. W. H.
YARDLEY	...	Swinburn, F. T.
Yardley-Hastings ...	...	Cockett, F. J.
Yarmouth, St. Nicholas ...	...	Freshfield, J. M.
„ „ ...	...	Gott, J.
„ „ ...	...	Holme, A. P.
„ „ ...	...	Richmond, T. K.
York, St. John	...	Karney, G. S.
„ St. Mary Bishophill-Junior		Buncombe, C. G.
„ „ ...	...	Palmer, H. V.
„ St. Michael-le-Belfry	...	Straffen, G. M.
„ St. Paul	...	Medland, W.
York, Archbishop Holgate's School		Hewison, G. H.
„ Training College ...	...	Jones, J.
„ County Hospital ...	...	Short, N. N.
Ystradffyn	...	Davies, D.
Ystradyfodwg	...	Gower, J.

Printed by John Crockford, 10, Wellington-street, Strand, London.

A NEWLY-INVENTED APPLICATION OF CORALITE GUM-COLOURED

INDIA-RUBBER,

AS A BASE FOR ARTIFICIAL TEETH, GUMS, AND PALATES.

BY HER MAJESTY'S ROYAL LETTERS PATENT.

1861, Just Published, Post Free Three Stamps.

GABRIEL ON THE LOSS AND ONLY EFFECTUAL MEANS OF RESTORING THE TEETH, explains their patented system of supplying artificial masticators, which are warranted to prove successful when all other methods fail, without springs, wires, or metal, and without any operations, and also shows how the best materials with first-class workmanship may be obtained at less than half the usual charge.

MESSRS. GABRIEL,

DENTISTS TO THE PRINCE D'OTTAJANA,

Established 1815 (*See Diploma*),

134, DUKE STREET, LIVERPOOL;

110, REGENT STREET, LONDON; 33 AND 34, LUDGATE HILL, CITY, LONDON; AND

65, NEW STREET, BIRMINGHAM.

AMERICAN MINERAL TEETH from 4 to 7 GUINEAS.

Also, just published, cloth bound, direct of the Authors by post, twelve stamps, or through any bookseller,

A PRACTICAL TREATISE ON ARTIFICIAL TEETH,

And the only effectual mode of supplying them.

HUMAN TEETH,

the diseases to which they are liable, and their remedy.

IMPORTANCE and VALUE of the TEETH in RELATION to HEALTH:

" What great events from little causes spring, | Dark eyes have caused a revolution,
Trifles light as air huge disasters bring: | And absent TEETH a broken constitution.

Daily Attendance from Ten to Five o'clock, at

LONDON, LIVERPOOL, AND BIRMINGHAM,

Now ready, Royal Octavo, cloth boards, price 7s. 6d.

Crockford's Scholastic Directory for 1861,

BEING AN ANNUAL WORK OF REFERENCE FOR FACTS RELATING TO

EDUCATORS, EDUCATION, AND EDUCATIONAL ESTABLISHMENTS

(PUBLIC AND PRIVATE) IN THE UNITED KINGDOM;

CONTENTS :

1. SCHOOL STATISTICS.
2. The UNIVERSITIES, with Names of HEADS of COLLEGES, &c., &c.
3. TRAINING COLLEGES.
4. THEOLOGICAL COLLEGES.
5. DISSENTING COLLEGES and SCHOOLS.
6. CATHOLIC COLLEGES and SCHOOLS.
7. An Alphabetical List of the Names and Addresses of the PRINCIPALS of COLLEGES and PUBLIC SCHOOLS, with full particulars of Appointments formerly held, Titles of Books published, University Honours and Degrees, &c.
8. An Index of the Towns and Cities having PROPRIETARY and ENDOWED SCHOOLS, with Dates of Foundation, Names of Patrons, Amount of Income and Endowment, kinds of Instruction given, Fees, Exhibitions, Scholarships, &c.
9. A List of PAROCHIAL SCHOOLS, with Dates of Foundation, Income, &c.
10. NATIONAL SOCIETY'S SCHOOLS (a notice).
11. BRITISH AND FOREIGN SOCIETY'S SCHOOLS (a notice).
12. An Alphabetical List of the Names and Addresses of Principals of PRIVATE SCHOOLS for GENTLE-
MEN, with the designation of the School in each case.
13. A similar List of PRIVATE SCHOOLS for LADIES.
14. List of Persons who receive PRIVATE PUPILS.
15. List of CONTINENTAL and other FOREIGN SCHOOLS.
16. Names and Addresses of SCHOLASTIC AGENTS.
17. List of School and other Educational Books published during the Year 1860.
18. An Appendix, alphabetically arranged under the Names of Towns and Cities, containing the Advertisements of Schools and Colleges, and of those who receive Private Pupils. In each case the entry of the Name in the Directory will have a reference mark to its corresponding Advertisement in the Appendix. Thus those who consult the Lists of Names and Addresses of Schools will at once be guided to the further information given in the Advertisement Pages.
19. Advertisements of School Books and Works on General Literature—Insurance Offices, Public Companies, and other business announcements.

May be had by order of any Bookseller—or a copy will be sent in return for a remittance of 7s. 6d., by

JOHN CROCKFORD, 10, WELLINGTON-STREET, STRAND, LONDON, W.C.

SUPERIOR

PRIVATE EDUCATION ON THE CONTINENT.

A beautiful and interesting part of the Coast of France.

DIRECT COMMUNICATION WITH ENGLAND ALMOST DAILY.

THE BRITISH CHAPLAIN AT HAVRE DE GRACE receives into his family Four Young Lads, whose Religious and Literary Education he takes charge of, acting towards them in every respect *in loco parentis*, and securing to them as far as possible the benefits and comforts of their own homes.

Havre affords superior Educational advantages, Professors of the highest qualifications residing here.

The Chaplain's Residence is most healthfully situated in one of the best localities in the suburbs, and close to the sea baths.

TERMS from £80 to £100 per annum.

The highest references given and required. For fuller information apply to the British Chaplain, Havre.

N.B. *The prepaid postage from England to France is 4d. for letters under quarter of an ounce, and 8d. for letters over quarter and under half an ounce.*

d in the United Kingdom
ghtning Source UK Ltd.
)UK00001B/9/A